LATIN-AMERICAN
MILITARY AVIATION

First Edition

LATIN~AMERICAN
MILITARY AVIATION

John M. Andrade

Midland Counties Publications

Warning!

The hobby of aircraft spotting can be misunderstood in countries where it is not as widely accepted as in the UK and this has lead to a number of unfortunate incidents over the past few years.

We therefore remind readers of the advice contained in the official booklet *Essential Information for British Passport Holders:* 'Hobbies like *aircraft*, train or ship spotting, and even bird watching, are liable to misinterpretation and may lead to your being arrested for spying in some countries abroad. If in doubt you should enquire from the local authorities or a British consular officer'.

Edited and Published by
Midland Counties Publications (Aerophile) Limited
24, The Hollow, Earl Shilton, Leicester,
LE9 7NA, England.

Copyright © 1982
Midland Counties Publications (Aerophile) Limited

ISBN 0 904597 30 X (Hardback)
      0 904597 31 8 (Paperback)

Printed by W. & J. Linney Limited,
121 Newgate Lane, Mansfield, Notts, NG18 2PA
and David Green Printers Limited,
Newman Street, Kettering, Northants, NN16 0TU.
Bound by F.F. Allsopp & Company Limited,
Union Road, Nottingham, NG3 1FU, England.

Contents

Cover photographs: Dassault Mirage IIIEV 2843 of
the Venezuelan Air Force at Maracay in July 1976
(D.Hughes) and Mil Mi-8 OB-E-996 of the Peruvian
Air Force at Iquitos in 1976 (C.Ballantine).

Prefacio

La América Latina, tierra ideal para el desarrollo de la aviación, ha dado al mundo una contribución valiosísima en esta material, desde el primer vuelo de Santos-Dumont hasta la exploración de la floresta virgen que cubre mucho del continente, además del perfeccionamiento de la técnica de vuelo a gran altitud (en Bolivia) y las primeras tácticas de la guerra aérea (por ejemplo en México). Así siendo, es lamentable verse que muy poco se conoce en otros países sobre la historia de la aviación militar latinoamericana.

Es seguro que hay obras de gran valor, como la Historia Oficial de la Fuerza Aérea Expedicionaria Mexicana del Teniente-Coronel Sandoval Castarrica, los Aportes para la Historia de la Fuerza Aérea Uruguaya del Coronel Jaime Meregalli, la Historia de la Fuerza Aérea Brasileña del Teniente-Brigadero Lavanère-Wanderley, o la Historia de la Fuerza Aérea de Chile publicada por la Revista de la FACh. Además uno de los mejores periódicos de aviación, la revista 'Manche', se publica en Brasil. Pero la mayoría de los estudiantes de la historia aeronautica no conoce el castellano o el portugués, y muchos libros de interés son muy difíciles de hallar fuera de sus países de origen. Los pocos artículos publicados en la prensa especializada anglo-americana son en general incompletos, y no pocos son inexactos.

El presente libro fué escrito para los aficionados de la aviación militar en América Latina, y para aquellos en el resto del mundo que hay muchos anos deseaban una fuente de referencia fácilmente asequible. No obstante los esfuerzos más grandes para obtener información detallada y corrigir los errores más óbvios, hay muchos detalles que no fueran inclusos por razones de espacio, y otros cuya precisión no puede ser garantizada, por causa de las contradiciones halladas en los documentos consultados. El autor invita los lectores a dirigir comentarios correciones y informaciones suplementarias a los editores; con la ayuda de todos, estamos seguros que la segunda edición será aún mejor y más completa que la primera.

N.R. La revista 'Manche' se llama actualmente 'South American Aviation News'.

Prefácio

A América Latina, terra ideal para o desenvolvimento da aviação, tem dado ao mundo uma contribuição valiosísima nesta matéria, desde o primeiro voo de Santos-Dumont até ao desbravamento da floresta virgem que cobre muito do continente, passando pelo aperfeiçoamento da técnica de voo a grande altitude (na Bolívia) e das primeiras táticas de guerra aérea (por exemplo no México). Assim sendo, é lamentável ver-se que se conhece muito pouco nos países estrangeiros sobre a história da aviação militar latino-americana.

É certo que há obras de grande valor, como a História da Força Aérea Brasileira do Tenente-Brigadeiro Lavanère-Wanderley, a História Oficial da Força Aérea Expedicionária Mexicana do Tenente-Coronel Sandoval Castarrica, os Subsídios para a História da Força Aérea Uruguaia de Coronel Jaime Meregalli, ou a História da Força Aérea Chilena publicada pela Revista da FACh. Por outro lado, uma das melhores publicações periódicas aeronáuticas, a revista 'Manche', publica-se no Brasil. Mas a maioria dos estudiosos da história aeronáutica não conhece a língua portuguesa ou castelhana, e de resto muitos livros de interesse são muito difíceis de adquirir fora dos seus países de origem. Os poucos artigos publicados na imprensa especializada anglo-americana são em geral incompletos, e não poucas vezes contém inexatidões.

O presente livro foi escrito para os entusiastas da aviação militar da América Latina, e para aqueles que em todo o mundo há muitos anos desejavam uma fonte de referéncia facilmente acessível. Não obstante os maiores esforços para obter informações pormenorizadas e corrigir os erros mais evidentes, há muitos detalhes que não puderam ser incluídos por razões de espaço, e outros cuja precisão pode deixar um pouco a desejar, visto que os documentos consultados eram por vezes contraditórios. Assim, o autor convida os leitores a dirigir comentários, correções e informações suplementares aos editores; com a ajuda de todos, temos a certeza que a segunda edição será ainda melhor e mais completa que a primeira.

N.R. A revista 'Manche' chama-sa actualmente 'South American Aviation News'.

Introduction

This book is the seventh in our *Military Air Arms* series, which aim to present a historical background and an extensive survey of current and more recent organisation and equipment of the various air arms, supported by a wide-ranging photographic coverage, base maps, unit insignia etc. As always, data of a technical nature such as aircraft performance, dimensions and armament is deliberately kept to a minimum since this may easily be found in other reference books such as the 'Janes' and 'Observers' series.

This particular book has been a long time in preparation, but has been considerably expanded by new information which has continued to flow in from many sources — not least because of the most recent activities in the Falkland Islands which have lent an unexpected topicality to the subject. However, perhaps it is appropriate to set the scene with a more general review of the geographical area covered and the aeronautical history of the region.

Latin America is the name normally given to the Spanish and Portuguese speaking countries of the American continent — Mexico in North America; Costa Rica, Guatemala, Honduras, Nicaragua, Panama and El Salvador in Central America, and Argentina, Bolivia, Brazil, Chile, Colombia, Ecuador, Paraguay, Peru, Uruguay and Venezuela in South America.

The area they occupy is naturally suited for the development of aviation, comprising large uninhabited zones, forests and vast plains. This, together with the barrier to communications by land formed by the massive chain of the Andes, made the aircraft an essential tool of progress — in fact the first Pan-American Aeronautical Conference took place in Santiago, Chile as early as 1916. Airfields were opened where necessary, regardless of difficulties; for example, Bolivia has the world's highest airport at La Paz and some of the country's airfields are as high as 25,000 feet. The military use of the aircraft was also quickly understood; there was military flying during Mexico's revolutionary period (circa 1911) which comprised not only the usual observation missions previously performed by balloons but also the first ground attack raids.

Latin America is particularly important because of its largely unexplored natural resources as well as its enormous strategic significance. The Panama Canal for instance, although no longer vital because of the development of air power, is a major strategic waterway and whoever controls it can dictate political changes in the whole of Latin America. Similarly the interests which the super-powers have in Chile and Argentina are understandable because, if the Canal were to be closed for some reason, the only alternative route between the Atlantic and the Pacific would be around Cape Horn or through the Straits of Magellan - controlled by those countries.

Latin American countries are economically interdependent which is not surprising as most of them separated themselves from the Spanish Empire in the early nineteenth century; this in turn made them strategically interdependent as a way to counteract their vulnerability (industrial and population centres are usually concentrated, due to insufficient road communications). National economies are mainly agricultural although industrial power in Argentina, Brazil and Chile — and to some extent Mexico — is constantly expanding.

President James Monroe expressed in 1823 the principles of United States policy towards Latin America (Monroe Policy) — European interference or expansion within the area would from then on be actively opposed. Changing strategic considerations led to the First International Conference of the American States in 1889-1890, which concluded with the creation of the Pan-American Union and an escalation of United States influence in Latin America. Following the Japanese raid on Pearl Harbor on 7 December 1941, the US government obtained defence concessions from the Latin American countries and an Inter-American Defense Board was formed early in 1942 to co-ordinate defence plans against possible Axis invasions; some IADB members eventually took an active part in the war on the Allied side. In September 1947 the United States and the Latin American states signed the Inter-American Treaty of Reciprocal Assistance ('Rio Pact') which in the aeronautical field had as a consequence the supply of badly-needed military aircraft in exchange for defence concessions to the US government; US Military Aid Advisory Groups (MAAGs) were deployed to the Rio Pact signatory countries.

The Organisation of the American States/Organización de los Estados Americanos (OAS/OEA) was formed in April 1948 within Article 51 of the United Nations Charter, absorbing the IADB (which still exists to monitor joint military exercises). Five non-Latin American countries are currently OAS members — Barbados, Haiti, Grenada, Jamaica and Trinidad and Tobago. Cuba withdrew from the Organisation in March 1960 although it remains in theory a member state.

Five Central American states — Costa Rica, Guatemala, Honduras, Nicaragua and El Salvador, the original provinces of the Spanish Captaincy-General of Guatemala — formed in 1962 a parallel organisation, ODECA (Organización de los Estados Centro-Americanos, Organisation of the Central American States), which co-operates with the OAS when necessary and has its headquarters at San Salvador. A Central American Defense Council (CONDECA, Consejo de Defensa Centro-Americano) was formed at Guatemala City in 1963 to co-ordinate defence planning against Cuban-sponsored guerilla activities, with a substantial US technical and financial backing; the Cubans retaliated in 1966 with the formation of the Latin American Organisation for Solidarity (OLAS, Organización Latino-Americana de Solidariedad) to give training and logistic support to the various Latin American guerilla factions. OLAS's success has been rather limited and Cuba's new commitments in Africa may limit its activities.

More recently, United States influence in Latin America has declined dramatically, mainly due to political changes at government level and weapons and aircraft have been obtained more from Europe and the Soviet Union. Jimmy Carter's 'human rights' external policies forced traditionally pro-American countries such as Brazil to seek arms suppliers elsewhere, and some friendly countries had US support terminated altogether — in the case of Nicaragua, with radical changes in the strategic scenario. However, it is now apparent that with the election of Ronald Reagan as US president and the increased activity of guerillas in such countries as El Salvador, the United States is reverting to their traditional policy as essential to their survival as a major power by the suppression of the spread of communist influence from the south.

The invasion of the Falkland Islands by Argentina and their subsequent recapture by British forces during April to June 1982 has undoubtedly greatly affected relationships both within the Latin American countries, some of whom were more supportive to Argentina than others, and externally, particularly with the United States and the EEC countries, whose stance favoured the British side, though at the time of writing it is too early to assess the long term effects.

Turning now to the content of this book in more detail, we must first acknowledge that a few of the countries included are not strictly Latin American — Barbados, Guyana, Haiti, Jamaica, Surinam and Trinidad and Tobago —but they are incorporated since they fall in the same general geographical area.

We are pleased to have been able to assemble a more extensive range of photographs than ever before in this series, and these are arranged to be close to the relevant text. However, for reasons of printing economy, the colour section and some of the black and white photographs are grouped on pages 97 to 112, so please don't forget to look at those pages as well !

The Base Maps are presented for each country with the relevant air force text, but do include the naval and army aviation bases as appropriate.

We have made particular efforts to include notes on colours and markings which we hope will be useful especially to modellers. In general it should be noted that in earlier years, although nationality markings were worn, very few countries specified camouflage or livery details, and that most aircraft flew in their factory or delivery colours. It was not until after the Second World War that painting specifications were taken seriously in Latin America, largely because of growing US influence. Even today US camouflage regulations are widely followed. We have included as many unit bades as possible, and except for Chile the tones used are constant in the colours to which they refer. Please note that, as always, some of the drawings may vary from the form of insignia to be seen on individual aircraft, as these are not always painted in the same form.

As always, we are aware that there may be errors and omissions in this book, which is only natural as information is not as freely available as in most of Europe. Corrections and additions, as well as news, will therefore be welcomed by the publishers.

Midland Counties Publications   June 1982

Abbreviations

The abbreviations used in this book will already be familiar to most readers :

b/u	broken up
c/n	constructor's number
dbf	destroyed by fire
dbr	damaged beyond repair
d/d	delivered
f/f	first flight
soc	struck off charge
toc	taken on charge
wfu	withdrawn from use
w/o	written off

Acknowledgements

This book would never have been written without the co-operation of a large number of individuals, many of whom shall remain nameless — military aircraft enthusiasts are not viewed too favourably in some Latin American countries and their activities are often misunderstood. However, mention must be made of the following, to whom we are more than grateful for their assistance : Peter J. Bish, Fritz Braun, Denir Lima de Camargo (Manche magazine), Pierre Cortet, Jorge P. DiPaolo (Aero Espacio magazine), Jose Luis Gonzalez Serrano, J.M.G.Gradidge, Peter Hambrook, Noam Hartoch, Karl E.Hayes, Paul A.Jackson, Robert J.Kean, Ted Koppel, Graham G.Matthews, David W.Menard, Nery Mendiburu, Alberto Mirkin (AeroMundial), Alex Reinhard, Theron Rinehart (Fairchild Republic historian), Michael Robson, Santiago Flores Ruiz, Lineu Carneiro Saraiva, Walter J.Silveira, Stephen Simms, R.W.Simpson, Jerry E.Vernon, Peter L. Vickery and Johan van der Wei, plus the various magazines such as Small Air Forces Observer, South East Air Review, British Aviation Review which regularly publish material on military aviation in the area, and of course the various aircraft manufacturers who have helped.

The photographs in this book have been gathered from many sources. Our thanks go to the following individuals : A.Annis, C.Ballantine, P.J.Bish, M.Burton, W.J.Bushell, J.Guthrie, P.Hambrook, D.Head, A.Heape, D.Hughes, P.A.Jackson, D.Kettlety, I.MacFarlane, N.Mendiburu, I.W.O'Neill, H. Oehninger, R.Power, S.Simms, R.W.Simpson and J.Suarez. Other photographs have come from MAP and from Helicopter Magazine, and from the Ministerio de Obras General de Aviación Civil, Costa Rica, and from the following manufacturers: Aeritalia, Beech, Bell Helicopter Textron, British Aerospace, CASA, de Havilland Canada, Embraer, Fokker, Gates Lear, Pilatus, Sikorsky, Swearingen and Westland Helicopters. To all go our thanks.

Language Glossary

Although most Spanish and Portuguese names are translated in the text, the following glossary may be found helpful, especially for the more technical terms which are not to be found in smaller dictionaries. It must be stressed however that a given word may have different meanings in different countries and that even within the same country its meaning may vary. Such is the case with *escuadrilla* which may mean flight or squadron - the appropriate translation is then found in the main text.

ENGLISH	SPANISH	PORTUGUESE
Air	(n.) Aire	(n.) Ar
	(adj.) Aéreo, Aérea	(adj.) Aereo, Aérea
Air Base	Base Aerea	Base Aérea
Aircraft	aeroplano,	aeroplano,
	avión (pl. aviones)	avião (pl.aviões)
Aircraft, jet	avión a chorro	avião a jacto (Brazil, jato)
Airfield	campo de aterrizaje	campo de aterragem,
		campo de pouse (Brazil)
Air Force	Fuerza Aérea	Força Aérea (Brazil, ex Fôrça)
Airport	aeropuerto	aeroporto
Armed Forces	Fuerzas Armadas	Forças Armadas (Brazil, ex Fôrças)
Army	Ejército	Exército
Army co-operation	cooperación con el ejército	cooperação com o exército
Attack	ataque	ataque
Aviation	aviación, aeronáutica	aviação, aeronáutica
Basic training	instrucción básica	instrução básica
Battalion	batallón (pl.Batallones)	batalhão (pl.batalhões)
Bomber	bombardero	bombardeiro
Bombing	bombardeo	bombardeio, bombardeamento
Brigade	brigada	brigada
Combat	combate	combate
Command	Comando, Mando	Comando
Communications	comunicaciones	comunicações
Company	compañía	companhia
Constructor's number	número de construcción	número de construção
Crew	tripulación, equipaje	tripulação, equipagem
Defence	defensa	defesa
Directorate	Dirección	Direcção (Brazil, Direção)
Fighter, fighting	caza	caça
Fighter-bomber	caza-bombardeo	caca-bombardeio, (bombardeiro)
Flight (unit)	escuadrilla	esquadrilha
(act of flying)	vuelo	voo (Brazil, ex vôo)
General headquarters	Cuartel General, Comando General	Quartel General
General Staff	Estado Mayor	Estado Maior
Group	Grupo	Grupo
Helicopter	helicóptero	helicóptero
Liaison	enlace	ligação
Maintenance	mantanamiento	manutenção
Ministry, Minister	Ministerio, Ministro	Ministério, Ministro
Multi-engined	multimotor polimotor(pl.polimotores)	multimotor (pl. multimotores)
Museum	Museo	Museu
Naval	Naval	Naval
Navy	Marina, Armada (Marines are Fucileros Navales)	Marinha, Armada (Marines are Fuzileiros Navais)
Observation	Observación	Observação
Paratroop	paracaidista	paraquedista
Patrol	patrulla	patrulha
(aircraft)	patrullero	patrulheiro, avião de patrulha
Photographic	fotográfico	fotográfico
Reconnaissance	reconocimiento exploración	reconhecimento
Regiment	Regimiento	Regimento
Registration	matrícula (civil)	matricula (civil)
Runway	pista	pista
School	Escuela	Escola
Search and Rescue	Búsqueda y Rescate (- y Salvamento)	Busca e Salvamento
Section	sección	secção (Brazil, seção)
Serial number	matrícula, número de serie	número de série
Service	Servicio	Serviço
Special	especial (pl. especiales)	especial (pl.especiais)
Squadron	Escuadrón(pl.escuadrones) also Escuadrilla	Esquadrão (in Brazil: pl. Esquadrões)
Tactical support	apoyo táctico	apoio táctico (Br.tatico)

ENGLISH	SPANISH	PORTUGUESE
Tail surfaces	cola	cauda
Training	instrucción, entrenamiento	instrução, treino
Transport	transporte	transporte
(freight-)	- de carga	- de carga
Troops	Tropas	Tropas
Wing (unit)	Ala (pl. Alas)	Ala (pl. Alas)
(flying surfaces)	Ala (pl. Alas)	Asa (pl. Asas)

The following words are related to colours and markings :

red	rojo	vermelho (encarnado)
orange	naranja	laranja (alaranjado)
yellow	amarillo	amarelo
green	verde	verde
blue	azul	azul
purple	morado	violeta (roxo)
white	blanco	branco
black	negro	preto
grey	gris	cinza (cinzento)
silver	plateado	prateado
light-	- claro	- claro
dark-	- oscuro	- escuro
olive green	verde oliva	verde oliva (verde azeitona)
camouflage	camuflaje	camuflagem
mottle	moteado	malhado
shading	sombreado	sombreado
colour scheme	pintura	pintura
gloss	brillante	brilhante
matt	mate	mate (baço)

As a rule the adjectives follow the noun and agree with it in gender and number. The regular plural form is obtained by adding an 's' if the word ends in a vowel; exceptions are not uncommon and some are listed above. The Portuguese spoken and written in Brazil differs somewhat, both phonetically and graphically from the Portuguese of Portugal, although a recent orthographic reform has unified some of these differences — for instance, *Fôrça* is now written *Força* as in Portugal. On the other hand, the simplification of the Portuguese language was introduced in Portugal several years before it became accepted in Brazil; thus some earlier Brazilian reference sources may have such words as *Photographico* (instead of *Fotográfico*) or *Nacionaes* (instead of *Nacionais*). The name of the country, now spelled Brasil, was written as Brazil until as late as the mid-1940s, although it was written with an 's' in Portugal from the early 1930s.

ARGENTINA

Area	2,776,643 sq km
Population	26,393,000
Capital	Buenos Aires
Civil registration	LV- LQ- (Govt owned)

The Argentine Republic, named after the Río de la Plata (Silver River) which was discovered by Juan Díaz de Solís in 1515, became independent from Spain in 1816, after a struggle which began with a popular uprising in 1810, but did not achieve internal stability until 1853. The population is mainly of white European origin, race mixing being much less pronounced than in other Latin American countries. Argentina's modernisation began during the rule of General Juan Domingo Perón, who was one of the very few New World leaders to develop a political doctrine with massive popular support - the Justicialismo, or quest for justice - and his prestige was such that, although overthrown by the military in 1955, he was re-elected as president in 1973, and his ideology is still very much alive. Argentina also possesses a proud military tradition and conscription is in existence; all males over twenty are required to serve for a year (two in the Navy), plus up to nine years in the Reserves, and in the case of war another ten years in the National Guard and five (40-45 age group) in the Territorial Guard. Argentina also has claims over a substantial Antarctic territory, and the British colony of the Falkland Islands (Islas Malvinas), culminating in an Argentine invasion on 2 April 1982, and there is a dispute with Chile over the possession of the islands south of Tierra del Fuego. Argentina's economy is based on cattle-raising — some forty per cent of its territory consists of pasture land — and agriculture, but its industrial potential is considerable and is constantly being developed, despite some political unrest and hostility from certain countries to the policies of the current regime.

Funds were first collected in June 1912 for the purchase of military aircraft, and on 8 September an Escuela de Aviación Militar (Military Aviation School) was established at El Palomar, Buenos Aires with a mixture of Blériot XI and Morane-Saulnier monoplanes and Henry Farman biplanes. This was to be the nucleus of the Servicio de Aviación Militar (Military Aviation Service), and such was the will to succeed that the Escuela soon became famous throughout South America, training pilots for the emerging air arms of Paraguay, Peru and Uraguay. The Escuela was the recipient of a couple of presentation Blériot XI during 1913; one was funded by the Aero Club Argentino, another, named 'Centenario' (centennial) was presented by a tobacco company, which also donated a Henry Farman. Two Morane-Saulniers in use were purchased in France. Other aircraft obtained during 1913-14 included additional Blériot XI, a Nieuport 2G named 'América', two Nieuport IV and at least one Deperdussin monoplane. The first Army manoeuvres incorporating military aircraft took place in the province of Entre Ríos in 1914.

The First World War period substantially delayed the expansion of the Argentine air service, as there was no question of procuring aircraft in Europe, and the USA was too far away and lagging behind in aeronautical matters; in any case, Argentina had closer links with Europe. It was thus decided to await the end of hostilities. In the meantime, the Escuela workshops turned out three additional Henry Farmans; and in 1916 a Voisin biplane was actually received from Italy. It was also during 1916 that the embryo of what was to become a naval air arm first appeared — a Henry Farman was assembled by the River Plate Naval Arsenal and allotted to the Parque y Escuela de Aerostación y Aviación de la Armada (Naval Balloon and Aircraft Depot and School) at Puerto Barragán, which had a short life, being closed down in 1918, by which time there were three Henry Farman on charge.

As soon as the war was over, an Italian mission arrived in Argentina, establishing itself at El Palomar and bringing along six Ansaldo SVA biplane fighters, four Caproni Ca 33 trimotor bombers, two Fiat BR.2 light bombers and two Ansaldo SVA.10 reconnaissance biplanes, in addition to two Savoia-built Farman biplane trainers, all of which were presented to the Argentine government. The mission included a Naval detachment, with two Macchi M.7 and two M.9 and two Italian-built Löhner L3 flying-boats which established a naval air base at San Fernando, where a Naval Air Service was founded on 17 October 1919.

Not to be outdone, the French sent an air mission in April 1919 to reorganise the Servicio de Aviación Militar. France had previously, in 1918, provided a handful of war-weary machines — a few Voisin and Caudron G.III, a Caudron 80 which was used as an instructional airframe, and two aircraft for the future naval air arm, a Nieuport 12 and a Georges Lévy 40 Hb2 flying boat, which were in such poor condition that they were never taken on charge. But this time the French were more generous: four SPAD VII and XIII fighters, half a dozen Caudron G.III (which were to supplemented by another fifteen assembled at El Palomar), a pair of Morane-Saulnier MS.35 parasol trainers — later followed by two MS.139 for evaluation — and two Nieuport 28 C1 fighters, which were used for experimental flying.

The Escuela de Aviación Militar became Grupo de Aviación I in 1922, with provision for fighter, bomber/reconnaissance and training squadrons, and a small number of Nieuport-Delage NiD.29 C1 sesquiplane fighters were taken on charge in 1925; a reorganised Escuela was activated in January of that year, receiving ten Avro 504K (including E9428, E9430, H1913, H2024, H2026, H6603, H7422, H7492, H7497) which arrived from Britain with some Bristol F.2b Fighters. Grupo de Aviación III was formed at Paraná in January 1926, heralding the first significant expansion of the service.

The first of eighteen Breguet 19 A1 and B2 reconnaissance bombers arrived in January 1926, being allotted to the I Grupo de Observación; another fourteen were subsequently taken on charge (serials 1 to 30, 33 and 38 have been confirmed, but some of these may be re-numbered rebuilds), and the last machines were not retired until 1937. From France — already Argentina's main source of aircraft — came also twenty-five Dewoitine D.21 single-seat fighters, which remained in use until 1938. At this time, Argentina realised how vital it was to be self-sufficient in the military field and a decision was taken to establish an aircraft factory, which was inaugurated in October 1927 as the Fábrica Militar de Aviones (FMA, Military Air-

craft Factory) at Córdoba. FMA's first contracts were for thirty-two Dewoitine D.21, to be fitted with engines built by the factory's powerplant division; forty Bristol F.2b Mk.III general-purpose biplanes; and a hundred Avro 504R trainers, to enable the new Escuela de Aviación Militar to standardise on a single basic training type. These in fact followed thirty-three licence-built Avro 504K and ten 504R purchased in Britain. As the Dewoitine fighters became surplus to requirements, they were as a rule stored or dismantled for spares, but five were overhauled and presented to the Navy, and three found their way to Paraguay for use in the Gran Chaco war. It is interesting to note that the first seven D.21 to be delivered (as AC-1 to AC-7) were actually built by Dewoitine's Swiss associate company EKW.

By 1930, the FMA engineering staff had amassed enough experience to initiate production of the firm's own designs, which were to equip many Servicio units and show a degree of reliability which was unexpected for such a newcomer to the aeronautical industry. FMA designs included :

Ae.C.1	basic training monoplane; thirteen built for state flying schools.
Ae.C.2	development of the above, initially as a civilian trainer (hence the C designation) with a 165hp Wright R-540, but later modified as the Ae.ME.1 military trainer. Two Ae.C.2 prototypes were followed by seven Ae.ME.1, six of which were delivered to the Argentine demonstration unit 'Escuadrilla Sol de Mayo' (Sun of May Flight) for goodwill flights to neighbouring countries.
Ae.MB.1	light bomber monoplane; 715hp Wright SGR-1820-F3, four 7.65mm guns (two dorsal, one ventral, one in nose) and 400kg of bombs. Prototype only.
Ae.MB.2	production version of the Ae.MB.1 with detail modifications. Fourteen were built in 1936, serialled 201 to 214; one converted for observation duties with serial O-203.

Ae.MO.1 observation version of the Ae.ME.1 with a 235hp Wright R-760-E1. Twelve built for Grupo de Observación N° 1, being taken on charge in July 1934.

Ae.MOe.1 observation/training version of the Ae.MO.1; six were built.

Ae.MOe.2 as Ae.MEe.1 but with re-designed tail surfaces and detail changes; fourteen were built.

Ae.MS.1 ambulance version of the Ae.MOe.1 with a 330hp Wright R-975. Only one was built, flying for the first time in December 1935.

Orders were also placed abroad — for example, the Breguet 19 B2 of the I Grupo de Bombardeo Ligero (I Light Bomber Group) at El Palomar were replaced in 1933 by five Junkers K.43 monoplanes, serialled 101 and 103 to 106, nicknamed 'Vaquitas' (little cows), which served at Paraná, the Grupo's new base, until 1938, and were eventually converted to transports, broadly similar to the single Junkers W.34 (serial 102) ordered at the same time. A K.43 serialled 103 was still on charge as late as 1943. Additionally, evaluation of promising types continued. In October 1936, Cierva C.30a autogiro LV-CEA was used during manoeuvres for artillery spotting, and two similar Avro 671 were acquired late in 1937 (c/ns 1031 and 1032). These served for some time and c/n 1031 eventually became LV-FBL; it is now preserved at the Museo Nacional de Aeronáutica.

The Servicio de Aviación Militar comprised the following first-line units in 1934:

I Grupo de Caza	El Palomar
II Grupo de Caza	Los Tamarindos, Mendoza province
I Grupo de Bombardeo Ligero	El Palomar (later Paraná)
II Grupo de Bombardeo Ligero	Los Tamarindos
I Grupo de Reconocimiento	El Palomar
II Grupo de Reconcimiento	Paraná, Entre Ríos

FMA production capacity was boosted in 1937, a contract for a staggering 500 Focke-Wulf FW 44j Stieglitz primary training biplanes being placed, although only 190 were actually built, powered by the FMA-built IAe.Sh.14, a licence-built version of the Siemens Sh.14. The first few were rolled out in 1938; in 1945 a prototype of an all-wood variant was completed as the IAe.23. Another Focke-Wulf type was adopted for Servicio use — the twin-engined Fw 58B-2 crew-trainer; three arrived from Germany (c/ns 2694 to 2696) and FMA built another thirty-eight. As the prospect of war in Europe increased, a fighter force began to take shape, FMA receiving an order for twenty Curtiss 75-O Hawk fighters, a fixed-undercarriage version of the USAAC P-36 (RAF Mohawk). The first Hawk to be taken on charge, in actual fact the Hawk 75H demonstrator (c/n 12328 ex NR12771) became C-601; it was followed by twenty-nine Curtiss-built Model 75-O c/n 12769 to 12797 which became C-602 to C-630. FMA production comprised C-631 to C-650. The Hawks remained in use as fighters at El Plumerillo until 1953, the survivors being then transferred to the Escuela de Aviación Militar as advanced trainers until grounded in 1954.

Argentina was one of the first Latin American countries to rationalise its serialling system. Un-prefixed block allocations were introduced in 1932 with rôle prefixes being added later. These included
A for Ataque/Attack
B for Bombardeo/Bomber
C for Caza/Fighter
E for Escuela/Trainer
O for Observación/Observation
T for Transporte/Transport
This system remains in use, although the very frequent reallocations and renumberings make positive aircraft identification rather complicated.

The Servicio had its structure gradually modified to suit the new strategic needs, operational Grupos being controlled by Air Regiments since 1938:

I Regimiento de Aviación at El Palomar
I Grupo de Caza
I Grupo de Reconocimiento
Escuadrilla de Transporte

II Regimiento de Aviación at Paraná
I Grupo de Bombardeo Ligero
II Grupo de Reconocimiento
Escuadrilla de Observación

III Regimiento de Aviación at Los Tamarindos
II Grupo de Caza
II Grupo de Bombardeo Ligero

IV Regimiento de Aviación to be formed at Villa Mercedes.

The Escuela de Aviación Militar comprised by then two separate establishments and was shortly afterwards to receive thirty North American NA.16-4P (NA.34) general purpose trainers (c/n 34-389 to 418), an early version of the famous AT-6 Texan. A medium bomber force was in the process of receiving twenty-five Martin 139WA twin-engined monoplanes which were serialled B-501 to B-525; the first machine was actually the Martin 139WA demonstrator, the others being 139WAA (WAA for Military Export, Argentine Army). Observation Grupos were about to re-equip with the Douglas 8A-2, an export version of the USAAC's Northrop A-17, thirty of which were delivered in the spring of 1938 and serialled O-401 to O-430 (c/ns 348 to 377). These equipped a Grupo de Ataque of the I Regimiento de Aviación at El Palomar (later under the control of the IV Brigada Aérea at El Plumerillo), and were replaced by Argentine-designed Calquíns during the early 1950s.

The small transport force, which was to become much larger as its role grew in importance, received Lockheed 10E Electra c/n 1125 and 12B Electra Juniors c/ns 1228 and 1249. Plans were also in hand to modernise the training units and a Curtiss-Wright CW.A14D Osprey c/n 14-2001 ex NX433W was acquired for evaluation with the serial E-439. At the same time, older civil aircraft were taken on charge, including a Fokker Universal which became T-201, Consolidated 17 Fleetster T-202 (believed to be ex-Naval 2-Gt-3) and Douglas Dolphin T-203 (ex-Navy). Two Fairchild 82 were used for photo-survey as 151 and 152.

The US involvement in the Second World War brought Argentina a number of problems. The country felt no hostility towards the Axis powers, having many citizens of German or Italian origin; but tended to be mistrustful of US plans for South America, and it was only logical that efforts were made to remain neutral. As a result, Argentina did not benefit from Lend-Lease deliveries, and had no other way of procuring aircraft in the USA. The obvious solution was to exploit the FMA's capabilities to the full.

The FMA, which had been renamed the Instituto Aerotécnico (IAe, Aerotechnical Institute) in October 1943, built a prototype of an all-metal advanced trainer, the IAe.21, which, combining a North American NA.16-1P fuselage with a new wing and retractable undercarriage, was found to be satisfactory but could not be built in quantity because of the shortage of light alloys. It was then redesigned with a wooden structure as the IAe.22DL, powered by the IAe.16 El Gaucho nine-cylinder radial engine with provision for armament. Two hundred IAe. 22DL were built for the Argentine Air Force, with serials Ea-701 to Ea-900, a number eventually becoming IAe.22C with the 475hp Armstrong-Siddeley Cheetah 25 radial; a factory demonstrator was also completed and later delivered to the Brazilian Air Force. A twin-engined attack bomber which was not unlike the de Havilland Mosquito, the IAe.24 Calquín (Royal Eagle) was also developed but did not fly until July 1947; a hundred were built (A-01 to A-100) for the IV Brigada Aérea at El Plumerillo with two 1050hp Pratt & Whitney R-1830-SC3G radials, saw service during the 1955 troubles (during which two were brought down by ground fire) and were phased out in 1958. Plans to build another hundred were abandoned for financial reasons.

The service had already been upgraded to Army Command status, when the campaign to give it full autonomy finally succeeded. It was renamed the Fuerza Aérea Argentina (Argentine Air Force) on 4 January 1945, an Air Ministry being formed on the same day. The country was divided into six Air Zones, with headquarters at Buenos Aires, El Palomar, Paraná, Córdoba, Villa Mercedes and Tandil

respectively, and provision was made for the existence of six Air Regiments. The FAA was on its way to becoming the most powerful air arm in Latin America.

The USA had vast numbers of surplus aircraft for disposal, and supplied thirty Beechcraft AT-11 Kansan crew trainers, eight Douglas C-54 Skymaster and the first few Douglas C-47 for a future transport command. Britain benefitted from larger orders, for fifteen Avro Lancaster I and thirty Lincoln B. Mk.2 bombers, one hundred Gloster Meteor F.Mk.4 jet fighters — the first to be exported anywhere in the world — and batches of Bristol 170 Freighter, de Havilland DH.104 Dove and Vickers Viking transports, in addition to a hundred Percival Prentice trainers. Italy, desperately trying to build up a new aeronautical industry, was delighted to receive orders for Fiat G.46 and G.55 trainers, and a G.59-2A was also delivered for evaluation. A Supermarine Spitfire HF.IX was also obtained, but ten Spitfire T.Mk.9 which were to follow were in fact cancelled.

New aircraft were only part of the FAA's plans for expansion. In 1947 it signed on a technical adviser of international repute, the former Luftwaffe General and fighter ace Adolf Galland, who was to direct the force's organisation throughout the Perón régime; other German refugees, headed by Dipl.Ing. Kurt Tank, helped bring the IAe up to modern standards, two generally similar jet types being designed: the IAe.27 Pulqui by the French expatriate Émile Dewoitine, and the IAe.33 Pulqui II by Kurt Tank himself. The IAe.27 was Latin America's first jet design; it first flew in August 1947 with an imported Rolls-Royce Derwent 5 turbojet. The IAe.33 derived from the wartime Focke-Wulf Ta 183 project (which also inspired the Soviet MiG 15) and five prototypes were built. It was at one time planned to produce the IAe.33 as a Meteor replacement, although the type proved disappointing during its flight test programme and never went beyond experimental status.

Four operational commands were established — Air Defence, Strategic, Tactical and Air Transport. The IAe was absorbed in 1952 by the Industrias Aeronáuticas y Mecánicas del Estado (IAME, State Aeronautical and Mechanical Industries), although government policies, which included plans for the production of a cheap 'people's car', the Justicialista, reduced aircraft manufacturing to a trickle. The IA.35 Huanquero (originally 'Justicialista del Aire') twin-engined light transport, first flown in September 1953 with 1st Lt Jorge Conan Doyle (a descendant of the writer) at the controls, did enter production and became quite successful, several versions being built; but other projects were shelved when Perón was ousted from power, the German engineering team disbanded, and the IAME restyled as the National Directorate for Aircraft Manufacture and Research (DINFIA), the Córdoba factory assuming its traditional name of FMA in July 1956.

Unbuilt projects included the IA.37 Pulqui III twin-turbojet, delta-wing all-weather fighter, designed by Dipl.Ing. Reimar Horten; the IA.38 four-engined flying wing transport, also a Horten creation, a prototype being actually tested in flight (as was a full-scale glider version of the IA.37); the IA.30 Ñancú twin-engined single-seat fighter, powered by two Rolls-Royce Merlin 604, a prototype being completed; and the IA.31 Colibrí tandem-seat primary and aerobatic trainer, three prototypes flying with either the 155hp Blackburn Cirrus Major 3 or the 145hp de Havilland Gipsy Major 10.

Perón's downfall, although undoubtedly a victory of democracy, almost ruined the country. Foreign currency was so scarce, and the likelihood of an economic revival made so doubtful by political agitation, that the FAA had to make do with whatever aircraft it had for a number of years. The Meteors, which were due to be replaced in 1956-57 by Canadair Sabres, were destined to soldier on until December 1971, an initial order for thirty-six Sabres being cancelled due to lack of funds. The number of different types in service also caused additional problems connected with spares availability, although some earlier machines — such as four Air France airliners interned in June 1940, Dewoitine 333 F-ANQB c/n 1 and F-ANQC c/n 2, and Dewoitine 338 F-AQBR c/n 18 and F-AQBT c/n 20, which served as military transports during the war — had already been disposed of.

Argentina's quasi-self-sufficiency days in military aviation had now come to an end, and it became obvious that US military assistance was essential. Efforts were still made to maintain the traditional links with Europe, and ten Holste MH.1521C Broussard light communications aircraft were ordered in 1956 (although only seven were actually taken on charge), followed by forty-eight Morane-Saulnier MS.760A Paris light jet transports in the following year; but it was not enough and the country's resources did not allow for extensive foreign contracts. From the USA came Beechcraft T-34A Mentor basic trainers, Bell, Hiller and Sikorsky helicopters, a few assorted light aircraft and additional Douglas C-47 transports. The FMA was kept busy through contracts for the assembly of seventy-five Beechcraft T-34A and the licence production of thirty-six MS.760A Paris, using French-supplied sub-assemblies; and limited manufacture of the IA.35 Huanquero and such civil types as the IA.46 Ranquel and the El Boyero (The Cowboy) series of high-wing monoplanes was also undertaken.

Even under such difficult conditions, the FAA did not become wholly dependent on US assistance. France was a favourite alternate supplier, releasing sixty Sud Fennecs which were allocated to the Navy in 1966-67; other aircraft came from Canada (DHC.2 Beaver, DHC.3 Otter and more recently the DHC.6 Twin Otter) and the Netherlands (with Fokker F.27 Friendship and in 1975 the F.28 Fellowship). It was initially planned to order eight Hawker-Siddeley HS.748 for the Fuerza Aerea Argentina, but financing problems led to the adoption of the Friendship instead. Three former Aerolíneas Argentinas Sud SE.210 Caravelle VIN twin-jet airliners were also obtained. A contract signed in August 1970 called for ten Dassault Mirage IIIEA interceptors and two IIIDA operational trainers, and serious thought was given to the local manufacture of the type for an interceptor force of eighty aircraft, although once again economics dictated otherwise. Ten BAC Canberra B.Mk.62 and two T.Mk.64 were ordered in mid-1969 and delivered in 1971-72. The older helicopters were supplemented by such modern types as the Sud SA.315B Lama from France, and the Bell 212, Hughes 500M and Sikorsky S.61 from the USA, although three Vertol CH-47C were initially embargoed by the Carter administration.

At the same time, the FMA kept up with the latest requirements, and evolved the twin-turboprop IA.50 Guaraní II light transport from the IA.35 Constancia via the Guaraní I prototype (LQ-HER), which retained the earlier type's twin fins and rudders; although the IA.50 was a promising type, it was never destined to be built in large numbers, the few machines actually completed being allocated to the FAA (one was temporarily used by the Navy). More recently, the IA.58 Pucará (Fortress) twin-turboprop close-support aircraft has won a production contract and is now in service; it was also offered for export, where its success appeared to be assured as there were no direct competitors. After a disappointing start — an order from Mauritania was cancelled for financial reasons, another from Nicaragua due to the overthrow of the Somoza regime, and a projected contract for twenty-five for the Peruvian Air Force failed to materialise — small numbers were eventually sold to the Dominican Republic, Uraguay, Venezuela and an unspecified Middle-eastern country, and the type was also evaluated in July 1980 by the Brazilan Air Force. Subsequent versions included the more heavily-armed and improved IA.58B and the IA.66 with two Garrett-AiResearch TPE331, a dual-control variant of the latter being also developed for use by the Instituto Nacional de Aviación Civil (INAC, National Civil Aviation Institute). The latest design is the IA.63 basic jet trainer, developed in close co-operation with Dornier. Four prototypes were ordered, three with the Garrett AiResearch TFE731-3, the fourth with a Pratt & Whitney JT15D-5 for comparative tests.

The Argentine aeronautical industry is not limited to the FMA. Apart from the Aero Talleres-built Aero Boero series (not to be confused with the IAe.20 El Boyero, light Cessna types are assembled by TENSA at Córdoba, Chincul SA at Mendoza builds Piper Cherokee versions (including a military trainer version of the Cherokee Arrow 200 with provision for armament, which at the time of writing is still in the prototype stage) as well as the Aztec, Navajo and Seneca twins, and RACA is Argentina's Hughes licensee. An earlier project was not so successful; Aviones Lockheed-Kaiser SA were formed in 1960 as a subsidiary of Industrias Kaiser Argentina, the Argentine branch of Kaiser Industries, to build the Lockheed CL.402 high-wing transport. A prototype, c/n 3001 LV-PXI later LV-GOL, was followed by eleven of the planned five hundred production aircraft, as CL.402-2-4 four-seaters and CL.402-2-5 six-seaters, before lack of interest caused the plan to be terminated. The CL.402 was built in Mexico as the Lockheed-Azcarate LASA.60, and had a much more successful career in Italy, where it was built by Macchi as the AL.60.

The first Argentine aircraft to land in the Antarctic, in 1962, marked the beginning of an ambitious scheme to explore part of the continent and claim it for Argentina. An Air Force branch, the Fuerza Aérea de Tareas Antártcias (Antarctic Air Task Force) was formed at El Palomar in 1966 with US-supplied Douglas LC-47 transports, and was eventually supplemented by an Antarctic-based unit, the I Grupo Antártico at Base Aérea Militar Benjamín Matienzo. Aircraft flown to or in the area included besides the LC-47, the DHC.2 Beaver, DHC.3 Otter, DHC.6 Twin Otter, Douglas C-54 and DC-6, Grumman HU-16 and helicopters, with the larger aircraft operating from BAM Vice-Comodoro Marambio.

The most recent events which have had a most significant effect on the Argentine forces are the Argentine invasion of the Falkland Islands and its dependencies in April 1982 and the re-taking of the islands by British forces during May and June. The various actions and aircraft losses are described in an appendix which appears on page 285, though of course at the time of going to press the details are not as complete as we should like. For this reason we have not in general attempted to include all of the losses in the 'Aircraft Review' sections which follow.

There will of course be longer term implications arising from the conflict, particularly in respect of relationships with other countries, some of which were more supportive to the Argentine cause than others, and in terms of revision of the disposition of forces in future. Broadly, the European nations lined up behind Britain and imposed sanctions which included the embargoing of arms awaiting delivery, notably the balance of the Super Etendard force from France, and of course Lynx helicopters from Britain. Likewise the United States declared itself as supporting Britain, and is unlikely to be considered as a source of supplies for some time to come. However, the Soviet Union, an unlikely ally of a militarist right-wing government, is known to have supplied electronic equipment, and through its Cuban allies may have sent further support. A loan of Bandeirantes for maritime patrol was made by Brazil, and Peru acted as an intermediary for the supply of other weaponry. Venezuela also declared its support for Argentina, and may offer future assistance. Israel and South Africa have also been mentioned as probable sources of military supplies.

FMA badge - appears on the fin of most FMA-built aircraft.

Current Organisation

The Fuerza Aérea Argentina is currently organised into four commands:

Comando de Operacions Aéreas (Air Operations Command)
Comando de Regiones Aéreas (Air Regions Command)
Comando de Material (Material Command)
Comando de Personal (Personnel Command)

The Comando de Operaciones Aéreas comprises the following units.

I Brigada Aérea at BAM El Palomar, Buenos Aires province comprises:
STAM (Servicio de Transportes Aéreos Militares, Military Air Transport Service) made up of:
I Escuadrón de Transporte   Lockheed C-130, IA.50 Guarani II, Boeing 707
LADE (Líneas Aéreas del Estado, State Airlines) with Fokker F.27/F.28 and Twin Otter.
Departamento de Aviones Presidenciales with Fokker F.28, Sabre 75A and Sikorsky S.58T.

II Brigada Aérea at BAM General Justo José de Urquiza, Paraná, Entre Ríos province.
I Escuadrón de Bombardeo   Canberra 62/64
I Escuadrón Fotográfico   IA.50 Guaraní II, Lear Jet 35A

III Brigada Aérea at BAM Reconquista:
II Escuadrón de Exploración y Ataque   IA.58 Pucará

IV Brigada Aérea at BAM El Plumerillo, Mendoza province:
I Esc. de Caza-Bombardeo   Douglas A-4P
II Esc. de Caza-Bombardeo   MS.760A Paris
III Esc. de Caza-Bombardeo   MS.760A Paris

V Brigada Aérea at BAM General Pringles, Villa Reynolds, San Luis province:
IV Esc. de Caza-Bombardeo   Douglas A-4P
V Esc. de Caza-Bombardeo   Douglas A-4P

VI Brigada Aérea at BAM Tandil, Buenos Aires province:
II Escuadrón de Caza   IAI Dagger
III Escuadrón de Caza   IAI Dagger

VII Brigada Aérea at BAM Doctor Mariano Moreno, Moron, Buenos Aires province:
I Escuadrón de Exploracion y Ataque   Hughes 500M, Bell UH-1H

VIII Brigada Aérea at BAM Doctor Mariano Moreno, Moron, Buenos Aires province:
I Escuadrón de Caza   Mirage IIIEA/DA

IX Brigada Aérea at BAM Comodoro Rivadavia has a communications squadron in formation.

X Brigada Aérea is to be activated shortly.

There are also the following units :
I Escuadrón de Búsqueda y Salvamento at BAM El Palomar with detachments elsewhere, using Grumman HU-16B and SA.315B Lama.

I Escuadrón Antártico at BAM Benjamín Matienzo and BAM Río Gallegos, Córdoba province with Sikorsky S.61R, DHC.2 Beaver, DHC.6 Twin Otter and Douglas LC-47.

SADEN, Servicios Aéreos del Estado Nacional (National State-operated Air Services) at BAM Rio Gallegos, Cordoba with Aero Commander 500U).

Grupo Aéreo Escuela, at BAM Córdoba comprising
Escuela de Aviación Militar with Beechcraft T-34A and MS.760A Paris.
Escuela de Especialidades (Specialists School)
Escuela de Paracaidistas (Paratroop School)
I Escuadrón de Comunicaciones Escuela with T-34A, MS.760A Paris, IA.35 Huanquero.

The military airline LADE (Líneas Aéreas del Estado) was formed on 23 October 1945 by the merger of two Air Service organisations, the Línea Aérea del Sudoeste (LASO, Southwest airline) and the Línea Aérea del Noreste (LANE, Northeast airline), both of which had been activated during the Second World War to set up a comprehensive internal airline network. LADE aircraft, which are controlled by the I Air Brigade, are flown and serviced by air force personnel, but have civilian cabin attendants and stewardesses, and their operations come under the supervision of the Department of Civil Aviation.

LADE - light blue/white disc with red letters. Two-tone brown eagle with a yellow beak.

Military Air Bases

1	Buenos Aires (El Palomar)
2	Morón
2A	Tandil
3	Rosario
4	Santa Fe
5	Paraná (General Urquiza)
6	Orán
7	Jujuy
8	Salta
9	San Miguel de Tucumán
10	Resistencia
11	San Juan
12	El Plumerillo
13	Córdoba
14	Villa Mercedes
14A	Villa Reynolds (General Pringles)
15	Santa Rosa
16	Mar del Plata
17	Bahía Blanca
18	Comodoro Rivadavia
19	Rio Gallegos
20	Rio Grande

Antarctic bases are Tnte.Benjamin Matienzo and Vicecomodoro Marambio. During the Falklands campaign bases were established in the islands at Port Stanley (Puerto Argentino - BAM Malvinas), Goose Green, San Carlos, Fox Bay and Pebble Is.

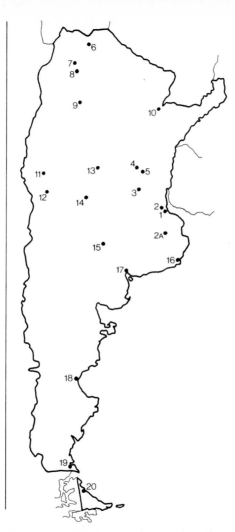

Aircraft Review

COLOURS AND MARKINGS

The colours of the flag designed in 1812 by General Manuel Belgrano (light blue/white/light blue) were reproduced in roundel form and initially applied to the wings only, although since 1945 the rule has been that the roundel should also appear on the fuselage sides. Horizontal light blue/white/light blue rudder stripes, with the 'Sun of May' insignia which commemorates the May 1810 republican uprising, on the white stripe, have now been superseded by a reproduction of the state flag as a fin flash, but presidential aircraft as a rule have the national coat of arms as their only fin marking; the arms are based on those of liberator General José de San Martin's Army of the Andes.

Several camouflage schemes have been used in recent years, including a dark green/dark brown disruptive scheme and a green/grey close support scheme, with light grey undersides in both cases, but the USAF tactical scheme of dark green, green and tan with light grey undersides is also used, as is a regulation for low-visibility inscriptions. Thus, *Fuerza Aérea Argentina* and serial numbers may appear in tan on green and green on tan, blending nicely in with the camouflage.

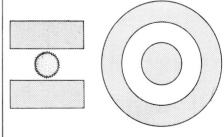

SERIAL NUMBERS

Argentine Air Force aircraft are serialled in (often

re-allocated) blocks of three digits, with a letter prefix to indicate their primary role, as follows:

A	Ataque	attack
B	Bombardeo	bomber
BS	Búsqueda y Salvamento	search and rescue
C	Caza	fighter
E	Escuela	trainer
Ea	Escuela avanzada	advanced trainer
F	Fotográfico	photographic
H	Helicóptero	helicopter
I	Intercepción	interception
O	Observación	observation
P	Polar	Antarctic use
PG	Propositos Generales	general purpose
S	Sanitario	ambulance
T	Transporte	transport
TA	Transporte Antártico	Antarctic transport
TC	Transporte de Carga	freight transport
TS	Transporte Sanitario	medical transport

MAINTENANCE NUMBERS

It is known that many FAA aircraft have, in addition to their serial numbers, a maintenance number, which is only occasionally painted on the aircraft, and consists of a type prefix, followed by a sequential number, not necessarily related to the serial. Some known examples of this practice are the following :

Douglas C-47	241	e.g. 241-15 TC-17
		241-16 TC-18
Douglas A-4P	243	243-07 C-207
North-American F-86	251	251-06 C-108
		251-20 C-124
		251-23 C-123
MS.760A Paris	271	271-04 E-205
		271-13 E-215
		271-21 E-224
		271-22 E-225
		271-24 E-227
		271-27 E-230
		271-29 E-233
		271-30 E-234
		271-32 E-236

Beechcraft T-34A	283	283-37 E-048
		283-39 E-052
IA.50 Guaraní II	293	293-03 T-110 (and retained when used by the Navy 5-T-30)
		293-05 T-115
		293-10 T-120
		293-12 T-122
		293-15 F-31
DH.104 Dove	311	311-17 T-87
Grumman HU-16B	331	331-01 BS-01
		331-02 BS-02
		331-03 BS-03

AIRCRAFT USED

Aircraft known to have been used by the Argentine Air Force in post-war years include the following. Note that some have been preserved at the Museo Nacional de Aeronáutica, Aeroparque Jorge Newbery Buenos Aires, better known as the Aeroparque.

AERO COMMANDER 500U

Fourteen aircraft delivered in 1968, primarily for use by SADEN :

T-131	c/n 1742-38
T-132	1743-39
T-133	1744-40
T-134	1745-41
T-135	1746-42
T-136	1748-43
T-137	1749-44
T-138	1757-46
T-139	1758-47
T-140	1759-48
T-141	1768-51
T-142	1769-52
T-143	1770-53
T-144	1771-54

T-145 to T-153 are known to exist but are not identified. An earlier aircraft T-130 c/n 545-214 ex LQ-MAY is a model 500S delivered in 1956.
T-133 and T-134 were later used by the Comando de Material and T-140 by the Dirección de Circulación Aérea y Aeródromos (Air Traffic Control and Airfields Directorate), crashing on 25.1.78. An Aero Commander has also been reported as BS-11.

AIRSPEED AS.65 CONSUL

Ten were delivered in 1947, c/ns 5140 to 5144 and 5152 to 5156, probably all equipped as ambulances. Known serials included S-7, S-12 and S-21.

AVRO LANCASTER B.Mk.1

Fifteen were obtained for use by the II Grupo de Bombardeo of the III Brigada Aérea, replacing the old Martin 139WAA from mid-1948; the last machine was retired in 1968. A chronic lack of spares limited their use to a considerable extent. Three were converted to transports.

B-031	ex PA375/G-11-14	wfu
B-032	PA376/G-11-15	wfu
B-033	PA377/G-11-16	wfu
B-034	PA350/G-11-17	to TC-034; w/o
B-035	PA348/G-11-18	wfu
B-036	PA349/G-11-19	w/o 15.11.57
B-037	PA344/G-11-20	w/o 9.55
B-038	PA369/G-11-21	to T-038, TC-038; wfu
B-039	PA346/G-11-22	wfu
B-040	PA365/G-11-23	to T-040; w/o 16.12.65
B-041	RA265/G-11-24	wfu
B-042	RA798/G-11-25	w/o
B-043	RA788/G-11-26	wfu
B-044	RA789/G-11-27	wfu
B-045	PA378/G-11-28	wfu

Two Lancastrian transports were also used :

T-101	ex TX287/LV-ACU	c/n 1402 wfu
T-102	TX289/LV-ACV	1403 w/o 11.12.60

AVRO LINCOLN B.Mk.2

Thirty were delivered, the first on 19 September 1947 and the remainder during 1947-48 for use by the I Grupo de Bombardeo of the V Brigada Aérea. They were declared obsolete on 1 August 1967. The first twelve came from RAF stocks; the remainder were specially built by Armstrong-Whitworth and had no previous RAF identity.

B-001	c/n 1405	ex RE343	w/o 1947
B-002	1406	RE349	w/o 1949
B-003	1407	RE350	to T-101; w/o 15.8.60
B-004	1408	RE351	wfu 8.67
B-005	1409	RE352	wfu 9.65
B-006	1410	RE353	wfu 7.64
B-007	1411	RE354	w/o
B-008	1412	RE355	w/o 5.63
B-009	1413	RE356	w/o 12.55

B-010	1414	RE408	wfu 3.66
B-011	1415	RE409	w/o 17.5.61
B-012	1416	RE410	w/o 1949
B-013	1489		wfu 1.65
B-014	1490		w/o 5.65
B-015	1491		wfu 11.64
B-016	1492		wfu 1.68
B-017	1493		wfu 6.65
B-018	1494		w/o
B-019	1495		w/o 3.50
B-020	1496		w/o 1.66
B-021	1497		w/o 5.58
B-022	1498		wfu 6.67
B-023	1499		w/o 11.54
B-024	1500		w/o 11.64
B-025	1501		wfu 1.65
B-026	1502		w/o 5.60
B-027	1503		w/o 1953
B-028	1504		w/o 9.55
B-029	1505		w/o 1.65
B-030	1506		w/o 1952

B-022 was converted to a tanker. B-003 became a transport serialled T-101 and named 'Cruz del Sud' (Southern Cross), being used for supply dropping over the Antarctic bases as well as more routine jobs; it was temporarily registered as LV-ZEI and was written off on 15.8.60. B-017 was preserved at Villa Reynolds. The Lincoln at the Aeroparque museum carries serial B-010, but this is believed not to be its true identity.

BEECHCRAFT C-45H EXPEDITOR

One aircraft, previously on the civil register, was obtained in 1967 and serialled T-78.

BEECHCRAFT AT-11 KANSAN

Thirty were delivered to the Escuela de Aviación Militar with serials E-101 to E-130. One became LV-GFU; others were re-serialled, examples being Ea-11, F-2 (operated by the Navy), F-3, S-4, T-91, T-101 (solid nose). E-117 was modified with a solid nose. The type was retired in 1967-68, and E-110 preserved at the Aeroparque.

BEECHCRAFT 45 MENTOR (T-34A)

Fifteen were delivered from Wichita and serialled E-001 to E-015; another seventy-five were assembled by FMA from Beechcraft-supplied components, as follows :
E-016 to E-035 c/n CG.180 to 199
E-036 to E-090 CG.224 to 278
They were mainly used by the Escuela de Aviacion Militar, but a few went to the I Grupo de Ataque of the VII Brigada Aérea (two of these were written off on 25.11.70 and 15.10.72 respectively). About thirty remained in use by late 1979. Known losses included :

E-013	w/o	29.5.68
E-047		14.6.67
E-051		1.11.71
E-054		3.10.68
E-058		6.10.67
E-061		7.6.67
E-077		20.3.68

BEECHCRAFT BONANZA 35

One was used in 1967; details not known.

BELL 47G/J

At least half a dozen were taken on charge, and four were still in use by 1977-78. Three 47G-2A, c/ns 2698 to 2700, were handed over to SADEN by the Argentine National Bank. Two Bell 47J were H-52 and H-53.

BELL UH-1D/H IROQUOIS

Four UH-1D, serialled H-10 to H-13, were delivered for communications and attached to the I Brigada Aérea. The three UH-1H, serialled H-14 to H-16, went to the I Escuadrón de Exploración y Ataque; H-16 c/n 11885 is ex US Army 69-15997. Another six UH-1H may have been delivered at a later date.

BELL 212

Eight aircraft, serialled H-81 to H-88; c/ns are believed to be 30603 to 30610.

BOEING 707

A 707-387B c/n 21070 was acquired for the Escuadrilla Presidencial as T-01 and later converted to a freighter with the serial TC-91. This was followed by an ex Aerolíneas Argentinas 707-372C c/n 20077 ex LV-LGP which was serialled TC-92 in mid-1980, and 707-387C TC-93 c/n 19962, ex Aerolíneas Argentinas LV-JGP on 5.1.82.

BRISTOL 170 FREIGHTER

Thirty were to be delivered, commencing in November 1946, but in the event only fifteen were taken on charge :

T-27	c/n 12737	ex LV-XII	to TC-270; wfu
T-28	12750	LV-XIL	w/o 8.7.49
T-29	12749	LV-XIJ	wfu 1958
T-30	12751	LV-XIM/LV-AEY	to TC-330; wfu
T-31	12752	LV-XIN	wfu 1959
T-32	12753	LV-XIO/LV-AEZ	wfu 1959
T-33	12754	LV-XIP/LV-AEX	wfu 1959
T-34	12758	LV-XIQ	wfu 1959
T-35	12760	LV-XIR	wfu 1959
T-36	12764	LV-XIS	wfu 1959
T-37	12765	LV-XIT	w/o 25.9.51
T-38	12768	LV-XIU	wfu 1959
T-39	12769	LV-XIV	w/o 31.8.49
T-40	12770	LV-XIW	wfu 1959
T-41	12771	LV-XIX	w/o 8.53

TC-330 was preserved at the Aeroparque.

CESSNA A.182J/K

Acquired mid to late 1960s. Known aircraft are PG-341, PG-342, PG-344, PG-348, PG-349, PG-351, PG-353, PG-355, PG-356, PG-357, PG-358, PG-367, PG-369, PG-370, PG-373, PG-374, PG-375, PG-376, PG-378, PG-379; PG-373 an A.182K was written off 28.1.78; another crashed on 3.9.68.

CESSNA 310

At least one used, serial PG-386.

DASSAULT MIRAGE IIIEA/DA

A contract placed in August 1970 called for ten Mirage IIIEA, serialled I-003 to I-012, and two Mirage IIIDA, serialled I-001 and I-002. Another two IIIEA were never delivered, and plans for licence production were dropped. Seven replacement IIIEA were ordered in 1977, serials I-013 to I-019, and delivered during 1979-80. The 'I' prefix was to have been changed to 'C' during 1978, but this was not implemented. An unidentified aircraft crashed March 79.

DE HAVILLAND DH.104 DOVE 1/2

Forty-three Dove 1 and a single Dove 2 (T-99) were delivered
though initial plans had called for fifty aircraft. None remain
in service; three were handed over to the Prefectura Nacional
Marítima, and one to the Paraguayan Air Force.

T-51	c/n 04145	ex LV-XZZ	to T-66
T-54	04027	LV-XWH	to T-67
T-55	04069	LV-XWS	
T-56	04039	LV-XWO	to T-68
T-57	04042	LV-XWL	to T-83
T-58	04067	LV-XWQ	to T-72
T-59	04046	LV-XWN	to T-76
T-60	04070	LV-XWT	to T-80
T-61	04095	LV-XWK	
T-62	04109	LV-XWZ	
T-63	04108	LV-XWY	
T-64	04146	LV-YAD	
T-68	04178	LV-YAL	
T-69	04066	LQ-XWP	to LV-IDM
T-69	04165	LV-YAJ	to F-4, F-11
T-70	04093	LV-XWV	
T-70	04142	LV-XZW	
T-71	04198	LV-YBO	
T-72	04204	LV-YBS	
T-73	04202	LV-YBR	to Paraguay AF T-73
T-74	04200	LV-YBQ	
T-75	04216	LV-YBH	
T-77	04136	LV-XZS	dbf 12.68
T-78	04045	LQ-XWM	
T-79	04137	LV-XZT	to T-73, LV-XZT, w/o 7.71
T-79	04197	LV-YBN	
T-81	04138	LQ-XZU	
T-81	04191	LV-YAT	
T-82	04237	LV-YBJ	
T-83	04214	LV-YBU	
T-84	04215	LV-YBG	
T-85	04197	LV-YBI	
T-86	04232	LV-YBF	
T-87	04248	LV-YBT	to LQ-YCP
T-90	04156	LV-YAI	to F-5, F-12, LV-ALA
T-90	04188	LQ-YAQ	to T-99
T-95	04110	LV-XXD	to LV-XXD
T-96	04130	LV-XXE	to LV-XXE
T-97	04187	LV-YAP	
T-98	04180	LV-YAN	
T-99	04206	LV-YBT	to T-90
S-1	04230	LV-YBD	
S-2	04203	LQ-YAX	to LQ-YAX
S-3	04231	LV-YBE	

DE HAVILLAND CANADA DHC.2 BEAVER

Six acquired for I Grupo Aéreo Antártico. Four were actually written off in the Antarctic, one of them on 14.10.76,
and the remains of P-05 were preserved at the Aeroparque
museum.

P-01	c/n 1437	w/o
P-02	1438	wfu
P-03	1480	w/o
P-04	1494	w/o
P-05	1506	w/o 9.8.68; remains preserved
P-06	1508	wfu

DE HAVILLAND CANADA DHC.3 OTTER

Two were delivered in February 1965 for Antarctic use by
the Grupo Aéreo Antártico :

P-11	c/n 447	to Paraguay AF T-05 9.11.71
P-12	448	wfu 1972

DH CANADA DHC.6 TWIN OTTER 200

Seven aircraft for LADE and Antarctic use, the first five
delivered in November and December 1968, and the other
two in October 1969 :

T-81	c/n 165	
T-82	167	
T-83	170	
T-84	172	
T-85	173	
T-86	225	
T-87	230	w/o 7.8.77

DOUGLAS C-47

About forty delivered, of which about six were still in use in
1978-79. Known aircraft include :

T-01			
T-02			to TA-02
T-03			
TS-04			
T-05			
T-08	c/n 12850	ex LV-ABY	
T-09	13150	LV-ADJ	
T-10			to CP-1622 1980
T-11			to TC-11
T-12	11920	LV-AQP	

T-13			
T-14			
T-15			to TC-15
T-16			
T-17			to TC-17; w/o 5.70
T-18			to TC-18
T-19	4754	PP-ASQ	to T-39, LQ-JNB
T-19	16790/33538	LV-ACG	
T-20	2012	PP-YQL	to TC-20
T-21			to TC-21
T-22	12190	PP-YQV	to PP-JAC
T-23			
T-24			to TC-24
T-25			to TC-25
T-26			
T-27	13621	PP-YQA	to Paraguay AF T-27
T-27			to TC-27
T-28	13783/25228	PP-YQJ	to TC-28;w/o 5.5.69
T-29	4825	PP-AVI	
T-30	14426/25871	PP-YQM	
T-31			to TC-31
T-32	4365	PP-ANM	to TA-05 'El Montañes' and preserved at Aeroparque.
TC-32			
TA-33	9254	N148A	w/o 10.12.64
TC-33			
T-34			to TC-34
T-35			to TC-35
T-36	12025	PP-YQB	to TC-36
T-37	4957	PP-NBJ	to TC-37
T-38	4280	PP-ANS	to TC-38, LQ-IPC
T-39	19438	PP-ANF	to N48FN (VIP interior)
T-40			
T-42			
T-48			
T-69			
TC-89			
T-101			
T-102			
T-103			
S-2	14010/25455	LQ-ACF,LQ-MSP	
S-3			
E-301			
E-304			
VR-10			
VR-11			
VR-12			

To these must be added EC-47 TA-06 and TA-07 transferred
from the USAF in 1966 for Antarctic use; an EC-47 serialled
VR-14 used by the Instituto Nacional de Aviación Civil (Nat-

Bell 212 H-85 of the VII Brigada Aérea, in a colour scheme of mid-green and tan camouflage.

English Electric (BAC) Canberra B.62 B-101, seen in 1970 when it wore the marks G-AYHO for participation at Farnborough prior to delivery.

ional Civil. Aviation Institute) in military markings for navaid checking; and DC-3-294 T-145 which was operated by Air France as F-ARQJ (c/n 2122) on the Buenos Aires-Mendoza-Santiago service in 1940 and was impressed into Argentine military service. TA-05 was preserved at the Aeroparque in 1971. Aircraft used for communications at Air Brigade level included T-23 of the I Brigada Aérea; one of the IV Brigada Aérea was written off on 16.4.70; and one of the V Brigada Aérea written off on 8.8.71. Most Argentine AF C-47s were C-47A or C-47B, but T-19, T-32 and T-38 were R4D-1 (the US Navy model), T-29 a C-53, T-20 a DC-3-228, T-37 a DC-3-435A and TA-33 an LC-47A conversion. Ambulances S-2 and S-3 were delivered in 1967. There was another C-47 flown as LQ-IOS.

DOUGLAS C-54 SKYMASTER

Eight were delivered in 1947 for I Brigada Aérea use, with serials T-41 to T-48, later TC-41 to TC-48. None remain in service.

TC-41		
TC-42	c/n 10328 ex 42-72223/LV-XFZ to LV-JPG 1970	
TC-43		
TC-44		
TC-45		
TC-46		
TC-47		w/o 10.5.64
TC-48		w/o 4.11.64

The TC-48 was the first Argentine AF aircraft to fly over the South Pole.

DOUGLAS DC-6

The first three DC-6 were ex Aerolíneas Argentinas aircraft obtained in 1966 for the II Grupo de Transporte; the other two were DC-6A purchased in the USA. All ended their operational lives with the I Brigada Aérea, the survivors being sold in the USA in April 1973.

T-51	c/n 43030	ex LV-ADR	to N21CA
T-52	43032	LV-ADT	to N23CA
T-53	43033	LV-ADU	to N26CA
TC-54	44102	N8102H	to N8CA
TC-55	44114	N6114C	w/o 7.11.68

DOUGLAS A-4P SKYHAWK

Conversion of the US Navy A-4B/C; 25 were ordered in 1966 serialled C-201 to C-225, another 25 in 1970, serialled C-226 to C-250, and 25 more in 1975, serialled C-251 to C-275. The first fifty were converted A-4B, the remainder converted A-4C. They were used by the I, II, IV and V Escuadrones de Caza-Bombardeo, and six were allocated to the V Brigada's aerobatic team, the 'Halcones Azules' (Blue Falcons). C-213 was written off on 27.12.78; at least another nine have been lost, three of them on 13.11.71, 5.9.72 and 25.6.73. The IV Brigada Aerea lost two in 1981, on 10.1.81 and 19.8.81. Many Skyhawks were lost during the Falklands conflict. See page 285.

ENGLISH ELECTRIC (BAC) CANBERRA

Ten Canberra B.Mk.62 serialled B-101 to B-110, and two T.Mk.64 (B-111 and B-112) were ordered in mid-1969 and delivered during 1970-71, entering service with the I Escuadrón de Bombardeo.

B-101	exWJ616/G-27-111/G-AYHO	d/d 16.11.70
B-102	WJ713/G-27-112/G-AYHP	16.11.70
B-103	WJ714/G-27-113	16.11.70
		w/o22.11.71
B-104	WH913/G-27-114	d/d 26.2.71
B-105	WH702/G-27-127	26.5.71
B-106	WJ609/G-27-165	26.5.71
B-107	WH727/G-27-162	26.5.71
B-108	WH886/G-27-164	9.9.71
B-109	WH875/G-27-163	9.9.71
B-110	WJ619/G-27-166	9.9.71
B-111	WT476/G-27-121	26.2.71
B-112	WJ875/G-27-122	26.2.71

Two replacement/additional aircraft were ordered in 1981 for completion and delivery in November 1982 from BAe at Samlesbury; delivery now seems improbable :

B.2/B.62	WH914/G-27-373	
T.4/T.64	XH583/G-27-374	

FIAT G.46-5B

About forty were delivered in 1949. Serials Ea-426 to Ea-461 have been confirmed. One is preserved at the Aeroparque as Ea-441, though this may not be its true identity.

FIAT G.55

Rebuilt wartime G.55 fighters; thirty G-55A single-seaters serialled C-001 to C-030, and fifteen G-55B two-seaters, serials C-031 to C-045 later C-31 to C-45, delivered in 1948 as advanced trainers.

FIAT G.59-2A

One only, delivered for evaluation in 1949.

FMA IA.35 HUANQUERO

Four aircraft were built as prototypes in crew-trainer configuration (Ea-001 to Ea-004) to replace the AT-11; one which had a solid nose, LQ-FMA 'Constancia 3' ex Ea-003, was written off on 21.7.63. The initial production models were the IA.35-Ia crew-trainer (known serials E-501 to E-530) and the IA.35-Ib primary trainer/close support aircraft (known serials A-301 to A-323). The IA.35-II was a seven-passenger light transport; one, T-551, converted from IA.35-Ia E-522, was used by the FAA's Cuartel-Maestro General (Quartermaster General), and production examples differed from T-551 in having a solid nose. The IA.35-III was an ambulance version with provision for four stretchers, also referred to as the IA.35B; its prototype, the IA.35-X-III T-550, once an IA.35-I prototype, was allocated to the I Brigada Aerea. Other ambulance aircraft were serialled TS-11, S-12, TS-13 and TS-14. The IA.35-IV was the photo-survey model; known machines included F-504, F-505, F-506, F-524 and F-22. IA.35Ib A-316 was preserved at the Aeroparque in 1976. One known write-off was a transport conversion of the IA.35-Ia, T-509 of the V Brigada Aérea, lost on 16.7.67.

FMA IA.50 GUARANÍ II

Two prototypes were produced : TX-01, ex LV-X-27 first flown on 23.4.63, and TX-110 which used for a time by the Navy as 5-T-30. Production aircraft comprised eighteen transports (T-111 to T-128 c/ns 13 to 20), five photo-survey models (F-31 to F-35 for II Brigada Aérea use), and two navaids calibration aircraft (VR-15 and VR-16) which were delivered to the Instituto Nacional de Aviación Civil. T-125 was test-flown with wheel/ski undercarriage units for possible Antarctic use; T-119 was transferred to a government agency as LQ-JXY, and T-122 was allocated to the FAA's Comandancia General (GHQ). T-123 was written off on 27.5.69 while on I Brigada Aérea charge. TX-01 remains in service with the Centro de Ensayos de Vuelo (Flight Test Centre).

FMA IA.58 PUCARÁ

Two prototypes of this twin turboprop close-support aircraft were built (AX-01 and AX-02) followed by a pre-production machine (AX-03) which was written off on 5.8.77 and replaced by a production aircraft. An initial production batch of thirty IA.58A was ordered, serials being A-501 to A-530 (scheduled for change to A-01 to A-30, although this may not have been implemented; however, A-501 to A-507 were contemporaries of A-19). Others were ordered later, serials up to A-539 having been confirmed and it seems that sixty IA.58A are being built, followed by perhaps forty of the improved IA.58B version with 2 x 30mm DEFA 553 cannon. A production IA.58A was converted as the IA.58B prototype in 1979 and re-serialled as AX-05. Known write offs prior to the Falklands conflict were on 1.6.79, 7.5.80 and 25.10.81. Perhaps fifteen were lost in the Falklands, including A-528 at Port Stanley on 1.5.82.

FOKKER F.27 FRIENDSHIP

Sixteen aircraft have been delivered since 1968, of various models, for use by the IV Escuadrón de Transporte and LADE. These include new aircraft taking up serials formerly used by aircraft no longer in service.

		c/n	ex	d/d	
T-43	Srs.600	10451	PH-EXA	28.12.71	
T-44	600	10454	PH-EXB	28.12.71	
T-79	400	10345	PH-FLR	16.8.68	to T-41
				w/o 17.4.72	
T-80	400	10346	PH-FLS d/d 12.8.68		to T-42
TC-71	400M	10403	PH-FOB	9.6.69	
TC-72	400M	10404	PH-FOC	9.6.69 w/o 16.3.75	
TC-72	500	10619	PH-EXH	20.11.81	
TC-73	400M	10407	PH-FOF	24.7.69	
TC-74	400M	10408	PH-FOG	31.7.69	
TC-75	400M	10411	PH-FOK	12.8.69	
				w/o 10.6.70	
TC-75	500	10621	PH-EXM d/d 18.12.81		
TC-76	400M	10412	PH-FOL	26.8.69	
TC-77	400M	10416	PH-FOP	29.9.69 w/o 2.12.69	
TC-78	400M	10418	PH-FOS	17.10.69	
TC-79	400M	10368	PH-FMP	15.8.75	to T-45
TC-79	400M	10575	PH-EXG	8.2.79	

FOKKER F.28 FELLOWSHIP

An F.28-1000, T-01 'Patagonia' was acquired for the Escuadrilla Presidencial, and five F.28-1000C for LADE. Another F.28-1000 was transferred to the FAA in November 1977.

Four of the F.28-1000C were retro-fitted in 1977 with a cargo loading door on the forward fuselage.

	c/n	ex	d/d	
T-01	11028	PH-EXA	28.12.70;	to T-02 in 3.76, damaged by bomb 18.2.77 but repaired and back in service by 19.12.77
T-03	11048	LV-LZN d/d 12.12.77		
TC-51	11076	PH-EXY	13.1.75	
TC-52	11074	PH-EXG	30.1.75	
TC-53	11020	PH-EXX	7.5.75	
TC-54	11018	PH-EXW	23.7.75	
TC-55	11024	PH-EXZ	6.10.75	

GLOSTER METEOR F.Mk.4

Fifty ex RAF aircraft were delivered as I-001 to I-050, followed by fifty built to order as I-051 to I-100. Initially classified as interceptors, they were eventually designated as fighters and their serials were accordingly changed to C-001 to C-100. They were used by the I, II and III Grupos de Caza of the VII Brigada Aérea, the last few machines in service being struck off in the second half of 1971 and replaced by Dassault Mirages. C-068 was the first of several Meteors to be fitted by FMA with underwing bomb-racks. I-056 had a longer-span Meteor III wing and pressurised cockpit and was used for high-altitude research until it was written off in June 1958. Meteors were among the first aircraft to be given the FAA's new tactical camouflage. C-095 was displayed outside the FAA headquarters in Buenos Aires. When I-062 crashed, another I-062 was built with parts of the first machine and of an earlier write-off I-064; this explains why there are two I-062 in the list which follows :

	ex		
I-001	RA384	w/o 11.66	
I-002	RA386	wfu 30.12.71	
I-003	RA388	w/o 3.58	
I-004	RA389	w/o 4.63	
I-005	RA390	wfu 30.12.71	
I-006	RA391	w/o 10.58	
I-007	RA370	w/o 6.58	
I-008	RA385	w/o 11.58	
I-009	RA392	wfu 28.8.69	
I-010	RA393	wfu 12.5.71	
I-011	RA395	wfu 12.5.71	
I-012	RA396	w/o 1953	
I-013	EE570	wfu 6.3.70	
I-014	EE575	wfu 12.5.71	
I-015	EE551	w/o 6.65	
I-016	EE569	w/o 1951	
I-017	EE554	w/o 1.56	
I-018	EE571	w/o 3.48	
I-019	EE553	wfu 12.5.71	
I-020	EE546	wfu 12.5.71	
I-021	EE544	wfu	
I-022	EE552	w/o 11.62	
I-023	EE576	w/o 1.56	
I-024	EE548	w/o 1953	
I-025	EE532	w/o 10.62	
I-026	EE572	w/o 9.56	
I-027	EE527	wfu 30.12.71	
I-028	EE535	w/o 1954	
I-029	EE537	wfu 30.12.71	
I-030	EE542	wfu 23.10.62	
I-031	EE588	wfu 25.11.69	
I-032	EE581	w/o 20.3.67	
I-033	EE582	w/o 11.54	
I-034	EE574	wfu 16.3.66	
I-035	EE580	w/o 7.60	
I-036	EE577	w/o 2.5.68	
I-037	EE583	wfu 30.12.71	
I-038	EE587	wfu 12.5.71	
I-039	EE585	w/o 5.60	
I-040	EE589	w/o 11.62	
I-041	EE586	wfu 12.5.71; preserved Aeroparque.
I-042	EE526	w/o 1952	
I-043	EE540	w/o 5.56	
I-044	EE534	wfu 25.11.66	
I-045	EE547	w/o 11.55	
I-046	EE543	w/o 1950	
I-047	EE533	w/o 1951	
I-048	EE539	w/o 1.66	
I-049	EE536	w/o 4.60	
I-050	EE541	w/o 8.55	
I-051	c/n G5/151	wfu 12.5.71	
I-052	G5/152	w/o 5.56	
I-053	G5/153	w/o 6.62	
I-054	G5/154	w/o 8.57	
I-055	G5/155	w/o	
I-056	G5/156	w/o 6.58	
I-057	G5/157	wfu 30.12.71	
I-058	G5/158	w/o 10.55	
I-059	G5/159	w/o 1949	
I-060	G5/160	w/o 1954	
I-061	G5/161	w/o 11.57	
I-062	G5/162	w/o	
I-062	(rebuilt)	w/o 4.61	
I-063	G5/163	w/o 3.5.66	
I-064	G5/164	w/o 16.6.55	
I-065	G5/165	w/o 16.3.66	
I-066	G5/166	wfu 28.8.69	
I-067	G5/167	w/o 1951	
I-068	G5/168	w/o 8.63	
I-069	G5/169	w/o 9.60	

Fokker F.27M Srs.400M TC-72. This was written off in March 1975.

Douglas EC-47D Skytrain TA-06, an Antarctic aircraft seen in November 1966.

Morane-Saulnier MS.760A Paris E-221, one of thirty-six completed by FMA from French parts.

Boeing 707-387B TC-91 was formerly serialled T-01 as the presidential aircraft, but converted as a freighter in which guise it is seen here at East Midlands Airport in 1978.

FMA IA.58 Pucara A-19, which was displayed at the 1978 Farnborough show.

Swearingen SA226AT Merlin IVA T-01 seen prior to delivery in 1978 with test registration N5438M.

De Havilland Canada DHC.6 Twin Otter 200 T-83, one of seven delivered to the FAA.

Douglas A-4P Skyhawks C-213 and C-214, both from the first of three batches of twenty-five aircraft supplied by the USA.

I-070	G5/170	w/o 1949
I-071	G5/171	wfu 30.12.71
I-072	G5/172	w/o 10.62
! 073	G5/173	wfu 30.12.71
I-074	G5/174	w/o 7.56
I-075	G5/175	w/o 6.58
I-076	G5/176	wfu 29.1.70
I-077	G5/177	w/o 6.56
I-078	G5/178	w/o 1952
I-079	G5/179	w/o 9.55
I-080	G5/180	w/o 9.58
I-081	G5/181	wfu 12.5.71
I-082	G5/182	w/o 1952
I-083	G5/183	w/o 10.67
I-084	G5/184	wfu 26.11.70
I-085	G5/185	w/o 4.60
I-086	G5/186	wfu 5.3.68
I-087	G5/187	w/o 3.58
I-088	G5/188	wfu 30.12.71
I-089	G5/189	w/o 11.64
I-090	G5/190	wfu 16.3.66
I-091	G5/191	w/o 10.64
I-092	G5/192	w/o 1951
I-093	G5/193	wfu 30.12.71
I-094	G5/194	wfu 30.12.71
I-095	G5/195	wfu 30.12.71
I-096	G5/196	w/o 7.60
I-097	G5/197	w/o 1951
I-098	G5/198	w/o 1951
I-099	G5/199	wfu 30.12.71
I-100	G5/200	w/o 10.62

GRUMMAN HU-16B ALBATROSS

Three delivered as BS-01 to BS-03; BS-03 was withdrawn from use in 1977, but at least one remains in use with the I Escuadrón de Búsqueda y Salvamento. One of the trio was used by LADE from 12.1.72 on a regular service between Comodoro Rivadavia and Puerto Stanley in the Malvinas (Falklands). BS-01 and BS-03 were temporarily attached to the Fuerza Aérea de Tareas Antárticas (FATA).

HAWKER-SIDDELEY HS.748

One series 221 only, T-01, c/n 1597 ex LV-PGG, delivered on 20.12.66 for presidential use. It became T-02 in January 1971, and then T-03 in July 1975, before being sold as C-GQWO to Austin Airways. Eight HS.748 series 240 (c/ns 1648 to 1655, to have been TC-71 to TC-78) were ordered but cancelled in November 1967 in favour of Friendships.

HILLER OH-23 (UH-12L)

Three aircraft, serialled H-41 to H-43, later H-01 to H-03. No longer in service.

HOLSTE MH.1521C BROUSSARD

Ten were ordered by the government in 1956 and delivered during the following year :

c/n 20C	LV-FYA	d/d 5.4.57
21C	LQ-FZH	23.3.57
22C	LQ-FZJ	4.57
23C	LV-FYB	4.57
24C	LQ-FZL	13.5.57
25C	LQ-FZM	13.5.57
26C	LQ-FYS	23.2.57
27C	LQ-FZO	21.6.57
28C	LQ-FZN	9.57
29C	LQ-FZP	21.6.57

At least eight were eventually taken on FAA charge as PG-331 to PG-334, PG-336 to PG-338 and PG-340. PG-334 of the IV Brigada Aérea was written off on 9.12.70.

HUGHES 369

Fourteen helicopters of which H-20 and H-21 were model 369HE, and the rest 369HM :

H-20	c/n 890106E	d/d 11.11.69
H-21	890107E	11.11.69
H-22	390032M	25.4.69
H-23	390033M	26.4.69
H-24	390034M	26.4.69
H-25	390035M	26.4.69
H-26	490045M	6.69
H-27	490046M	6.69
H-28	490047M	6.69
H-29	490048M	7.69
H-30	490049M	7.69
H-31	490050M	7.69
H-32	490051M	8.69
H-33	490052M	8.69

IAI DAGGER

An initial twenty-six of this Israeli-built version of the Dassault Mirage V were ordered for use by the re-activated VI Brigada Aérea. Serials are C-401 et seq. One reportedly crashed in mid-1979. A reported second order in 1981 for twelve plus four trainers is denied by Israel.

LEAR JET 35A

Two were delivered to the II Brigada Aérea during 1977 for communications and photo-survey :

| T-21 | c/n 35.115 |
| T-22 | 35.136 |

Another two, equipped for airways calibration, were ordered early in 1980 :

| T-23 | c/n 35.319 | d/d 20.10.80 |
| T-24 | 35.333 | 9.12.80 |

A further aircraft was delivered in 1981 for radio-calibration (hence the VR - Verificación Radio - serial) :

| VR-17 | 35.369 |

LOCKHEED C-130 HERCULES

A total of ten aircraft have been delivered to the I Brigada Aérea :

TC-61	C-130E	c/n 4308	d/d 11.68
TC-62	C-130E	4309	12.68 w/o 28.8.75
TC-63	C-130E	4310	12.68
TC-64	C-130H	4436	1971
TC-65	C-130H	4437	1971
TC-66	C-130H	4464	1971
TC-67	C-130H	4576	3.3.75
TC-68	C-130H	4578	10.3.75
TC-69	KC-130H	4814	24.4.79
TC-70	KC-130H	4816	10.5.79

Two are believed to have been lost in the Falklands dispute, one at Port Stanley on 1.5.82, and one shot down 1.6.82.

MORANE-SAULNIER MS.760A PARIS

Forty-eight were ordered in 1957. The first twelve were French-built, and delivered between May and December 1958; the first nine were initially given attack serials, but later reclassified as advanced trainers.

A-01	c/n 3	to	E-201
A-02	4		E-202
A-03	7		E-203
A-04	10		E-204
A-05	11		E-205
A-06	13		E-206
A-07	15		E-207
A-08	16		E-208
A-09	17		E-209
E-210	18		
E-211	21		
E-212	22		

The remaining 36 aircraft were completed by FMA from French-supplied parts and with FMA c/ns (e.g. E-225 was c/n 271-22 and E-234 was c/n 271-30), and were serialled E-213 to E-248. Seven MS.760A, including E-229, were used in 1970 by an EAM aerobatic team, the Escuadrilla Aguila (Eagle Flight); others were camouflaged. Two IV Brigada Aérea machines were lost in 1968 (21.2.68 and 20.6.68), and two from the II Grupo de Caza-Bombardeo collided in flight on 30.3.73 and were written off. An unidentified aircraft crashed on 11.2.81. A number of aircraft remain in service, although the III Escuadron de Caza-Bombardeo of the IV Brigada Aérea at El Plumerillo, which did operate the type, has been disbanded.

NORTH AMERICAN T-28A

At least thirty-six USAF surplus T-28A were transferred to the Argentine Air Force and serialled E-601 to E-636; they were taken over by the Grupo Aéreo Escuela, but none remains in service. Their USAF serials were 51-3487, 3492, 3501, 3524, 3547, 3574, 3614, 3653, 3675, 3718, 51-7498, 7514, 7523, 7525, 7546, 7573, 7600, 7630, 7659, 7663, 7686, 7721, 7725, 7751, 7771, 7836, 7842, 7843, 7853, 7860, 7862, 7890, 52-1188, 1189, 1197, 1236. Serial tie-ups are unknown, except for E-608 which was 51-3574 and is now preserved at the Aeroparque.

NORTH AMERICAN F-86F SABRE

Twenty-eight were delivered in 1960 for use by the I, II and III Grupos de Caza-Bombardeo and serialled C-101 to C-128. The last twelve were withdrawn from use in December 1976 and were to have been sold to the Uruguayan Air Force, but this was vetoed by the US government in 1977 and the aircraft were still being offered for sale as scrap by Argentina in 1981. Six aircraft were used by the Escuadrilla Acrobatica Cruz del Sur (Southern Cross Aerobatic Flight) in 1962-63 in a distinctive silver/blue/red/yellow livery. Known write-offs are on 6.10.67 and 5.10.72, and on 8.5.68 when two I Grupo aircraft collided in mid-air.

PERCIVAL PRENTICE T. Mk.1

One hundred were delivered between September 1948 and January 1950 for Grupo Aéreo Escuela use, with serials E-301 to E-400. C/ns were PAC/F/089, 099 to 102, 107, 117 to 120, 122 to 123, 141, 144 to 146, 148, 151, 152,

155, 157, 159, 160, 162, 163, 165, 167 to 169, 172, 171, 173 to 177, 184, 180 to 183, 178, 188, 191 to 193, 196, 198, 200, 202, 204, 206, 210, 209, 212, 213, 217 to 219, 221, 222, 227 to 231, 233, 243, 245, 246, 248, 249, 254, 256 to 258, 262 to 270, 275, 278, 277, 279 to 283, 288 to 289, 293, 294, 296, 297 and 300 respectively. They were gradually replaced by T-34 Mentors. E-390 is preserved at the Aeroparque.

PIPER PA-31 NAVAJO

Three have been reported :
TS-01 an ambulance version; no further details
PG-396 a PA-31P c/n 31P-7300130
PG-397 model and further details unknown

ROCKWELL SABRE 75A

One only, c/n 380-3 ex N8467N, delivered as TC-10; became T-10 of the Comando General, and seen as such 3.75.

SIKORSKY S.55/UH-19A

Nine were delivered as H-01 to H-09, later H-1 to H-9. H-01 c/n 55.791 was delivered in August 1954. H-4, ex USAF 51-3886, once used by the I Brigada Aérea, was preserved at the Aeroparque in 1971. Another I Brigada Aérea aircraft was written off on 25.2.68. Four UH-19A remain in service.

SIKORSKY S.58T

Two ex West German Army CH-34 converted by Carson Helicopters to S.58T configuration, were delivered as H-01 and H-02 for presidential use, with VIP interiors.

SIKORSKY S.61

Two were delivered to the VII Brigada Aérea, S.61NR H-71 and S.61R H-72.

SUD SE.210 CARAVELLE VIN

Three ex Aerolíneas Argentinas aircraft delivered in 1973 to the I Brigada Aérea. They were used for a short time only, and sold to International Air during 1974-5.

T-91	c/n 19	ex LV-HGX	to N45SB, F-GBMI
T-92	149	LV-HGZ	N46SB, F-GBMJ
T-93	180	LV-III	N49SB, F-GBMK

SUD SA.315B LAMA

Six helicopters delivered in 1972 and equipped for search and rescue; three replacement machines assumed the serials of lost Llamas (note local spelling) :

H-61	c/n 2267	
H-62	2282	w/o
H-62	2459	w/o 12.76
H-63	2299	w/o
H-63	2496	
H-64	2302	
H-65	2327	w/o
H-65	2499	
H-66	2328	

One was written off 1.4.81 in Mendoza province.

SWEARINGEN SA226AT MERLIN IVA

Two were delivered in 1978 :
T-01 c/n AT063 ex N5438M
T-02

VICKERS VIKING

Twenty-two Viking 1B and a Viking 1 c/n 113 were taken on charge. The first thirteen were the only ones intended from the outset for FAA use, the others being obtained from British sources of the airline FAMA (Flota Aérea Mercante Argentina). Most were disposed of in September 1959, but three remained in use until 1962. T-9 was eventually preserved as T-09 in I Brigada Aérea markings at the Aeroparque.

T-1	Srs620	c/n 113	ex LV-XEN	d/d 1.7.46	w/o 30.11.46
T-2	615	135	LV-XEQ	5.10.46	wfu 30.9.59
T-3	615	151	LV-XER	22.11.46	w/o 13.5.57
T-4	615	161	LV-XES	23.1.47	w/o 17.9.47
T-5	615	181	LV-XEV	27.3.47	w/o 28.6.56
T-6	615	180	LV-XEU	2.4.47	w/o 9.6.53

T-7	615	182	LV-XEW	18.4.47	wfu 30.9.59
T-8	615	183	LV-XEX	30.4.47	w/o 27.9.50
T-9	615	163	LV-XET	18.4.47	wfu 30.9.59
T-10	615	187	LV-XFD	28.5.47	wfu 30.9.59
T-11	615	188	LV-XFE	23.6.47	w/o 11.1.57
T-12	615	190	LV-XFG	27.6.47	wfu 30.9.59
T-13	615	189	LV-XFF	30.6.47	wfu 30.9.59
T-50	615	193	LV-XFJ,		
			LV-AFF		wfu 30.9.59
T-64	615	194	LV-XFM		w/o 27.10.52
T-77	615	192	LV-AFI		w/o 11.11.51
T-88	615	200	LV-XFL,		
			LV-AFU		wfu 30.9.59
T-90	635	294	G-AMNS	26.1.56	to T-94
					wfu 1962
T-91	610	258	G-AJDI	26.1.56	wfu 1962
T-92	610	239	G-AJBM	26.1.56	w/o 7.8.59
T-93	610	244	G-AJBS	26.1.56	wfu 30.9.59
T-184	615	184	LV-AEW		wfu 1962
T-185	615	185	LV-AEV		to T-76,
					wfu 1962

VERTOL CH-47C CHINOOK

Three Vertol model 308 ordered for Antarctic use with increased fuel capacity and weather radar, with the first aircraft delivered in December 1979. Serials are H-91 to H-93 and c/ns CG-001 to CG-003 respectively. H-92 was written off 28.1.82 at Marambio in the Antarctic.

OTHER AIRCRAFT

Other aircraft used by the Argentine Air Force include a number of sailplanes on Escuela de Aviación Militar charge (One is SZD 30 Pirat V-06), and LQ- and LV- registered light aircraft such as :
Cessna 180 LV-ZKD and LV-ZKE; also LQ-ZKQ which went which went to the Escuela Regional de Aviación Civil (Regional Civil Aviation School) on 20.12.69.
Cessna A182J LQ-IXB operated by SADEN; LQ-JAL operated by the Comando de Regiones Aéreas (Air Regions Command).

The Instituto Nacional de Aviación Civil (INAC), part of the Air Regions Command, uses various aircraft for calibration work including two Chincul PA-A-34 Senecas delivered on 5.12.81, two Chincul PA-A-28-201R Arrow delivered on the same date — all have PG- prefixed serials — and two RACA-Hughes 500 delivered 4.6.81 with PGH- prefixes.

Argentine Army

The Argentine Air Force gained full autonomy from the Army on 4 January 1945, and for a number of years no aircraft were operated by the Army itself. However, in 1957 a new Comando de Aviación del Ejército Argentino (Argentine Army Aviation Command) came into being, to serve the Army, which is a National Militia, with compulsory service for all able-bodied male citizens aged twenty and over, and comprising three levels — the active Army, the National Guard (30 and over) and the Territorial Guard (ages 35 and over), the latter being mobilised only in the case of war.

One of the first aircraft to be acquired was an executive Cessna 310C, which was allocated to the War Ministry (Ministerio de la Guerra) in May 1957 with the serial number MG-1E; it later became ME-1E when the Ministry was renamed as the Ministry of the Army (Ministerio del Ejército) and was subsequently given a standard AE (for Aviación del Ejército)- prefixed serial. Other early procurements included two Cessna 180A, eleven Piper Super Cubs and five Piper Apache 160.

The Army operates from three Buenos Aires airfields — Campo de Mayo (the main one), Ezeiza and Aeroparque, as well as numerous airstrips throughout the country, and is organised on US Army Aviation lines. Its main unit was the Batallón de Aviación del Ejército 601 at Campo de Mayo, with aircraft allocated to Batallones (battalions) and Compañías (companies) attached to field units. In 1981 the 601 General Aviation Support Company formed to operate all fixed-wing aircraft, with the 601 Combat Aviation Battalion (i.e. the original unit mentioned above, apparently renamed left to operate all helicopters. Most aircraft originated in the US but embargoes have resulted in purchases elsewhere, e.g. Pumas until Chinooks arrived. A light tactical transport requirement was fulfilled by an order for three Aeritalia G.222. Also from Italy have come an initial nine Agusta A.109A Hirundo

helicopters, of which more are on option. Aircraft of local manufacture, such as the single-engined Aero Boero types were used for a time but are no longer in service.

Argentine Army aircraft are identified by the word *Ejército* on the fuselage sides; sometimes *Ejército Argentino* is used. Colour schemes are based on those of the US Army, with an overall olive green livery (with white tops on passenger transports) used as standard.

Aircraft known to have been used by the Comando de Aviación del Ejército include the following:

AERITALIA G.222

Three aircraft, all delivered in 1977, the first being on 29 March :
AE-260	c/n 4010
AE-261	4011
AE-262	4021

AERO COMMANDER 680

Two early-production 680 were used, SG-50E c/n 469-139 ex N6201D, operated by the Dirección General de Fabricaciones Militares (General Military Supply Directorate) and eventually written off, and SG-51E, c/n 547-215 ex LV-PLW and N6277D, which became AE-255 and then LQ-JOL. There was also an Aero Commander 680V, AE-104 c/n 1681-63, delivered in November 1967 and eventually renumbered as AE-129. Five locally-assembled Aero Commander 690A were also reportedly procured; two are believed to be AE-128 and AE-129.

AGUSTA A.109A HIRUNDO

Nine were ordered, with another nine expected to follow :
AE-331	c/n 7138
AE-332	7140
AE-333	7142
AE-334	7144
AE-335	7148
AE-336	7150
AE-337	7152
AE-338	7158
AE-339	7160

Aeritalia G.222 AE-260, the first of three delivered to the Argentine Army in 1977.

De Havilland Canada DHC.6 Twin Otter 200 AE-259, which was written off on 5 January 1975.

BEECHCRAFT C-45 EXPEDITOR

Known examples include AE-250 (withdrawn from use), and AE-253 and AE-254 used by the Instituto Geográfico Militar.

BEECHCRAFT QUEEN AIR B80

Two aircraft used by the Instituto Geográfico Militar :
AE-102 c/n LD. ..... to AE-256
AE-109 LD.461 to AE-257

BEECHCRAFT KING AIR 100

One only, AE-100 c/n B.82 damaged on 13.8.71 but later rebuilt.

BELL 47G/OH-13H

At least three were obtained, and two remain in service. One is AE-396, c/n 1660 ex 55-4631.

BELL UH-1H IROQUOIS

Twenty are believed to have been delivered: serials AE-400 to AE-415 are confirmed. Two aircraft are :
AE-412 c/n 13559 ex 73-22076
AE-415 13567 73-22084
An unidentified UH-1H crashed on 6.5.79.

BELL 206A JET RANGER

Seven were delivered; details not known.

BELL 212

Two believed delivered circa 1976; no details

CESSNA 180

Two Cessna 180A were delivered in April 1957 :
ME-20 c/n 32803 ex N9506B to AE-200
ME-21 32817 N9520B to AE-201

Another LV-FZZ, c/n 32815 ex N9518B, was used by the Secretaría del Ejército (Secretariat of the Army).

CESSNA 182J/A182J

Over a dozen Cessna and FMA-built aircraft were obtained. US-built 182J included :
AE-202
AE-203
AE-204
AE-205 w/o 9.75
Locally-built A182J included :
AE-210
AE-214
AE-215 used by Instituto Geográfico Militar

CESSNA T207 SKYWAGON

Six aircraft :
AE-216
AE-217
AE-218
AE-219 d/d late 1978
AE-220 d/d late 1978
AE-221 d/d early 1979

CESSNA 310C

One only, c/n 35517 ex N5317A, taken on charge in May 1957 as MG-1E; became ME-1E, AE-1E and AE-101, and was struck off charge in September 1966.

CESSNA 500/550 CITATION

A Cessna 500 was delivered in January 1978 for use by the Instituto Geográfico Militar, equipped with Wild RC.10 survey cameras :
AE-185 c/n 500-0356 ex N36848
An executive Cessna 550 Citation II was delivered 11.79:
AE-129 c/n 550-0106 exN2665A

CESSNA T-41D

At least five aircraft serialled AE-051 to AE-055; AE-059 has since been reported also.

CESSNA U-17B

Fifteen believed delivered; confirmed serials are AE-202, 208 (written off 15.4.73), 209, 210, 212, 213 and 214. 208 and 209 were operated by Batallón de Aviación 601.

DHC.6 TWIN OTTER

Three DHC.6-200 were delivered in August 1968 :
AE-257 c/n 136 ex AE-100, AE-106
AE-258 138
AE-259 140 w/o 5.1.75
A single DHC.6-300 was delivered in July 1978 :
AE-263 594

DOUGLAS C-47

One was operated as AE-100, though is no longer current, and may have been a former Air Force machine.

FAIRCHILD-HILLER FH.1100

Seven were delivered, serialled AE-300 to AE-306. AE-303 is known to have been written off.

PIPER PA.18 SUPER CUB 150

Eleven were delivered in May and June 1957, and most re-serialled later, including one converted as a trainer, which became AE-015. Last two retired early in 1981.
ME-7-OB c/n 18-5699
ME-8-OB 18-5765
ME-9-OB 18-5770 to AE-90B
ME-10-OB 18-5772
ME-11-OB 18-5778
ME-12-OB 18-5780 to AE-120B
ME-13-OB 18-5785
ME-14-OB 18-5789
ME-15-OB 18-5793
ME-16-OB 18-5797
ME-17-OB 18-5802

PIPER PA.23 APACHE 160

Five were delivered in March 1957 :

ME-2E	c/n	23-974
ME-3E		23-975
ME-4E		23-976
ME-5E		23-978
ME-6E		23-979

All were withdrawn during the 1960s, though one which had been re-serialled AE-105 was still in use as late as 1968.

PIPER PA.23 AZTEC 250C

Six were delivered in July 1964 but are no longer current :

AE-115E	c/n 27-2602	to AE-115
AE-116E	27-2606	AE-116
AE-117E	27-2611	AE-117
AE-118E	27-2614	AE-118
AE-119E	27-2617	AE-119
AE-120E	27-2621	AE-120

One aircraft, attached to the III Army Corps was written off on 23.2.68.

PIPER PA.31 NAVAJO

Five were delivered :

AE-101	c/n 31-429	wfu
AE-102	31-432	wfu
AE-103	31-435	wfu
AE-104	31-438	wfu
AE-105	31-441	w/o 10.8.70

PIPER PA.34 SENECA 200

One aircraft, c/n 34-7570136, reported as ER-106.

ROCKWELL SABRE 75A

One only, AE-175, c/n 380-13 ex N65761, allocated to the Comando Especial de Aquisiciones (Special Procurements Command).

SUD SA.315B LAMA

Six were ordered in November 1974, and delivered 27.11.75.

AE-385	c/n 2424
AE-386	2425
AE-387	2427
AE-388	2429

AE-389	2431
AE-390	2432

Another twelve were ordered in 1978. One was shot down at Grytviken, South Georgia on 2 April 1982.

SUD SA.330J PUMA

Ten delivered, serialled AE-501 to AE-510, of which AE-507 is c/n 1559. Another twelve are on order.

SWEARINGEN MERLIN

Two SA.226T Merlin IIIA were delivered in July 1977 :
AE-176
AE-177
Three SA.226AT Merlin IVA followed in October 1977, one of which was fitted out as an ambulance.
AE-178
AE-179
AE-180
Two of these were c/n AT064 ex N5439M and c/n AT071E ex N5656M.

VERTOL CH-47C CHINOOK

Two were delivered during 1980 :

AE-520	c/n CG101
AE-521	CG102

Gendarmeria Nacional

The National Gendarmerie which has a personnel strength of about 12,000 has its own Air Division (Division de Aviacion) mainly for communications and border patrol duties. Their aircraft have 'GN-' prefixes, and have included the following :

BELL 47G-3B-1

Two helicopters, delivered in June 1967 :

GN-1H	c/n 6633
GN-2H	6634

CESSNA 172

Five aircraft were said to be in use.

CESSNA 182H

Five aircraft were delivered in November 1965 :

GN-5E	c/n 56663	ex N8563S	
GN-6E	56664	N8564S	w/o 23.6.67
GN-7E	56665	N8565S	
GN-8E	56669	N8569S	
GN-9E	56670	N8570S	

CESSNA 185A

One only, GN-2A, c/n 185-0477, delivered in July 1962.

CESSNA U206

Two aircraft :

GN-802	c/n 206-0269	ex N5269U
GN-803	206-0270	N5270U

CESSNA 210

One was reported as GN-2E.

CESSNA 310

One Cessna 310G delivered in July 1962 :
GN-1B c/n 310G-0125 ex N2925R
One Cessna 310H delivered 1963 :
GN-13E 310H-0069

CESSNA 337

Two were delivered in November 1965 :
GN-3E c/n 337-0236
GN-4E 337-0237

CESSNA 402

One aircraft only, serialled GN-701.

HILLER FH.1100

One ex-Army machine was serialled GN-351.

PILATUS PC.6/B TURBO-PORTER

Three aircraft :
GN-804 c/n 786
GN-805   787
GN-806

PIPER PA.23 AZTEC 250

One aircraft was serialled GN-702.

PIPER PA.31 NAVAJO 310

Two aircraft are known to have been delivered:
GN-700   imported from the USA
GN-750   assembled by Chincul

Argentine Navy

A Sección de Aviación (Air Section) was created in 1921 within the I Región Naval at Puerto Belgrano (Bahía Blanca), comprising an operational unit with six Curtiss PN-5 patrol flying boats, and a Naval Aviation School (Escuela de Aviación Naval, or ESAN) with four US Navy-trained instructors and a pair of Curtiss HS.2L flying boats; fourteen Avro 552 floatplane trainers (serialled E-1 to E-14, the prefix E indicating Escuela) were later acquired. A naval balloon school, with SCA and Avorio-Prassoni balloons, was formed at Puerto Barragán (Ensenada) in the following year, but was transferred to Punta Indio (Estación Verónica) in 1925, when it was decided to concentrate all training units within a single base.

The first few years were spent building up the new air arm. Small orders were placed for new aircraft as funds allowed, initial deliveries consisting of a few Huff-Daland Petrel and Keystone 24 Pelican biplane trainers from the USA, and in May 1923, four Napier Lion powered Vickers 84 Viking IV amphibians, which flew with the serial/registrations R-3 to R-6 (Argentina was at the time using the prefix R for interim civil registrations, the current prefix LV- being adopted at a later date).

In due course, half a dozen Supermarine Southampton III bomber-reconnaissance flying-boats arrived to replace the obsolete F.5L (PN-5), entering service in 1928. Italy provided ten Savoia-Marchetti S.59bis flying boat trainers (serialled HR-1 to HR-10) which for the sake of standardisation — not unexpectedly, there were already spares and maintenance problems — were like the Southampton powered by twelve-cylinder 450hp Lorraine-Dietrich engines, well-known to Argentine mechanics. The S.59bis had an eventful service life: HR-4 was written off on 27 February 1930, HR-9 on 10 July 1930, and the survivors were transferred to ESAN with the serials E-18 to E-25. Other aircraft to be obtained included a couple of Dornier Do J Wal

patrol flying boats and Vickers Valparaiso general purpose biplanes (for evaluation), and a Savoia-Marchetti S.57 flying boat formerly used by the Italian military attaché in Buenos Aires, which was classified as a fighter (!) with the serial HC-1 (HC for Hidroavión de Caza, or Fighter Seaplane), although it was shortly afterwards transferred to ESAN as E-10. The first real fighter unit was formed in 1927 with five Lorraine-Dietrich powered Dewoitine D.21 released by the Aviación Militar; another two were delivered in 1928 (serials C-101 to C-107 are confirmed).

Commercial relations between Argentina and Britain were extensive at this time, Britain having important financial interests in the country; this explains why US trade penetration took longer than in most other Latin American countries. Britain was also a traditional source of military aircraft: six Fairey IIIF Mk.IIIM, again powered by Lorraine-Dietrich engines, were delivered on floats with the serials AP-1 to AP-6 (c/ns F.1122/1127, later reserialled as R-50 to R-55); being eventually re-engined with Armstrong-Siddeley Panther VI radials, the same engine that powered the single Fairey Seal (c/n F.2111) procured for evaluation.

The mid-1930s saw the arrival of more modern types, this time from the United States — twelve Vought V.65F versions of the O2U Corsair biplane (serialled R-61 to R-72) which was also in use as a lower-powered advanced trainer (serials included R-57 to R-60); fourteen Vought V.142A (first was R-73) based on the SBU scount-bomber biplane then in US Navy service; six Consolidated P2Y-3 patrol flying boats to replace the elderly Southamptons of the Escuadrilla de Patrulleros (Patrol Squadron), which was since 1936 under the Aviación de la Escuadra de Mar (High Seas Fleet Aviation); eight Grumman JF-2 Duck armed reconnaissance amphibians (serialled M-O-1 to M-O-8); ten Stearman 76D1 advanced training biplanes (E-40 to E-49) delivered in June 1936 and followed by another six in August 1937; small numbers of Curtiss-Wright CW.16E basic training biplanes, Consolidated 17 Fleetster and Fokker F VII/3m transports, a single Douglas Dolphin amphibian (T-203 c/n 1281) delivered in 1934; and most important of all, twelve Martin 139WAN twin-engined monoplane bombers (3-B-1 to 3-B-12) which gave the service a genuine offensive capability. Three Curtiss CT32 twin-engined transport biplanes were also acquired: 1-E-301 (c/n 63) was delivered in 1935 as a crew-trainer, serving until 1947: 2-Gt-11 (c/n 64) and 3-Gt-1 9c/n 65) were freighters and were broken up in 1949. A Consolidated 17 Fleetster (2-Gt-3) is believed to have become T-202 in Air Force service. Other aircraft taken on charge during this period included at least one Junkers W34 (1-E-305); Lockheed 10E Electra c/n 1115; two Fairchild 45A light transports (c/n 4007 and 4008) and a second-hand Fairchild 82B (c/n 65 ex CF-AXP); and a Stinson SR.10E Reliant (c/n 5-5954), operated as 1-E-66 until sold in October 1949 as LV-FBE.

By 1939, the Servicio de Aviación Naval (Naval Air Service) as the force was now called, comprised an Escuadra Aérea de la Defensa del Río (River Plate Air Defence Squadron) at Punta Indio, consisting of a fighter Escuadrilla with Dewoitine D.21 and the P2Y-3 equipped Escuadrilla de Patrulleros; an Escuadrilla de Caza de la Área Naval del Plata (River Plate Area Fighter Flight) at Mar del Plata with Dewoitines; a Grupo de Transporte and bomber and reconnaissance Escuadrillas at Puerto Belgrano, Punta Indio and Ushuaia; the Escuela de Aviación Naval at Puerto Belgrano, and a patrol detachment and a medical centre at Mar del Plata. There were also Grumman JF-2 equipped detachments aboard the cruisers ARA Almirante Brown and ARA Veinticinco de Mayo, and the then recently-delivered cruiser ARA La Argentina had two Supermarine Walrus biplane amphibians on board.

The Second World War brought the Servicio some serious problems, as it had to fly regular neutrality patrols along Argentina's long coastline in obsolete aircraft which had to be kept serviceable despite a chronic shortage of spares. The fact that these duties were maintained throughout the war

speaks highly for the air and ground crews of the Aviación Naval. However, by the end of the war, replacement of the existing aircraft had become an urgent necessity. In August, five Douglas DC-2 operated by the airline AVENSA were purchased, so as to relieve the few old transports in service, but more clearly had to be done. Thus it was that US assistance, which followed the signature of the Rio Pact in 1947 and comprised technical advisers (who later helped to re-organise the service) and small numbers of aircraft, was very welcome. Deliveries included ten Vought F4U-5 Corsair fighters, later supplemented by radar-equipped F4U-5N and -5NL; ten Grumman F6F-5 Hellcats, some of which were later presented to the Paraguayan Navy; eight Martin PBM-5A Mariner patrol amphibians for the Escuadrilla Aeronaval de Exploración (Naval Air Reconnaissance Squadron); twenty-three Stearman PT-17 primary training biplanes; nine Vought OS2U-3 Kingfisher observation seaplanes (ex USN Bu5932 to 5940); and small numbers of Beechcraft C-45 and Grumman JRF Goose light transports, Beechcraft AT-11 crew-trainers, and Vultee BT-13 and North American AT-6/SNJ Texan trainers — some of the latter, fitted with underwing racks for light bombs, serving briefly as coastal patrol aircraft.

In 1946, a civil-owned Consolidated PBY-5A Catalina was sold by its Canadian pilot to the Argentine Navy, which was so pleased with its performance and reliability that it was decided to equip the Escuadrilla Aeronaval de Exploración with the type. Twelve US Navy surplus PBY-5A Catalinas were accordingly obtained in 1947, refurbished with parts from other machines, and put into service with the Escuadrilla, under the control of the 2ª and 3ª Escuadras Aeronavales, at Base Aérea Naval (BAN) Comandante Espora and BAN Punta del Indio respectively. They were extensively used for patrol, training, photo survey, rescue and transport, being relegated to training duties as the PBM-5A Mariners and Lockheed P2V-5 Neptunes became available. By 1962, there were only two still in use, both as transports with the Escuadrilla

Aeronaval de Propósitos Generales (General Purpose Squadron).

In 1948, the Argentine Navy became the first Latin American naval air arm to introduce helicopters into service, six Bell 47D having been delivered to the II Escuadra Aeronaval. A specialised helicopter unit, the Escuadrilla Aeronaval de Helicópteros, was formed in October 1955, still within the II Escuadra Aeronaval; in 1979 it was split into two separate Escuadrones.

A significant step forward was taken in 1958 with the purchase of the British light aircraft carrier HMS Warrior which became the ARA Independencia. Its first deployed unit was the F4U-5 equipped 2ª Escuadrilla de Ataque, which thus became the first carrier-based squadron of any Latin American air arm.

The Argentine Navy, like the other services, benefited from the long rule of Juan Domingo Peron to a great extent. Peron's aim was to establish Argentina as a self-sufficient country, with its own aeronautical industry and powerful armed forces; and, luckily enough, his successors, however opposed they might be to Justicialismo principles, were also keen on maintaining this policy. In 1958, eight ex Royal Air Force Coastal Command Lockheed P2V-5 Neptunes were acquired for the I Escuadrón de Exploración of the II Escuadra Aeronaval at Puerto Belgrano, eventually replacing the surviving PBM-5A Mariners. During the same year, twenty ex US Navy Grumman F9F-2 Panther jet fighters — the Aviación Naval's first jets — were delivered for use by the 1ª Escuadrilla Aeronaval de Ataque; and ten years later, an adequate tactical support force was formed with sixty Sud Fennecs (a ground-attack conversion of the North American T-28A), which were divided between the Escuela de Aviación Naval and the 2ª Escuadrilla Aeronaval de Ataque. The latter unit eventually operated from the 16,000 ton ARA 25 de Mayo, formerly the Dutch aircraft carrier HrMs Karel Doorman.

In the 1960s, obsolete aircraft were gradually disposed of and replaced by more modern equipment. Acquisitions comprised replacement P2V

Neptunes, a trio of Grumman HU-16B Albatross amphibians, and eight Macchi MB.326GB jet trainers with attack capability to replace the surviving F9F-2 Panthers. The first three helicopters (Sikorsky S.55), to which numbers of Bell 47 were later added, were replaced by Sikorsky HSS-1 and Sud Alouette III, followed by four Sikorsky S.61D-4 (the export version of the SH-3D in US Navy service). Two Westland Lynx Mk.23 were ordered in 1972 (though delivery did not in the event take place until 1978), and in early 1980 an order was placed for three late-model SA.330 Pumas. The US supplied Douglas A-4Q Skyhawks were complemented by fourteen Dassault Super Étendard strike fighters, ordered in the first part of 1980, but not all delivered by early 1982, when many aircraft were lost in the Falklands conflict. See the appendix on page 285.

Current Organisation

The present-day Comando de Aviación Naval has about three thousand personnel and is organised in six Escuadras Aeronavales (Naval Air Groups):

1ª Escuadra Aeronaval at BAN Punta del Indio
Escuela de Aviación Naval	Beechcraft T-34C
4ª Escuadrilla Aeronaval de Ataque	Beechcraft T-34C (codes 1-A-401 etc)
Escuadrilla Aeronaval Aerofotográfica	Beechcraft Queen Air (1-F-21)
1ª Escuadrilla Aeronaval de Propósitos Generales	Beechcraft King Air 200 (1-G-41/42)

2ª Escuadra Aeronaval BAN Comandante Espora (Puerto Belgrano)
1ª Escuadrilla Aeronaval de Exploracion	Lockheed SP-2H (2-P-110 etc)
2ª Escuadrilla Aeronaval de Propósitos Generales	Beechcraft King Air 200 (2-G-47/48, possibly 46)

3ª Escuadra Aeronaval BAN Comandante Espora (Puerto Belgrano)
2ª Escuadrilla Aeronaval de Caza y Ataque	Super Étendard (3-A-201 etc)
3ª Escuadrilla Aeronaval de Caza y Ataque	A-4Q Skyhawk (3-A-301 etc)
1ª Escuadrilla Aeronaval de Helicópteros	Alouette III (3-H-112 etc); Lynx (3-H-41 etc)
2ª Escuadrilla Aeronaval de Helicópteros	Sikorsky S.61D-4 (2-H-231 etc)
3ª Escuadrilla Aeronaval de Propósitos Generales	Queen Air (3-G-82/83) possibly now King Airs

4ª Escuadra Aeronaval at BAN Punta del Indio
1ª Escuadrilla Aeronaval de Ataque	MB.326GB (4-A-101 etc); MB.339A (4-A-110 etc)
4ª Escuadrilla Aeronaval de Propósitos Generales	Beechcraft King Air (probably two of 4-G-43/45)

5ª Escuadra Aeronaval at Ezeiza (Buenos Aires airport)
1ª Escuadrilla Aeronaval de Sosten Logistico	Lockheed Electra (5-T-1 etc)
2ª Escuadrilla Aeronaval de Sosten Logistico	Fokker F.28 (5-T-10 etc); HS.125 (5-T-30); Beechcraft King Air 200 (5-T-31/32)

6ª Escuadra Aeronaval BAN Almirante Zar (Trelew)
6ª Escuadrilla Aeronaval de Propósitos Generales	Pilatus PC.6 (6-G-2/4) seconded to the Escuadrilla Aeronaval Antártico at Petrel, Antarctica. C-45H (6-G-16); S-2A; Queen Air (6-G-81 etc)

Detachments on board the *ARA 25 de Mayo* whose home base is Puerto Belgrano include the Skyhawks and Super Étendards, Trackers and S.61Ds. The Lynx are used on *ARA Hercules* and *Santisima Trinidad*, whilst Alouettes are detached to the icebreaker *General San Martin*.

1ª Escuadrilla Aeronaval de Ataque - blue and white quartered disc, a red dragon, silver sword with black shading and yellow handle.

2ª Escuadrilla Aeronaval de Ataque - red outer ring, white centre. Green bird with red head and yellow beak, brown gauntlet and boots and a dark green club.

3ª Escuadrilla Aeronaval de Ataque - red outer ring, white lightning and dart and trail on a blue sky; black bird with a white eye and yellow beak. An inscription below the badge reads 'Firmiter in Re'.

2º Escuadron de Exploracion - a 'comet' in black.

Aircraft Review

COLOURS AND MARKINGS

Argentine naval aircraft carry roundels similar to those of the air force, though of a more complex design, consisting of the light blue/white/light blue rings and a central motif, often on a white background, comprising a black anchor, a black and red Republican symbol (Phrygian cap on a pole) and the 'Sun of May'. Anchors are carried on the wings in place of roundels; the fin markings are similar to those of the air force.The common inscription is *Armada* though in some cases *Armada Argentina* or *Armada Nacional* is used. Naval aircraft are painted according to US Navy regulations, most operational machines having gull grey upper surfaces and white undersides.

SERIAL NUMBERS AND CODES

The permanent identification of Argentine Navy aircraft is made by means of a four-digit serial number, usually painted on the fin or the rear fuselage. An often-changed unit code is also worn, consisting of a digit indicating the Escuadra Aeronaval to which the aircraft is assigned, a role code and an individual number. In the aircraft review which follows, aircraft codes which are known are shown are quoted with the oldest code first, and the most recent last. Role codes include :

A	Ataque	attack
AS	Anti-submarino	anti-submarine
B	Bombardeo	bomber
BP	Bombardeo en Picada	dive bomber
BS	Búsqueda y Salvamento	search and rescue
C	Caza	fighter
E	Escuela	trainer
F	Fotográfico	photographic
G	Propósitos Generales	utility
GT	Generales y Transporte	utility transport
H	Helicóptero	helicopter
HT	Helicóptero de Transporte	transport helicopter
O	Observación	observation
P	Patrullero	patrol
T	Transporte	transport

Not all of the above are current, Multi-letter codes are occasionally used, with CTA for Comando de Transportes Aeronavales or EAN for Escuela de Aviación Naval, followed by a number.

BEECHCRAFT C-45/SNB EXPEDITOR

At least twenty-eight were used, including :

0518	1-G-12	
0519	EAN-307	
0520	1-G-15, 1-G-54	
0521	1-G-51	
0523	1-G-50	
0524	4-G-15	
0525	4-G-12	
0526	1-G-55	
0528	EAN-301, 4-G-12	
0529	4-G-13	
0531	4-G-14	
0543	1-F-11, 4-F-11	
0544	1-F-12	
0545	1-G-56	
	1-A-59	
	3-A-12	
	1-G-23	
	1-G-52	EAN-303
	1-G-53	EAN-304
	4-G-18	EAN-305
	5-G-15	EAN-306

Two TC-45H were presented to the Uruguayan Navy in November 1979, and six offered for sale in November 1981.

BEECHCRAFT QUEEN AIR B80

The first delivered was equipped for photographic duties :

0679	4-F-21, 1-F-21, 1-G-81	c/n LD.447

Another four were utility transports :

0687	3-G-81, 1-G-81	LD.449
0688	3-G-82, 1-G-82	LD.450
0689	3-G-83, 1-G-83	LD.452
0690	1-G-84	LD.453

BEECHCRAFT KING AIR 200

Two delivered initially as staff transports :

0697	5-T-31	c/n BB.54
0698	5-T-32	BB.71

Another six were ordered late in 1978 as utility transports plus two more later :

1-G-41	
1-G-42	
4-G-43	
4-G-44	
4-G-45	BB.488
2-G-46 (unconfirmed)	
2-G-47	
2-G-48	

BEECHCRAFT T-34C-1 TURBO-MENTOR

Fifteen were ordered, deliveries being completed in 1980 :

0719	1-A-401
0720	1-A-402
0721	1-A-403
0722	1-A-404
0723	1-A-405
0724	1-A-406
0725	1-A-407
0726	1-A-408
0727	1-A-409
0728	1-A-410
0729	1-A-411
0730	1-A-412
0731	1-A-413
0732	1-A-414
0733	1-A-415

BELL 47D/G

Six Bell 47D were delivered in 1948, being allocated to the II Escuadra Aeronaval :

```
0284   E-1, 1-HO-1, 2-HE-1, 2-PH-401. w/o 5.6.59
0285   E-2, 1-HO-2. w/o 12.5.54
0286   E-3, 1-HO-3, 2-HE-2, 2-PH-402
0287   E-4. w/o 1951
0288   E-5, 1-HO-4, 2-HE-3, 2-PH-403
0289   E-6, 1-HO-5, 2-HE-4, 2-PH-404
```
The 2- prefixed codes referred to the Escuadrilla Aeronaval de Helicópteros, activated in October 1955.
Two Bell 47D were subsequently refurbished :
```
       4-H-1           wfu
       4-H-2 c/n 27  to N208B
```
Three Bell 47G were delivered in August 1964 :
```
0536   4-H-3 c/n 3158 w/o 6.1.65
0537   4-H-4        3160 to Prefectura PA-23
0538   4-H-5        3162 to Prefectura PA-24
```

CONSOLIDATED PBY-5A CATALINA

At least fourteen aircraft from US Navy surplus stocks plus an ex Canadian civil aircraft. First deliveries took place in June 1946, the type being used by the Escuadrilla Aeronaval de Exploración and assigned to the 2ª and 3ª Escuadras Aeronavales (codes 2-P- and 3-P- respectively). Known aircraft include :
```
0261   3-P-1, 2-P-1
0262   3-P-2, 2-P-2
0263   3-P-3, 2-P-3
0264   3-P-4, 2-P-4
0265   3-P-5, 2-P-5, 5-P-5
0266   3-P-6, 2-P-6, 5-P-6
       2-P-7                w/o 10.56
       2-P-8, 5-P-8
       2-P-9, 5-P-9
       2-P-10
       2-P-11
       2-P-12
       2-P-13
       2-P-17
       2-P-18
       2-P-20
```
Two surviving machines were allotted to the Escuadrilla Aeronaval de Propósitos Generales as follows :
```
       1-G-2, 2-G-2         wfu 1968
       3-G-1, 1-G-1         preserved BAN Punta Indio
```
An unidentified PBY-5A was operated in 1946 as 2-P-23.

DASSAULT SUPER ETENDARD

Fourteen aircraft ordered early 1980 to equip the 2ª Escuad-

rilla Aeronaval de Ataque. First five delivered to Landivisiau, France 26.3.81 for crew-training. It is believed that only five or six reached Argentina before the Falklands issue resulted in an embargo on further deliveries.
```
0751   3-A-201
0752   3-A-202
0753   3-A-203
0754   3-A-204
0755   3-A-205
0756   3-A-206
0757   3-A-207
0758   3-A-208
0759   3-A-209
0760   3-A-210
0771   3-A-211
0772   3-A-212
0773   3-A-213
0774   3-A-214
```

DE HAVILLAND CANADA DHC.2 BEAVER

A Beaver 0502/3-G-6 c/n 1432 was delivered on 7.10.60 for use by the Grupo Naval Antártico; it was later used by the Escuadrilla Aeronaval de Helicópteros and became 4-G-1. It was damaged in 1968 but repaired and flown as 4-AA-101 until sold as N5230G. An earlier Beaver IAA-101 c/n 129 ex N1523V was operated by the Instituto Antártico Argentino and serviced by the Navy, being retired by 1974.

DHC.6 TWIN OTTER 200

One only, 0640/1-G-101, c/n 171 delivered in 1969 and used by Fuerza Aeronaval No.2; it later became a paratroop trainer. It was subsequently converted for photo-survey duties in the Argentine Antarctic territories, with the code 1-F-1 until transferred to the state oil prospecting organisation as LV-LNY.

DOUGLAS DC-2

Five ex AVENSA aircraft were purchased on 16.8.46. They were DC-2-243 (USAAC C-39) :
```
c/n 2057   ex YV-AVG   to YV-AVG
    2074      YV-AVH   to LV-GGU
    2083      YV-AVK   to LV-GGV
    2085      YV-AVL   wfu
```

and a Douglas DC-2-267 (USAAC C-42) :
```
    2060      YV-AVJ   to LV-GGT
```

DOUGLAS C-47 SKYTRAIN

About a dozen were used by the I and II Escuadrones de Transporte, and one flew with Comando de Transportes Aeronavales number CTA-15. The last machine in service was 5-T-22 'Cabo de Hornos' of the 2ª Escuadrilla Aeronaval de Transporte, which had been delivered in 1947; it was retired in August 1979 and preserved at Ushuaia. Known aircraft included :
```
0171   5-T-21, 5-T-26
0172   5-T-22
0188   5-T-24
0264   5-T-11
0278   5-T-26        to Paraguay Navy T-26 in 1979
       2-Gt-14
       2-Gt-21       c/n 4680, ex 41-18555
0652   5-T-10        c/n 12678 ex LQ-GJT
       5-T-12
       5-T-13
       5-T-19
       5-T-23
       5-T-25
```
CTA-15 is on display at Buenos Aires - Ezeiza in Grupo Naval Antártico markings.

DOUGLAS C-54 SKYMASTER

At least a dozen were used. One, coded 2-Gt-1 was the first Argentine aircraft to cross the Antarctic Circle on 13.12.47 and was also the last naval C-54 to be disposed of. At least three had CTA- numbers, CTA-1 to CTA-3, although the latter also flew as TA-3. Known examples included :
```
0297   5-T-40, 5-T-1   c/n 10402  ex 42,72297, LV-XGD
       2-Gt-10         10301   42-72196
       2-Gt-11         10385   42-72280
       2-Gt-12         3093    41-37302
       2-Gt-21
       4-T-40, 4-T-1
       4-T-41, 4-T-2
       4-T-42, 4-T-3
       4-T-43, 4-T-4
       4-T-44, 4-T-5
       5-T-2
       5-T-3
       5-T-4
       5-T-5
```

DOUGLAS A-4Q SKYHAWK

Sixteen aircraft converted to Argentine Navy requirements from A-4B standards by McDonnell Douglas at Santa Monica and initially allocated to Fuerza Aeronaval No.2 at BAN Comandante Espora, operating from the *ARA 25 de Mayo* (whose deck had to be lengthened by sixteen metres for the purpose) with the codes of the 3ª Escuadrilla Aeronaval de Caza y Ataque.

0654	3-A-301, 3-A-201	
0655	3-A-302, 3-A-202	
0656	3-A-303, 3-A-203	
0657	3-A-304, 3-A-204	
0658	3-A-305, 3-A-205	
0659	3-A-306, 3-A-206	
0660	3-A-307, 3-A-207	
0661	3-A-308, 3-A-208	
0662	3-A-309, 3-A-209	
0663	3-A-310, 3-A-210	w/o
0664	3-A-311, 3-A-211	w/o 18.7.77
0665	3-A-312, 3-A-212	
0666	3-A-313, 3-A-213	w/o
0667	3-A-314, 3-A-214	
0668	3-A-315, 3-A-215	w/o 25.6.73
0669	3-A-316, 3-A-216	w/o

Several other aircraft were lost in the Falklands dispute.

FMA IA.50 GUARANI II

The second prototype was on loan from the air force for a while, flying as 5-T-30; it returned to the air force as TX-110.

FOKKER F.28 FELLOWSHIP 3000M

Three aircraft procured in 1979 :

0740	5-T-10 c/n 11147 ex PH-EXW	d/d 1.8.79
0741	5-T-20	11145	PH-EXV	5.4.79
0742	5-T-21	11150	PH-EXX	1.8.79

GRUMMAN JRF GOOSE

Known examples include a JRF-4 :
0186 c/n 1100   ex Bu3846 to Paraguay Navy 0128
and two JRF-5

B.29	37776	Paraguay Navy 0127
B.53	37800	Paraguay Navy 0126

One JRF-5 was serialled 0254.

GRUMMAN HU-16B ALBATROSS

Four aircraft equipped the Escuela Aeronaval de Búsqueda y Salvamento (Naval SAR school), and were withdrawn from use when the Escuela closed down in November 1978.

0533	4-BS-1, 2-G-201	
0534	4-BS-2	
0535	4-BS-3	
0645	4-BS-4	d/d 10.70

GRUMMAN F9F PANTHER/COUGAR

Twenty F9F-2 Panthers were delivered to the 1ª Escuadrilla Aeronaval de Ataque at BAN Punta Indio (under the control of the 2ª Escuadra Aeronaval. The first flight from BAN Comandante Espora took place on 4.12.58, and the aircraft were gradually grounded from 1969 onwards due to lack of spares and finally replaced by Macchi MB.326GBs.

0442	2-A-01, 2-A-101, 3-A-101	
0443	2-A-02, 2-A-102, 3-A-102	
0444	2-A-03, 2-A-103, 3-A-103	
0445	2-A-04, 2-A-104, 3-A-104	
0446	2-A-05, 2-A-105, 3-A-105	
0447	2-A-06, 2-A-106, 3-A-106	
0448	2-A-07, 2-A-107	w/o 4.63
0449	2-A-08, 2-A-108, 3-A-108	
0450	2-A-09, 2-A-109, 3-A-109	
0451	2-A-10, 2-A-110, 3-A-110	
0452	2-A-11, 2-A-111, 3-A-111	
0453	2-A-12, 2-A-112, 3-A-112	preserved at the Museo Naval de la Nación
0454	2-A-13, 2-A-113, 3-A-113	
0455	2-A-14, 2-A-114, 3-A-114	
0456	2-A-15, 2-A-115, 3-A-115	
0457	2-A-16, 2-A-116, 3-A-116	
0458	2-A-17, 2-A-117, 3-A-117	
0459	2-A-18, 2-A-118, 3-A-118	w/o 1959
0460	2-A-19, 2-A-119, 3-A-119	
0461	2-A-20, 2-A-120, 3-A-120	

The Argentine Navy also had two F9F-8T Cougar trainers:

0516	3-A-151	
0517	3-A-152	w/o

GRUMMAN S-2 TRACKER

Six S-2A were delivered and operated from the *ARA 25 de Mayo* until withdrawn from use in the summer of 1979:

0510	3-AS-2, 2-AS-2
0511	2-AS-1

0512	2-AS-3
0513	2-AS-5
0514	2-AS-4
0515	2-AS-6

An aircraft coded 3-AS-11 was also reported.
Six S-2E were supplied from US Navy stocks in January of 1978 - the US Navy Bu.number tie-ups are not confirmed :

0700	2-AS-21	ex Bu.152346
0701	2-AS-22	152829
0702	2-AS-23	153565
0703	2-AS-24	153569
0704	2-AS-25	153577
0705	2-AS-26	153581

HAWKER-SIDDELEY HS.125 Srs.400B

One only, 0653/5-T-30 c/n 25251 used as an executive transport. It was damaged in 1977, but repaired and returned to service.

LOCKHEED P-2 NEPTUNE

Eight ex Royal Air Force Neptune MR.Mk.1 (P2V-5) were delivered in 1958. Their radio callsigns are shown in the fourth column below :

0408	2-P-30, 2-P-101 ex WX502	c/s LO-TAC	
0409	2-P-31, 2-P-102	WX512	LO-TBA	scrap 6.71
0410	2-P-32, 2-P-103	WX513	LO-TCP	scrap 1966
0411	2-P-33, 2-P-104	WX527	LO-TGV	scrap 1966
0412	2-P-34, 2-P-105	WX549	LO-TIJ	scrap 1966
0413	2-P-35, 2-P-106	WX516	LO-TJY	scrap 1966
0414	2-P-36, 2-P-107	WX522	LO-TKF	w/o 7.11.65
0415	2-P-37, 2-P-108	WX524	LO-TOW	

These aircraft were operated from BAN Bahía Blanca by the I Escuadrón de Exploración of the II Escuadra Aeronaval. Four replacements to full SP-2E standards were delivered between 1966 and 1972; survivors offered for sale 11.81 :

0541	2-P-101	
0644	2-P-102		w/o 15.9.75
0682	2-P-104	ex Bu. 131532	b/u 1977
0683	2-P-105	131523	

A batch of four P-2H followed, the first two (0708 and 0709) on 6.8.77, the others in 1978 :

0706	2-P-110	148349
0707	2-P-111	148361
0708	2-P-112	150280
0709	2-P-114	148348

The last aircraft appears to have been re-serialled as 0718 at a later date.

North American AT-6 Texan 0208/EAN-219

Douglas C-47 Skytrain 0264/5-T-11

Lockheed L.188A Electra 0692/5-T-2, one of three converted to L.188PF standards.

Grumman S-2A Tracker 0514/2-AS-4 was one of six operated from the *ARA 25 de Mayo.*

Hawker-Siddeley HS.125 Srs.400B 0653/5-T-30. It is the only example of the type in Argentine service.

Pilatus PC.6/B.H2 Turbo-Porter 0684/4-G-2 in an overall bright red scheme for use by the IV Escuadra Aeronaval in the Antarctic.

Douglas A-4Q Skyhawk 0669/3-A-216, one of sixteen acquired for use from the *25 de Mayo.*

Beechcraft T-34C-1 Turbo Mentor 0720/1-A-402, the second of fifteen delivered from 1978 to 1980.

LOCKHEED 188A ELECTRA

Three model L.188A-08-10 were delivered in December 1973 and converted to L.188PF standards during the early part of 1974.
0691 5-T-1 c/n 1102 ex N6124A 'Antártica Argentina'
0692 5-T-2 1120 N6129A 'Ushuaia'
0693 5-T-3 1122 N6131A 'Río Grande'
A fourth machine, L.188A-08-02 c/n 1005 ex N5501E, was handed over to the Taller Aeronaval Central (Central Naval Air Workshops) in 1977 as a source of spares.

LUSCOMBE 8E SILVAIRE

At least one, serialled 0270, no longer current.

MACCHI MB.326GB

Eight aircraft were delivered to replace the F9F-2 Panthers of the 1ª Escuadrilla Aeronaval de Ataque (3ª Escuadra Aeronaval). They were later transferred to the 4ª Escuadra Aeronaval jurisdiction and recoded accordingly.
0613 3-A-101, 4-A-101
0614 3-A-102. 4-A-102
0615 3-A-103, 4-A-103
0616 3-A-104, 4-A-104
0617 3-A-105, 4-A-105
0618 3-A-106, 4-A-106
0646 3-A-107, 4-A-107
0647 3-A-108, 4-A-108
0646/3-A-107 was originally painted as 0619, and 0647 probably as 0620; this may have been a Macchi error.

MACCHI MB.339A

Ten were ordered in 1980 for delivery during 1981 :
0761 4-A-110
0762 4-A-111
0763 4-A-112
0764 4-A-113
0765 4-A-114
0766 4-A-115
0767 4-A-116
0768 4-A-117
0769 4-A-118
0770 4-A-119

MARTIN PBM-5A MARINER

Eight were used by the Escuadrilla de Patrulleros until replaced by P2V-5 Neptunes in 1958-59. One was coded as 2-P-21.

NORTH AMERICAN AT-6/SNJ TEXAN

Over thirty aircraft are believed to have been operated, of which the following are known :
0208 EAN-219
0212 EAN-223
0344 4-G-125
0345 EAN-224
0349 3-A-26, 4-G-126
0355 EAN-001 Preserved at BAN Punto Indio
0374
0416 4-G-115
0425 4-G-113
0427 4-G-117
0431 4-G-123
0437
0442 4-G-75 Preserved at Museo Naval de la
0459 4-G-101 Nación
0461 4-G-103
0462 4-G-78
0466 4-G-110, 4-G-108 w/o 20.3.68
0520
0525
       4-G-102
       4-G-104
       4-G-109
       3-A-12
       1-E-221
       1-E-222
       EAN-212
       EAN-232
Two aircraft were transferred to the Bolivian Navy 28.5.69 as FNB-001 and FNB-002.

NORTH AMERICAN T-28A (FENNEC)

Sixty Sud Aviation converted Fennecs were transferred from French Air Force stocks to the Argentine Navy, forty-three in 1966 and seventeen in 1967. Although serial tie-ups are not known, their Fennec numbers were as follows :

No.	Serial	No.	Serial	No.	Serial	No.	Serial
11	ex 51-7680	14	52-1204	17	51-7817		
12	52-1198	15	52-1238	19	51-7812		
13	52-1199	16	52-1232	20	52-1231		
21	51-7845	74	51-3741	107	51-7645		
25	51-7834	75	51-3493	108	51-7504		
26	51-7799	78	51-3603	109	51-3795		
28	51-3635	79	51-3638	112	51-7518		
29	51-3647	80	51-3634	113	51-7782		
30	51-3652	83	51-3592	117	51-7798		
31	51-3677	86	51-3535	123	51-3719		
34	51-3703	87	51-3582	126	51-7532		
35	51-3710	88	51-3646	127	51-7660		
36	51-3715	89	51-3672	134	51-7742		
40	51-3488	91	51-3585	136	51-7606		
62	51-3625	94	51-3594	137	51-7640		
65	51-3704	95	51-3641	138	51-7820		
66	51-3674	97	51-3641	139	51-7649		
69	51-3569	101	51-3702	141	51-7655		
70	51-3644	102	51-3598	144	52-1205		
71	51-3686	106	51-3711	145	51-7613		

The Fennecs entered service with the 2ª Escuadrilla Aeronaval de Ataque in July 1966, after modification for carrier operations by Hamilton Aircraft. When the Escuadrilla was deactivated in late 1977, most of its aircraft went to the Escuela de Aviación Naval, which had previously operated a few Fennecs, including EAN-101/105, 112, 114, 117, 119 and 121/122. The serial block is believed to be 0553 to 0612; known aircraft and codes are :
0553 1-A-261
0568 1-A-263
0570
0575 4-G-55
0580 4-G-60
0583
0587
0588
0589 4-G-58
      1-A-260 w/o 10.2.71
      1-A-274
      3-A-210 w/o 20.4.71
      3-A-221 w/o 2.8.70
      3-A-222
Two more 2ª Escuadrilla aircraft crashed on 23.8.73 and 13.11.73. Nine surplus Fennecs were presented to Uruguay early in 1980, and nine more in 1981. Two engineless aircraft were offered for sale in November 1981.

PILATUS PC.6/B.H2 TURBO-PORTER

Four were obtained for use by the IV (later VI) Escuadra:
0674 4-G-1, 6-G-1 c/n 2034 w/o 20.1.78
0684 4-G-2, 6-G-2 2045
0685 4-G-3, 6-G-3 2046
0686 4-G-4, 6-G-4 2047

ROCKWELL SABRE 75

One only, coded 5-T-10. Serial and c/n unknown.

SIKORSKY S.55/UH-19

Twelve were delivered, mainly for use in Argentina's Antarctic territories and aboard the ARA *General San Martin*. The first three, delivered on 10.11.53, 1.12.53 and 8.12.53 respectively, were S.55 :

0369	HG-1, 2-HT-1; w/o 1960	c/n 55.585
0370	HG-2, 2-HT-2, 2-PH-404, 2-PH-411,	55.610
	2-H-11, 4-H-11; soc 1973.	
0371	HG-3, 2-HT-3, 2-PH-405, 2-PH-412	55.633
	2-H-12, 4-H-12; soc 1971.	

Four H-19A followed in 1960-61, and a fifth, 0508, was acquired at the same time but not put into service until 1964 when it replaced 0504 :

0504   2-PH-413, 2-H-13; w/o 11.63
0505   2-PH-414, 2-H-14, 4-H-14; soc 1973
0506   2-H-15, 4-H-15; soc 1973
0507   2-H-16, 4-H-16; soc 1973
0508

One UH-19B obtained in late 1968 but used very little due to a lack of spares :

0639   4-H-20

Also delivered in 1968 were three UH-19D :

0610   4-H-17; soc 1973
0611   4-H-18; soc 1973
0612   4-H-19; soc 1971

One of the H-19s ditched on 15.3.68 whilst being operated by the Antarctic force.

SIKORSKY S.58 (HSS-1)

Only one was actually delivered, on 17.10.57 :
0407   2-HT-10, 2-PH-406, 2-H-10; w/o 25.4.61 .c/n58.611

SIKORSKY S.61D-4 (SH-3D)

Four were delivered to the I Escuadrón Aeronaval de Helicópteros, and recoded when transferred to the II Escuadrón during 1978 :

0675   4-H-31, 2-H-31, 3-H-31, 3-H-231
0676   4-H-32, 2-H-32, 3-H-32, 3-H-234
0677   4-H-33, 2-H-33, 3-H-33, 3-H-233
0678   4-H-34, 2-H-34, 3-H-34, 3-H-234

A fifth machine with a VIP interior was later delivered :
0696   2-H-35, 3-H-35, presently uncoded.

STEARMAN PT-17

Twenty-three were delivered during the late 1940s and used until 1958. Six were transferred to the Bolivian Air Force on 18 April 1958.

SUD SA.316B ALOUETTE III

Three were ordered in March 1969 for the Escuadrilla Aeronaval de Helicópteros and the Grupo Aeronaval Antártico, and delivered on 31 October in that year, all SE.3160 :

0641	4-H-21, 4-H-1, 2-H-1; w/o 14.5.76	c/n 1616
0642	4-H-22, 4-H-2, 2-H-2, 3-H-2	1623
0643	4-H-23, 4-H-3, 2-H-3, 3-H-3; w/o 4.3.79	1624

Four SA.316B were ordered in January 1970, the first two being delivered on 28 May, and the others on 16 September:

0648	4-H-4; w/o 7.9.70	1730
0649	4-H-5, 2-H-5, 3-H-5	1734
0650	4-H-6; w/o 28.1.71	1766
0651	4-H-7, 2-H-7, 3-H-7	1767

Another two SA.316B ordered in April 1971, were delivered on 18 November :

0680	4-H-8; w/o 7.1.73	1847
0681	4-H-9, 2-H-9, 3-H-9	1851

They were followed by a final SA.316B, ordered in December 1974 and delivered on 18 June 1975 :

0699   2-H-10, 3-H-10   2250

Four uprated SA.319B with ASW capability were ordered in January 1978 and delivered late in the year :

0736	3-H-11	ex F-WTNB	2345
0737	3-H-12	ex F-WTNJ	2346
0738	3-H-14		2349
0739	3-H-15		2350

The Alouette III replaced the elderly S.55 and UH.19 in service, and currently undertake such varied rôles as search and rescue, ASW and close support.

SUD SA.330J PUMA

Three were reportedly ordered early in 1980.

VOUGHT F4U-5 CORSAIR

The first ten F4U Corsairs, four F4U-5N and six F4U-5NL, were delivered in 1956, forming the 2ª Escuadrilla Aeronaval de Combate (later 'de Ataque') on 9.9.56, which was scheduled to develop into a Grupo de Caza de Noche (Night Fighter Group). An additional twelve machines, eight F4U-5 and four F4U-5NL were delivered in 1958. Initially coded as 3-C-1 to 3-C-22 (3-C-4 was an F4U-5N), they were recoded 2-A-201 to 2-A-222 under 2ª Escuadra Aeronaval control, and finally 3-A-201 to 3-A-222, of which the following are identified :

3-A-201	F4U-5NL	ex Bu 124705
3-A-204	F4U-5NL	124541
3-A-211	F4U-5	124576

Known crashes are 3-A-214 on 23.1.63; 3-A-216 on 16.2.64; an unidentified machine on 16.10.59; and 3-A-210 on 9.11. 65 during a short conflict with Chile over disputed territory, Killing the 2ª Escuadra's CO, Teniente de Navio Jorge A. Pittaluga. All surviving Corsairs were grounded on 16.12.65 and the Escuadrilla disbanded in January (it was reformed in 1968 with Sud Fennecs). Most of the Corsairs were then scrapped, but one became an instructional airframe at the Escuela de Mecanica de la Armada (Naval Mechanical School) and one, F4U-5NL 3-A-204 was preserved at the Museo Naval de la Nacion.

WESTLAND LYNX Mk.23/87

Two were ordered in 1972 for the 4ª Escuadrilla Aeronaval, for deployment aboard the missile-armed destroyers ARA *Hércules* and ARA *Santísima Trinidad*. The order was cancelled in late 1973, mainly due to production delays, but was reinstated in 1978, the two machines being delivered on 27.8.78 to BAN Comandante Espora :

0734	3-H-41	c/n WA.035 ex G-BFDT
0735	3-H-42	WA.036

Eight Mark.87 were ordered later, but are now unlikely to be delivered as a result of the Falklands conflict. The first two were built early in 1982 :

3-H-143   c/nWA.249, test-flown as G-17-10, to G-BKBL
3-H-144   WA.256

An unidentified Curtiss C-46 Commando, registered LV-FIB was also flown by the Argentine Navy on medium-term lease between 1956 and 1960.

Argentine Coast Guard

The Prefectura Naval Argentina (Argentine Naval Agency, known as the Prefectura Nacional Marítima or National Maritime Agency until 1970), which has around 9,000 personnel and about sixty patrol craft and comes under the Secretary of the Navy, initially operated a few government-owned Nord 1203 Norecrin light transports (one was LQ-FDP c/n 281) and ex Argentine Navy Grumman JRF-6 Goose amphibians on coast guard and communications duties, with serials initially prefixed PM-, currently PA-. Its first helicopter was a Sikorsky S.51 (PM-20),originally procured for use by the Dirección Nacional de la Aviación Civil (National Directorate for Civil Aviation), which was based at the Mar del Plata seaside resort for rescue duties - in fact, the first rescue missions were flown while it was still under DNAC control. The Prefectura's División de Aviación (Air Division) currently has six Hughes 500M utility helicopters and four Short Skyvan light transports.

Aircraft used have included the following :

BELL 47G

Two were obtained from the Argentine Navy in 1969 :
PM-23 (later PA-23)   ex 0537/4-H-4
PA-24   0538/4-H-5

BELL 47J-2A

Two aircraft, the second as a replacement for the first.
PM-21   w/o 1.64
PM-22 (later PA-22) c/n 3320 d/d 7.65, w/o c.1969

DE HAVILLAND DH.104 DOVE 1

Three ex Argentine Air Force aircraft :
PM-10
PM-11 (later PA-11)   wfu 1970/71
PM-12 (later PA-12)   wfu 1970/71

DE HAVILLAND CANADA DHC.2 BEAVER

One only, PA-05, on loan from the Navy circa October 1972.

DOUGLAS C-47

At least two ex- Argentine Air Force - PM-15 and PM-16, which became PA-15 and PA-16 respectively.

HUGHES 500M

Six were delivered, serialled PA-30 to PA-35.

SHORT SKYVAN 3M-400-7

Five aircraft, one destroyed at Pebble Island 15.5.82 :
PA-50	c/n SH.1887	ex G-14-59	d/d 2.6.71
PA-51	SH.1888	G-14-60	2.6.71
PA-52	SH.1889	G-14-61	16.7.71
PA-53	SH.1890	G-14-62	17.7.71
PA-54	SH.1891	G-14-63	16.7.71

SUD SA.330L PUMA

Three helicopters delivered :
PA-11   c/n 1587   ex F-WXFJ
PA-12
PA-13

Short Skyvan 3M-400-7 PA-50, one of five used by the Prefectura Naval Argentina.

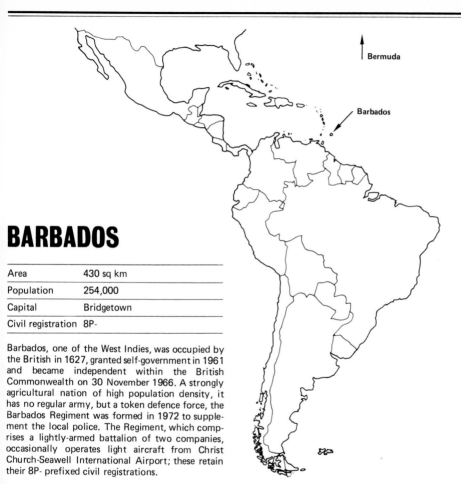

Bermuda

Barbados

BARBADOS

Area	430 sq km
Population	254,000
Capital	Bridgetown
Civil registration	8P-

Barbados, one of the West Indies, was occupied by the British in 1627, granted self-government in 1961 and became independent within the British Commonwealth on 30 November 1966. A strongly agricultural nation of high population density, it has no regular army, but a token defence force, the Barbados Regiment was formed in 1972 to supplement the local police. The Regiment, which comprises a lightly-armed battalion of two companies, occasionally operates light aircraft from Christ Church-Seawell International Airport; these retain their 8P- prefixed civil registrations.

BERMUDA

Area	55 sq km
Population	57,000
Capital	Hamilton
Civil registration	V R-B

A British colony, Bermuda comprises about 150 small islands, only twenty of which are permanently inhabited. The economy is based on agriculture and related activities, the main revenue being provided by tourism. Defence is provided by the Bermuda Regiment, of about 500 personnel, and the local police force. There is no military aviation, and the civil register is quite small, many aircraft being temporarily registered in the colony for reasons of convenience.

BELIZE

Area	22,965 sq km
Population	150,000
Capital	Belmopan
Civil registration	VP-H

Belize, known as British Honduras until June 1973, was occupied by British settlers in the seventeenth century against Spanish opposition, and became a colony in 1862, attaining self-government in 1964 and independence after several delays during 1981. The country's economy is rather primitive; about half of the total land area is covered with forests, some of the remainder growing sugar cane, bananas, grapefruit and oranges. A third of the population lives in Belize City, the country's main seaport and international airport. There are no armed forces, internal order being maintained by a police force of about four hundred.

Guatemala has long claimed sovereignty over Belize, which it calls the 'Province of Belice', and from time to time threatens to annexe the country by force; several attempts to reach a settlement have been unsuccessful. There has been a British military detachment in Belize (currently known as British Forces Belize) since 1975, which presently numbers over 2,000 personnel. This includes a small Royal Air Force contingent of about two hundred personnel and a number of aircraft, which are normally based at Airport Camp, at Belize International Airport, to the northwest of Belize City, but periodically operated from airstrips in the hot and damp interior. Typical aircraft complement includes six Harrier GR.3 (forming 1417 Flight, initially known as 'Strike Command Detachment') for border security and interception duties — more than adequate against the token Guatemalan offensive force — and three or four Puma HC.1 medium transport helicopters. Logistic support is regularly provided by Hercules C.1 from RAF Lyneham. The Army Air Corps also maintains a couple of observation helicopters, initially Westland Scout AH.1, but probably now replaced by Gazelles.

BOLIVIA

Area	1,098,575 sq km
Population	6,113,000
Capital	La Paz
Civil registration	CP-

The Bolivian Republic was proclaimed on 6 August 1825. For a country with a capital whose name means 'peace', it has a very turbulent history, being the only country in the world to have had five presidents on one single day, 3 October 1970. It has been through many revolutions ('cuartelazos') so far — the one on 17 July 1980 being the 189th! — not to mention several unsuccessful boundary disputes; it lost its only seaport, Arica, to Chile in 1884, some areas to Brazil and Peru, and in the disastrous Chaco War (1932-35) it lost most of the Gran Chaco and its only port on the Paraguay River, an indirect outlet to the Atlantic. Postwar politics have alternated military, leftist and nationalist dictatorships. A degree of stability was at last achieved when the August 1971 military takeover brought Colonel Hugo Banzer Suárez to power, with wide Nationalist support, but he was deposed in July 1978 by a coup d'état with Air Force participation and replaced by General Juan Pereda Asbun, who was destined to be ousted from power some four months later.

Bolivia is still largely undeveloped, its main source of income being agricultural undertakings, closely followed by cattle raising. Economic limitations reflect themselves on the country's defence budget. Although there is little need for concern about external aggression — due to Bolivia's high altitude and the formidable natural barriers of the Andes — there is always the threat of civil unrest, sparked off by Cuban guerillas and their Peruvian auxiliaries, who infiltrate the country from time to time (the Cuban guerilla expert 'Che' Guevara was actually killed in Bolivia), and also by the Communist-inspired workers' militias in the mines.

A law passed in 1943 provided for a permanent military force of 15,000 (currently some 18,000), under the control of the Head of State as Captain-General of the Armed Forces. All males aged nineteen or over are liable to conscription, although in practice this is limited by budgetary allowances. There is no independent Navy, but a small, 1500-strong river patrol force, under partial Army command, exists for surveillance of Lake Titicaca and the country's major waterways. The National Police Corps and the paramilitary Carabineros total some 5,000 personnel. There are eight military districts, with headquarters at Camiri, Cochabamba, Oruro, Riberalta, Roboré, Santa Cruz, Viacha and Villa Montes; and regional headquarters at La Paz, Sucre (Bolivia's second capital), Cobija, Potosí, Tarija and Trinidad. The paratroop regiment (CITP) is under Army control.

Military aviation in Bolivia began in 1917, with the training of three Army officers at the El Palomar school in Argentina; one of these officers was killed before gaining his brevet. Two US surplus DH.4 (serialled AM-1 and AM-2) were acquired in 1919, and two Blériots were donated by industrial tycoon Simón Patiño, but the Cuerpo de Aviadores Militares Bolivianos (Bolivian Military Aviatiors Corps) was not officially formed until August 1924, during the celebrations of Bolivia's first centenary of independence. An Escuela de Aviación (Flying School), which had been inaugurated at Alto La Paz (La Paz Heights) in 1915, was then absorbed into the Cuerpo de Aviadores (later renamed as Cuerpo de Aviación, or Air Corps). Alto La Paz, chosen as being conveniently close to the capital, was less than ideal as a training airfield, at an altitude of 13,500 feet - 1,640 feet higher than La Paz itself - and over a dozen student pilots were actually killed in accidents directly related to this. Despite such an obvious problem, Alto La Paz remained as Bolivia's only training airfield until Cochabamba and Villa Montes were activated in the late 1920s, and is still very much in use with the name of Base Aérea General Jorge Jordán.

The forty-odd obsolete aircraft which the Cuerpo had at the time of its inception were long overdue for replacement, but aircraft procurement was made rather difficult both by the shortage of funds and the need for machines suitable for operation from extreme altitudes. France supplied small numbers of Morane-Saulnier MS.39 and Caudron 97 trainers for the flying schools, which by this time formed the Grupo Escuela (School Group). Three Breguet 19 reconnaissance bombers (later

named 'Batallón Colorados', 'Boquerón' and 'Ingavi') formed the Grupo de Guerra, or Combat Group, which later received three 520hp Hispano-Suiza-powered Fokker C VC, and may have had another dozen or so Breguets with Hispano-Suiza or 450hp Lorraine-Dietrich engines, although sources are contradictory in this respect. In any case, by the Spring of 1933 there were only two Breguet 19 on charge.

In 1928, Vickers secured a substantial (by South American standards) contract from the Bolivian Government for an extensive re-equipment of the Cuerpo de Aviación, which only did not become total because of the escalation of the Gran Chaco dispute with Paraguay and related economic considerations. Three Vickers 155 Vendace III biplane trainers were obtained in October 1928 with 300hp Hispano-Suiza engines, followed by six Type 149 Vespa III army co-operation biplanes (mainly used as conversion trainers) and six Type 143 'Bolivian Scouts', the service's first single-seat fighters, designed to Bolivian requirements and powered, like the Vespas, by the 450hp Bristol Jupiter VI radial. The Vickers representative, F/O W.H.R.Banting, later used a Vespa to break the South American altitude record by reaching 27,000 feet without oxygen or supercharger - an amazing feat by any standards.

By this time the Gran Chaco dispute had evolved into a shooting war. When all-out hostilities began in 1932, additional aircraft had been procured in the USA and Germany, the latter country also providing technical advisers. The Grupo de Guerra now had a mixture of Curtiss Hawk II single-seat fighters (nine were delivered to the 'Punta Alas' squadron, with c/ns H.23/26, H.64/65 and seaplanes c/ns SH.27/29), Falcon two-seat reconnaissance biplanes (seven delivered, one of which was later presented to Brazil), CW.19R Osprey two-seat general-purpose biplanes (also used by the 'Punta de Alas' squadron) and three Junkers W.34/K.43 monoplane bombers (serialled 101/103). Seven unregistered Junkers Ju 52/3mde used by the national airline Lloyd Aéreo Boliviano (including c/n 4008 'Juan del

Valle', 4009 'Huánuni', 4018 'Chorolque' and 4061 'Bolívar') were shared with the Cuerpo de Aviación which at its peak had sixty aircraft on charge.

The war ended in 1935. Bolivia was defeated and economically exhausted, and it was clearly impossible to carry on the long-delayed re-organisation of the Cuerpo, at least without outside help. This materialised in 1937 in the shape of an Italian military mission, but no further aircraft were obtained. The late 1930s saw a large-scale political offensive by the USA to steer Latin America away from European influences, and this led Bolivia to purchase small numbers of Curtiss CW.19R and CW.22 advanced trainers, followed by a single Ryan STA Special primary training monoplane for evaluation (c/n 199 ex NC18905). The latter, which crashed shortly after being delivered, was unsuitable for operation from Alto La Paz, and plans to order a number for the Grupo Escuela had to be dropped. In May 1941, when the USA were fully into the so-called 'armed neutrality' which was to lead to Pearl Harbor, Bolivia took over the German-controlled Lloyd Aéreo Boliviano and handed over its trio of Junkers Ju 86Z-7 transports to the Cuerpo de Aviación.

A US military mission replaced the Italian one in November 1941 and began by supplying three North American NA.16-3 (AT-6) Texan advanced trainers. Bolivia was divided into four Regiones Aéreas (Air Regions), each of which was to have a Grupo Aereo of two seven-aircraft Escuadrillas :

1ª Región Aérea — HQ El Alto (La Paz)
2ª Región Aérea — HQ El Trompillo (Santa Cruz)
3ª Región Aérea — HQ La Florida (Sucre)
4ª Región Aérea — HQ El Tejar (Tarija), later Trinidad

The Grupo Escuela comprised an Escuela de Pilotaje (Pilot Training School) at Colcapirua (Cochabamba), and an Escuela de Aplicación (Operational Training School) at El Alto (La Paz).

Bolivia started receiving Lend-Lease aircraft after Pearl Harbor; these included eight Interstate L-8A liaison monoplanes (ex USAAF 42-88658/88665), and small numbers of Douglas C-47 transports,

Ryan PT-16, Stearman PT-17, Vultee BT-13 and Beechcraft AT-11 trainers, and a couple of Stinson 105 Voyager light communications aircraft, as well as two early-model Republic P-47D Thunderbolts and at least one Grumman JRF-6B Goose amphibian. The Cuerpo de Aviación was further re-organised in 1944 along USAAF lines to become the Fuerza Aérea Boliviana (Bolivian Air Force), with most of its aircraft of US manufacture. The FAB was at first under partial Army control, but became totally independent in 1957.

Bolivia signed the Rio Pact in 1947 and the usual Military Assistance Program deliveries followed — initially small numbers of North American AT-6 Texan trainers and B-25J Mitchell bombers, followed in mid-1956 by seven Boeing B-17G Fortress bomber/transports. Further aircraft came from Brazil, henceforth a regular source of equipment for the FAB; eleven Fábrica do Galeão-built Fairchild PT-19 (Model 3FG) primary trainers. Small numbers of aircraft were subsequently procured at irregular intervals, as and when defence budgets allowed it, and the USA remained the main supplier followed by Brazil and Europe. Brazil made available eight Fokker S 11 basic trainers, a few North American T-6G Texans, and later eighteen Aerotec A122A Uirapuru primary trainers for what is now the Colegio Militar de Aviación (COLMILAV, Military Aviation College). Other aircraft came from Uraguay and Venezuela, and in 1973 the FAB entered the jet age with the first of fifteen Canadair T-33 Mk.3 Silver Star advanced trainers. Transport aircraft were purchased from foreign civil markets, and included six Convair 440-61 twin-engined civil airliners disposed of by Aviaco of Spain early in 1972; during 1978, six Fokker F.27-400M Troopships were ordered from the manufacturers. Various attempts to set up a realistic combat element have so far been unsuccessful; an order for ten Hispano HA.220 close-support jets was cancelled, as was an option on a small number of Embraer EMB.326GB Xavantes, due to lack of funds. In December 1980 permission was granted for the acquisition of twenty-four fighters, the Mirage, Jaguar and Kfir C2 all being considered, but little seems to have come of this, and there were reports during late 1981 that ex-Belgian Air Force Starfighters may be acquired. However, recent purchases of modern equipment have been made, principally of twenty Pilatus Turbo-Trainers to re-equip the Escuadrón Basico of COLMILAV.

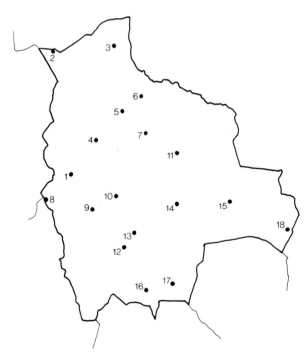

Military Air Bases

1   La Paz (El Alto)
2   Cobija
3   Riberalta
4   San Borja
5   Santa Ana
6   San Joaquín
7   Trinidad
8   Charaña
9   Oruro
10 Cochabamba (Colcapirua)
11 Ascensión
12 Potosí
13 Sucre (La Florida)
14 Santa Cruz (El Trompillo)
15 San José de Chiquitos
16 Tarija (El Tejar)
17 Villa Montes
18 Puerto Suárez

Current Organisation

The Fuerza Aerea Boliviana currently comprises the following units :

Grupo Aereo de Caza N° 1 at Base Aerea de El Trompillo, Santa Cruz de la Sierra, with North American F-86F Sabres.

Grupo Aereo de Caza N° 2 at Base Aerea General Jorge Jordan, El Alto (La Paz), with Canadair T-33 Mk.3 Silver Stars.

Grupo Aereo de Cobertura N° 1 (No.1 Tactical Support Group) at Base Aerea Capitan Arturo Valle, El Tejar (Tarija) with North American AT-6G Texans.

Grupo Aereo Mixto (GAMX, Mixed Air Group) at Base Aerea de Colcapirua (Cochabamba) with Bell UH-1H and Sud SA.315B Lamas.

Grupo de Operaciones Aereas Especiales (GOAE - Special Air Operations Group) at Base Aerea de Reboré with Hughes 500M.

Grupo Aéreo de Transporte, incorporating the **Transporte Aéreo Militar, TAM** at Base Aerea General Walter Arze, El Alto (La Paz), with Douglas C-47, C-54 and DC-6, Convair 440 and 580, IAI 201 Arava.

Colegio Militar de Aviación (COLMILAV) at Base Aérea de El Trompillo, Santa Cruz de la Sierra, due to move to Santa Rosa by 1982, and consisting of:

Escuadrón Primario with Aerotec A122A Uirapurus
Escuadrón Básico with T-6G Texans, North American T-28s and Pilatus PC-7 Turbo-Trainers.

Servicio Nacional de Aerofotogrametría (National Photogrametric Service) at Base Aerea General Walter Arze, El Alto (La Paz) with Lear Jet 25B, Cessna 402.

Escuadrilla Ejecutiva at Base Aerea Walter Arze, El Alto (La Paz) with Beechcraft King Air 200, Cessna 414 and Lockheed 188A Electra. This unit was formerly known as the Escuadrilla Presidencial.

There are also several liaison Escuadrillas flying light aircraft. The Grupo de Operaciones Aéreas Especiales was formed at Reboré with armed T-6G Texans and later re-equipped with a dozen armed Hughes 500M helicopters, although it was to have re-equipped with eighteen Embraer Xavantes. The Grupo Aereo de Transporte incorporates since 1978 the Transporte Aéreo Boliviano (TAM), which operates regular freight services, often on charter to commercial enterprises, with military aircraft in civil marks but flown and serviced by FAB personnel; their aircraft comprise three Lockheed Hercules and a Convair 580. The FAB also controls an infantry regiment for airfield defence.

Aircraft Review

COLOURS AND MARKINGS

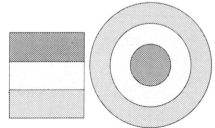

The colours of the national flag — red for the animal kingdom, yellow for the mineral kingdom and green for the vegetable kingdom — appear in roundel form on the wings, and optionally on the fuselage sides, and as rudder stripes or fin flash on camouflaged aircraft. Camouflage schemes follow the US model, using two tones of green with light grey undersides.

SERIAL NUMBERS

Serial numbers most commonly consist of a three-digit number, though TAM aircraft have two-digit numbers prefixed by TAM-.

AEROTEC A122A UIRAPURU

Eighteen were delivered to equip the Escuadrón Primario of of the COLMILAV, the first seven being taken on charge on 9 May 1974.

160	c/n 076
161	077
162	078
163	079
164	080
165	081
166	082
167	083
168	084
169	085
170	086
171	087
172	088
173	089
174	090
175	092
176	093
177	094

BEECHCRAFT C-45G

One was serialled 809, c/n AF.366 ex 51-11809, written off on 20 September 1959.

BEECHCRAFT KING AIR 90

One, serialled 006, was operated by the Escuadrilla Presidencial, and written off on 26 April 1979. A new aircraft, model F90 serial 018 was seen at the factory prior to delivery in March 1981.

BEECHCRAFT KING AIR 200

Two aircraft for the Escuadrilla Presidencial :
001 c/n BB.125   (also reported as 001A)
002   BB.11   ex N200MM

BELL UH-1H IROQUOIS

Six were delivered to the Grupo Aéreo Mixto :
720
721
722   w/o 8.8.77
723
724
725

BELL 212

Two were reported as delivered :
101 c/n 30514 ex N7103J·
102   30515   N7119J

BOEING B-17G FORTRESS

Seven were delivered in mid-1956 for use as transports, ex-USAAF 44-6393, 6556, 83750, 83809, 85774, 85817 and 85840.

CESSNA 172K/T-41D

At least three 172K, delivered about 1970 :
120 c/n 57606
121   57607
122   57608
These were followed by a batch of ex—USAF T-41D :
123   R172-0386 ex 69-7274
124   R172-0387   69-7275
125   R172-0388   69-7276
126   R172-0389   69-7277
127   R172-0390   69-7278
128   R172-0391   69-7279

CESSNA 180C

One was delivered in October 1960, serial 001, c/n 50884 ; it is no longer current, becoming CP-1056 in 1973

CESSNA 185/U-17A

Deliveries comprised at least fifteen civil Cessna 185, the first seven being A185E :
219 c/n 185-1344 d/d 3.68 w/o 25.11.72
220   185-1345   3.68
223   185-1346   3.68
224   185-1435
225   185-1436   w/o 18.4.72
226   185-01858
227   185-   w/o 18.6.71
These were followed by eight A185F :
230   185-02211
231   185-02221
232   185-02229
233   185-02234
234   185-02240   w/o 6.11.73
235   185-02252
236   185-02255
237   185-02256
Eleven ex US military U-17A were also known to have been delivered including :
205   185-0580 ex 63-9796
208   185-0584   63-9800
209   185-   63-
215   185-0999   66-8036 w/o 18.4.72
216   185-
218   185-0592   63-9805
238   185-   w/o 5.8.79

CESSNA 195

One only, serialled 372, c/n 7342 ex N4319V, eventually disposed of as CP-646.

CESSNA U206

Seven U206C were reported as delivered, but not all seem to have been taken on charge. At least one U206F was later acquired. Known aircraft :
221 U206C c/n 206-   w/o 23.9.72
222 U206C   206-0980
229 U206F   206-01735

At the end of the 1970s a batch of U206G were acquired :
237   206-05929
238   206-05996
239   206-06046
240   206-06075
241   206-06089
242   206-06098
243   206-06121

CESSNA T210

Two model T.210L acquired mid-1970s :
238 c/n 59975 re-serialled as 261
262   59983 to CP-1213 in 1975
One model T.210N acquired 1981 :
244   64302

CESSNA 310

At least one seems to have been used, though no details are known.

CESSNA 402B

At least two aircraft, taken on charge early 1970s :
003 c/n 402B-0108 ex N7858Q
012   402B-   w/o 1.7.78

CESSNA 414

One only, for the Escuadrilla Ejecutiva :
002 c/n 414-0170

CESSNA 421B

One serialled 005 for the use of the Escuadrilla Ejecutiva. It is believed that a second machine was later procured.

CONVAIR 440-61

Six ex-Aviaco machines, delivered on 21.5.72.
TAM-43 c/n 330 ex EC-APV w/o 27.10.75
TAM-44   328   EC-APT
TAM-45   406   EC-AQK w/o 24.1.78

TAM-46	373	EC-APU	
TAM-47	445	EC-ARP	w/o 21.12.73
TAM-48	457	EC-ARQ	

CONVAIR 580

Four aircraft bought from US civil operators around 1974 for use by TAM :

TAM-70	c/n 39 ex N4803C to N81MR 24.10.79		
TAM-71	370	N2046	wfu
TAM-72	54	N73127	to N5822 12.80
TAM-76	41	N73122	to N5590L 4.80

Additionally, Convair 580 N5836 c/n 169 was delivered to Transporte Aéreo Boliviano, in full camouflage with the civil registration CP-1330.

CURTISS C-46 COMMANDO

Four aircraft were used by TAM :

TAM-29	d/d 10.68
TAM-38	
TAM-60	c/n 26683 ex 41-24762, LV-FTX, acquired 1964, w/o 17.2.71
TAM-61	c/n 26771 ex 42-3638, N91364, acquired 12.69, and sold as CP-1080 in 1977.

TAM-60 was a model C-46C and TAM-61 a model C-46A.

DOUGLAS C-47 SKYTRAIN

About forty are believed to have been used, with about fourteen remaining in service. Known aircraft are :

TAM-01	c/n 1934 ex N17319		w/o 14.4.72
TAM-02			wfu
TAM-03			w/o 15.10.58
TAM-04			w/o 20.1.58
TAM-05			w/o 8.11.58
TAM-09	9030	42-32804	w/o 1.8.60
TAM-11			w/o 12.2.70
TAM-12			
TAM-14	4569	41-18477, PP-YPL	
TAM-15	15939	44-76355 to CP-1417 in 1978.	
TAM-16			wfu
TAM-17			wfu
TAM-18			
TAM-20			
TAM-21			wfu
TAM-22			w/o 4.5.71

TAM-23			w/o 28.9.72
TAM-24			w/o 25.9.72
TAM-25	15878	44-76294	w/o
TAM-27			
TAM-28			wfu
TAM-30			w/o 19.1.74
TAM-32			
TAM-33			
TAM-34			w/o 11.11.74
TAM-35			wfu
TAM-36			

One aircraft is c/n 13371 ex CP-680/42-93457. Three unidentified machines were sold to civilian operators in 1980 :

c/n 16240/32988 ex 44-76656	to CP-1419
c/n 19344	42-100881	CP-1418
c/n 19395	42-100932	CP-1470

DOUGLAS C-54 SKYMASTER

Five aircraft were used by TAM :

TAM-01		
TAM-51	c/n 36004 ex 45-551	wfu 1980
TAM-52		w/o 10.1.74
TAM-53		
TAM-54	10649	42-72544 wfu 1980

The TAM-51 was a C-54G, and TAM-54 a C-54D.

DOUGLAS DC-6B

Two aircraft were delivered to TAM in 1980. One was TAM-63 c/n 43543 ex CP-715, and is now withdrawn from use. The other was c/n 43272 ex CP-740, and did not acquire a serial, being for spares use only.

FAIRCHILD PT-19 (MODEL 3FG)

Eleven supplied by Brazil, from surplus air force stocks :

0340	ex PP-GBO
0376	
0385	
0389	PP-HQO
0402	
0452	
0469	
0482	PP-HQS
0484	
0489	
0529	

FOKKER F-27-400M TROOPSHIP

Six were ordered for TAM use as C-47 replacements :

TAM-90	c/n 10578 ex PH-EXL/PH-FTN	d/d 1.5.79
TAM-91	10580	PH-EXM	29.5.79
TAM-92	10584	PH-EXH/PH-FTM	17.4.79
TAM-93	10599	PH-EXC	20.5.80
TAM-94	10600	PH-EXD/PH-FTV	7.2.81
TAM-95	10601	PH-EXE/PH-FTW	7.2.81

The last two aircraft were embargoed in August 1980 due to the coup d'état in Bolivia, but delivered in February 81.

FOKKER S 11-4 INSTRUCTOR

Eight ex Brazilian Air Force aircraft delivered in 1972 and serialled 151 to 158; withdrawn from use in 1976.

GRUMMAN JRF-6B GOOSE

At least one, c/n 1150 ex Royal Navy FP500 , later sold in the USA as N5548A.

HILLER UH-12B/OH-23

Seven to twelve were reported as delivered, including three UH-12B, of which one was serialled 603. Another, referred to by some sources as an SL4, was 604, and was written off on 21 May 1967. No Hillers remain in service.

HUGHES 500M

Twelve armed helicopters delivered in 1978 to re-equip the Grupo de Operaciones Aéreas Especiales. Ten remained in use in 1980.

IAI 201 ARAVA

Six aircraft for TAM use :

TAM-75	c/n 0021 ex 4X-IAT	d/d 12.9.75
TAM-76	0024	4X-IAW	28.10.75 w/o 2.3.76
TAM-77	0026	4X-IAY	14.12.75 w/o 16.3.77
TAM-78	0027	4X-IAZ	4.5.76
TAM-79	0032	4X-IBE	21.6.76
TAM-80	0042	4X-IBO	10.11.76

LEAR JET 25

Lear Jet 25B 008 c/n 25.192 was delivered in July 1975 to the FAB Comando General (General Headquarters) for use by the Servicio Nacional de Aerofotogrametría.
Lear Jet 25D 010 c/n 25.211 ex N3514F was delivered in December 1976.

LOCKHEED T-33 (CANADAIR T-33 Mk.3)

The aircraft used were actually Canadair T-33 Mk.3 Silver Stars converted to T-33A-N standards with provision for armament. The first fifteen (600 to 614) were delivered in 1973-74; another five (615 to 619) followed through Northwest industries in 1977, traded in part for six surviving F-51D Mustangs. The Silver Stars form the current equipment of the Grupo Aéreo de Caza de El Alto.

600	c/n 287 ex-CAF	133287	w/o 19.4.77
601	162	133162	w/o 19.8.77
602	492	133492	
603	616	133616	w/o 10.73 on delivery
604	432	133432	
605	208	133208	w/o 9.8.77
606	158	133158	
607	530	133530	
608	468	133468	
609	475	133475	
610	459	133459	
611	338	133338	
612	627	133627	
613		133.....	
614		133.....	
615	150	133150/C-GWHM	w/o 21.2.80
616	580	133580/C-GWHN	
617	488	133488/C-GWHL	
618	464	133464/C-GPEG	
619	329	133329/C-GWHO	

LOCKHEED L-188A ELECTRA

One aircraft TAM-69, model L-188A-08-10 c/n 1125 ex CP-853 delivered in 1973; to the Escuadrilla Ejecutivo in May 1975 as TAM-01.

LOCKHEED C-130H HERCULES

Two aircraft, model L.382C-72D, were delivered in July and October 1978 respectively, and subsequently handed over to Transporte Aéreo Boliviano with civil registrations :
TAM-90 c/n 4744 to CP-1375 w/o 28.9.79
TAM-91 4759 CP-1376
A third C-130H, model L.382G-45C, c/n 4833 ex N4083M was delivered to Transporte Aéreo Boliviano on 23.10.79.

NORTH AMERICAN AT-6 TEXAN

Some eighty of all models delivered. The first fifteen AT-6B arrived in December 1942, and a batch of fifteen AT-6D (ex 44-81175 to 81189) in December 1944. At least five T-6G were obtained from the Brazilian Air Force, and two AT-6C from the Argentine Navy in June 1960. Serials included 100 to 119 (reported as SNJ-6B) and 301 to 359 (AT-6B, C, D and T-6G). About a dozen remain in service, most with armament, but only two on COLMILAV charge.

NORTH AMERICAN F-51D MUSTANG

The first four aircraft came from the Uraguayan Air Force in 1960; others followed later, including three (plus a TF-51D) in 1966, and eight Cavalier-rebuilt F-51D in 1968 under Project Peace Condor - although only four of these were to full Cavalier Mustang standards. The last operational machines, in service with Grupo Aéreo Nº2 at Colcapirua and the Grupo Aéreo de Caza de Santa Cruz, were retired in 1977 and replaced by T-33A-N Silver Stars. Six were sold in Canada to Northwest Industries :

506 ex	44-63807/Uraguay	to C-GXUO
511	45-11453	(C-GXUP), N59038
519	67-22579	C-GXRG
520	67-22580	C-GXUQ
521	67-14866 (TF-51D)	C-GXUO
523	67-22581	C-GMUS

A TF-51D was serialled 510. An F-51D was written off on 30.7.70. Other F-51D were two former Nicaraguan Air Force machines 44-72059 (ex Swedish AF 26146 and N6150U) and 44-72291 (ex Swedish AF 26055 and N6140U); 44-86455/N6362T delivered in 1966; an unidentified TF-51D ex N6326T; and Cavalier F-51D 67-22582.

NORTH AMERICAN B-25J MITCHELL

Thirteen were delivered. Three, 541 to 543, were in service with TAM as late as 1979, converted to transports.

NORTH AMERICAN F-86F SABRE

Nine ex Venezuelan Air Force aircraft, serialled 650 to 658, delivered for use by the Grupo Aereo de Caza de Santa Cruz.

NORTH AMERICAN T-28D

Six aircraft, serialled 401 to 406; most reported as withdrawn from use during 1978.

PILATUS PC.6 PORTER

PC.6 Porter 160, c/n 349 ex HB-FAY, and Fairchild PC.6/C Turbo-Porter 009, c/n 2070 ex N5307F, are known to have been delivered. Sixteen PC.6/B2-H2 Turbo-Porters have been ordered recently.

PILATUS PC.7 TURBO-TRAINER

Twenty-four have been supplied in two batches of twelve, one in 1979 and one in 1981, to re-equip the Escuadrón Básico of the COLMILAV :

450	c/n 110 ex HB-HAZ	d/d 10.4.79	
451	111	HB-HCA	10.4.79	
452	112	HB-HCB	10.4.79	
453	113	HB-HCC	10.4.79	
454	114	HB-HCD	18.5.79	
455	115	HB-HCE	18.5.79	w/o 7.5.80
456	116	HB-HCF	18.5.79	
457	117	HB-HCG	18.5.79	
458	118	HB-HCH	6.79	
459	119	HB-HCI	6.79	
460	120	HB-HCK	11.8.79	
461	121	HB-HCL	11.8.79	
462	245	HB-HLC	16.6.81	
463	246	HB-HLD	16.6.81	
464	247	HB-HLE	16.6.81	
465	248	HB-HLF	8.7.81	
466	249	HB-HLG	8.7.81	
467	250	HB-HLH	8.7.81	
468	251	HB-HLI	28.7.81	
469	252	HB-HLK	28.7.81	
470	253	HB-HLL	25.8.81	
471	254	HB-HLM	28.7.81	
472	255	HB-HLN	25.8.81	
473	256	HB-HLO	25.8.81	

Cessna A185E FAB225 seen at Wichita in October 1968 before delivery; it was written off on 18.4.72.

Pilatus PC.7 Turbo-Trainer 450 seen as HB-HAZ on delivery through Reykjavik in April 1979.

ROCKWELL SABRE 60

One aircraft serialled 001, c/n 306-115 ex N2118J, delivered on 24.8.76 to the Departamento Aéreo de la Presidencia de la República (Air Department of the Presidency of the Republic) for use by the Escuadrilla Presidencial. It is no longer current, and may have been replaced by Sabre 65A c/n 465-60 ex N2580E.

SIAI-MARCHETTI SF.260CB

Six aircraft delivered in 1978, serialled 180 to 185. 181 was written off on 26.3.79.

SIKORSKY HH-19B

Two were used; details not known.

STEARMAN PT-17

About twenty believed delivered, including ex-USAAF 41-864, 41-923 (which was serialled FAB 05), 41-8459 and 41-25727 to 25731; and six ex Argentine Navy machines delivered on 18.4.58.

SUD SA.315B LAMA

Five were delivered early in 1979 to supplement a similar number already in use with the Grupo Aéreo Mixto. The first three of the 1979 batch were :
723 c/n 2420
724   2422
725   2426
Six examples of the Brazilian-built Lama, the Helibras Govião (Kestrel) were ordered for delivery during 1981; they are known as 'Gavilán' (Spanish for kestrel) in FAB service. FAB-732 was written off on 16.6.81.

Curtiss C-46 Commando TAM-29 seen at Miami on 7 March 1969.

Army & Carabinero

The Ejército Boliviano has recently operated at least one Cessna 421 serialled EB-1001, and two aircraft delivered during 1981 were Beechcraft King Air 200 c/n BB.209 ex N5450M for the Commander in Chief of the Army as EB-001, and Piper PA-31T Cheyenne II EB-004 c/n 31T-8120017 ex CP-1678.

The Carabinero are known to operate at least a Cessna 421B, serialled CB-001.

Bolivian Navy

The Bolivian Navy's aeronautical pretensions have been very modest and equipment consists of two AT-6s received as a gift from the Argentine Navy in May 1969, serialled FNB-001 and FNB-002 and a Cessna U.206G FNB-003 c/n U206-05516 ex-N4624X was delivered in November 1980.

BRAZIL

Area	8,511,968 sq km
Population	126,000,000
Capital	Brasília
Civil registration	PP-, PT-

Brazil was discovered by Portuguese navigator Pedro Álvares Cabral in April 1500 and soon became Portugal's most prosperous colony. It became an independent kingdom on 13 May 1822, ruled by the King of Portugal's son, who was chosen as Emperor of Brazil in October as Pedro I. He was succeeded by Pedro II who was dethroned in November 1889 when Brazil became a republic. A federal system of government (the country was known as the United States of Brazil for a number of years) has since been modified through consitutional reforms. Brazil is the only Latin-American country speaking Portuguese and the largest Latin-American country — in fact it is one of the world's largest countries, with abundant and largely unexplored natural resources and an ever-expanding industrial potential. Most of its exports are still agricultural (rubber, coffee, cocoa, sugar) but there has been an increase in the export of manufactured goods and indeed a Brazilian aircraft, the Embraer Bandeirante (flag-bearer) light transport, has become an export best-seller. Although inflation is a problem and there is some political agitation, in common with most Latin-American countries, the country has a potentially brilliant future, being already self-sufficient in most respects. Brasília, the new capital city built out of nowhere through an incredible effort, is the world's most modern city.

Military aviation in Brazil may be said to have begun in June 1867 during the war against Paraguay, when a balloon purchased in the United States of America by the Brazilian Army was successfully used for observation. This in itself is not surprising because one of the world's earliest lighter-than-air pioneers, Bartolomeu de Gusmão, came from Brazil to the Portuguese Court, and the country's aeronautical tradition was confirmed when Alberto Santos-Dumont made the first officially-recognised heavier-than-air flight in Europe in October 1906. Purists may even give more credit to Santos-Dumont than to the Wright brothers, because the Brazilian's aircraft took off with no external aids and was directionally controllable in the air.

The Brazilian Army continued to employ balloons

for observation purposes, although there was a gap between the Paraguay war and 1907 when funds were made available for the creation of a Parque de Aerostação (Balloon Park) and for the purchase of four French balloons. An Escola Brasileira de Aviação (Brazilian Flying School) was formed in February 1914 with the Army's first aircraft – five Bleriot monoplanes and three Farman biplanes. However, government funds which had been promised did not come and the school had to close down after five months of operations due to heavy losses. A few Army sergeants and Naval junior officers received some flying training. Later in 1914 and during the first few months of 1915, a few Army aircraft (most from the Escola, others from the Brazilian Aeroclub) including an Italian-built Bleriot-SIT and a Morane-Saulnier monoplane were employed in action against insurgents in the Santa Catarina state. A few airstrips were opened up but little else could be achieved because, due to the war in Europe, aircraft procurement was a near-impossibility. This was not really likely to discourage the Brazilians : Army Captain Marcos Villela built two aircraft of his own design in 1917-18, naming them Aribu (vulture) and Alagoas (after his native state).

Steps were taken to form an Army Air Service in late November 1918. A French air mission arrived to help to organise an Escola de Aviação Militar (Military Aviation School), which was to incorporate a Companhia de Aviacao (Aviation Company). The Escola was formally inaugurated on 10 July 1919 with a small complement of French aircraft; additional machines were delivered in 1920-21. The first Brazilian Army trainers were seven Nieuport 82 (c/n 2380, 4767, 8049, 8064, 8065, 8069, 8070), fourteen Nieuport 83 (c/n 8877, 8889, 8890, 8894, 8901, 8902, 8908/8910, 8915, 8917, 8919, 8921, 8922), three Sopwith 1A2 (the French version of the 1½ Strutter; c/n 3061, 3514, 3633) and a single Morane-Saulnier MS.21 'rouleur' or ground trainer, capable of taxying at high speed but not of flying (c/n 1345). Their c/ns served as serial numbers. The first combat aircraft to be received were thirty

Breguet 14 A2 and B2 (c/n 1855/1872, 1958/1962, 1965/1971), although not more than half a dozen were ever used at the same time, twenty SPAD VII fighters (c/n 2952/2961, 2971/2980) and six Nieuport 24bis (c/n 3042, 3064, 3318, 3889, 4648 and 5149) the latter being used as operational trainers.

The development of the Air Service proceeded satisfactorily. In June 1922 a Grupo de Esquadrilhas de Aviação (Group of Air Squadrons) was activated comprising a 1ª Esquadrilha de Bombardeio (1st Bomber Squadron) with four Breguet 14 B2, the 1ª Esquadrilha de Caca (1st Fighter Squadron) with nine SPAD VII and the 3ª Companhia Provisória de Parque de Aviação (3rd Provisional Air Material Company), all at Santa Maria in the state of Rio Grande do Sul, and the 3ª Esquadrilha de Observação (3rd Observation Squadron) at Alegrete with six Breguet 14 A2. The Grupo was disbanded in March 1928 and its aircraft were returned to Campo dos Afonsos, where the Escola was operating and which by that time had been considerably expanded.

The 1920s saw the arrival of more French aircraft. Two Caudron G.IV were delivered to the Serviço Geográfico do Exército (Army Geographical Service) in December 1920 and were used for photo-survey until mid-1922. In January 1921 the Escola de Aviação Militar (EscAvM) received some new equipment – ten Nieuport 80 (c/n 8001/8010), eight Nieuport 81 (c/n 8101/8108) and eight Nieuport 21 (c/n 2101/2108); another ten Nieuport 81 and twelve Nieuport 21 (including c/n 7090, 7096, 7103, 7112, 7114, 7117, 7118, 7128) followed at a later date. A few Nieuport 81 were eventually converted to taxying trainers with most of their wing covering removed. In June 1924, eight SPAD 54 trainers were taken on charge (c/n 3686/3693; at this time there was a serious revolutionary attempt in São Paulo state and the SPAD 54s were sent into active service with the Esquadrilha de Aperfeiçoamento (Operational Conversion Squadron) at Mogi das Cruzes before they were ever used as school aircraft (this did not happen until 1927). The Esquadrilha was in fact an offshoot of the EscAvM, which also formed the 1ª Companhia de

Parque de Aviação and supplied six Breguet 14 A2 and two Nieuport 21. Both units returned to Campo dos Afonsos in July 1924, only to return, incorporated in the Destacamento de Aviação (Air Detachment). Some operational experience was gained in August-September, but at the cost of a delay in the service's expansion plans.. An earlier SPAD 34 had been in service since early 1922 at the EscAvM.

The service was upgraded to Arma de Aviação de Exército (Army Air Arm) in January 1927. The EscAvM was further modernised with the assistance of another French mission. Further aircraft were purchased: a Morane-Saulnier MS.137 was obtained from a French civilian living in Argentina; ten MS.35 trainers and six Breguet 19 A2/B2 bombers arrived from France in April 1928 followed in September by six Potez 25 A2 and three Caudron 59 trainers in October.

A decision dated January 1929 tried to introduce a basic designation system for military aircraft but in the event this did not become a reality; however it did succeed in introducing a coherent serialling system to replace the then current identification by c/n or type number. Aircraft were to receive a three-digit serial with a letter prefix denoting its current unit – A to J for operational squadrons and K for the EscAvM. The only letters to be used in practice were A for the Grupo de Combate of the EscAvM – on Potez 25 A2 serialled A111 et seq, and K for EscAvM aircraft which were serialled in blocks according to types:

K111/120	Morane-Saulnier MS.35
K121/126	Morane-Saulnier MS.147
K127	Morane-Saulnier MS.149
K128/139	Morane-Saulnier MS.147
K211/225	Morane-Saulnier MS.130
K231	Caudron 140
K241/243	Caudron 59
K251/252	Farman 74
K311/318	Potez 33
K331/337	Schreck-FBA 17
K411/415	Wibault 73 C1
K421/424	Nieuport-Delage NiD 72
K511/515	Potez 25

K521   Breguet 19
K611/613 Lioré et Olivier LeO 25 Bn4
K621/624 Amiot 122 Bp3

The K prefix was retained after the system was modified in November 1933, although aircraft operated by the Regimentos de Aviação (Air Regiments) had no prefixes. Trainers in Regimento use however, had a four-symbol serial comprising the Regimento number, the letter T, and two digits (2T05, for example was the fifth trainer used by the 2° Regimento de Aviação — an MS.130).

Fifteen Morane-Saulnier MS.130 were delivered to the EscAvM in March 1929, eight Potez 33 between June and November (c/n 1415/1417, 1543/1546, 1728); they were joined in 1930 by two ex-Argentine Potez 32, the first three of seven Schreck-FBA 17 Ht2 flying boats in October, a single Caudron 140 (c/n 6363) in November and six of a total of eighteen Morane-Saulnier MS.147 in December. Five Wibault 73 C1 parasol fighter-trainers arrived at about the same time.

1930 was an eventful year, although it began on a positive note with the delivery of a Morane-Saulnier MS.149 (c/n 58) and later of eighteen Potez 25 TOE (c/n 1816/1833). It was then that a revolution took place in three states, bringing Getúlio Vargas to power; he was to rule Brazil until 1945 and again between 1951 and his suicide in 1954. Two Potez 25 TOE were among the aircraft which flew for the revolutionaries; others included a Farman 192 acquired from a civilian, which had a very short service life, and a long-range Breguet 19GR formerly registered P-BARR (c/n 1748). At about the same time, three Lioré et Olivier LeO 253Bn4 night-bombers arrived from France (K611 *Itororó*, K612 *Avahy* and K613 *Tuiuty*) but were little used. The new Brazilian government, owing much to São Paulo state, did not forget it, a Destacamento de Aviação (Air Detachment) being permanently based in the city of São Paulo. It eventually evolved into the 2° Regimento de Aviação.

The first operational Army air unit to be formed, the Grupo Misto de Aviação (Mixed Air Group),

became a reality at Campo dos Afonsos in May 1931, comprising a combat Esquadrilha with ten Potez 25 TOE and an Esquadrilha de Treinamento (Training Squadron) with a handful of Curtiss Fledglings, which were later used to build up the Correio Aéreo Militar (Military Air Mail Service); Fledgling K263 is preserved at the Museu Aeroespacial. The Grupo became the 1° Regimento de Aviação in 1933 — but first, Brazil had to go through a difficult period.

In July 1932 a part of the armed forces in São Paulo state rose against the Vargas government. Aircraft were used from the very beginning, many EAvM (note the new abbreviation) aircraft being transferred to the Grupo Misto de Aviação. Apart from the types mentioned above, there were others: two Farman 74 instrument trainers delivered in November 1931, four Amiot 122 Bp3 bombers delivered early in 1931, and four Nieuport-Delage NiD 72 fighters which arrived in March-April; in addition to fifteen de Havilland DH.60T Moth trainers (c/n 3000/3014) from Britain and forty-one Waco CSO armed reconnaissance biplanes from the USA (ten were acquired initially and later used for the Air Mail service). Orders were placed for Boeing 256 (P-12) fighters and Vought V.65 observation biplanes, but these arrived after the insurgents had surrendered. Before that, they had been able to obtain nine Curtiss Falcon observation aircraft from Chile, two of them being actually used in combat; they operated alongside two Potez 25 TOE, two Waco CSO and a single NiD 72, mainly from Campo de Marte (Mars Field) in São Paulo.

As the country returned to peacetime, the Aviação Militar was once more re-organised, in March 1933, with provision for seven Regimentos de Aviação (RAv) within three Zonas Militares Aéreas (Military Air Zones):

1ª Zona Militar Aérea (HQ Rio de Janeiro)
1° RAv at Rio de Janeiro (Campo dos Afonsos)
6° RAv at Recife (Campo da Tablada)
7° Rav at Belém (Campo do Instituto)
2ª Zona Militar Aérea (HQ São Paulo)
2° RAv at São Paulo (Campo de Marte)
4° RAv at Belo Horizonte

3ª Zona Militar Aérea (HQ Porte Alegre)
3° RAv at Porto Alegre (Canoas)
5° RAv at Curitiba (Campo de Bacachery)
The Regimentos were gradually activated; the 7° did not form until June 1936. In January 1934 the now familiar-looking Brazilian star insignia — a green and yellow five-pointed star with a white/blue disc on its centre — was introduced, with proportions which were modified to their present standards in May 1941. The green/yellow rudder stripes were introduced in January 1937, prior to that date rudders had been painted blue, green and yellow in a number of variations.

New aircraft types in service comprised a few Bellanca 31-42 Pacemaker light transports, thirty Waco CPF (c/n 4250/4259, 4340/4359 delivered in 1935 and still in use in March 1943), a single Stinson Model O observation aircraft and twenty-three Boeing F4B fighter biplanes (fourteen model 256 serialled I101/114 and nine model 267 serialled I115/123). Some of these again saw action, this time against communist rebels who had begun their revolution in November 1935 by the summary execution of a number of officers. A raid by Vought Corsairs was instrumental in securing the surrender of the rebels. Other Waco purchases totalled twenty RNF, twenty CTO, twenty-five CJC and a single UMF. Fifteen Avro 626 advanced training biplanes were obtained in May 1937 (c/ns 952-966), twenty-four Stearman A76C3 advanced trainers serialled in the K210 block in July (K210 was preserved at the Museu Aeroespacial, c/n 76015 became PP-LBK and 76032 PT-AUV), and two Lockheed 12A staff transports in October. The first modern primary trainer to be designed in Brazil, the Muniz M.7, was adopted by the Army in May 1938, one other being placed for twenty. In February of that year, the three Savoia-Marchetti S.79T tri-motor bombers of the *Sorci Verdi (Green Mice)* team which, commanded by Mussolini's son Bruno, had flown from Italy to Brazil (I-BISE, I-BRUN and I-MONI) were presented to the Brazilian government and allocated to the Army. Fifteen Waco EGC7 cabin biplanes were bought in September 1938, with another fifteen following in March 1940 and then seven more built locally. In February 1939 the first really modern Army aircraft were purchased — ten Vultee V.11GB-2 bomber/reconnaissance monoplanes, which type became known as the *Vultizão (Big Vultee)*. A few were actually V11TS twin-float seaplanes.

With the outbreak of the Second World War, Brazil was in a difficult position and consequently tried to remain neutral for as long as possible. Although the government was ideologically inclined to support the Axis powers the country was clearly in the American sphere of influence and the United States were busy consolidating their influence all over Latin America. Even Brazil's main airline, Panair do Brasil, was US-owned ! It was finally decided to maintain a state of armed neutrality and as a result orders were placed for more aircraft. The EAvM, which had been renamed as Escola de Aeronáutica Militar (Military Aeronautical School) in December 1938 and again in 1940 as the Escola de Aeronáutica do Exército (Army Air School) re-equipped with twenty Stearman A75L3 primary trainers (c/n 75599/75618 delivered in July 1940 and serialled in the K130 block; K132 is preserved at the Museu Aeroespacial), and thirty North American NA.44 advanced trainers (charge number NA.72; c/n 72-3077/3096 and 72-4757/4766). Two Panair do Brasil Consolidated Commodore flying boats were obtained for transport and patrol duties; and two Bellanca Skyrocket were bought in March for photo-survey work. Small detachments of Vought Corsairs were sent to Belém and Recife for anti-submarine patrols although their efficiency was little more than a show of force.

The Air Ministry came into being in January 1941 merging the Army and Navy air forces into the Forças Aéreas Nacionais (National Air Forces), which in May became the Força Aérea Brasileira (Brazilian Air Force) a name which it still has. The former naval units were accordingly renamed: the Bases de Aviação Naval became Bases Aéreas (Air Bases) and the Oficinas Gerais de Aviação Naval (General Naval Aviation Workshops) became the Fábrica do Galeão (Galeão Factory) which was to build a considerable number of trainers for military use. The 1° RAv was transferred from Campo dos Afonsos to Rio de Janeiro's Bartolomeu de Gusmão airport, which became known as Base Aérea de Santa Cruz; Campo dos Afonsos was then occupied solely by what was now the Escola de Aeronáutica. The inscriptions *EXÉRCITO* and *MARINHA* disappeared from FAB aircraft.

Five Zonas Aéreas (Air Zones) were created in October 1941, the 1ªZA (HQ at Belém), 2ªZA (HQ Recife), 3ªZA (HQ Rio de Janeiro), 4ªZA (HQ Porto Alegre) and the 5ªZA (HQ Campo Grande), with separate commands activated in 1942. By then Brazil was following United States policy in its understanding of what a neutral country is supposed to be. Following the formation of a coastal patrol network with US assistance, there were a few attacks on U-boats found within Brazilian territorial waters. Not unexpectedly, Germany retaliated by torpedoing some Brazilian ships, and Brazil was logically forced to declare war on both Germany and Italy, although the government was careful enough not to include Japan, on 31 August 1942. Immediately afterwards, facilities were given to the USA for the establishment of air bases in Brazil, both for ferry purposes and for use by US Navy patrol squadrons. The USA also supplied during the war a total of 946 aircraft under Lend-Lease arrangements, which permitted an unprecedented expansion of the FAB — 40 Aeronca L-3, 34 Beechcraft UC-43 and GB, 15 AT-7, 10 AT-11 and 9 C-45, 33 Cessna UC-78, 89 Curtiss P-40, 31 Douglas A-20, two B-18 and 11 C-47, 10 Fairchild UC-61 and 190 PT-19, 10 Grumman JRF Geese (and later a few J4F-2 Widgeon), 2 Lockheed A-28, 8 C-60 and a PV-2, 19 Noorduyn UC-64, 50 North American B-25 and 125 AT-6, 21 Piper L-4, 88 Republic P-47D, 120 Vultee BT-15 and 29 A-35B. The Salvador air base was activated on 5 November 1942 and operational flying — anti-submarine patrols — began on the same day, with AT-6 Texans.

The Fábrica de Galeão was modernised and started assembly of the Fairchild PT-19 in 1944, licence production following in 1946; the Ranger engines were built by FNM (Fábrica Nacional de Motores), which has more recently built heavy lorries under Alfa-Romeo licence. The São Paulo-based Escola Técnica de Aviação (Air Technical School) was reorganised by United States advisers and received nine 'war-weary' aircraft to act as instructional airframes (two Curtiss P-40, two North American B-25 and single examples of the Douglas A-20 and B-18, Lockheed B-34, Republic P-47 and Vultee A-35, as well as a Curtiss O-52 ex USAAF 40-2696.

A number of FAB personnel were sent to the USA in January 1944 for training prior to being sent to Europe on active duty; they formed the 1° Grupo de Caça (1st Fighter Group) of the Força Expedicionária Brasileira (FEB, Brazilian Expeditionary Force) and equipped with P-47D Thunderbolts. The 1° Grupo de Caça was allocated to the USAAF's 350th Fighter Group of the Twelfth Air Force, arriving at Tarquinia in Italy in October 1944 and becoming fully operational in November; it moved to Pisa-San Giusto in December and there it remained until the end of the war, by which no less than 2560 operational sorties had been flown mainly against ground targets, for the loss of seventeen aircraft and five pilots.

The United States Naval Task Force 44 (Fourth US Fleet) was assigned to Brazil in late 1943. It comprised Fleet Air Wing 16 at Rio de Janeiro (VP-211 with Martin PBM-3), Fortaleza (VB-127 with Lockheed PV-1, later replaced by VB-130), Natal (VB-107 with Consolidated PB4Y-1, VB-145 with PV-1, VP-83 — later VP-94 — with Consolidated PBY-5A, Recife (VB-143 with PV-1) and Salvador (VB-129 with PV-1, VP-74 — later VP-203 — with PBM-3), and Fleet Airship Wing 4 with squadrons ZP-41 at São Luís and ZP-42 at Maceió.

The war did not prevent — rather the opposite — further re-organisataions of the FAB. The most significant one took place in January 1944; the Grupo was defined as the basic operational unit, divided in Esquadrilhas and making up Regimentos de Aviação (equivalent to USAAF Wings); two or more Regimentos made up a Brigada de Aviação (Air Brigade). Grupos were classified according to their primary rôle — Caça (fighter), Bombardeio (bomber — Leve/light, Médio/medium, Picado/dive), Ataque (attack), Observação (observation), Reconhecimento (reconnaissance), Patrulha (patrol) Torpedeiros (torpedo) and Transporte (transport). The following units were officially activated between 17 August and October 1944:

1ª Zona Aérea

1º Grupo de Patrulha at Belém with Consolidated PBY-5

2ª Zona Aérea

1º Grupo Misto de Aviação at Natal with various fighter and bomber types

2º Grupo de Caca at Natal with Curtiss P-40

4º Grupo de Bombardeio Médio at Foraleza with North American B-25 Mitchell

6º REGIMENTO DE AVIAÇÃO :

1º Grupo de Bombardeio Médio at Recife with Lockheed A-28/PV-1

2º Grupo de Bombardeio Médio at Salvador with Lockheed A-28/PV-1 and B-25 Mitchell

3ª Zona Aérea

1º Grupo de Transporte at Rio de Janeiro-Santos-Dumont with Douglas C-47

2º Grupo de Transporte at Rio de Janeiro-Campo dos Afonsos with Lockheed C-60, Beechcraft C-43 and C-45

1º REGIMENTO DE AVIAÇÃO :

1º Grupo de Bombardeio Picado at Santa Cruz with Vultee A-35

4º REGIMENTO DE AVIAÇÃO :

2º Grupo de Patrulha at Rio de Janeiro-Galeão with Consolidated PBY-5

3º Grupo de Bombardeio Medio at Rio de Janeiro-Galeão with Lockheed A-28/PV-1

4ª Zona Aérea

1º Grupo Misto de Instrução at Sao Paulo with assorted trainer types

2º Grupo de Bombardeio Leve at Sao Paulo with Douglas A-20

2º REGIMENTO DE AVIAÇÃO :

2º Grupo de Bombardeo Picado at São Paulo with Vultee A-35

5ª Zona Aérea

3º REGIMENTO DE AVIAÇÃO :

1º Grupo de Bombardeio Leve at Canoas with Douglas A-20

3º Grupo de Caça at Canoas with Curtiss P-40

5º REGIMENTO DE AVIAÇÃO (which never became a reality) :

1º Grupo de Caça at Curitiba with Republic P-47D

3º Grupo de Bombardeio Picado at Curitaba with Vultee A-35

In October 1944 the 2º Grupo de Caca moved to Santa Cruz and became part of 1º RAv.

By the end of the war, the FAB operated over 1,100 aircraft, some three hundred of which were front-line types, but its strength was soon reduced. Between August and December 1945, further unit changes brought the FAB to a peacetime order of battle: the 1º RAv at Santa Cruz was given the 1º and 2º Grupos de Caca; the 2º RAv at Cumbica the 1º and 2º Grupos de Bombardeio Leve; the 5º RAv at Curtiba was to have operated the Vultee A-35 of the 1º and 3º Grupos de Bombardeio Picado, but the type had by then been found totally unsuitable for use and these units were never activated. The 1º Grupo Misto de Aviação was replaced by a 5º Grupo de Bombardeio Medio, and the 2º Grupo de Bombardeio Picado was disbanded.

Mention must be made of another expeditionary unit, which performed an important, if rather less glamorous, rôle in Italy — the 1ª Esquadrilha de Ligação e Observação (1ª ELO, 1st Liaison and Observation Squadron), formed in July 1944 with Piper L-4 Cubs and the FAB's first specialised artillery spotter unit. The Piper Cubs flew with mixed crews — FAB pilots and Army observers. The unit returned to Brazil at the end of the war and was disbanded in October 1945.

The early postwar years brought some considerable problems. The FAB had to expand the airline routes in the country, occupy and maintain the bases left over by the United States Navy and to uphold Brazilian sovereignty — all this with less aircraft, personnel and funds. The situation was improved by the signing in 1947 of the Rio Pact, which brought more US aircraft, spares and technical assistance to Brazil, and with the formation of the Escola de Comando e Estado Maior da Aeronáutica (ECEMAR, Air Command and General Staff School) in December 1947. The Escola de Especialistas da Aeronáutica (Specialised Crew-Training School) was expanded and moved from Galeão (which then became Rio de Janeiro's international airport) to Guaratinguetá in São Paulo state. The Air Ministry's operating procedures were streamlined. An Escola Preparatória de Cadetes do Ar (Air Cadets' Training School) was inaugurated at Barbacena, and Construções Aeronáuticas SA at Lagoa Santa assembled eighty-one North-American AT-6D (NA.119, c/ns 119-40086 to 40166).

A major unit re-organisation took place in March 1947, and the Regimentos de Aviação were replaced by Grupos de Aviação (GAv), sixteen being provided for — 1º GAv Rio de Janeiro, 2º GAv Belém, 3º GAv São Luís, 4º GAv Fortaleza, 5º GAv Natal, 6º GAv Recife, 7º GAv Salvador, 8º GAv Rio de Janeiro, 9º GAv Manaus, 10º GAv São Paulo, 11º GAv Santos, 12º GAv Curitiba, 13º GAv Florianópolis, 14º GAv Porto Alegre, 15º GAv Campo Grande, 16º GAv Belo Horizonte. Some of these Grupos still exist; some never came into being.

Aircraft procurement was of course reduced, but changed requirements demanded new equipment. A Centro de Treinamento de Quadrimotores (Four-engined Aircraft Training Centre) was formed in January 1951 at Galeão prior to the arrival of the first Boeing B-17G Fortresses; these were taken on charge in May and the Centro moved to Recife in June, SAR and photo survey sorties beginning shortly afterwards. The Centro became the 1º Esquadrão of the 6º GAv (1º/6º GAv) in October 1953. When additional machines were delivered in late 1954, the 6º GAv was expanded to incorporate two Esquadrões — the 1º for SAR duties, the 2º for photo survey and weather reconnaissance. The

Comande de Transporte Aéreo (COMTA, Air Transport Command) was formed at Galeão airport, consisting of the 1º and 2º Grupos de Transporte; it was also given the task of training Army paratroops and flying air mail. The 1º Esquadrão de Contrôle e Alarme (1st Control and Warning Squadron) was re-organised and co-ordinated with the 1º GAvCa at Santa Cruz. An aeronautical research establishment, the Centro Técnico de Aeronáutica (CTA) was formed at São José dos Campos, São Paulo state in November 1953.

The jet era became a reality with the purchase in Britain of sixty-two Gloster Meteor F.8 fighters and ten T.7 conversion trainers, which were delivered in 1953-54 and given FAB designations F-8 and T-7 respectively (a designation system based on the one used by the United States Air Force had already been introduced; this will be detailed later). In July 1953, an agreement was reached between the Brazilian government and NV Fokker in the Netherlands for the licence production of the Fokker S.11 primary trainer; one hundred aircraft were built by the Fábrica do Galeão, which also built a limited number of the S.12 (tricycle-undercarriage version) and further developed the design as the Guanabara, although none of the latter were ordered by the FAB. The Fábrica was for most of this period operated under contract by the Fokker subsidiary Fokker Indústria Aeronáutica SA.

During 1954 very little was achieved due to political changes. An enquiry into the shooting of a FAB officer led to the suicide of President Getúlio Vargas in August; he was succeeded by the Vice-President Café Filho, who dismissed an interim Air Minister and appointed another. The new president resigned due to illness, being replaced by a parliamentary leader who was deposed in November 1955, at which yet another Air Minister was appointed. Then there was an attempted coup d'état in February 1956 against the newly-elected President Juscelino Kubitschek, the founder of Brasília, which ended with the choice of another Air Minister. In spite of these serious political circumstances, the FAB still managed to obtain more aircraft — twelve

Fairchild C-82A tactical transports in July 1955. In December of the same year, the 1ª ELO was reformed at Campo dos Afonsos for army co-operation duties. 1956 was the fiftieth anniversary of the famous first flight of Santos-Dumont and among the celebrations (which included the expansion of the FAB's officer cadres) there was one of particular interest: the paratroop battalion (or, more precisely, the Infantry Battalion of the Nucleus of the Paratrooper Division — Batalhão de Infantaria do Núcleo da Divisão Aeroterrestre) was officially named after Santos-Dumont. Another innovation was more readily recognised by the general public: the FAB's official aerobatic team, the Esquadrilha da Fumaça (Smoke Flight; with the introduction of Esquadrão for squadron, Esquadrilha became flight) formed in May 1952 as part of the Escola de Aeronáutica, became an independent team, flying eight AT-6 Texans painted in a striking white, red and blue livery. The need for the creation of a naval air arm was finally acknowledged and in June 1956 the 2ª ELO was formed at Galeão for naval co-operation.

The 1º Grupo de Aviação Embarcada (1º GpAv Emb, later 1º GAE — 1st Shipborne Aviation Group) was formed — on paper — in February 1957, to be quartered at Santa Cruz pending the introduction of an aircraft carrier into service. Two tactical commands were formed in the following month — the Comando Aerotático Terrestre (CATTER) for co-operation with the ground forces, and the Comando Aerotático Naval (CATNAV) for naval co-operation. The Grumman SA-16 Albatross and the Douglas B-26 Invader were added to the FAB inventory, followed by the Lockheed P2V-5 Neptunes obtained from Royal Air Force Coastal Command, the first Grumman S2F-1 (S-2A; FAB designation P-16) for the 1º GAE, the Lockheed F-80C Shooting Star jet fighters and the Douglas C-54 Skymaster transports. A specialised troop transport unit, the 1º Grupo de Transporte de Tropas (1º GTT) was activated at Campo dos Afonsos (now Base Aérea dos Afonsos) in January 1958, and in November the 3ª ELO, another army co-operation flight, was formed at Pôrto Alegre.

In June 1960, the Belgian Congo became independent but it soon became clear that the Congolese leaders were too inexperienced and had too little authority to rule such a vast country. A bloody civil war ensued and the United Nations sent a peace-keeping force, mainly at the request of the Prime Minister Patrice Lumumba, who was alarmed by the secession of the province of Katanga, which had half of the country's mineral wealth and a pro-Western leader. Brazil agreed to co-operate with the United Nations, and its contribution included a FAB detachment which left in July 1960. A total of twenty-nine officers and NCOs were eventually assigned to a Douglas C-47 squadron under the command of a FAB major. Another three detachments were later flown to the Congo, with a combined personnel strength of 179, to fly Douglas C-47s. The FAB personnel were flown home in early 1964. During those years many things happened in Brazil: Kubitschek had been replaced by leftist President Jânio Quadros, who resigned in August 1961 and was replaced by João 'Jango' Goulart, whose policies were so markedly leftist that he was finally deposed in March 1964 and replaced by the first of a series of military rulers.

During mid to late 1965, seven Esquadrilhas de Reconhecimento e Ataque (ERA, Reconnaissance and Attack Flight) were formed with T-6 Texans: ERA21 at Natal (later Recife), ERA31 at Santa Cruz, ERA32 at Galeao (later Barbacena), ERA41 at Cumbica, ERA42 at Campo Grande, ERA51 at Canoas and ERA61 at Brasília (note that the first digit of the ERA's number was that of the respective Air Region). They were later upgraded to Esquadrão status with up to twenty T-6 each and were replaced in 1973 by mixed-complement EMRAs as explained later.

The subsequent expansion of the FAB owed much to the emerging Brazilian aeronautical industry concentrated in São Paulo state. One of the oldest aircraft manufacturers was Neiva at São José dos Campos and Botucatu, which finally became established through the production of substantial numbers of the Paulistinha high-wing monoplane, broadly similar to the Piper Cub, for both military and flying club use; later types included the L-42 Regente observation/Communications three-seater and the T-25 Universal primary trainer. Aerotec, formed in 1968 at São José dos Campos, concentrated on the production of their own Uirapuru (T-23) primary trainer, and currently the Tangará, but also undertook sub-contract work for their neighbours Embraer. Embraer (Empresa Brasileira de Aeronáutica, Brazilian Aeronautical Corp.) was formed at São José dos Campos in 1969 and now ranks as one of the world's major manufacturers of aircraft. Initially intended to build and develop the IPD.6504 (later EMB.110) Bandeirante twin-turboprop light transport, which has now become an export success as a third-level airliner, and undertake licence manufacture of the Macchi MB.326GB basic jet trainer as the EMB.326GB Xavante (the name of a local Indian tribe), Embraer also designed and built the Ipanema agricultural aircraft and the Urapema high-performance sailplane, and more recently the EMB.121 Xingu light transport/communications aircraft — and has plans for the introduction of more transport designs in the near future. Embraer also builds several Piper types under a licence awarded in 1974, for domestic sales only, each Piper model having an Embraer designation and an Indian name — EMB.710 Carioca for the Cherokee 235 (a low-cost version is nemed the Tupi), EMB.711 Corsico for the Cherokee Arrow 200, EMB.720 Minuano for the Cherokee Six 300, EMB.721 Sertanejo for the Cherokee Lance 300, EMB.810 Seneca for the Seneca 200T and EMB.820 Navajo for the Navajo Chieftain 350. The only Embraer design to enter FAB service was the Seneca, designated U-7. Entering production is the EMB.312 Tucano (T-27) turboprop powered basic trainer, of which a total of 168 are to be built for the air force, with first deliveries due in October 1982 to the Academia da Forca Aerea. The latest Embraer venture is the joint development with Aeritalia-Aermacchi of the AMX light-weight strike fighter, which is scheduled to enter production in 1984. A requirement exists for the delivery of up to 144 of the Brazilian (ABX) version to the FAB, funding being partially provided by Italy; Embraer will undertake one third of the research and development programme.

New aircraft were still acquired at regular intervals and sometimes from unexpected sources. In 1965 the Brazilian Navy agreed to hand over its fixed-wing aircraft (T-28A and Pilatus P.3) to the FAB. Other aircraft were obtained in the USA — thirty-six Northrop F-5E Tiger II tactical fighters and six two-seat F-5B — and in other countries, such as Canada, which supplied twenty-four DHC.5 Buffalo STOL transports. An important acquisition was that of sixteen Dassault Mirages which were to undertake the air defence of the country and were assigned to a specially-formed unit, the 1ª Ala de Defesa Aérea (1ªALADA, 1st Air Defence Wing), which became 1º Grupo de Defesa Aérea in 1979, and based at the new Base Aérea de Anápolis, near Brasília, and linked to an early-warning radar system known as SISDACTA (Air Defence and Air Traffic Control System) set up with French assistance. Initially covering the Rio de Janeiro-São Paulo-Belo Horizonte-Brasília polygon, it is to be expanded to cover the whole territory of Brazil. It is a little-known fact that the FAB considered the purchase from Britain of sixteen BAC Lightning interceptors but the Mirage was selected for budgetary reasons.

An executive transport unit — Grupo de Transportes Especiais (GTE, Special Transport Group) was formed, mainly for presidential use, with an initial complement of two Vickers Viscount airliners, but later equipping with the BAC One-Eleven, the HS.125 and more recently the Boeing 737-2N3. Political changes all over Latin America reflected themselves in a marked emphasis on close-support and anti-guerilla tactics; eighteen B-26 Invaders were modernised to B-26K counter-insurgency standards, some twenty-four Lockheed T-33A were armed to AT-33A standards and designated FAB TF-33, and there were plans to develop a single-seat ground-attack version of the Xavante, though in the event it was a two-seat model which became the standard equipment of many Esquadrões Mistos de Reconhecimiento e Ataque (EMRA, Mixed Reconnaissance and Attack Squadrons - initially formed in 1973 as Esquadrilhas) replacing the armed T-6 Texan.

The EMRAs were disbanded in 1980-81 and the units reformed as follows :

1º EMRA became 1º/8º GAv
2º EMRA became 2º/8º GAv
3º EMRA became 1º/13º GAv
4º EMRA became 1º/11º GAv
5º EMRA became 5º/8º GAv

The Esquadrilha da Fumaça aerobatic team, after flying T-6 Texans for nearly twenty years converted in 1968 to the Fouga Magister for a short period and is currently inactive, although it is expected that it will be re-formed during 1982-83 with the Embraer EMB.312.

Esquadrilha da Fumaça - outer ring red, inner ring white; a red lightning flash thinly edged in white on a light blue sky; yellow/brown eagle with white head, yellow beak and red tongue on a light blue sky. White clouds with light blue trim. The middle band is dark blue, with four light blue aircraft and white contrails.

Military Air Bases

1 Brasília
2 Anápolis
3 Goiânia
4 São Paulo (Pirassununga)
4A Cumbica
5 Santos
6 Curitiba
7 Florianópolis
8 Pôrto Alegre (Canoas)
9 Pelotas
10 Campo Grande
11 Corumbá
12 Rio Branco
13 Fonte Boa
14 Tefe
15 Manaus
16 Santarém
17 Belém
18 São Luís
19 Fortaleza (Ceará)
20 Natal
21 João Pessoa
22 Recife
23 Maceió
24 Salvador (Bahia)
25 Vitória
26 Belo Horizonte
26A Barbacena
27 Niterói
28 Rio de Janeiro (Galeão, Campo dos Afonsos, Santa Cruz)
29 São Pedro da Aldeia

Brazil comprises a Federal District (DF, Distrito Federal), twenty-one states and four territories. The states are abbreviated as follows : Acre AC, Alagoas AL, Amazonas AM, Bahia BA, Ceará CE, Espírito Santo ES, Goías GO, Maranhão MR, Mato Grosso MA, Minas Gerais MG, Pará PA, Paraíba PB, Paraná PR, Pernambuco PE, Piauí PI, Rio Grande do Norte RN, Rio Grande do Sul RS, Rio de Janeiro RJ (including the former state of Guanabara GB), Santa Catarina SC, São Paulo SP, Sergipe SG. Note that Mato Grosso state has recently been divided and the Mato Grosso do Sul state created.

1ªALADA - Yellow lightning flash; top segment blue with a yellow cross; lower segment red ; white aircraft. Yellow scroll with blue lettering.

1º/1ºGAvCa - red 'sky', white clouds, pink and white bird on a grey gun, white edged shield with white stars on a blue background. White shellburst in the sky.

2º/1ºGAvCa - red 'sky', white clouds; black and white penguin with yellow beak, feet and band and white cutlass, on a silver and green aircraft. Black shellbursts. Outer ring green; inner ring yellow.

1º/10ºGAv - white shield with black out-line and black lion. Black scroll with white lettering.

Current Organisation

The Força Aérea Brasileira has a personnel strength of about 35,000 all ranks and operates about six hundred aircraft. It is organised into the following units :

Comando de Defesa Aérea (COMDAER, Air Defence Command)
1º GpDA at Anápolis — 1º Esquadrão with Dassault Mirage IIIEBR/IIIDBR
— 2º Esquadrão with Dassault Mirage IIIEBR/IIIDBR

Comando Aerotático (COMAT, Tactical Air Command)
1º GAvCa at Santa Cruz — 1º Esquadrão 'Senta a Pua' with Northrop F-5E/B
— 2º Esquadrão 'Rompe Mato' with Northrop F-5E/B
4º GAvCa at Fortaleza — 1º Esquadrão with Embraer EMB.326GB Xavante
— 2º Esquadrão with Embraer EMB.326GB Xavante
8º GAv - dispersed — 1º Esquadrão with Bell UH-1H, Embraer Seneca at Manaus
— 2º Esquadrão with Bell UH-1H, Embraer Seneca at Recife
— 3º Esquadrão with UH-1H, SA.330 Puma at Campo dos Afonsos
— 4º Esquadrão to be formed
— 5º Esquadrão with Bell UH-1H, Embraer Seneca at Santa Maria
10º GAv - dispersed — 1º Esquadrão with Embraer EMB.326GB at Santa Maria
— 2º Esquadrão with Embraer EMB.326GB at Campo Grande
11º GAv at São Paulo — 1º Esquadrão with Bell UH-1H
13º GAv at Santa Cruz — 1º Esquadrão with Neiva U-42, Embraer Seneca
14º GAvCa at Canoas — 1º Esquadrão with Northrop F-5E/B
15º GAv at Campo Grande — 1º Esquadrão with Embraer EMB.110 Bandeirante

Comando Costeiro (COMCOS, Coastal Command)
6º GAv at Recife — 1º Esquadrão with RC-130E Hercules, Embraer Bandeirante
7º GAv at Salvador — 1º Esquadrão with Embraer EMB.111 'Bandeirulha'
— 2º Esquadrão formed at Florianópolis 2/82
10º GAv (Serviço de Busca e Salvamento (Search and Rescue Service); currently 'SALVAERO', Serviço Aéreo de Rescate (Air Rescue Service) — 2º Esquadrão with Embraer EMB.110P1 at Campo Grande
— 3º Esquadrão with Bell 47G and SH-1H at Florianópolis
GAE (Grupo de Aviacao Embarcada) — 2º Esquadrão with Grumman S-2E; shore-base is Santa Cruz

Comando de Transporte Aéreo (COMTA, Air Transport Command)
1º GT at Campo dos Afonsos — 1º Esquadrão with Lockheed C-130E/H Hercules
— 2º Esquadrão with Lockheed KC-130H Hercules
2º GT at Galeao — 1º Esquadrão with Embraer Bandeirante, HS.748
— 2º Esquadrão with Embraer Bandeirante
1º GTT at Campo dos Afonsos — 1º Esquadrão with DHC.5 Buffalo
— 2º Esquadrão with DHC.5 Buffalo

2° GTT at Galeão	1° Esquadrão with Lockheed C-130H Hercules
	2° Esquadrão with DHC.5 Buffalo detached at Campo Grande
2° GAv at Belém	1° Esquadrão with Consolidated PBY-5A
9° GAv at Manaus	1° Esquadrão with DHC.5 Buffalo
GTE at Brasília	1° Esquadrão with Boeing 737, Bell 206
	2° Esquadrão with HS.125, Embraer Xingu
1° ETA at Belém	with PBY-5A, Douglas C-47, Embraer Bandeirante
2° ETA at Recife	with Embraer Bandeirante, Seneca
3° ETA at Galeão	with Embraer Bandeirante, Seneca
4° ETA at Cumbica	with Embraer Bandeirante, Seneca
5° ETA at Brasília	with Embraer Bandeirante, Seneca
6° ETA at Porto Alegre	with Embraer Bandeirante, Seneca

1°/14°GAv - Outer ring green, inner ring yellow. Blue sky, white cloud and stars; black bomb with white nose & fins; flesh coloured pilot with green helmet, brown/yellow gun. Black lettering.

Comando de Formação e Aperfeiçoamento (COMFAP, Training and Development Command)

Academia da Força Aérea (AFA, Air Force Academy) at Pirassununga with Cessna T-37C (to be replaced by EMB.312 Tucano), Xavante and Bandeirante; includes the *Clube de Vôo à Vela (CVV, Gliding Club)* with Embraer Ipanemas, Fournier RF.5 motor gliders and Blanik, Libelle and Quero-Quero sailplanes.

Centro de Aplicação Tática e Recomplementação de Equipagens (CATRE, Tactical and Crew Training Centre) at Natal, with three Esquadrões de Instrução Aerea or Air Training Squadrons with Embraer Bandeirante, Xavante and Neiva Universal. The 3°EIA, initially with Xavantes, re-equipped with Bandeirantes.

Centro de Formação de Pilotos Militares (CFPM, Military Pilot Training Centre) at Natal with Xavante, Uirapuru and Neiva Universal.

Centro de Instrução de Helicópteros (CIHel, Helicopter Training Centre) at Santos with Bell 206 and Bell UH-1D, Hughes OH-6.

Centro Técnico de Aeronáutica (CTA, Air Technical Centre) at Sao Jose dos Campos with Bandeirante, Xavante, Neiva U-42 etc.

Escola de Comando & Estado Maior da Aeronáutica (ECEMAR, Air Force Command and General Staff School) at Canoas - non-flying.

Escola Preparatória de Cadetes do Ar (EPCAR, Air Cadets' Training School) at Barbacena with Uirapuru and Bandeirante.

Grupo Especial de Inspeção e Vigilância (GEIV, Special Inspection and Checking Group) at Rio de Janeiro with Embraer Bandeirante and Douglas EC-47.

Escola de Aperfeiçoamento de Oficiais da Aeronáutica (EAOAer, Air Officers' Training School) at São Paulo - non-flying.

Escola de Especialistas da Aeronáutica (ESPAER, Air Force Technical School) at Guaratinguetá, São Paulo state - non-flying.

1°/7°GAv - green outer yellow inner ring; black scrolls, white lettering. Red griffon with yellow/orange cape and yellow crown on white ground.

2°/10°GAv - yellow border, light blue background, white lifebelt with red rope etc, and black lettering. White pelican with yellow beak and feet.

COMTA - white edging, blue shield with white 'COMTA', green leaves, red circle with light blue interior, green map with black lines. White scroll with black lettering.

The following are the most commonly used abbreviations for types of unit :

ELO	Esquadrilha de Ligação e Observacao	GpDA	Grupo de Defesa Aérea
ETA	Esquadrão de Transporte Aéreo	GT	Grupo de Transporte
GAv	Grupo de Aviação	GTE	Grupo de Transportes Especiais
GAvCa	Grupo de Aviação de Caca	GTT	Grupo de Transporte de Tropas

1°/9° GAv - Black outer, red inner circles; pale green background;flesh coloured boy with red skirt, green armbands and headphones; white Buffalo with black 'face' and detail.

1°/1°GT - red shield, yellow lettering; black eagle with white head and feet; blue globe with brown continents.

AFA - blue shield with yellow border/lettering; yellow eagle with brown wings, red on head. On eagle's tail two brown oars with white handles, two black cannon, white anchor, two brown lances red/white pennants. Red shield, with white star. yellow sword/wings,

Clube de Voo a Vela - white outer rings edged in black, and black lettering. Green and yellow segments in the outer ring. Mid-blue centre with white birds and black 'AFA'. Eagle is white with brown feathers.

1ªELO (as formed 1955) - yellow outline; yellow eagle on red shield; black/white bridge; three white/red bayonets on red shield.

1°ETT - green outer, yellow inner borders to shield; white inner with black bird with yellow feet. Red shield with white parachute; red scroll with white lettering.

1°ELO - green outer and yellow inner rings; mid-blue centre, black lettering but white 'Olho Nele'; white clouds and uniform to man with brown boots and cap peak and belt. Yellow wings. White binoculars, and grey barrel.

2ªELO - red outer circle, mid-blue sky, dark blue sea, yellow sword and wings with black detail, white anchor and lettering.

4°ETA - pale blue outer circle with black edging and lettering; mid-blue centre with gold/brown stylised '4' and white lettering.

1°ETA - yellow outer and red inner circles; white centre with blue turtle with brown shell and yellow wings. Black lettering.

6°ETA - black '6' on a red symbol of Brasilia.

4°EMRA - black outline on white only.

...é pei a...

2°/5°GAv - black outer, yellow inner rings, sky blue centre, white cloud, yellow/brown/black jaguar; black/grey bomb with red stripe vertically with black lettering and yellow horizontal stripe. Black lettering 'é pei a'.

5°GAv - red bordered blue shield with red bombs and yellow segment with green lines; red lettering.

ERA 32 - yellow border; red centre. Yellow bird carrying black bombs. White lettering.

ERA 32 - (earlier badge) - yellow-bordered shield; top part blue, lower part red/yellow/white; black bombs with white tops. Lettering 'ERA' in white and '32' in yellow.

Aircraft Review

COLOURS AND MARKINGS

Brazilian military aircraft were at first identified by their serial numbers and high-visibility colour schemes, although Naval aircraft were from the very beginning flown with green/yellow/blue roundels on the wings and (often) fuselage sides, and green/yellow/blue rudder stripes. The first Army Air Force star was introduced on 31 January 1934 and was superseded during the war by a similarly-coloured star of different proportions. This was based on the USAAF star and in fact 1°GAvCa Thunderbolts flew in Italy with US markings, but with the white stars painted in Brazilian colours.

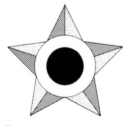

First Brazilian Army AF star - as defined by an order of the War Minister dated 31.1.34. The diameter of a circle drawn around the points of the star would be 85% of the wing chord. The outer diameter of the white circle is 49% of the circle joining the points, and the inner blue circle has a diameter of 31% of the outer.

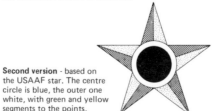

Second version - based on the USAAF star. The centre circle is blue, the outer one white, with green and yellow segments to the points.

Prewar inscriptions were *EXÉRCITO* (Army) and *MARINHA* (Navy), soon to merge into a unified service — *FORÇA AÉREA BRASILEIRA* then appeared, as it does now, on most transport (and other) aircraft. Both the Army Air Force and the FAB favoured green/yellow rudder stripes, replaced by fin flashes from the late 1950s onwards. The fuselage stars are still often omitted.

Camouflage schemes have always followed US practice, and the current US tactical scheme has been adopted as standard, as it is ideally suited to most areas of Brazil, first on Xavantes and Bandeirantes, and from 1979 on some of the Hercules. Trainers are overall yellow or — the current standard, based on wartime practice — have chrome yellow wing and tailplane upper surfaces. Army co-operation aircraft are usuallly olive green overall, transports have a white fuselage top and blue cheat line, and aircraft imported from abroad or transferred from US stocks usually retain their delivery colours. Patrol Bandeirantes wear a naval style scheme of gull grey uppers with light grey undersides.

DESIGNATIONS

A designation system for FAB aircraft based on the United States Air Force system, was introduced in 1950. Aircraft were designated within a number of classes — A amphibian, B bomber, C transport, F fighter, H helicopter, L liaison, P patrol, T trainer, to which M maritime, O observation, R reconnaissance, S search and rescue, U utility and Z sailplane were added. For a limited period, aircraft without USAF designations retained their original designations with an appropriate USAF-type prefix: the AT-Fw 44 and AT-Fw 58 trainers and the UC-J4F2 light transport were examples of this. There was even an impressed Stinson SR-10E Reliant, serial 2653, which flew with the designation UC-SR10 ! It is now preserved at the Museu Aeroespacial.

Thereafter, aircraft without an equivalent USAF designation were given FAB designations, mainly by taking up unused or little-used numbers in the USAF sequences. Examples are :

C-8	Beechcraft Queen Air 80 (ex U-8)
C-26	Piper Aztec 250
C-41	Morane-Saulnier MS.760A Paris 1
C-42	Neiva 591 Regente (to L,42, U-42)
C-55	Beechcraft Baron 55
C-90	Vickers Viscount
C-91	HS.748 Srs.2A
C-92	BAC One-Eleven 423ET
C-93	HS.125
C-95	Embraer EMB.110 Bandeirante
C-96	Boeing 737-2N3
C-115	DHC.5A Buffalo
CA-10	Consolidated PBY-5A (to C-10)
F-8	Gloster Meteor F.8
TF-33	Lockheed AT-33A
F-103	Dassault Mirage III
H-4	Bell 206 Jet Ranger
H-5	Hiller FH.1100
H-33	Sud SA.330J Puma
L-3	Pilatus P.3 (to O-3)
L-6	Neiva 56 Paulistinha (to O-6)
L-7	Neiva N.582 Campeiro
L-8	Neiva N.591 Regente (prototype)
L-42	Neiva N.591 Regente-ELO (to U-42)
M-16	Grumman HU-16 (ex A-16, U-16)
O-3	Pilatus P.3 (ex L-3, to U-3)
O-6	Neiva 56 Paulistinha (ex L-6)
P-15	Lockheed P2V-5 Neptune
P-16	Grumman S2F Tracker
T-7	Gloster Meteor T.7
T-17	Aerotec A132 Tangará
T-21	Fokker S.11
T-22	Fokker S.12
T-23	Aerotec 122 Uirapuru
T-24	IPD Guanabara (later CM.170 Magister)
T-25	Neiva Universal
AT-26	Embraer EMB.326GB Xavante
T-27	Embraer EMB.312 Tucano
U-3	Pilatus P.3 (ex L-3 and O-3)
U-7	Embraer EMB.810C Seneca
U-8	Beechcraft Queen Air 80 (to C-8)
U-9	Embraer EMB.121 Xingu
U-19	Embraer EMB.201 Ipanema
U-37	Cessna 185
U-45	Beechcraft C-45 (after 1970)
U-93	HS.125
TZ-3	Fournier RF.5
TZ-13	LET L.13 Blanik

Although the use of prefixes to denote a change in rôle initially follows USAF conventions (the transport conversion of the B-25 for example, was correctly designated as the CB-25), it later became usual for a change of designation prefix to take place without a change in the number. Thus, the Embraer Bandeirante was the C-95 transport, P-95 patrol aircraft and R-95 photo-survey model; the B-26 Invader's transport conversion was the C-26; and the Neiva Regente was C-42 in pre-production stages, L-42 early in its production and subsequently U-42 when the L prefix became redundant and was replaced by O or U, again following USAF practice. Aircraft to fly with USAF designations included : Grumman A-16 (to U-16 and M-16), Boeing B-17, North American B-25, Douglas B-26, Lockheed B-34, Vultee BT-15, Beechcraft C-43 and C-45, Curtiss C-46, Douglas C-47 and C-54, Lockheed C-60, Fairchild C-61, Noorduyn C-64, Lockheed C-66, Fairchild C-82 and C-119, Douglas C-118, Lockheed C-130, Northrop F-5, Lockheed F-80, Sikorsky H-3, H-19 and H-34, Cessna L-19 and O-1, Curtiss P-36 and P-40, Republic P-47, Fairchild T-19 and PT-26, North American T-6, Beechcraft T-11 (AT-11), North American T-28, Lockheed T-33, Cessna T-37, Grumman U-16 (to M-16).

SERIALS

FAB serials consist of four digits and are allocated within nine blocks according to primary rôle:

0	Primary trainers
1	Basic/advanced trainers
2	Transports
3	Liaison/observation
4	Fighters
5	Bombers
6	Amphibians (latterly SAR)
7	Patrol
8	Helicopters

Aircraft which have been used by the Força Aérea Brasileira since the end of the Second World War include the following :

AEROTEC A122 UIRAPURU (T-23)

Following the flight-testing of prototypes PP-ZTF (c/n 001) and PP-ZTT (c/n 002), a hundred Uirapurus were ordered for FAB use. The first two, 0940 and 0941 (C/ns 004 and 005) were pre-production aircraft, followed by 0942 to 0999 (c/ns 006 to 063) and 1730 to 1739 (c/ns 064 to 073). Production deliveries began in January 1969. Existing aircraft were modified during 1978/79 with a re-designed engine cowling, nosewheel and canopy, and increased fuel capacity.
T-23 0968 suffered structural damage and became an instructional aircraft at ESPAER. An unidentified crash took place on 3.7.73. Other known losses include :

0942	c/n 006	w/o 1.11.68
0957	021	10.5.72
1730	064	10.8.77
1735	069	23.8.72
1736	070	18.3.77

The second prototype PP-ZTT is preserved at the Museu Aeroespacial..
An improved version of the T-23, the A132 Tangará (originally known as the Uirapuru II) with a re-designed rear fuselage and tail unit, was first flown in prototype form as YT-17-1000 on 27.2.81. The test programme has now been completed and the type will replace the Uirapuru, with probably one hundred being built. The surviving T-23s will be refurbished and modified as glider tugs for issue to gliding clubs.

BAC ONE-ELEVEN 423ET (VC-92)

Two aircraft acquired in 1968 for GTE use; they were both sold to the Ford Motor Company in the UK in 1977.

2110	c/n 154		to G-BEJW
2111	118	ex G-16-2	G-BEJM

BEECHCRAFT UC-43/GB (UC-43)

Thirty-four UC-43, GB-1 and GB-2 were delivered under Lend-Lease, including GB-2 Bu.33044, 33045, 33052, 3305 33055 to 33057, 33061 to 33065. A few remained in use after the war; one serialled 2778 was preserved in the Museu Aeroespacial.

BEECHCRAFT C-45/MODEL 18

An initial batch of nine C-45 arrived in 1942-43 (ex USAAF 43-35725, 35883, 35916, 44-46476, 47064, 47646, 47672, 47740, 87117) together with a number of AT-7 and AT-11 crew trainers, some of which were eventually converted to C-45 standards and redesignated accordingly. About fifty Model D18S were delivered after the war, receiving the designation C-45 which was replaced by U-45 in 1970. Known examples include :

2820	c/n A.296	
2821	A.301	
2822	A.306	
2823		w/o 27.12.67
2824	A.329	w/o 30.10.56
2825	A.330	w/o 27.7.51
2826	A.331	w/o 12.9.75
2827	A.332	wfu
2828	A.334	
2829	A.335	to PT-KUV
2830		
2831		
2832		
2833	A.402	
2834	A.403	
2835	A.404	
2836	A.405	w/o 23.6.61
2837	A.409	
2838	A.410	
2839	A.411	w/o 29.12.48
2840	A.417	
2841	A.418	
2842	A.419	w/o 10.3.66
2843		
2844		
2845		
2846		
2847		
2848	A.446	
2849	A.447	
2850	A.448	
2851	A.449	to PT-KYI
2852		
2853	A.514	
2854	A.515	
2855	A.516	
2856	A.517	
2860		
2862		
2867		
2868		
2869		
2870		
2871		
2872		

Earlier aircraft included 2787 (w/o 21.2.67), 2788, 2789 (w/o 26.1.67). T-7 and T-11 converted to C-45 included 1350, 1354, 1438, 1444, 1446, 1510, 1518, 1598. About thirty later Model E18S and H18 were eventually procured; serials 2885 onwards were tri-gear models, designated TC-45T and (after 1970) U-45T. Aircraft 2909 was an EC-45T before becoming a U-45T. Some TC-45T were referred to as C-45T.

2876	c/nBA.203	to PT-KXN
2877	BA.204	to PT-KVQ
2878	BA.205	w/o 5.12.67
2879	BA.214	to PT-KXP
2880	BA.266	
2881		
2882	BA.356	to PT-KUU
2883		
2884		
2885	BA.672	to PT-KXH
2886	BA.673	to PT-KVY
2887	BA.674	
2888	BA.675	to PT-KXQ
2889	BA.676	to PT-KXG
2890	BA.677	to PT-KXK
2891	BA.678	w/o 20.8.74 (was UC-45T)
2892	BA.679	to PT-KVZ
2893	BA.680	to PT-KXA
2894	BA.681	to PT-KXB
2895	BA.682	to PT-KXC
2896	BA.683	to PT-KXL
2897	BA.684	to PT-KXM
2898	BA.687	to PT-KXE
2899	BA.686	to PT-KXD
2908	BA.703	to PT-KXI
2909	BA.685	to PT-KXJ

Aircraft 2885 was for a time a Esquadrilha da Fumaça support machine. Preserved aircraft are 2875 at Nova Iguacu, 2850 at the Museu de Armas, Veículos Motorizados e Avioes Antigos 'Eduardo Andrèia Matarazzo'(Museum of Weapons Motor Vehicles and Old Aircraft) at Bebedouro, São Paulo state, and 2856 at the Museu Aeroespacial.

BEECHCRAFT AT-7 (T-7)

At least fifteen were delivered during the war and about ten (including 1510 to 1518) in 1947. A few, including 1510 and 1518, were converted to C-45 standards. Previous USAAF serials included 42-2459, 43461, 56730, 56808, 56837, 43-33288, 33297, 33328, 33347, 33367, 33370, 33373, 33394, 33407, 33435, 33450, 33535, 33619, 49969, 49983, 49992, 50027, 50093.

BEECHCRAFT AT-11 KANSAN (T-11)

Over thirty believed delivered; FAB serials included 1348 to 1375 and 1519 to 1530. Previous USAAF serials included 42-36863, 37175, 37220, 37256, 37468, 37473, 37624, 37696, 37699, 37700, 37704, 37712. Two confirmed tie-ups are 1363 ex 42-37592 (and sold as PT-KUT) and 1524 ex 42-37220 (sold as PT-KUS). Several, including 1350, 1354, 1438, 1444, 1446 were converted to C-45 standards. 1371 is preserved at the Museu Aeroespacial.

BEECHCRAFT QUEEN AIR B80 (U-8, C-8)

Eight believed delivered, serialled 2101 to 2108. Two were EU-8 navaid checking aircraft :

2101	c/n LD.379	ex PP-FOC	to PT-KYG	
2102	LD.378	PP-FOB	PT-KYH	

BELL 47 (H-13)

Three HTL-3 ex US Navy Bu.144693 to 144695 were delivered, as were numbers of OH-13E, G H and J. Known aircraft include :

8500	47D-1	c/n 618	
8501	47D-1	652	
8502	47D-1	651	
8510	47J		preserved at Museu Aeroespacial
8512	47J	1794	
8513	47G-2	2454	to HK-1302-E
8514	47G-2	2456	
8515	47G-2	2455	
8516	47G-2	2458	
8517	47G-2	2461	
8518	47G-2	2459	
8519	47G-2	2462	
8520	47G-2	2464	
8521	47G-2	2465	
8522	47G-2	2467	
8523	47G-2	2469	
8524	47G-2	2470	

An unspecified number of ex US Army OH-13G were later delivered, with serials in the 8600 block. 8600 (ex 56-2234) was acquired late in 1972, but damaged beyond repair and is now preserved by Ala 435 at Santos AB, São Paulo state; 8633 was written off in May 1974. Other known write-offs are a Bell 47G on 13.1.74, an OH-13J on 24.3.70,

Bell 206A Jet Ranger (VH-4) 8570. Note the presidential seal in place of the fuselage star.

Aerotec A122 Uirapuru (T-23) 0946 photographed at Galeao in April 1968.

BAC One-Eleven 423ET (VC-92) 2111, later sold to Ford Motor Co. as G-BEJM.

Consolidated PBY-5A Catalina (CA-10) 6526 at Miami in September 1970.

Curtiss C-46A Commando 2058 was operated from 1948 to 1968 and although earmarked for preservation, was allocated the export markings PT-LBP in 1981.

and two in a mid-air collision on 28.6.72.

BELL UH-1 IROQUOIS (H-1)

Six SH-1D, eight UH-1D and thirty-six UH-1H are known to have been delivered. Known examples :

```
8530  SH-1D  c/n 3202
8531  SH-1D      3203   w/o 15.9.80
8532  SH-1D      3204
8533  SH-1D      3205
8534  SH-1D      3206
8535  SH-1D      3207
8536  UH-1D
8537  UH-1D
8538  UH-1D
8539  UH-1D
8540  UH-1D
8541  UH-1D          3ºEMRA;armed
8542  UH-1D
8543  UH-1D          converted to SH-1H
```

The UH-1H serials include 8650 to 8671, of which 8662 was written off on 4.6.80, 8663 on 28.5.80 and 8668 on 29.4.75. A few UH-1H were fitted with armament as AH-1H; examples include 8659, 8660, 8663, 8664 (w/o 5.12.80), 8666, 8667 and 8668 all used by the 4ºEMRA.

BELL 206A JET RANGER (H-4)

Three were purchased as presidential transports (VH-4), with the fuselage star replaced by the presidential seal; four more were bought as communications helicopters (LH-4, later OH-4), and it is reported that three more followed.

```
8570  VH-4  c/n 159
8571  VH-4      169
8572  VH-4      173
8580  OH-4      245   d/d 6.68    w/o 12.3.74
8581  OH-4      249       6.68
8582  OH-4      250       7.68
8583  OH-4      251       7.68    w/o 17.4.78
```

BOEING SB-17G FORTRESS (B-17)

Twelve in all for use by the 6ºGAV's two squadrons, and serialled 5400 to 5411. The first five were delivered in May 1951, and the remainder in late 1954. 5400 was ex 44-83663 and 5408 (which is preserved at Natal) was ex 44-83462). Other previous USAAF serials included 44-8891, 83378, 83718, 83764, 85494, 85583, 85602 and 85836. A few were used as transports in the early 1960s.

BOEING 737-2N3 (VC-96)

Two only, for GTE :
```
2115  c/n 21165  d/d 31.3.76
2116      21166      13.4.76
```

CESSNA O-1A/E BIRD DOG (L-19, O-1)

Ten L-19A (O-1A, serials 3060 to 3069) and ten L-19E (O-1E, serials 3150 to 3159) are believed to have been delivered for service with the ELO's (O-1E 3152 for example was operated by the 3ªELO. They were eventually replaced by Neiva Universals. A Cessna 180B was also taken on charge as an 'L-19' with the serial 3100; it was c/n 50458 ex PT-BDV, sold as PT-IJZ).

CESSNA T-37C (T-37C)

Forty initially purchased directly from Cessna (one of the first to be delivered in May 1968 had the ferry registration N7044C) and serialled 0870 to 0909. Another twenty-five were delivered in 1969-70 as 0910 to 0934. Most were used by the AFA. Known losses include :
```
0871  w/o
0872  w/o 29.8.72
0889  w/o 9.11.70
0899  w/o 27.4.71
0900  w/o 31.5.77
0901  w/o
0911  w/o 14.10.76
0914  w/o 13.6.72
0915  w/o 26.7.77
0929  w/o 4.8.77
```
plus unidentified losses on 15.5.73, 31.7.76, 28.1.69, two in a mid-air collision on 10.7.71 and another two on 13.10.76. The T-37C was withdrawn from service towards the end of 1980, mainly due to spares shortages, and temporarily replaced by the Xavante pending the delivery of the ultimate replacements, the Embraer EMB.312s. Most of the surviving machines are expected to be returned to the USA, but two are to be preserved in Brazilian museums.

CESSNA 185 (U-37)

One was serialled 2905. It was c/n 185-0433, and was sold as PT-KZN.

CONSOLIDATED C-87 LIBERATOR (C-87)

One only, serialled 2054, used by the 1º Grupo Misto de Instrução, mainly as an instructional airframe.

CONSOLIDATED PBY-5A CATALINA (CA-10)

Some thirty PBY-5 Catalinas were transferred from the US Navy to the FAB in 1942-44; one of them, serialled PBY-14, attacked and destroyed submarine U.199 in July 1943. Subsequent deliveries included twenty-eight PBY-5A (FAB designation CA-10, later CA-10A and C-10A) serialled 6500 to 6527 of which 6520 was ex Bu.46582, and two PBY-5 (FAB CA-10 later C-10) serialled 6550 and 6551. A few remain in use with the 1ºETA. Civilianised examples are PP-PCW c/n CV.429, PP-PCX c/n CV.240, PP-PDR ex Bu. 48419 and PP-PEC ex Bu.08068. PBY-5A 6509 and 6527, in 1ºETA markings are preserved at the Museu Aeroespacial. Known write-offs include 6514 on 13.4.72, 6521 on 8.2.68 and 6550 on 4.10.78.

CURTISS P-36A (P-36A)

Ten aircraft delivered under Lend-Lease on 8 March 1942 :
```
FAB1   ex 38-54   c/n 12468
FAB2      38-39       12453
FAB3      38-43       12457
FAB4      38-159      12573   w/o 30.9.43
FAB5      38-51       12465
FAB6      38-158      12572
FAB7      38-175      12589
FAB8      38-106      12520
FAB9      38-60       12474
FAB10     38-53       12467   w/o 8.5.42
```

CURTISS P-40 (P-40)

Eighty-nine P-40 of all models were delivered: six P-40E (FAB1 to 6), thirty P-40K (FAB7 to 36), ten P-40M and forty-one P-40N, plus two P-40K instructional airframes. The last flyable examples were withdrawn from use in 1954. A P-40N with the post-war serial 4064 (ex 44-7700) has been preserved in the markings of the 1º/14ºGAv, the last squadron to operate the type.

CURTISS C-46A COMMANDO

Two aircraft acquired in 1948 and operated by the 2°GT :
2057 c/n 44 ex PP-XBS, 43-46973 w/o 13.12.49
2058 155 PP-XBR, 43-47084
The latter was withdrawn from use in 1968 and scheduled for preservation in the Museu Aeroespacial, but became PP-ZBE and was overhauled at Campo dos Afonsos in the early part of 1980, ostensibly for sale in Bolivia, and was allotted the registration PT-LBP for export in 1981.

DASSAULT MIRAGE III (F-103)

Twelve Mirage IIIEBR (FAB designation F-103E) serialled 4910 to 4921 and four two-seat Mirage IIIDBR (F-103D), serials 4900 to 4903 were ordered in 1972 for use by the 1ª ALADA. An additional five Mirage IIIEBR were ordered in 1977 and delivered in 1979-80; serials were 4922 to 4926.
Known losses are :
4900   20.11.80
4912   28.6.79
4920   2.9.75
4921   5.9.74

DHC.5A BUFFALO (C-115)

Twenty four were delivered in 1969-70, of which about eighteen remain in service with the 2° Esquadrão of GTT.
2350 c/n 15
2351   17   temporarily to CF-DJU
2352   18
2353   20
2354   22
2355   24
2356   26   w/o 18.10.74
2357   27
2358   28
2359   29
2360   30
2361   31
2362   32
2363   33
2364   34
2365   35
2366   36   w/o 18.9.74
2367   37
2368   38

2369   39
2370   40
2371   41
2372   42   w/o 23.2.73
2373   43

DOUGLAS A-20 HAVOC/BOSTON (B-20)

Thirty-one A-20 of various models were delivered, including A-20K 6085 c/n 23762 ex 44-539 which is preserved at the Museu Aeroespacial, and ex Royal Air Force Boston III AL336 c/n 2203.

DOUGLAS B-26 INVADER (B-26)

Upwards of thirty aircraft were taken on FAB charge, mainly around 1957, and comprised both B and C models, with serials in the 5140 to 5176 range. The aircraft noted as 'R' in the list below were amongst sixteen dispatched to Tucson, Arizona in 1968-70 for rework to approximate B-26K standards; after their return they were operated by 1°Esquadrao of 10°Grupo, replacing that unit's RB-25s. The type was phased out in 1976 in favour of the AT-26 Xavante.
Confirmed aircraft are :
5140   B-26B   R
5143   w/o 31.10.68
5145   B-26B   R
5146   w/o 17.7.67 at Natal
5147   B-26B   R
5149   B-26B   R
5150   B-26B   R   ex 44-34196
5152   B-26B
5153   B-26B   R
5156   B-26B   R   to museum at Pirassununga
5157   B-26B   R
5158   B-26B
5159   B-26C   to Museu Aeroespacial
5160   B-26B   R
5161   R
5162   B-26C   R
5170   B-26C   R
5171   B-26C   R
5172   B-26C   R
5173   B-26C
5174   B-26C   ex 44-34749. To instructional, ESPAER.
5175   B-26C
5176   C-26B   ex 44-34134, N115RG, seized at Brasília 21.6.66 for smuggling and handed over to the FAB. Sold to museum at Bebedouro in January 1975.

DOUGLAS B-18 BOLO (B-18)

Two only, 6300 (ex USAAF 36-300) and 7032 (ex 37-32) for use by the Agrupamento de Aviões de Adaptação, a provisional conversion training unit set up under Lend-Lease. They were later used for anti-submarine patrols and were struck off charge by the end of the war. Another B-18 was used as an instructional airframe.

DOUGLAS C-47 SKYTRAIN (C-47)

Eighty-two C-47 and DC-3 of various models were taken on charge, the first nineteen being Lend-Lease aircraft, and serialled between 2009 and 2092 — note that 2054 was a Consolidated C-87, and 2057 and 2058 were Curtiss C-46A. All DC-3 models were designated as FAB C-47, including an unserialled machine C-53 PP-EDL, c/n 4910 ex 42-6458, which was operated during 1974-76 as 'C-47 EDL' until sold as PT-KVP. The exceptions were EC-47 2088 and 2089 (C-47 2065 was eventually converted to EC-47 standards).

Serial	C/n	Ex	
2009	14234/25679	43-48418	to Museu Aeroesp'l.
2010	14235/25680	43-48419	w/o 6.72
2011	14236/25681	43-48420	
2012	14237/25682	43-48421	
2013	14238/25683	43-48422	wfu 1969
2014	14239/25684	43-48423	to PT-KVM
2015	14240/25685	43-48424	
2016	14241/25686	43-48425	w/o 1945
2017	15476/26921	43-49660	to PT-KZG
2018	15477/26922	43-49661	
2019	15478/26923	43-49662	w/o 14.4.45
2020	17003/34266	45-1000,PP-CCW	to PT-KZE
2021	17004/34267	45-1001	to PT-KYW
2022	17038/34303	45-1035	to PT-KUW
2023	17108/34373	45-1105,N2025A	
2024	20555	43-16089	
2025	13952/25397	43-48136	to PT-KVI
2026	20459	43-15993	wfu 1969
2027	20466	43-16000	
2028	11843	42-92082	w/o 1952
2029	9246	42-23384	w/o 1.12.58
2030	9985	42-24123	to PT-KVR
2031	20206	43-15740	to Museu Aeroesp'l
2032	20414	43-15948	
2033	13971/25416	43-48155	
2034		43-30672	w/o 3.9.67
2035	13821/25266	43-48005	to PT-KYX
2036	13973/25418	43-48157	
2037	13981/25426	43-48165	wfu 1967

Dassault Mirage III EBR (F-103E) 4921. Note the 1^{a}ALADA badge on the fin.

De Havilland Canada DHC.5A Buffalo (C-115) 2360. The FAB had twenty-four of this type.

Douglas EC-47 2088 photographed at Galeão in December 1969.

Embraer EMB.110 Bandeirante (SC-95B) 6542, an example of the latest SAR version.

Embraer EMB.810C Seneca (U-7) 2631, the licence built Piper aircraft incorporating Robertson STOL modifications.

Embraer EMB.111A(A) Bandeirulha (P-95) 7052 was shown at Farnborough in September 1978; it is the maritime patrol version of the Bandeirante.

Embraer EMB.110A Bandeirante (EC-95) 2178, one of four of this navaid calibration variant.

Embraer EMB.121E Xingu (VU-9) 2651. Note the 6°ETA badge on the fin.

2038	11837	42-92077	to PT-KYZ
2039	19775	43-15309	to PT-KZV
2040	20048	43-15582	wfu 1968
2041	20451	43-15985	to PT-KVH
2042		43-30693	
2043	13538	42-108969	to PT-KZJ
2044	9932	42-24070	to PT-KUR
2045	10177	42-24315	
2046	10172	42-24310	to PT-KZH
2047		43-30690	w/o 4.3.75
2048	9777	42-23915	w/o 11.7.52
2049		43-30711	w/o 1954
2050	11811	42-92053	w/o 13.11.74
2051	13109	42-93221	w/o 17.10.56
2052	18993	42-100530	to PT-KVN
2053	19305	42-100842	to PT-KVL
2055	4473	41-18411,PP-FVA	w/o 25.3.61
2056	19055	42-100592,PP-ETE	to PT-KXR
2059	20055	43-15589	to PT-LBL
2060	20074	43-15608	w/o 1960
2061	20210	43-15744	to PT-KVX
2062	20216	43-15750	w/o 1958
2063	20410	43-15944	wfu 1963
2064	20428	43-15962	to PT-KVS
2065	19217	42-100754	w/o 13.9.75
2066	13636	42-93696,PP-AXK	w/o 14.3.61
2067	15624/27069	43-49808	wfu 1963
2068	17020/34284	45-1017,PP-AXY	w/o 15.6.67
2069	20244	45-15778,PP-NBL	to PT-KZF
2070	13822/25267	43-48006,PP-ANZ	w/o 1.3.59
2071	15624/27069	43-15670,PP-AKD	to PT-KVB
2072	20136	Bu.05064,PP-ANY	to PT-KVA
2073	4756	44-77241,PP-AKB	wfu 1965
2074	16825/33573	43-16053,PP-ANQ	
2075	20519	42-92355,PP-AXF	to PT-KVT
2076	12146	42-92544,PP-AXE	to PT-KVU
2077	12356	Bu.05063,PP-YPN	
2078	4755	41-18579,PP-ANR	
2079	4704	45-1031,PP-ANE	to N9049Y
2080	17034/34299	45-1028,PP-SPN	to PT-KVK
2081	17031/34296	45-1096,PP-CCW	
2082	4621	41-18529,PP-SQM	to PT-KZM
2083	17099/34366	42-100545,PP-CDB	to PT-KUY
2084	19008	42-93264,PP-CDN	to PT-LBK
2085	13156	43-16120,PP-CEB	to PT-LBM
2086	20586	41-18578,PP-CCT	
2087	4703	45-1002	to PT-KZW
2088	17005/34268	16788/34249 45-985	
2089	16788/34249	45-985	
2090	27198	PP-ENB	
2091	2134	PP-PED	to PT-KZB
2092	42980	PP-NAM	to PT-KVC

The various models were :
DC-3A-279 2091   DC-3D 2092
C-47   2055, 2079, 2082, 2087
C-47A 2024 to 2053, 2056, 2059 to 2066, 2069, 2070,
       2072, 2075, 2076, 2077, 2084 to 2086
C-47B 2009 to 2023, 2035, 2067, 2068, 2088, 2089
R4D-1 2073, 2078

The last twenty-one aircraft in service were retired in 1976 and sold in the civil market. The C-47 preserved at the Escola de Paraquedistas do Exército, Campo dos Afonsos, is an ex-Varig airliner PP-AKA c/n 20193 ex 43-15727 and N4908V.

DOUGLAS C-54G SKYMASTER (C-54)

Twelve were delivered for 1°/2°GT use, the squadron being activated on 21.9.59. Four were transferred to the Colombian Air Force as FAC640 to 643 in 1970.

2400	c/n 35978	ex 45-525	to Colombia FAC641 1970
2401	36025	45-572	w/o 11.12.60
2402	35956	45-503	to Colombia FAC640 1970
2403	36028	45-575	to N2168 in 1956
2404	35957	45-504	b/u 1970
2405	35963	45-510	b/u 1970
2406	36054	45-601	b/u 1970
2407	36068	45-615	to Colombian AF 1970
2408	36019	45-566	to Colombian AF 1970
2409	36050	45-597	b/u 1970
2410	35935	45-482	b/u 1970
2411	35964	45-511	b/u 1970

DOUGLAS DC-6B (C-118)

Five obtained from Varig Airlines in 1968:
2412	c/n 44166	ex PP-YSI	to Paraguay AF T-91
2413	43745	PP-YSJ	wfu 1973
2414	43746	PP-YSL	w/o 28.4.71
2415	43822	PP-YSM	to Paraguay AF T-87
2416	43824	PP-YSN	to Paraguay AF T-89

EMBRAER EMB.810C SENECA (U-7)

Twelve U-7 Embraer licence-built Piper Senecas, serialled 2600 to 2611 were delivered between 27.12.77 and 5.6.78, and later fitted with weather radar. They were used for communications with the ETAs (for example 2608 went to the 4°ETA), ELOs (2602 went to the 2°ELO) and the 1ª ALADA. U-7 2602 had c/n 810.137.

Another twenty Senecas with Robertson STOL modification incorporated, were ordered in 1980 as U-7A, and these were serialled 2612 to 2631, of which 2616 was c/n 810.371 and 2617 was 810.380.

EMBRAER EMB.121E XINGU (VU-9)

Six Xingus were delivered in April-May 1978, initially with serials 2250 to 2255, later 2650 to 2655. Users included the GTE and the 6°ETA, the latter receiving 2651 and 2654.
2650	c/n 121.002	ex PP-ZXI
2651	121.003	
2652	121.004	
2653	121.005	
2654	121.006	
2655	121.008	

EMBRAER EMB.110 BANDEIRANTE (C-95)

Embraer's successful light twin transport operates in several guises for the FAB.
Two YC-95 prototypes (model EMB.100):
2130	c/n 01	wfu 1975; to the Museu Aeroespacial
2131	02	wfu 8.78; preserved São Paulo

C-95 production transports delivered between January 1973 and November 1976 (model EMB.110) :
2132	110.002	
2133	110.001	
2134	110.003	
2135	110.007	
2136	110.008	
2137	110.014	
2138	110.015	
2139	110.019	
2140	110.020	
2141	110.027	
2142	110.028	
2143	110.029	w/o 14.10.80
2144	110.034	
2145	110.035	
2146	110.036	
2147	110.039	
2148	110.040	
2149	110.041	
2150	110.042	
2151	110.043	
2152	110.044	
2153	110.045	
2154	110.048	
2155	110.052	

2156	110.053		
2157	110.057	w/o 3.6.77	
2158	110.058		
2159	110.051		
2160	110.054		
2161	110.060		
2162	110.061		
2163	110.066		
2164	110.064		
2165	110.067		
2166	110.068		
2167	110.071		
2168	110.073		
2169	110.075	w/o 23.4.77	
2170	110.077		
2171	110.078		
2172	110.080		
2173	110.093		
2174	110.094		
2175	110.095		
2176	110.097		

Two EC-95 navaid calibration aircraft (model EMB.110A):

2177	110.099
2178	110.100

Further production C-95 :

2179	110.103
2180	110.104
2181	110.105
2182	110.109
2183	110.110
2184	110.113
2185	110.114
2186	110.117
2187	110.118
2188	110.121
2189	110.122

Two further EC-95 :

2190	110.123
2191	110.124

R-95 photo survey aircraft for operation by the 1°/6°GAv, delivered July-August 1977 (model EMB.110B) :

2240	110.133
2241	110.134
2242	110.135
2243	110.138
2244	110.140
2245	110.141

P-95 'Bandeirulha' patrol aircraft, delivered during 1977-1978, manufacturer's designation EMB.111A(A), initially given transport serials, but renumbered as patrol types and given the names of Brazilian sea birds :

2260	110.142	to 7050 'Gavião de Urua'
2261	110.151	7051 'Pelicano'

2262	110.155	7052	'Taiaçú'
2263	110.159	7053	'Petrel'
2264	110.163	7054	'Martim Pescador'
2265	110.167	7055	'Talha-mar'
2266	110.171	7056	'Albatroz'
2267	110.179	7057	'Falcão Pescador'
2268	110.182	7058	'Alca'
2269	110.185	7059	'Biguá'
2270	110.188	7060	'Gaivota'
2271	110.191	7061	'Alcatraz'

C-95A transports, the improved EMB.110K1 version, with deliveries commencing September 1977 :

2280	110.139	
2281	110.148	
2282	110.149	
2283	110.143	ex PT-GLA
2284	110.152	
2285	110.160	
2286	110.164	
2287	110.168	
2288	110.169	ex PT-GLE
2289	110.170	
2290	110.172	
2291	110.173	
2292	110.174	
2293	110.175	
2294	110.176	
2295	110.177	
2296	110.178	
2297	110.180	
2298	110.181	
2299	110.183	
2300	110.246	ex PT-SAM
2301	110.247	
2302	110.25..	
2303	110.2....	

C-95B transports, model EMB.110P1K, still in production:

2304	110.269	
2305	110.276	ex PP-ZKK
2306	110.282	
2307	110.291	
2308	110.299	
2309	110.306	
2310	110.3....	
2311	110.320	
2312		
2313		
2314	110.337	

An SC-95B search and rescue version has recently been introduced, with deliveries to 2°/10°GAv during 1981 :

6542
6543
6544
6545
6546
6547
6548
6549

EMBRAER EMB.326GB XAVANTE (AT-26)

An initial order for 112 of these licence-built Aermacchi MB.326 aircraft was subsequently increased to an overall total of 182, with serials beginning at 4460. The first Xavante entered FAB service on 28 March 1972; the hundredth to be delivered was 4561, 4497 having been retained by the manufacturers. The final deliveries were made in late 1981, being replacements for export aircraft relinquished by FAB from earlier contracts.

Known serials include 4460, 4463/4470, 4475, 4483, 4493, 4497/4499, 4504/4506, 4511, 4522, 4532, 4533, 4544, 4549/4553, 4556/4563, 4565/4570, 4580/4590, 4594/4595. They are used primarily by the EMRAs and CATRE, examples of use being 4483 and 4544 with 3°EMRA, 4504, 4560, 4563, 4595 with 4°EMRA, 4522 and 4533 with CATRE and 4546, 4569 with CTA.

Attrition has been high. Known write-offs are :

4497	w/o 4.8.77	
4504	5.7.77	
4511	18.9.74	
4522	8.10.76	
4532	10.10.79	(c/n 74071314)
4533	5.7.77	
4544	5.79	(c/n 75083326)
4547	22.3.80	
4549	16.9.79	(c/n 75083331)
4552	20.7.76	
4553	20.7.76	
4556	10.10.78	
4559	12.8.76	

plus unidentified crashes on 5.6.73, 20.10.73, 19.6.75, 31.7.75, 3.9.75, 15.7.76 and 27.10.76. Two collided on 10.9.75.

A number of CATRE aircraft were named after Brazilian Indian tribes and caciques (chiefs) :

4462	Apoena	4471	Tupinambá
4467	Yawalapiti	4484	Ipurinan

4496	Xacriabá		4573	Juruna
4498	Kalapalo		4575	Potiguara
4505	Surui		4576	Bororó
4514	Jirió		4579	Parasi
4524	Opaié		4581	Mawé
4527	Kaiabi		4590	Javaé
4537	Puxiti		4592	Xavante
4542	Kuikuru		4605	Kraho
4571	Apinaié		4607	Karajá
4572	Akuen		4608	Xerente

4596 was named 'Joker' after CATRE's call-sign prefix.

EMBRAER EMB.312 TUCANO (T-27)

An Air Ministry development contract was awarded, covering a prototype (serialled 1300, first flown 16.6.80) and a static test airframe of this turboprop powered trainer. A contract was signed in October 1980 for a total of 168 (118 and 50 options) with production deliveries to begin in October 1982. The first recipient is to be the Academia da Força Aérea, other machines being probably used to re-form the Esquadrilha da Fumaça aerobatic team.

EMBRAER EMB.201 IPANEMA (U-19)

An agricultural aircraft, but three procured as glider tugs for the Clube de Vôo à Vela :
0151 c/n 201......
0152
0153

FAIRCHILD UC-61A (UC-61A)

Ten were delivered; one became 2683 and is now on show at the Museu Aeroespacial.

FAIRCHILD PT-19 (T-19)

190 PT-19 were supplied under Lend-Lease during the war, including es USAAF 40-2464/2465, 42-3437, 42-82969, 82974 and 83184. Additionally, the Fábrica do Galeão built the type as their Model 3FG in 1946-49 (serials up to 0422 in 1946, 0423 to 0461 in 1947, 0462 to 0518 in 1948 and 0519 to 0556 in 1949.
0321 c/n 3FG- 056

0322	057	to PP-GFZ	0376	116	to Bolivian AF
0323	058	to Paraguay AF	0377	117	
0324	059	to PP-GGB	0378	108	
0325	061	to PP-GFO	0379	109	
0326	062	to PP-GFQ	0380	112	to PP-GFJ
0327	064	to PP-GGD	0381	113	to PP-GFS
0328	066		0382	114	
0329	077		0383	118	
0330	078		0384	119	
0331	079		0385	120	to Bolivian AF
0332	080		0387	122	
0333	081	to PP-HNJ	0388	123	
0334	082	to PP-GGA	0389	124	to PP-HQO, Bolivian AF
0335	083	to PP-HQC	0390	125	
0336	084	to PP-GVF	0391	130	
0337	085		0392	131	to PP-HNN
0338	086		0393	132	to PP-HQR
0339	087		0394	121	
0340	088	to PP-GBO, Bolivian AF	0395	126	
0341	089		0396	127	
0342	090	to PP-HMZ	0397	128	
0343	091		0398	129	
0344	092		0399	133	
0345	093		0400	134	to PP-GLH
0346	094		0401	135	
0347	095	to PP-GFM	0402	136	to Bolivian AF
0348	096		0403	137	to PP-GIC, PP-GZI
0349	067		0404	138	
0350	068		0405	139	to PP-GGG
0351	069	to Paraguay AF	0406	140	
0352	065	to PP-GGE	0407	141	
0353	070		0408	142	
0354	071		0409	143	
0355	073	to PP-GFP, PP-GQM	0410	144	
0356	075		0411	145	to PP-GZF
0357	072	to PP-HLE	0412	146	
0359	060	to PP-HNM	0413	147	
0360	063	to PP-GGF	0414	148	
0361	074	to PP-HQB	0415	149	
0362	097	to PP-GFW	0416	150	
0363	098	to PT-GBN	0417	151	
0364	099	to PP-GBP	0418	152	
0365	100		0419	153	
0366	101		0420	154	
0367	102		0421	155	to Paraguay AF
0368	103		0422	156	to Paraguay AF
0369	104	to Paraguay AF	0423	157	
0370	105	to PP-GQV	0424	158	to Paraguay AF
0371	106	to PP-GFK	0425	159	to PP-HPV
0372	107		0426	160	
0373	110		0427	161	
0374	111		0428	162	
0375	115	to PP-HQC	0429	163	

0430	164		0483	217		0536	269	
0431	165	to PP-HNP	0484	218	to Bolivian AF	0537	270	
0432	166	to PP-GZJ	0485	219		0538	271	
0433	167	to Paraguay AF	0486	220	to PP-HNX	0539	272	
0434	168		0487	221		0540	273	
0435	169		0488	222	to PP-GGR	0541	274	
0436	170	to Paraguay AF	0489	223	to Bolivian AF	0542	275	to PP-HNV
0437	171		0490	224	to PP-HNZ	0543	276	
0438	172	to PP-GZL	0491	225		0544	277	to PP-HOD
0439	173		0492	226	to PP-GEI	0545	278	to PP-HND
0440	174	to PP-GIB	0493	227	to PP-GEJ	0546	279	
0441	175	to PP-HLC	0494	228	to PP-GEK	0547	280	
0442	176		0495	229	to PP-GEL	0548	281	to PP-GUF
0443	177		0496	230	to PP-GEM	0549	282	to PP-GUH
0444	178	to PP-GGH	0497	231	to PP-GEN	0550	283	to Paraguay AF
0445	179	to PP-GFL	0498	232	to PP-GEO	0551	284	
0446	180		0499	233	to PP-GEP	0552	285	to PP-HNC
0447	181	to PP-HQD	0500	234	to PP-GEQ	0553	286	
0448	182		0501	235	to PP-GER	0554	287	to PP-GZM
0449	183	to PP-GOZ	0502	236	to PP-GES	0555	288	
0450	184	to PP-HQE	0503	076	(wooden monocoque prototype)	0556	289	to PP-HQN
0451	185	to PP-GUE	0504	237	to PP-GET			
0452	186		0505	238	to PP-GEU			
0453	187	to Bolivian AF	0506	239	to PP-GEV			
0454	188	to PP-HNQ	0507	240				
0455	189	to PP-HPX	0508	241				
0456	190	to PP-GZN	0509	242				
0457	191		0510	243	to PP-GEW			
0458	192		0511	244	to PP-GEX			
0459	193		0512	245	to PP-GEY			
0460	194		0513	246	to PP-GEZ			
0461	195		0514	247	to PP-GHA			
0462	196	to PP-HNR	0515	248	to PP-GHB			
0463	197	to PP-GGO	0516	249	to PP-HQG			
0464	198	to PP-HNS	0517	250				
0465	199	to Paraguay AF	0518	251				
0466	200		0519	252	to PP-GOE			
0467	201	to PP-HMA	0520	253	to PP-HQT			
0468	202		0521	254				
0469	203	to Bolivian AF	0522	255	to PP-HOA			
0470	204		0523	256	to PP-GGS			
0471	205		0524	257				
0472	206	to PP-GFY	0525	258				
0473	207		0526	259	to PP-HOC			
0474	208		0527	260	to PP-GUD			
0475	209		0528	261	to PP-GOY			
0476	210	to PP-GQL	0529	262	to Bolivian AF			
0477	211	to PP-HLB	0530	263				
0478	212	to PP-GGT	0531	264	to PP-HOB			
0479	213	to PP-HNA	0532	265	to PP-HLA			
0480	214	to PP-GLF	0533	266	to PP-GZG			
0481	215	to PP-HNT	0534	267				
0482	216	to PP-HQS, Bolivian AF	0535	268	to Paraguay AF			

At least one of the Lend-Lease machines was allocated a civil registration : 0225, ex 42-3437, which became PP-HQA. Another, 0222 was preserved at the Museu da AFA, Pirass-ununga. 0310 was preserved at the Museu Aeroespacial.

___

FAIRCHILD C-82A PACKET (C-82)

Twelve aircraft; entered service on 20.9.55 with the 1°GTT and were withdrawn from use on 9.7.67. The first machine was delivered as 2065 but re-numbered as 2200. The following have been identified :

2200	c/n 10219	ex 48-584	to PT-DLP
2202	10220	48-585	
2204	10215	48-580	
2205	10222	48-587	
2207	10213	48-578	to PT-DNZ and w/o 10.70

___

FAIRCHILD C-119G (C-119)

Eighteen were delivered with serials 2300 to 2317. Only four remained in service by late 1975, and all had been retired by 1977. Further information :

2303	preserved at Deodoro, RJ
2304	preserved at Deodoro, RJ
2305	preserved at Museu Aeroespacial
2307	w/o 27.6.74
2310	ex 51-8066
2312	ex 51-8077

Embraer EMB.110K1 Bandeirante (C-95A) 2300 a camouflaged example of the improved transport version, shown here at the Chilean Air Force 50th anniversary display.

Potez CM.170-2 Magister (T-24) 1723 at Galeão in April 1968 when with the Esquadrilha da Fumaça.

Morane-Saulnier MS.760A Paris I (C-41) 2922 in Esquadrilha da Fumaça markings.

Fokker S.12-2 (T-22) 0806, one of fifty built between 1960 and 1962.

Fairchild C-82A Packet 2203; the type was used from 1955 to 1967.

FOCKE-WULF Fw 58K-2 (AT-Fw58)

At least three of these former naval crew trainers were used after the war with the irregular designation AT-Fw58 :
```
1191 c/n 210   to PP-EBF, PT-BHL
1509           to PP-EBG, PT-BHM
1530           to PP-FDD
```
Other civilianised machines were PP-FDE c/n 171 and PT-BHN c/n 220 ex PP-ECD.

FOKKER S.11-4 (T-21)

Ninety-five were built by Fokker Indústria Aeronáutica under licence from the Dutch parent company from 1955 to 1959, with serials 0705 to 0799. These in fact followed five Dutch built aircraft which were only assembled in Brazil, serialled 0700 to 0704. Five aircraft were transferred to the Bolivian Air Force. Further details are :
```
0705 c/n 001   w/o 12.2.68
0706     002   w/o 19.12.67
0707     003   to PP-KAM
0716     012   to PP-KAF
0720     016   to PP-KAP
0724     020   to PP-KAN
0729     026   to PP-KAJ
0748     044   to PP-KBA
0750     046   to PP-KBA
0754     050   to PP-KAG
0758     054   to PP-KAO
0765     061   w/o 26.7.68
0770     066   to PP-KAY
0772     068   w/o 17.1.68
0782     078   w/o 27.10.69
0789     085   preserved at Museu Aeroespacial
0795     091   instructional airframe at ESPAER
```

FOKKER S.12-2 (T-22)

Fifty were built between 1960 and 1962 with serials 0800 to 0849; the last aircraft was built as the 8FG Guanabara (YT-24) prototype. Further details of individual aircraft :
```
0800 c/n 001   to PP-KAT
0805     006   to PP-KAZ
0806     007   to PP-KAE
0807     008   to PP-KAK
0811     012   preserved at Museu Aeroespacial
0818     019   to PP-KAI
0828     029   to PP-KAS
0833     034   to PP-KBT
```

```
0843     044   to PP-KAL
```
An unidentified aircraft became PP-KAQ.

FOURNIER RF.5 (TZ-3)

At least one, serial 8003, for the use of the Clube de Vôo à Vela.

GLOSTER METEOR (F-8, T-7)

Sixty Meteor F.Mk.8 (F-8) and ten Meteor T.Mk.7 (T-7, later TF-7) were delivered; the two squadrons of the 1° GAvCa exchanged their Thunderbolts for Meteors on 23.10.53. Meteor F.Mk.8 serials were 4400 to 4459, of which 4455 to 4458 were ex Royal Air Force WK877, WK887, WK888 and WK889 respectively; T.Mk.7 serials were 4300 to 4309 (ex RAF WS142 to WS151, although some sources, perhaps mistakenly, identify 4300 and 4301 as WL485 and WL486 respectively). An additional F.Mk.8 was built up from spares by the Parque de Aeronáutica (Air Park) at São Paulo serialled 4460 and used by the 1°GAvCa for target-towing; it was eventually camouflaged in a three-tone scheme and finally presented to the Museu Aeroespacial on 22.4.74. Other preserved Meteors include F-8 4409 and 4442 at the Bebeduoro museum, 4413 at the Museu da AFA, Pirassununga, 4438 at Galeão, 4439 and 4448 at Canoas, 4440 at the Museu Aeronáutica de São Paulo, 4441 at Santa Cruz, and 4452 at Curitiba; TF-7 4308 is on display at Manaus. An unidentified Meteor was written off on 19.11.70.

GRUMMAN J4F-2 (UC-J4F2)

Fourteen delivered during the war, originally as FAB 01 to 14, later reserialled 2667 to 2680.
```
2667 c/n 1271 ex Bu. 09805   w/o 21.4.48
2668     1272    09806   w/o 17.8.54
2669     1275    09807   wfu
2670     1276    09808   w/o 2.48
2671     1279    09809   wfu
2672     1280    09810   wfu
2673     1283    09811   w/o 29.4.52
2674     1284    09812   w/o 1.9.49
2675     1285    09813   w/o 11.45
2676     1286    09814   w/o 5.45
2677     1287    09815   w/o 18.9.47
2678     1288    09816   w/o 19.8.47
2679     1289    09789   wfu
2680     1290    34584   to (PP-HPU),PP-GQV
```

GRUMMAN HU-16A ALBATROSS (U-16, M-16)

Fourteen delivered in 1959 with serials 6530 to 6543; initially designated A-16, they became U-16, M-16 in 1976 and S-16 in 1977, by which time ten remained in use with the 2°/10°GAv. The type was retired in late August 1980. 6530 was earmarked for preservation at the Museu Aeroespacial, but 6528, 6529, 6532, 6533 and 6538 were broken up at the São Paulo Parque de Material Aeronáutico. S-16 6541 was written off on 23.12.77.

GRUMMAN S-2 TRACKER (P-16)

For use by the 1°GAE. Thirteen S-2A were delivered with serials 7014 to 7026, ex US Navy Bu.149037 to 149049; they were designated as P-16 and eventually as P-16A. 7024 and 7025 were converted for COD duties as UP-16A. Two at least were written off : 7014 on 3.9.69, 7022 on 28.1.69. 7026 is currently derelict at Rio - Santos Dumont Airport. Eight S-2E (P-16E) from surplus US Navy stocks were later delivered, serialled 7030 to 7037. Of these, three are identified : 7030 ex Bu.152329, 7031 ex 152352 and 7032 ex 152356.

HAWKER SIDDELEY HS.748 Srs.2A (C-91)

Two batches of six aircraft in 1962/63 and 1975, for use by the 2°GT. The second batch were series 281 with wide doors.
```
2500 Srs.204 c/n 1550 d/d 17.11.62
2501     205    1551     26.2.63
2502     205    1552     20.3.63
2503     205    1553     18.4.63
2504     205    1554     4.7.63
2505     205    1555     28.9.63
2506     281    1729     24.1.75
2507     281    1730     27.3.75
2508     281    1731     16.5.75
2509     281    1732     20.6.75
2510     281    1733     31.10.75
2511     281    1734     18.12.75
```

HAWKER SIDDELEY HS.125 (C-93, U-93)

Six HS.125-3B/RA and five HS.125-403B were delivered, the last in July 1974. The VC-93 and VU-93 were allocated to the GTE; the EC-93 and EU-93 are specialised navaid checking aircraft.

2119	EU-93 Srs	403B c/n	25274	ex G-5-20
2120	VC-93	3B/RA	25162	
2121	VC-93	3B/RA	25165	
2122	VC-93	3B/RA	25166	w/o 18.6.79
2123	VC-93	3B/RA	25167	
2124	VC-93	3B/RA	25168	
2125	EC-93	3B/RA	25164	
2126	VU-93	403B	25277	ex G-5-11
2127	VU-93	403B	25288	
2128	VU-93	403B	25289	ex G-5-16
2129	VU-93	403B	25290	

IAe DL.22

A basic trainer, of which one only was presented by the Argentine government, serial 1436 c/n 11.

LET L.13 BLANIK (TZ-13)

Ten sailplanes, serialled 8004 to 8013, for the Clube de Vôo à Vela. 8009 was written off on 28.10.79.

LOCKHEED 10A ELECTRA (VC-66)

Two only, 2008 and 2009; the latter was c/n 2148, ex USAAF 42-13567.

LOCKHEED 12A (UC-40)

Eight were purchased in 1939, c/ns 1234, 1235, 1278, 1279, 1288 to 1291. The first two were allocated to the Directorate of Army Aviation and coded DAe.01 and DAe.02 respectively. C/n 1278 became DAe.03 and later UC-40 2658, being disposed of as PP-VTA. C/n 1235 was civilianised as PT-CDU.

LOCKHEED 18 LODESTAR (C-60, C-66)

Eight L.18-56 were designated C-60 and serialled 2000 to 2007; 2005 was still in use as a VC-60 as late as 1967. There was also an L.18-10 FAB01, c/n 2148, ex 42-13567 and EW980, which was designated C-66 and serialled 2008 on 20.7.45, and was sold as N9928F in 1963. Lodestar 2006 was preserved at the Museu da AFA, Pirassununga, and later at the Museu Aeroespacial.

LOCKHEED PV-2

About thirty believed delivered; one was 1156. The FAB also operated a number of the earlier PV-1 and its USAAF equivalent the B-34, of which one was 5043, and at least six ex Royal Air Force Ventura II :

AJ311 c/n	4449	AJ358 c/n	4496
AJ351	4489	AJ360	4498
AJ356	4494	AJ361	4499

LOCKHEED P2V-5 NEPTUNE (P-15)

Fourteen ex Royal Air Force Coastal Command P-2V-5 Neptunes were acquired by the FAB between December 1958 and April 1959 via the USA; they were later brought up to P2V-5F (P-2E) standards. Operated by the $1^0/7^0$GAv in midnight blue and later in light grey and white, they were withdrawn from use between March 1972 and September 1976. The $1^0/7^0$GAv then spent eighteen months without aircraft, finally receiving EMB.111 Bandeirulhas in April 1978. Most P-15 (FAB designation) were given names after Brazilian sea birds or fish : 7000 Martim, 7002 Cação, 7004 Dourado, 7005 Mergulho, 7006 Melro, 7010 Salmão (later Gaivota), 7011 Espadarte (later Giant Petrel), 7012 Tubarão, 7013 Xeréu. They were used for several maritime patrol monoeuvres (Operation Unitas) between 1960 and 1972, and enforced Brazil's new 200-mile territorial water limits from March 1970. The defensive armament was removed in the early 1960s.

7000	ex 51-15956/WX505	Toc 15.12.58	Soc 22.3.73
7001	51-15935/WX509	15.12.58	w/o 21.7.62
7002	51-15957/WX515	16.12.58	Soc 17.9.73
7003	51-15943/WX519	12.12.58	Soc 21.6.76
7004	51-15959/WX521	15.12.58	Soc 30.7.75
7005	51-15942/WX523	25.1.59	Soc 8.6.76
7006	51-15928/WX529	26.1.59	w/o 16.4.67
7007	51-15925/WX525	22.1.59	w/o 21.8.59
7008	51-15931/WX543	20.3.59	w/o 29.8.63
7009	51-15948/WX544	20.3.59	Soc 3.9.76
7010	51-15952/WX548	20.3.59	Soc 8.10.74
7011	51-15949/WX553	24.4.59	Soc 27.3.73
7012	51-15960/WX555	25.4.59	Soc 30.3.72
7013	51-15964/WX556	25.4.59	Soc 29.10.74

7010 is preserved at the Museu Aeroespacial.

LOCKHEED F-80C SHOOTING STAR (F-80)

Thirty three were delivered with serials 4200 to 4232 (though serials up to 4247 have been reported). The first

was delivered on 31.3.58 and most were used by the 4^0 GAvCa until 1969/70. The F-80C was declared surplus to requirements in August 1973, mainly due to lack of spares. The last operational machine was then flown to the Museu da FAB on 16.8.73, but exploded in flight and was totally destroyed. However, two other machines have been preserved : 4201 at São José dos Campos, and 4225 at Fortaleza.

LOCKHEED T-33A (T-33)

Fifty eight were delivered, serialled 4310 to 4367, of which fifty seven were in use in 1973 and forty-five in 1975. At least twenty-four were converted to AT-33A standards for close-support duties, with the FAB designation TF-33A; known details include 4315, 4316, 4318, 4321/4323, 4325, 4327/4333, 4336, 4338, 4342, 4345, 4347, 4349/4351, 4359, 4362/4364 and 4367. The last TF-33A was withdrawn from use in February 1976. Two aircraft, 4313 and 4334, became instructional airframes at ESPAER, and at least three have been preserved : 4328 at the Museu da AFA, Pirassununga, 4336 at Canoas in $1^0/14^0$GAv markings, and 4364 at the Museu Aeroespacial.
TF-33As used by the 14^0GAvCa had playing card markings on the forward fuselage for plane-in-flight identification - known examples are 4222 (2 diamonds), 4327 (3 diamonds) 4331 (4 diamonds), 4321 (2 hearts), 4330 (4 hearts), 4323 (2 clubs), 4332 (4 clubs).
Known write-offs are 4312 on 22.6.67; 4314 on 22.10.75, 4330 on 4.11.70 ; 4353 on 3.5.73; 4359 on 3.6.69; 4366 on 30.9.70, and unidentified T-33As on 17.1.68 and 9.11.70.

LOCKHEED C-130 HERCULES (C-130)

A total of sixteen aircraft in various batches and variants : the first five were C-130E (model L.382-16B) for $1^0/1^0$GT, delivered in 1964-65 :

2450	c/n 4091	w/o 21.12.69
2451	4092	
2452	4093	w/o 26.10.66
2453	4113	w/o 7.11.72 ?
2454	4114	

They were followed by three more C-130E (one model L.382C-5D in 1965 and two L.382C-8D in August 1968) :

2455	4202
2456	4287
2457	4290

Three RC-130E (model L.382C-47D) equipped for search and rescue arrived in November 1968, to replace the SB-17G of $1^0/6^0$GAv :

Hawker Siddeley HS.125-403B (EU-93) 2119 at Hatfield prior to delivery in July 1974.

Lockheed C-130H Hercules 2465 of the 2^OGTT seen visiting Brize Norton on 16 November 1978.

Lockheed TF-33A 4328 visiting Curaçao on 15.2.68. Note the 'Two of Clubs' marking.

Neiva N.591 Regente (L-42) 3233, one of the later ELO versions with the cut away rear fuselage.

Pilatus P.3-04 3182 at Santos Dumont in 1969. Six aircraft of this type were transferred from the Navy in 1965.

Neiva N.621 Universal (T-25) 1880; over 150 of this type have been procured.

North American AT-6D 1485 at Santos Dumont in November 1969 when with 2^OELO.

Vickers 742D Viscount (C-90) 2100, delivered in 1957 and written off ten years later.

2458	4291	ex N7983R
2459	4292	
2460	4293	

Two KC-130H (model L.382C-47D) were delivered on 17.10.75 and 25.11.75 respectively :

2461	4625
2462	4626

They were preceded by three more transports, C-130H (model L.382C-45D) between March and October 1975 :

2463	4570
2464	4602
2465	4630

MORANE-SAULNIER MS.760A PARIS I (C-41)

Thirty were ordered in 1960 (the first eight in February) and assembled in Brazil. Eleven went to the GTE, and ten to the 5°GAv as jet trainers; others were allocated to base flights. In 1968, twenty-two machines were handed over to Sud Aviation as part-payment for seven Potez Magisters, and these were passed on to the French Air Force after an overhaul. The last five aircraft in FAB service were withdrawn from use in 1972.

2910	c/n 53	to French AF
2911	52	wfu 1972
2912	51	to French AF
2913	54	to French AF
2914	55	wfu 1972
2915	56	to French AF
2916	59	to French AF
2917	60	to French AF
2918	57	to French AF
2919	61	to French AF
2920	58	to French AF
2921	62	to French AF
2922	64	wfu 1972; preserved Santa Cruz
2923	63	wfu 1972
2924	65	to French AF
2925	66	wfu 1972
2926	67	w/o 29.10.62
2927	68	to French AF (CEV)
2928	70	to French AF
2929	71	to French AF
2930	74	w/o 25.5.62
2931	75	to French AF
2932	76	to Museu Aeroespacial
2933	77	to French AF
2934	78	to French AF
2935	79	to French AF
2936	80	to French AF

2937	81	to French AF
2938	82	to French AF
2939	83	to French AF (CEV)

NEIVA 56B PAULISTINHA (L-6)

Twenty were delivered with serials 3080 to 3099, c/ns 1001 to 1020, initially designated L-6 and later O-6. There was at least one other L-6, serialled 3107, c/n 1097, which was sold as PP-GYG, and an L-6A serialled 3109, c/n 1242, sold as PP-GYO. Other details of individual aircraft :

3082	c/n 1003	to PP-GYE
3086	1007	to PP-GYD
3091	1012	to PP-GYP
3092	1013	to PP-GYB
3093	1014	to PP-GYC
3094	1015	to PP-GYF
3095	1016	at Museu Aeroespacial
3099	1020	to PP-GYA

NEIVA N.591 REGENTE (C-42, L-42, U-42)

Two versions were built, the C-42 Regente light communications aircraft and the L-42 (later U-42) Regente-ELO utility aircraft with a cut away rear fuselage. The prototype C-42 (Regente N.591-360C) serialled 2941 was followed by seventy production C-42 (2220 to 2239 and 2941 to 2999). Known write-offs are 2232 on 2.8.73 and 2963 on 21.9.72. Aircraft 2970 became a YU-42 (initial designation L-8) although the first prototype of the Regente-ELO N.521-420L model was registered as PP-ZTP.

Forty production L-42 (U-42) were built, the first being YL-42 (later L-42) 3120, c/n 3501. Other known serials are 3144, 3210, 3211, 3213, 3222, 3227, 3228, 3229, 3231, 3233, 3236 (w/o 17.11.72), 3237, 3240 (w/o 13.9.77), 3245, 3246, 3247 and 3248. An unidentified aircraft was written off on 25.4.73. L-42 3120 was preserved at the Museu Aeroespacial.

NEIVA N.621 UNIVERSAL (T-25)

Initially 150 were ordered, with serials 1830 to 1979, but the order was subsequently reduced to 132, ten of which were diverted to the Chilean Army; eight replacement aircraft were eventually ordered in 1976. The prototype YT-25 (IPD.6201) had the serial 1830. Production aircraft were used by the 1°, 2° and 5°EMRAs, CATRE and CFPM. A T-25 was written off on 29.10.74; other known losses are :

1834	c/n 1004	w/o 24.7.77
1839	1009	w/o 7.11.79
1865	1035	w/o 22.3.77
1874	1044	w/o 25.3.77
1909	1079	w/o 19.1.77
1913	1083	w/o 29.8.80
1919	1089	w/o 13.12.78
1933	1103	w/o 24.7.80

A further twenty T-25 were ordered in July 1978. The prototype 1830 has been preserved at the Museu Aeroespacial, whilst the second aircraft, 1831 c/n 1001, was converted to N.622 Universal II, with a more powerful engine, detail changes and provision for armament, flying as such on 22.10.78 with the designation YT-25B and six underwing stores pylons; no orders have yet been placed for this version.

NOORDUYN UC-64A NORSEMAN (C-64)

Nineteen were delivered under Lend-Lease as FAB 01 to FAB 19; four were ex 43-35398/35401. A few remained in service in the immediate postwar years, one being 2805.

NORTH AMERICAN T-28 TROJAN (T-28)

Six armed T-28A were received from the Brazilian Navy, allotted serials 0860 to 0865 and used by the 2ª ELO for naval co-operation duties. Reports that twelve Fennecs (the Sud Aviation ground attack version) had been obtained from France have not been confirmed. 0862 is preserved at the Museu Aeroespacial.

NORTH AMERICAN B-25 MITCHELL (B-25)

Seven B-25B (ex USAAF 40-2245, 2255, 2263, 2306, 2309, 2310, 2316), twenty-nine B-25C and about sixty B-25J (including ex USAAF 43-27491, 27530, 27605, 27610, 27626, 27775, 27847, 27864, 27865, 27869, 27873, 27876, 27878, 27880, 27881, 28035, 28046, 28196, 28210, 28220, 35966, 36083, 36087, 36095, 36096, 36097, 36132, 36141, 36146, 36147, 36154, 36167 and 36224) were delivered.

Known B-25J serials are :

5127	preserved at Museu Aeroespacial
5133	at the Museu da AFA, Pirassununga
5136	

A few were converted to CB-25J (FAB designation CB-25) transports, including 5097 (now at the Bebeduoro museum) and 5164.

Identified aircraft are as follows :

5052	ex 43-29007	to ESPAER as instructional airframe
5063	43-29493	
5084	43-27610	
5096	43-28033	
5100	43-28220	
5140	43-30783	

The type was declared surplus to requirements during 1970. An unidentified aircraft was written off in June 1970.

NORTH AMERICAN AT-6 TEXAN (T-6)

436 Texans of six different versions were delivered to the FAB between 1943 and 1952 and used for both advanced training and coastal reconnaissance (with light armament); twenty ex US Navy SNJ-5C were delivered in 1960 for use by the 2ªELO, having arrester hooks, though in the event they were never operated from an aircraft carrier. With the formation of the ERAs in the early 1960s a number of T-6s were converted to close support aircraft. The T-6 was also standard equipment with the Esquadrilha da Fumaça since its formation in 1952, initially to introduce trainee pilots to aerobatic flight.

The T-6, nicknamed the 'T-Meia' (half-dozen T) by FAB personnel, was declared surplus to requirements in 1966-67, although disposals began earlier — on 26.5.75 sixty T-6D and G (twenty-eight airworthy, seventeen in need of repair and fifteen for scrap) were sold by auction. Fourteen T-6 were transferred to the Paraguayan Air Force in 1960.

Serial allocations comprised :

1193-1222	ZT-6	Model NA.72, c/ns 72-3077/3096, 77-4757/4766, initially serialled as FAB 01/30.
1223-1232	AT-6B	initially FAB 21/30
1233-1302	AT-6C	initially FAB 01/20, 31/80
1303-1347	AT-6D	initially FAB 81/125
1376-1395	AT-6D	built by Construções Aeronáuticas SA
1396-1435	AT-6D	refurbished
1447-1506	AT-6D	refurbished
1508	AT-6D	ex 42-43922, refurbished, d/d 1958
1531-1540	AT-6D	built by Construções Aeronáuticas SA
1542-1592	AT-6D	built by Construções Aeronáuticas SA
1600-1649	T-6D	
1650-1699	T-6G	
1700-1719	SNJ-5C	later to FAB T-6D

The NA.72 was the armed export version of the AT-6. All AT-6D later became T-6D. A few AT-6C and D (such as 1275 and 1320) were brought up to T-6G standards.

Previous USAAF serials included :

AT-6C	42-3950, 43922
AT-6D	41-34193, 34201, 34218, 34258, 34493, 34555, 42-44425, 44649, 84388, 84484, 84485, 84679, 84841, 85263, 85285, 85357, 85449, 85450, 85483, 85546, 85691, 85802, 85857, 85963, 86022, 86049, 86242, 86249, 86347, 86418, 86419, 86420, 86422/86427, 86461, 86485, 86535, 86544, 86555.
T-6G	49-2945, 2959, 2969, 3114, 3146, 3156, 3200, 3201, 3202, 3282, 3287, 3293, 3295, 3296, 3324, 3333, 3361, 3369, 3372, 3377, 3379/3381, 3385, 3388, 3389, 3398, 3399, 3403, 3412, 3418, 3419, 3440, 3445, 3455, 3457, 3460, 3523, 3537.

Other details of individual aircraft :

1223		preserved at EPCA
1235		wfu 1971
1242		w/o 4.1.73
1243		Esquadrilha da Fumaça
1252		w/o 30.1.67
1261		preserved at Paraguaçú, MG
1275		Esquadrilha da Fumaça; w/o 2.1.76
1296		'75' of 2ªELO
1319	ex 42-44585	temporarily to PP-GOX
1320		at Museu Aeroespacial
1323		w/o 18.8.70
1328		w/o 15.12.68
1339		at Bebeduoro museum
1344	ex 44-81306	to PP-GOW; w/o 14.7.56
1387		w/o 12.3.74
1390		Esquadrilha da Fumaça; at the Museu de Aeronáutica, São Paulo
1398		w/o 19.12.68
1403	c/n 88-9580	to PT-KVD
1409		w/o 15.3.73
1420		to instructional airframe at ESPAER
1427		Esquadrilha da Fumaça
1448		to instructional airframe at ESPAER
1455		Esquadrilha da Fumaça
1467		Esquadrilha da Fumaça
1471		to instructional airframe at ESPAER
1482		Esquadrilha da Fumaça
1497	c/n 78-7233	to PT-KSZ
1500		Esquadrilha da Fumaça
1506	c/n 78-7005	to PT-KVG
1508	ex 42-43922	Esquadrilha da Fumaça at Museu Aeroespacial
1517		5ºEMRA; w/o 24.7.75
1536		Esquadrilha da Fumaça
1539		Esquadrilha da Fumaça
1542		Esquadrilha da Fumaça
1550		Esquadrilha da Fumaça; w/o 26.6.65
1551		Esquadrilha da Fumaça; w/o 9.11.71

1559		Esquadrilha da Fumaça; preserved at Museu Aeroespacial
1565		AFA; w/o 7.67
1573		to instructional airframe at ESPAER
1575		at Bebedouro museum
1600		Esquadrilha da Fumaça; w/o 30.1.65
1612		Esquadrilha da Fumaça
1628		w/o 25.2.67
1631		Esquadrilha da Fumaça
1633	ex 42-85344	to Paraguay AF FAP 0101
1639	ex 44-81035	to PT-KUX
1640		w/o 18.12.71
1641		Esquadrilha da Fumaça; w/o 9.11.71
1643	ex 44-81564	Esquadrilha da Fumaça; to PT-TRB
1646		Esquadrilha da Fumaça
1647		w/o 18.6.69; remains at Pirassununga
1658	ex 49-3202	Esquadrilha da Fumaça; to PT-KVF
1661		w/o 26.2.72
1672	ex 49-3380	to PT-KQX
1679		w/o 26.4.71
1703	ex Bu43669	to PT-KRD
1704	ex Bu43684	to PT-KSX
1706	ex Bu85038	to PT-KRC
1708		Esquadrilha da Fumaça
1712	ex Bu112187	to PT-KVE
1713	ex Bu112119	
1714	ex Bu112256	
1715	ex Bu112118	
1716	ex Bu112004	
1717	ex Bu112295	
1718	ex Bu112230	preserved at Museu da AFA
1719	ex Bu112039	

Unidentified crashes took place on 8.9.68, 24.6.70, 9.5.71 and 29.5.71.

NORTHROP F-5 (F-5)

The following aircraft were delivered between June 1975 and February 1976; they equipped the two Esquadrões of the 1ºGAvCa.

Six F-5B :

4800	c/n X.1001	ex 74-1576	
4801	X.1002	74-1577	w/o 23.5.75
4802	X.1003	74-1578	
4803	X.1004	74-1579	
4804	X.1005	74-1580	
4805	X.1006	74-1581	

Thirty-six F-5E Tiger II :

4820	Y.1001	74-1582	
4821	Y.1002	74-1583	w/o 28.3.77

4822	Y.1003	74-1584	w/o 25.6.75
4823	Y.1004	74-1585	
4824	Y.1005	74-1586	
4825	Y.1006	74-1587	
4826	Y.1007	74-1588	
4827	Y.1008	74-1589	
4828	Y.1009	74-1590	
4829	Y.1010	74-1591	
4830	Y.1011	74-1592	
4831	Y.1012	74-1593	
4832	Y.1013	74-1594	
4833	Y.1014	74-1595	
4834	Y.1015	74-1596	
4835	Y.1016	74-1597	
4836	Y.1017	74-1598	
4837	Y.1018	74-1599	
4838	Y.1019	74-1600	
4839	Y.1020	74-1601	
4840	Y.1021	74-1602	
4841	Y.1022	74-1603	
4842	Y.1023	74-1604	
4843	Y.1024	74-1605	w/o 10.9.79
4844	Y.1025	74-1606	
4845	Y.1026	74-1607	
4846	Y.1027	74-1608	
4847	Y.1028	74-1609	
4848	Y.1029	74-1610	
4849	Y.1030	74-1611	
4850	Y.1031	74-1612	
4851	Y.1032	74-1613	
4852	Y.1033	74-1614	
4853	Y.1034	74-1615	
4854	Y.1035	74-1616	
4855	Y.1036	74-1617	

PIPER L-4 CUB (L-4)

Twenty one were delivered under Lend-Lease, mainly for use by the 1ª Esquadrilha de Ligação e Observação, attached to the Brazilian Expeditionary Force in Italy in 1944-45. One, c/n 12279 ex USAAF 44-79983, was eventually registered in Italy as I-MINK.

POTEZ CM.170-2 MAGISTER (T-24)

Seven acquired in 1968 for use by the Esquadrilha de Fumaça, with serials 1720 to 1726 (c/ns 556 to 560, 570, 571). Withdrawn from use early 1975 and sold to Aérospatiale.

REPUBLIC P-47D THUNDERBOLT (P-47D)

Eighty-eight P-47D were delivered under Lend-Lease for use by the 1º Grupo de Caça's four Esquadrilhas, and operated in Italy with their USAAF serial numbers and Esquadrilha codes (A1 to A6, B1 to B6, C1 to C6 and D1 to D6). Twenty-three aircraft were operational in April 1945, with another twenty-four in reserve; when the Grupo returned to Brazil, it brought along twenty-five Thunderbolts, most of which were put into service. Additional aircraft were delivered later to make up for attrition — twenty-five in late 1947 and twenty-three in October 1952. Known ex USAAF serials are 42-26706, 26757, 26759, 26766, 26771, 26773, 26775/26777, 26784, 26787, 44-19659, 19661, 19665, 19666, 20338, 20339, 33097, 90334, 90344, 90393, 90460, 45-49090, 49095, 49096, 49100, 49104, 49107, 49109, 49110, 49126, 49130, 49135, 49149, 49151, 49168, 49228, 49231, 49233/49247, 49249/49252, 49256, 49262, 49266, 49269, 49276, 49282, 49300, 49302/49303, 49325, 49346, 49352, 49357, 49359, 49361, 49380, 49406, 49411, 49430, 49436, 49489, 49491, 49508, 49523, 49526, 49535, 49541, 49542, 49548.

Postwar aircraft were serialled in the 4100 block; further details of individual aircraft are :

4104	ex 42-26450	4106	ex 42-26756
4107	on display at Santa Cruz air base		
4109	ex 42-26760, at Museu de Aeronáutica, São Paulo		
4110	ex 42-26762	4113	ex 42-26779
4114	ex 42-26786	4115	ex 42-26780
4116	ex 42-28986	4119	ex 44-19662
4123	ex 44-20850	4124	ex 44-20854
4127	ex 44-33093		
4184	preserved at the Museu Aeroespacial as 44-20339/D3 in wartime markings.		
4194	at the Museu da AFA, Pirassununga		

An aircraft is preserved at Fortaleza as '4181' which might not be a true identity.

The FAB did also receive an earlier 'razorback' Thunderbolt, possibly a P-47C, which was used as an instructional airframe.

The P-47D were progressively replaced by Gloster Meteors from 1953 onwards, but a few remained in use until 1960.

SIKORSKY UH-19D (H-19)

Six only, for use by the 10º GAv, with serials 8500 to 8505. A seventh aircraft, 8506, was purchased on the civil market.

SIKORSKY HSS-1N (H-34)

Six helicopters delivered under MAP, with serials 8050 to 8055 (ex USAF 60-5424 to 60-5429 respectively), were all transferred to the Brazilian Navy in 1965 as N-3001 to 3006.

SUD SA.330 PUMA (CH-33)

Six were ordered for delivery in May 1980 for operation by 3º/8º GAv.

8700	c/n 1624	ex F-ZKBI
8701		
8702		
8703		
8704		
8705		

VICKERS VISCOUNT (C-90)

Two aircraft delivered on 1.2.57 and 6.10.58 respectively for use as executive transports :

2100	Srs. 742D	c/n 141	ex (LN-SUN)	w/o 8.12.67
2101	789	345		wfu 1970

VULTEE A-35B VENGEANCE (A-35)

Twenty-nine A-35B-15-VN were delivered, ex USAAF 42-101437 to 101465, to equip three Grupos de Bombardeio Picado. The type was found to be unsuitable for service, and saw practically no use; the aircraft were left in open storage for a number of years before being scrapped.

VULTEE BT-15 (BT-15)

One hundred and twenty were delivered under Lend-Lease, including USAAF 41-10400/10404 and 42-41773 (which later became PP-GUK). A number were still in use in the late 1950s with serials in the 1000 block. Two, 1072 and 1137, ex 42-41773, were preserved at the Museu Aeroespacial, and a third, 1305, became PP-GRI. Other civilianised examples are :

c/n 3227 to	PP-GGZ	c/n 3263 to	PP-GGY
3229	PP-GOM	8079	PP-GRK
3232	PP-GRD	10365	PP-GGV
3258	PP-GGU		

Brazilian Army

Military service in Brazil is compulsory for males aged between twenty-one and forty-five and usually lasts for twelve months. The Brazilian Army (Exército Brasileiro) has a strength of 180,000 all ranks plus 60,000 first-line reserves, and comprises thirteen divisions — seven infantry, four mechanised, one armoured and one airborne. Although Army co-operation duties are undertaken by the Air Force, the Army has occasionally operated aircraft mainly for General Staff communications and these have the inscription *EXÉRCITO* on the fuselage sides. One such aircraft — no longer on charge — was Piper Aztec 250 (UC-26) serial 2904 (c/n 27-3368) one of two which later became FAB U-36 until disposed of in September 1980; another was a Beechcraft Baron C55 (FAB C-55) serialled 2903 (c/n TE.162 delivered 6.66), recently attached to the Army's 1°Grupamento de Engenharia e Construção (1st Engineering and Construction Detachment) at João Pessoa, Paraíba state.

The Escola de Paraquedistas do Exército (Army Paratroop School) is at Campo dos Afonsos, Rio de Janeiro. The crack unit of the Brazilian paratroops is the 26°Batalhão de Infantaria Paraquedista do Exército 'Santos-Dumont' (26th 'Santos-Dumont' Army Paratroop Infantry Battalion) at Deodoro, Rio de Janeiro, where the 20th Logistics Battalion is also stationed.

Brazilian Navy

The need for a Brazilian naval air arm is made clear by the country's very long and strategically important coastline (over 8,000 kilometres) as well as its extensive waterway network. Thus it is not surprising that Brazil was one of the first countries in the world to form a naval air force, the Aviação Naval, on 23 August 1916 (actually before the Army air service came into being), as a natural sequence to the inauguration in 1912 of the civil Escola de Aviação Brasileira (Brazilian Flying School) which had as its first instructor a naval officer-pilot. The Aviação Naval was initially based at the former Naval Arsenal (Arsenal de Marinha), being later transferred to Ilha das Enxadas (subsequently a commercial seaplane base) and finally Ponta do Galeão on the Governador island which was to become the present-day Galeão International Airport, Rio de Janeiro. Its first aircraft were three US-supplied Curtiss F-Boat trainers, which remained the sole complement of the Escola de Aviação Naval (Naval Aviation School) until early 1917, when additional machines were acquired.

In November 1917, a civilian-owned Borel float monoplane was purchased and serialled '4', but was disposed of in September 1918 due to its engine's poor reliability. The United States released a couple of Curtiss HS.2L flying boats and Aeromarine floatplanes, and Italy, where Brazilian naval pilots were being sent for operational training, supplied Macchi 7 and 9 flying-boats, and at least an SVA Ansaldo floatplane. Two Gosport-built Schreck-FBA Type B flying boats (later serialled 7 and 8) were obtained in Britain in June 1918, although in the event they had a short service life; the sole survivor, 7, was disposed of in August 1923.

More aircraft were procured in France after the war, an order being placed for two F.41 floatplanes and two F.51 flying boats. The F.41 (serials 20 and 21) served between 1919 and 1921, but the F.51 (serials 36 and 37) had worse luck, remaining crated until August 1921, and indeed 36 was never fully assembled. The US Navy provided fourteen Curtiss F.5L (PN-5) flying boats and a couple of Curtiss N.9 floatplane trainers (one was serialled 23).

The expansion of the Aviação Naval was initiated in 1922 following the publication of a Naval General Staff report, 'On the Organisation of the Air Defence of the Brazilian Coast'. A Naval Air Reserve was created; the British 'Gosport' training system was adopted and a batch of surplus Avro 504K purchased; these were serialled A1 to A17, of which the following are identified : A2 ex H2024, A3/H2026, A4/H7479, A6/H9608, A7/H2568, A8/H9660, A9/H7473, A10/J5496, A11/E9463, A12/H9618, A13/E4136, A14/H2504, A15/E446, A16/H2566, A17/H9591. These were supplemented in the 1930s by Avro 504Ns serialled A18 to A21 (c/ns 439 to 442). A fighter force was formed with seventeen ex-Royal Air Force Sopwith Snipes (serialled 1 to 4, 111, 112, 112A ex 113, 114, 115, 121 to 125, 131 to 133). The Ponta de Galeão base, housing the Escola and the Centro de Aviação Naval, was activated in November 1923 although its official inauguration did not take place until early 1925. By 1924 there were flying and technical training schools and some nine Esquadrilhas (flights) of four to six aircraft each; and by 1926 a few Avro 546 landplane trainers were in use and a Naval Aviation Directorate (Directoria de Aeronáutica da Marinha) had been formed.

The service was further expanded in October 1931 when it was renamed as the Corpo de Aviação da Marinha (Naval Air Corps) with, for the first time in its history, a permanent officers' cadre. In January of the same year, eleven Savoia-Marchetti S.55 flying-boats, led by the legendary General Italo Balbo, had made a non-stop flight from Rome to Rio de Janeiro, and were traded in for coffee by the Brazilian government, being assigned to the Naval Air Corps and eventually used for goodwill flights to Argentina and Uraguay. These aircraft were c/ns 45053, 45055/45057, 45059/45060, 45062, 45080/45083 and were numbered 1 to 11 (not in the same order). In 1932, the five remaining aircraft were serialled P1S-16 to 20 (P1S for patrol, 1st type, Savoia) and were finally withdrawn from use in 1936.

In March 1933 five Air Sectors (Setores Aéreos) were formed within the naval air command (Defesa Aérea do Litoral, or Coastal Air Defence) - Northern (Belém, comprising the states of Pará, Maranhão and Piauí), Northeastern (Natal, comprising the coastline of the states of Rio Grande do Norte, Alagoas, Bahia, Ceará, Paraíba, Pernambuco and Sergipe), Centre (Rio de Janeiro, coastline of Rio de Janeiro, Espírito Santo and São Paulo), Southern (Florianópolis, coastline of Rio Grande do Sul, Paraná and Santa Catarina), and Southeastern (Ladário, comprising the waterway borders of Mato Grosso state). These sectors were to be patrolled by five Divisions - the 1ªDivisão de Observação (1st Observation Division) at Centro de Aviação Naval do Rio de Janeiro, the 1ª Divisão de Esclarecimiento e Bombardeio (1st Reconnaissance and Bombing Division) at CAN de Ladário, the 2ªDEB at CAN de Florianópolis, the 3ªDEB at CAN de Santa Catarina, and the 4ªDEB at CAN do Rio de Janeiro. In the event however, a change in plans by the Ministry of the Navy prevented the implementation of the above.

In September 1933, the Observation and Reconnaissance and Bombing Divisions were disbanded and replaced by three operational Flotillas: the 1ª Flotilha de Aviões de Esclarecimiento e Bombardeio (1ªFEB, 1st Reconnaissance and Bombing Flotilla) with twenty Fairey Gordons recently purchased (c/ns F.1803/1812, F.1827/1836); the 1ªFlotilha de Observação (1st Observation Flotilla) with twelve Vought V.65 (O2U) Corsairs; and the 1ª Flotilha de Bombardeio e Patrulha (1ªFBP, 1st Bombing and Patrol Flotilla) with Savoias P1S-16 to 20 and two Curtiss PN-5. The aircraft were divided between the Fôrça Aérea da Esquadra (Fleet Air Force) — five Gordons and all the patrol bombers — and the Coastal Air Defence. There were also two Divisões (Divisions) : a Divisão de Aviões de Combate (Fighter Division) with eight Boeing 256 (F4B-4 coded 1-C-1 to 1-C-8) and a Divisão de Aviões de Treinamento (Training Division) with an equal number of Waco CSO conversion trainers, although at a later date the Boeing 256 and Vought Corsairs were combined into a Grupo de Observação e Combate (Observation and Fighter Group) for economy reasons; this was disbanded in August 1940. The first operational tour of duty of the Naval Air Corps took place in December 1934 during the Gran Chaco conflict between Paraguay and Bolivia when four Boeing 256 and six Vought Corsairs were deployed to Ladário to protect the Mato Grosso river borders; they returned to Rio de Janeiro after two weeks without firing their guns in anger.

The Naval Air Corps was reorganised in July of 1935. It now consisted of a Naval Air Directorate comprising technical and administrative commands as well as the General Staff and the Naval Air Force (Fôrça Aérea da Marinha) divided into Fleet Air Service and Base Air Service (the Naval Aviation Centres became Naval Air Bases —BAvN, Bases de Aviação Naval); there were also the Escola de Aviação Naval (EAvN), the Oficinas de Aviação Naval (OAvN) or workshops, an Almoxarifardo (AAvN) or quartermaster corps, and Special Services (Serviciós Especiais, SEAv). A number of auxiliary airstrips were established along the coastline and the small Correio Aéreo Naval (Naval Air Courier Service) was expanded. The training programme was substantially improved with the introduction into service of twelve North American NA.46 (BT-9C, c/ns 46-972 to 977 , 46-1991 to 1996); nicknamed Perna Dura (Stiff Legs) because of its fixed undercarriage, the NA.46 formed a new unit, the 1ªEsquadrilha de Adestramento Militar (1st Operational Training Squadron), in 1938. The Oficinas de Aviação Naval (OAvN) began licence manufacture of foreign designs in 1937 and was transferred to the Air Ministry in the following year — this because it built aircraft for both the Army and Navy, and the merger of both services was already envisaged. By 1939, the Oficinas had completed enough Focke-Wulf Fw 58K-2 Weihe twin-engined crew-trainers to enable the Navy to form a 2ªEsquadrilha de Adestramento Militar.

The locally-built Weihes were serialled V2AvN-209 to 223 and flew alongside eleven machines which had been assembled from German-supplied parts. Twenty-five de Havilland DH.60T Moth Trainers (c/ns 3015/3026 which became AI-5 to AI-16 and c/ns 3030, 3036/3047) and twelve DH.82A Tiger Moths (c/ns 3324/3335, coded 2-I-5 to 2-I-16) were also acquired for training, in addition to five DH.83 Fox Moths (c/ns 4027 to 4031) for communications duties. From the USA came ten Waco CPF floatplanes (c/ns 4360 to 4369, delivered 11 May 1935) and four CJC.

On 20 January 1941, the Army and Navy air services were merged under the Air Ministry with the interim title Fôrças Aéreas Nacionais (National Air Forces), soon to be replaced by Fôrça Aérea Brasileira. During the following seventeen years, no naval flying took place, although a reorganisation of the Navy in 1952 did suggest the re-establishment of a naval air service, and there was a Naval Air Observer specialisation for officers from 1955.

In 1957 the Royal Navy aircraft carrier HMS Vengeance was purchased by the Brazilian government and was extensively re-fitted and modernised at Rotterdam, Holland; the Dutch even supplied the first three post-war Brazilian naval aircraft, a trio of surplus TBM-3 Avengers which were used for carrier familiarisation training in the North Sea during the autumn of 1960. The HMS Vengeance was renamed as the NAeL (light aircraft carrier) Minas Gerais and was officially accepted in January 1961. The problem was to decide who was to operate the carrier-based aircraft; the Brazilian Air Force wanted to retain its monopoly of military flying and denied that the Navy had any need for aircraft. The recently acquired Grumman S2F-1 Trackers were thus taken on FAB charge and became the complement of a naval co-operation unit, the 1º Grupo de Aviação Embarcada (1st Shipborne Air Group). However the Navy was intent on having its own aircraft and six North American T-28 were literally smuggled into Brazil aboard Brazilian warships, being transported by road under cover of darkness, to the new naval air base at São Pedro da

Aldeia and assembled there for use by the 1º Esquadrao de Aviões de Instrução (1st Training Aircraft Squadron) of the Centro de Instrução Adestramento Aeronaval (CIAAN, Naval Air Training Centre). The same technique was used to obtain six Pilatus P.3 trainers from Switzerland (via Genoa, Italy) and single examples of the Fairchild PT-26 and Taylorcraft L-2K from miscellaneous sources.

The FAB was understandably upset about this and in an attempt to stop an impending inter-service war, a Presidential Decree dated January 1965 limited the Fôrça Aeronaval da Marinha do Brasil (Brazilian Naval Air Force) to helicopters, all fixed-wing aircraft being transferred to the air force. As there was no way out of this situation, the Navy acceded and set about the creation of a throughly modern and efficient helicopter force, at the same time tolerating the presence of FAB aircraft aboard the *Minas Gerais*. Its main base was to be São Pedro da Aldeia, Rio de Janeiro state, where all the shore-based squadrons were to be quartered. The inter-service ASW force, until then known as the 1º Esquadrão Misto de Aviões Anti-Submarinos e de Ataque (1st Mixed ASW and Attack Squadron) and incorporating the FAB Trackers of the 1º GAE, was named the Grupo de Caça e de Destruição (Location and Destruction Group) and its naval half, the 1º Esquadrão de Helicópteros Anti-Submarinos (ESQD HS-1; 1st ASW Helicopter Squadron), later renamed the 1º Esquadrão de Helicópteros de Ataque (1st Attack Helicopter Squadron) received six FAB Sikorsky SH-34J. The CIAAN was disbanded and most of its aircraft were taken on FAB charge, accordingly re-serialled.

The new Naval training unit was the 1º Esquadrão de Helicópteros de Instrução (ESQD HI-1, 1st Helicopter Training Squadron) at São Pedro da Aldeia with an initial complement of eleven Bell 47D and 47J; it was later to deploy individual aircraft aboard the oceanographic survey ships *Sirius* and *Canopus* under the control of the Naval Hydrographic and Navigation Directorate. The remaining helicopters on charge — two Westland Widgeons and six Westland Whirlwinds — were allocated to the 1º Esqu-

adrão de Helicópteros de Serviços Múltiplos, later renamed the 1º Esquadrão de Helicópteros de Emprêgo Geral (ESQD HU-1, 1st General Purpose Helicopter Squadron), which was to deploy helicopters aboard the cruisers *Almirante Tamandaré* (ex *USS St. Louis* CL49) and *Almirante Barroso* (ex *USS Philadelphia* CL41).

1º Esqd He A/S - green outer, yellow inner circles, pale blue sky, mid-blue sea with black waves; white pelican with yellow bill, dark green headset, yellow feet; all other detail and lettering in black.

Subsequent aircraft were procured in the United States and Britain, and it must be noted that no Brazilian designations are normally allotted, unlike in the FAB. ESQD HS-1 re-equipped with the Sikorsky S.61D-3, which is incidentally the only naval type to be maintained by the FAB; HI-1 now uses Bell 206B Jet Rangers, after a few years with Hughes 269A and A-1 models; and HU-1 still clings to the Westland Whirlwinds, although these are now the Gnome-powered Series 3, but are nevertheless due for replacement. Early in 1980, plans for a radical expansion of the Brazilian Navy were revealed, and include the construction of two new aircraft carriers, one of which is to replace the *Minas Gerais*. Both will carry a mixed complement of helicopters and fixed-wing V/STOL aircraft, which may indicate an interest in the acquisition of the Harrier/AV-8, possibly via the United States Navy.

Aircraft Review

COLOURS AND MARKINGS

Aircraft used since 1960 by the Naval air arm differ from FAB aircraft in being marked with green, yellow and blue roundels and fin flashes or rear fuselage bands, instead of the FAB stars and green and yellow rudders; this continues a pre-war tradition. Naval aircraft also have *MARINHA* and an anchor on the fuselage sides. Grey upper surfaces with light grey undersides have more recently been superseded by gull grey uppers and white undersides.

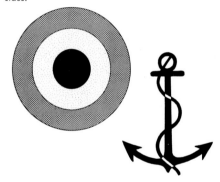

SERIALS AND AIRCRAFT USED

Aeronaval serials currently consist of four digits with an N- prefix. Aircraft used since 1960 include:

AÉROSPATIALE AS.350B ÉCUREUIL

Six ordered in 1980, to be serialled N-7050 to N-7055 and assembled by Helibrás as the Esquilo (the Portuguese word for the French écureil, squirrel). The first helicopter N-7050 c/n 1054 was actually assembled by CTA, as the Itajuba, MG plant of Helibrás was not completed at that time. Six more may be ordered.

Hughes 269A-1 N-5011 of ESQD HI-1 at Santos Dumont in November 1969.

Westland WS.55 Whirlwind Srs.3 N-7025, seen at Santos Dumont in January 1970.

Sikorsky S.61D-3 N-3007, seen prior to its delivery in 1970.

Westland Wasp HAS.1 N-7038 seen test-flying in 1977 as G-17-22; it was previously XS564.

BELL 47

About a dozen delivered, including three ex US Navy HTL-3 (Bell 47E) ex Bu.144693 to 144695. Known examples are the following Bell 47D-1 :
N-5001
N-5002
N-5003   c/n 464   ex Bu129965   Sold as PT-FAJ
N-5004
N-5005
N-5006
Also three Bell 47J :
N-7003   1728   N-7001   w/o
N-7004   1729   N-7002   Sold as PT-HDU
N-7005   1730   N-7003   w/o
There was also a Bell 47G,
N-7006   1023   Sold as PT-FAK
An unidentified Bell 47 was written off on 18.8.64, and another on 19.12.67

BELL 206B JET RANGER

Eighteen aircraft acquired in 1974. Ten for ESQD HI-1 for training (N-5021 to N-5030) and eight for ESQD HU-1 for communications (N-7028 to N-7035):

N-5021	c/n 1265	d/d 27.5.74
N-5022	1270	27.5.74
N-5023	1271	20.5.74
N-5024	1272	16.5.74
N-5025	1273	16.5.74
N-5026	1409	6.9.74
N-5027	1410	16.9.74
N-5028	1411	8.11.74
N-5029	1381	13.8.74
N-5030	1382	10.10.74
N-7028	1366	1.8.74
N-7029	1367	1.8.74
N-7030	1368	2.8.74
N-7031	1390	15.8.74
N-7032	1398	26.8.74
N-7033	1399	29.8.74
N-7034	1400	5.9.74
N-7035	1408	6.9.74

FAIRCHILD PT-26A CORNELL

One only, N-708, ex Royal Canadian Air Force FV607. It was withdrawn from use in 1965.

GRUMMAN TBM-3E AVENGER

The first three were delivered on 25.6.60 as N-501 to N-503; three more followed as N-504 to N-506. Serial tie-ups are unknown but the aircraft were :
Bu53142 ex Dutch Navy 073 for target towing
Bu53604   069
Bu85543   reported to N-502
Bu85549   067 to N-503
Bu85930   068
Bu86174   075 (TBM-3E2; target tug)

N-503 was ditched, but was salvaged and stored at Quartel dos Marinheiros (Naval Barracks), Rio de Janeiro, where it was later broken up.

HILLER FH.1100

Three only, disposed of to the Rio de Janeiro Police in 1977
N-7020   c/n 104   to PP-EGC
N-7021   105   PP-EGD
N-7022   106   PP-EGE

HUGHES 269A

Three 269A acquired for ESQD HI-1 :
N-5008   c/n 330181   to PT-HGX
N-5009   330182   to PT-HGY
N-5010   330183   to PT-HGZ

Also at least thirteen 269A-1 :
N-5005   1140015   to PT-HGP
N-5006   150020   ex N9841F, to PT-HGW
N-5007   150028
N-5011   1140017
N-5012   1140018   w/o 23.10.69 (collided with N-5017)
N-5013   1140035   to PT-HGR
N-5014   1140036   to PT-HGS
N-5015   1140037   to PT-HGT
N-5016   1140038
N-5017   1140039   w/o 23.10.69 (collided with N-5012)
N-5018   1140040   to PT-HGU
N-5019   1140041   to PT-HGV
N-5020   1140042   to PT-HHA

The Hughes 269A was at one stage to be designated as IH-2A within a projected US-based naval designation system which was never adopted.

NORTH AMERICAN T-28A

Six Nomair-converted T-28-R1 acquired for use aboard the *Minas Gerais*. They were eventually transferred to the FAB, and used by the naval co-operation unit 2ᵃELO at São Pedro da Aldeia.
N-701   to FAB 0860
N-702   0861
N-703   ex USAF 50-202   0862
N-704   0863
N-705   0864
N-706   49-1720   0865

PILATUS P.3-04

Originally allocated to Esquadrão de Aviação (Air Squadron) 1-1 and serialled N-501 to N-506. Transferred to the FAB in 1965 for use by the 2ᵃELO and designated O-3 (later O-3 and U-3). Two were named in FAB service : 3182 as 'Albatroz' (albatross) and 3180 'Ás de Ouros' (Ace of Diamonds).
N-501   c/n 331   ex HB-HOA   to FAB 3184
N-502   332   HB-HOB   3181
N-503   333   HB-HOC   3182
N-504   334   HB-HOD   w/o 25.3.64
N-505   335   HB-HOE   3183
N-506   336   HB-HOF   3180
3182 was preserved at the Museu Aeroespacial.

SIKORSKY HSS-1N (SH-34J)

Six helicopters, obtained from the FAB in 1965 :
N-3001   ex FAB 8050 and 60-5424
N-3002   8051   60-5425
N-3003   8052   60-5426
N-3004   8053   60-5427
N-3005   8054   60-5428   w/o 10.11.72
N-3006   8055   60-5429
Another was written off in the summer of 1965; the four surviving machines were withdrawn from use in 1970.

SIKORSKY S.61D-3 (SH-3D)

Four delivered in 1970, with two more later; equipped the ESQD HS-1 and usually operate from the *Minas Gerais*. The serials are N-3007 to N-3012. N-3008 was written off on 19.8.76 during a training flight.

TAYLORCRAFT L-2K

One only, possibly serialled N-707; withdrawn from use.

WESTLAND WS.51 WIDGEON

Two only, c/ns WA/H/142 and WA/H/143, the Aeronaval's first helicopters. Initially serialled H-4001 and 4002, they later became N-7001 and N-7002. H-4001 was delivered on 8.12.57; they are no longer in service.

WESTLAND WS.55 WHIRLWIND

Six Whirlwind Srs.2 were acquired :

N-3007	c/n WA.494	ex G-17-1	converted to Srs.3
N-3008	WA.495		converted to Srs.3
N-3009	WA.496		converted to Srs.3
N-7008	WA.394	ex G-17-1	
N-7009	WA.395		converted to Srs.3
N-7010	WA.396		converted to Srs.3

N-7009 and N-7010 were converted to Gnome-powered Srs. 3 as N-7026 and N-7027 (ex G-17-1 and G-17-2 respectively) the latter being written off on 11.2.79.

Two Whirlwind Srs.3 were also delivered :

N-7024	WA.692 ex G-17-1	
N-7025	WA.693 ex G-17-2	d/d 27.3.69

An example of the essentially similar Sikorsky S.55C was obtained in 1963, and serialled N-7014 c/n 55.1190 ex PT-HAJ, but was written off on 28.11.64.
Three Whirlwind Srs.3 are said to remain in service.

WESTLAND WASP HAS.Mk.1

The first three were obtained in 1966, for use by ESQD HU-1 aboard the newly-delivered frigates :

N-7015	c/n F.9614	ex G-17-1	w/o 15.7.67
N-7016	F.9615		w/o prior to delivery and replaced by.....
N-7016	F.9542	ex XS746	
N-7017	F.9616		

Another seven were ordered in 1977 from surplus Royal Navy stocks :

N-7036	F.9589	XT419	d/d 27.7.77
N-7037	F.9728	XV633	d/d 15.11.77
N-7038	F.9575	XS564	d/d 15.11.77
N-7039	F.9603	XT433	d/d 1978
N-7040	F.9557	XS530	d/d 1978
N-7041	F.9674	XT792	d/d 8.12.78
N-7042	F.9569	XS542	d/d 1.8.79

N-7036 and N-7037 were initially serialled as N-7018 and N-7019, and were test flown prior to delivery as G-17-1 and G-17-21 respectively.. N-7038 to N-7042 similarly used the marks G-17-22, -6, -7, -8, and -30 respectively prior to delivery. N-7037 and N-7038 were allocated to the frigate *A Defensora*, N-7041 to *Constituição*; N-7036 went to frigate *Marílio Dias* and was lost in the sea on 21.11.77, being replaced by N-7042.

An additional batch of four ex Royal Navy Wasps was acquired in mid-1980, including XT422, XT428 and XT788; they are believed to have taken up serials in the range N-7043 to N-7049.

WESTLAND LYNX HAS.Mk.21

Nine ordered to be deployed aboard *Niterói* class frigates, although a couple will remain at São Pedro da Aldeia for communications duties.

N-3020	c/n WA.018	ex G-17-11	d/d 30.3.78
N-3021	WA.025		31.7.78
N-3022	WA.029	G-BFAU	5.7.78
N-3023	WA.032		5.5.78
N-3024	WA.041	G-17-16	30.3.78
N-3025	WA.042	G-17-17	1978
N-3026	WA.048	G-17-18	1978
N-3027	WA.050	G-17-19	5.5.78
N-3028	WA.062	G-17-20	5.7.78

Westland Lynx HAS.21 N-3020 test-flying as G-17-11 in 1978.

CHILE

Area	756,943 sq km
Population	11,200,000
Capital	Santiago
Civil registration	CC-

The Republic of Chile became independent from Spain on 18 September 1810 and has had a remarkably stable history in comparison to most other Latin American countries. The first serious civil unrest in recent times came in the early 1960s with the growth of left-wing political activism which finally led to the election of the Socialist leader Salvador Allende Gossens with communist and progressive catholic backing. Allende's Popular Unity Movement at once started an extremist social programme which caused the takeover of Chile's vital resources and industries by armed bands. The ensuing economic collapse eventually led to a military intervention in September 1973; the armed forces and Carabineros, led by the Army's Commander-in-Chief General Augusto Pinochet Ugarte, overthrew Allende's regime and initiated a social counter-revolution, against extreme pressure from both capitalist and communist countries, but finally managed to control inflation and bring law and order to the country.

Chile's aeronautical history can be traced as far back as March 1785 when the French balloon pioneer La Perouse tested a hot-air balloon at Concepción, but the first Chilean to fly over his country was young Ygnez Clark, who successfully test flew a balloon of his own design in 1839.

The first aircraft to fly in Chile took off from Batuco on 21 August 1910 and later that year the government took the first steps towards the formation of an air service. An Escuela de Aeronáutica Militar was formed on 11 February 1913 at Lo Espejo (later renamed El Bosque), commanded by Chile's first military aviator, Capitán Don Manuel Avalos Prado. Initial equipment consisted of seven Blériots (two with 35hp engines, three with 50hp engines and two with 80hp engines), a Deperdussin monoplane, a Voisin biplane, four Breguet biplanes (three 80hp, one 100hp) and four examples of the Chilean-designed, French-built Sánchez Besa biplane. Flying training started on 7 March 1913 and the Servicio de Aviacion Militar de Chile was so firmly established a few months later that it organised South America's first flying display, at El Bosque, on 1 January 1915. Even more important was the participation of military aircraft in that year's Army manoeuvres.

Very few aircraft were obtained during the First World War. A Morane-Saulnier monoplane arrived during 1916 and a SPAD VII in 1918; but Britain supplied in 1918-19 twelve Bristol M.1C fighter monoplanes (from the C4901/5025 batch) to equip Chile's Primera Compañía de Aviación (First Aviation Company) at El Bosque. An M.1C retaining Royal Flying Corps markings and the serial C4988 was used by Teniente Dagoberto Godoy Fuentealba for the first aerial crossing of the Andes, between El Bosque and Mendoza in Argentina on 12 December 1918. An expansion of the service began in 1919-20, with the formation of an Inspectorate General of Aviation, the acquisition of additional aircraft (beginning with a Nieuport 17 and six Avro 504K serialled 82 to 87, c/ns 355 to 360 in 1920), and the establishment of a Meastranza Central (Central Workshops) at El Bosque, in charge of maintenance and eventually aircraft assembly — this later became the Fábrica Nacional de Aeronaves (FanAero - National Aircraft Factory). A British air mission arrived in 1921 to help to re-organise Chilean military aviation and aircraft procurement was subsequently intensified, although deliveries were rather slow. The Escuela de Aeronáutica was also re-organised, its aircraft being divided into two formations: Bandada de Instrucción (Primary Training Unit) and the Bandada de Entrenamiento (Advanced Training Unit). At this time, the school's Avro 504K were identified by both serial and name, examples being 77 Colchagua, 78 Capitán Avalos, 79 Mallico, 80 Chiloé, 81 Atacama, 82 Curicó.

Aircraft taken on charge during this period were a Nieuport 12, eight RAF SE.5a biplane fighters (one was E5814), twenty RAF-surplus Airco DH.9 and more Avro trainers including eight 504-O (another five 504-O serialled 20 to 24 were later built in Chile).

Four main airfields were in use by 1924 — El Bosque (Santiago), Los Cóndores (Iquique), Chamiza (Puerto Montt) and Maquehue (Temuco) — when

a German air mission arrived with two Junkers monoplanes (an F.13 and an A.20) which were used by the military for the establishment of an internal airline network, although the F.13 crashed at Antofagasta in the following year. German influence reflected itself in the placement of orders for Junkers A.20 army co-operation aircraft, F.13 and W.34 transports, six R.42 trimotor bombers (which were serialled 31 to 36) and a Dornier Do C Merkur bomber, the A.20, F.13 and R.42 and the Dornier equipping an Esquadrilla de Bombardeo (Bomber Squadron) formed on 12 July 1928.

Other machines however, came from North America — six Vickers Vedette V flying boats from Canada (serialled 1 to 6; three were c/n CV.92 ex G-CAUS, CV.98 ex G-CAUU, CV.99 ex G-CAUV) for an Escuadrilla de Anfíbios (Amphibian Squadron) formed at El Bosque on 27 July 1929, and four Curtiss Hawk II fighter biplanes (c/n 11767 and c/n SH.7 to SH.9 on floats) to replace the Vickers Wibaults of the Grupo Mixto de Aviación N° 1 (No.1 Mixed Air Group) at El Bosque. In the event eight P-1A and eight Hawk III (P-1B) fighters and thirty O-1E Falcon army co-operation aircraft were taken on charge and there were plans for series production of both types at the Fábrica de Aviones del Ejército (Army Aircraft Factory). Eight Falcons were subsequently transferred to Brazil.

Britain supplied sixty-four de Havilland Moth primary trainers (DH.60X G.1 to G.24 c/ns 651/671, 673/675; DH.60G G.25 to G.64 c/ns 930/969), which were widely used for communications duties as well, on wheels or floats; twenty Avro 626 advanced training biplanes (serialled 1 to 20 c/ns 828 to 847), which were plagued with maintenance troubles and had to be grounded in 1941; and a series of Vickers designs. These included a Type 147 Valiant army co-operation aircraft (ex G-EBVM), demonstrated as a Vixen replacement, one Type 102 Valparaiso I which broke the South American altitude record late in 1924 and was the prototype for a series of Portuguese developments; eighteen Type 116 Vixen V general purpose aircraft (serials 1 to 18) ordered in mid-1925, and twenty-six

Vickers-built Wibault 7 C1 monoplane fighters (Type 121, serials included W3 to W17, W22 to W27). Wibaults and Vixens were allocated to the Grupos Mixtos de Aviacion N°s 1 and 3 at El Bosque and Maquehue respectively. Other British aircraft which followed included seven Avro 504N, an additional twenty-one DH.60G Gipsy Moths (G.65 to G.85), and twelve Bristol 83B Lucifer biplanes (serialled B1 to B12) another four (B13 to B16) being built at the Maestranza de Aviación.

The military-operated LAN (Líneas Aéreas Nacionales) received eight Fairchild FC.2 light transports and three Ford 5-AT-C trimotors which flew in military markings.

The Army and Naval air arms merged on 21 March 1930 to form the Fuerza Aérea Nacional (National Air Force) — later renamed the Fuerza Aérea de Chile (FACH) — with a degree of independence and flexibility that made it the most efficient Latin American air force of the period. Equipment was plentiful and serviceable, and personnel training was of a high standard. The FAN comprised Grupo Mixto de Aviación N° 1 at Iquique with Curtiss Hawks and Falcons; Grupo de Co-operación Aeronaval N°2 at Quintero (the former naval air arm) with Fairey IIIF floatplanes and Dornier Wal flying boats; Grupo Mixto de Aviación N°3 at Maquehue with Vixens, Wibaults and Falcons; an Escuadrilla de Bombardeo Independiente at Chillán with Junkers and Dornier types; an Escuadrilla de Anfíbios at Chamiza (Puerto Montt) with Vedettes and Gipsy Moths, which became the Escuadrilla N° 1 when an Escuadrilla de Anfíbios N°2 was formed on 16 December 1930 at Punta Arenas with Falcons and a Junkers R.42; the Escuela de Aeronáutica Militar at El Bosque; and a Gabinete de Fotogrametría Aérea (Air Survey Bureau) with a specially-modified Vixen. There were also maintenance workshops and an aircraft factory.

German influence in Chile grew during the mid-1930s mainly as a result of Germany's pioneering work in the development of South American air transport, but also due to the fact that several German engineers and pilots had left for South

America as a result of political differences with the Weimar government. Thus it was logical that orders were placed for German aircraft, particularly after 1933 — and these included eight Junkers Ju 86K-1 bombers and a Ju 86Z-1 transport, fifteen Focke-Wulf Fw 44 primary trainers (which equipped the FAN's first aerobatic team) and six Arado Ar 95 general purpose aircraft, three Ar 95A-1 floatplanes and three Ar 95B landplanes. Italy supplied small numbers of Nardi FN.305 basic trainers and Breda Ba 65 attack aircraft (serials included 5, 7, 8, 13, and 17), but further purchases were limited by available funds, although both Germany and Italy were more than willing to help. Both countries were already firmly established in Argentina and Brazil where many Germans had settled and it was believed that European influence would be an effective counterpart to the ever-present American economic expansion. But world political changes eventually modified the service's procurement plans, although the German aircraft were very satisfactory in service; the same cannot be said about the Italian machines which were rather disappointing, perhaps because of poor maintenance.

Imports from the United States included a Loening amphibian and two Sikorsky S.43 flying boats, named *Chiloé* and *Magellanes*, for the Escuadrilla de Anfibios Nº1 and a Sikorsky S.38 for the Escuadrilla de Anfibios Nº2, which was eventually written off. In August 1940 an order was placed for twelve North American NA.44 attack bombers (charge number NA.74 c/ns 74-4745 to 4756).

In 1939 the Fuerza Aérea Nacional de Chile had its headquarters at Santiago and comprised:

1ª Brigada Aérea
Grupo de Aviación Nº1 — Los Cóndores (Iquique)
Grupo de Aviación Nº2 — Quintero (Valparaiso)
Grupo de Aviación Nº3 — Maquehue (Temuco)
Grupo de Defensa Antiaérea — El Bosque (Santiago)

2ª Brigada Aérea
Grupo de Aviación Nº4 — El Bosque (Santiago)
Grupo de Aviación Nº5 — La Chamiza (Puerto Montt)
Grupo de Aviación Nº6 — Magellanes (Punta Arenas)

Dirección de Entrenamiento (Training Directorate)
Escuela de Aeronáutica Militar — El Bosque
Escuela de Especialistas — El Bosque
Escuela de Mecánicos — El Bosque
Escuela de Armamentos — Quintero (Valparaiso)

The Grupos Nºs4, 5, and 6 were the former Escuadrilla de Bombardeo, Escuadrilla de Anfibios Nº1 and Escuadrilla de Anfibios Nº2 respectively.

United States expansion in South America, which had escalated following the outbreak of the war in Europe, reached its peak after the Japanese raid on Pearl Harbor in December 1941. Chilean military aviation was taken over by an American air mission which reorganised the FACH along USAAF lines and approved the delivery of Lend-Lease aircraft, 231 eventually being delivered — Consolidated PBY-5 and OA-10 Catalinas, Douglas A-24B attack bombers (at least thirteen serialled 700 to 712), Fairchild PT-19, PT-23 and PT-26 primary trainers, North American AT-6 Texan advanced trainers and B-25 Mitchell medium bombers, Republic P-47D Thunderbolt fighter-bombers, Vought OS2U-3 Kingfisher observation floatplanes and Vultee BT-13 basic trainers. The Grupos were allotted to four Brigadas Aéreas with headquarters at Antofagasta, El Bosque, Maquehue (later Puerto Montt) and Punta Arenas respectively, and a fighter-bomber conversion unit was formed at Los Cóndores. A single NAF N3N-1 primary training biplane (serial 500, ex Bu0719) was delivered for evaluation and later modified for glider towing.

When the war ended, the FACH was almost totally Americanised:

Grupo de Aviación Nº1 — North American AT-6 (incorporating an Escuela de Tiro y Bombardeo, or Gunnery and Bombing School)
Grupo de Aviación Nº2 — AT-6, PT-19, OS2U-3, PBY-5/OA-10, plus two Ar 95A-1 which flew for as long as there were spares.
Grupo de Aviación Nº3 — Gipsy Moth, AT-6 and BT-13.
Grupo de Aviación Nº4 — Junkers Ju 86K, AT-6 and Douglas A-24B.

Grupo de Aviación Nº5 — AT-6, BT-13, PT-19, plus a couple of Avro 626 returned to service.
Grupo de Aviación Nº6 — Sikorsky S.43, A-24B, AT-6.

The Escuela de Aeronáutica was also mainly equipped with US types, flying alongside a few Focke-Wulf Fw 44. No Italian aircraft remained in use.

The war's end presented Chile with a number of problems. United States influence had grown enormously, now that no European country was strong enough to expand overseas; the political scenario was completely changed, with different strategic requirements; and the country's economy was not exactly healthy. The United States training mission left Chile in 1946, following which procurements were limited to small numbers of trainers and light aircraft, often supplied under MAP agreements (an outstanding example was a single Ryan L17A Navion delivered in 1947 which remained in active service until 1961). An important requirement was the creation of a transport force separate from the state airline. A Grupo de Transporte was activated at Los Cerrillos on 29 December 1945 with a handful of Beechcraft C-45 plus a number of PT-19, BT-13 and AT-6 trainers, subsequently receiving the first few Douglas C-47 and becoming Grupo Nº10.

Despite the difficulties it was decided to expand the FACH, beginning with Grupo Nº7, formed at Los Cerrillos on 1 September 1949; this was later to become the first FACH jet unit, receiving five de Havilland DH.115 Vampire T.55 trainers in 1954, and Lockheed F-80C Shooting Stars in May 1959; the latter were also used for the *Cóndores de Plata (Silver Condors)* aerobatic team. On 6 February 1948, the P-47D Thunderbolts were grouped into Grupo de Caza Nº1 (later Nº5) which eventually became Grupo de Caza-Bombardeo Nº11; an additional twenty-eight Thunderbolts were delivered in 1952 to make up for attrition. Also in February 1948, Grupo 2 was restricted to an Escuadrilla de Exploración y Rescate (Search and Rescue Squadron) flying Catalinas from Quintero,

continued on page 113

Sikorsky S-61R 'H-72' of the Argentine Air Force's VII Brigada Aerea

Convair 440-61 TAM-43 of the Bolivian Air Force is ex-Aviaco EC-ARP, and was photographed in February 1979.

IAI 201 Arava TAM.80 seen on delivery to the Bolivian Air Force at Keflavik in 1976 was the last of six.

Embraer EMB.326GB Xavante of the Brazilian Air Force, seen during 1979.

Embraer EMB.110 Bandeirante C-95 2133 of the Brazilian Air Force at Rio/Santos Dumont in June 1978.

de Havilland Canada DHC.5A Buffalo (C-115) '2350' of the Brazilian Air Force

Embraer EMB.326GB Xavante '4563' of the Brazilian Air Force

Cessna A-37B J-630 ex-USAF 75-0438 prior to delivery to the Chilean Air Force from Wichita in May 1977.

Lockheed T-33A FAC-2013A for the Colombian Air Force seen at Marana, Arizona in March 1978.

North American/Cavalier P-51D Mustang of the Dominican Air Force at Sanisidro in June 1973.

Hawker Siddeley 748 Srs 260 FAC-1101 of Satena, the Colombian Air Force 'airline' at Bogota in 1977.

Bolivian Air Force aeriel survey **Learjet 25B '008'** and below, **Neiva T-25 Universal '101'** of the Chilean Army

Fokker F-28-1000 Fellowship '001', the Colombian Air Force presidential aircraft

Lockheed 188A Electra FAE.1040/HC-AZT of TAME, Ecuador at Quito in 1977.

Vought F4U-4 Corsairs 615, 614 etc of the Honduran Air Force at San Pedro Sula in May 1975.

Grumman HU-16D Albatross MP-106 of the Mexican Navy during a visit to San Antonio, Texas.

de Havilland Canada DHC-3 Otters 303 and 302 of the Panamanian Air Force at Tocumen on 20 June 1973.

Beech T-34C Mentor '0028' of the Ecudorian Air Force

Bell 206 Jet Ranger 'JDFH-4' of the Jamaica Defence Force, at Up Park Camp, Kingston, in April 1975

Mil Mi-8 EP-507 of the Peruvian Army at Lima in 1977.

Canadair CF-5A 6719 of Esc. Caza 36, Venezuelan Air Force at Palo Negro July 1976.

Cessna 337A TTDF-1, the first aircraft of the Trinidad and Tobago Defence Force, seen at Piarco in July 1968.

Hunting Jet Provost T.52 6780 of the Venezuelan Air Force EAM, at Maracay in July 1976.

de Havilland Canada DHC-6 Twin Otter 300, serialled '313' from the Peruvian Air Force

where the new, B-25 equipped Grupo de Bombardeo Mediano N° 8 was based.

Eight de Havilland Canada DHC.2 Beaver utility transports were ordered in 1952 for Grupo de Transporte N° 10, its Texans being at the same time disposed of to other units. In 1953 the Beechcraft T-34 Mentor was selected as the FACH's standard primary training aircraft, thirty-six being ordered, plus another thirty at a later date; maintenance and spares availability were made easier by Argentina's choice of the same type and its local manufacture, as relations between Chile and neighbouring Argentina were then, as now, quite friendly. Half a dozen Beechcraft D18S crew-trainers were added in 1955 to the C-45 and AT-11 in use, having in addition provision for photo-survey equipment. Five Beechcraft Twin Bonanza C50 followed in 1956, during which year an order was placed for fifty FanAero-designed Chincol primary trainers, although in the event they were never built. The obsolescent B-25 Mitchells were replaced from 1954 onwards by Douglas B-26 Invaders, which entered service with Grupo N° 8 at Cerro Moreno (Antofagasta) in December 1954; four B-26B and thirty-four B-26C were eventually delivered, most being written off in accidents, the last two surviving machines being converted to staff transports and allocated to Grupo N° 10 at Los Cerrillos.

Also during this period, FACH activities in the Chilean Antarctic Territories were organised. A Base Aérea Antártica named after Presidente Gabriel González Videla was activated at Bahía Paraíso in March 1952, serving until 1966 and again in 1968-69. In February 1955, BAA Presidente Pedro Aguirre Cerda was inaugurated at Isla Decepción, becoming the most important Antarctic base until it was destroyed by a volcanic eruption on 4 December 1967. The current FACH Antarctic base is a weather station, Centro Meteorológico Antárctico Presidente Eduardo Frei Montalva, inaugurated on 7 March 1969, and regular flights are made between it and the mainland, usually with Twin Otter light transports, although Lockheed C-130 Hercules have also operated from the base.

There are smaller Antarctic airstrips at Base General Bernardo O'Higgins, Base Presidente Gabriel González Videla, and Base Teniente Rodolfo Marsch.

Other aircraft obtained during the 1950s were five DHC.3 Otters in 1957, which like the Twin Bonanzas were allocated to Grupo N° 5 at El Tepual (Puerto Montt), and small numbers of Bell 47 and Sikorsky S.55 helicopters, which initially went to Grupo N° 10 but were later transferred to Grupo de Helicópteros N° 3, incorporating an Escuela de Helicópteros (Helicopter School). Partial reorganisations were occasionally made — Grupo 4 passed its Douglas A-24B to Grupo 6 and became Grupo de Caza-Escolta N° 4 (No.4 Escort Fighter Group) until its disbandment in 1956, and Grupo N° 2 specialised in ASW duties with the arrival of the first Grumman SA-16A Albatrosses in 1958 — but it was clear that some modernisation was urgently needed. A specialised SAR unit was activated on 2 August 1971, but the most important decision taken at the time was the choice of the Hawker Hunter jet fighter, an efficient and reliable aircraft well suited to the Chilean air defence scenario, as the FACH's standard fighter, supplementing (and later replacing) the Vampires and Shooting Stars. The latter, together with a number of T-33A trainers, formed Grupo N° 12 in February 1967 (this was disbanded in 1974 and reformed in 1977 with the Cessna A-37B; while the Hunters went to Grupo N° 7 at Los Cerrillos in 1964, then also to Grupo N° 8 at Cerro Moreno (which became the Unidad-Escuela de Caza-Bombardeo, or Fighter-Bomber OCU, as it still is) and in 1970 also to Grupo N° 9 at El Tepual. Interestingly enough, the Hunters, which had been ordered because the twenty-five North American F-86F Sabres promised under MDAP were not delivered, proved extremely successful in service and remain very active despite occasional spares shortages (usually the result of political argument). As recently as 1978 a plan to acquire up to a hundred ex Indian Air Force Hunters was said to be under consideration, and in April 1982 six or eight aircraft were reported to have been supplied from Royal Air Force stocks.

During Allende's revolutionary period, Chile was turned so much towards the Soviet Union that it was offered Mikoyan MiG-21F fighters on incredibly favourable terms to replace the ageing Hunters, but the military preferred the Northrop F-5E Tiger II, and, oddly enough, its export was approved by the United States government (although in the event the recipient was the anti-communist Pinochet regime). United States arms supplies have in later years been limited by political considerations and 'human rights' campaigns, but still continue, with numbers of Cessna T-37 jet trainers and A-37 close-support aircraft. US Navy surplus A-4B Skyhawk light attack aircraft were at one stage offered — a proposal which was made attractive by the use of the type in Argentina by both the air force and navy — but none were ever ordered.

An order for sixteen Dassault Mirage 5O fighter-bombers was approved by the French government in mid-1979. Initially these aircraft were thought to be ex-French surplus, ex-Israeli-order Mirage M5 re-engined with the SNECMA Atar 9K-50 turbojet, but are now believed to be newly-built; they are operated by Grupo N° 4, replacing Hunters, from a new base built at Santo Domingo de Las Rocas, though initially at Santiago's Arturo Merino Benítez International Airport (formerly known as Pudahuel). A number of Chilean pilots were sent to France in late 1979 for conversion training.

Early in 1980, the Piper Dakota 236 (a Cherokee variant) was selected as the standard Chilean primary trainer, and a number were ordered, to be assembled at the FACH's own workshops. Another Cherokee-based aircraft, the PA-28-300XBT Pillan has been developed as an aerobatic trainer and is also being built for the FACH by Indaer at Santiago, who are also to build a batch of up to fifty of the Spanish CASA C-101BB Aviojet (to be known as the T-36 Halcon in FACH service) after assembling the first batch of eight built in Spain; these are to replace the Cessna T-37s and A-37s.

Current Organisation

The Fuerza Aérea de Chile, which has about 11,000 personnel, consists of five Alas de Combate (Combat Wings), two independent Grupos, training and maintenance elements, a photo-survey service, a gliding school and a Regimento de Artillería Anti-Aérea (Anti-Aircraft Artillery Regiment) with headquarters at Colina and Grupos de Artillería Anti-Aérea N°s 21 to 25 attached to Alas 1 to 5 respectively. Units are :

COMANDO DE COMBATE (Combat Command)

Ala N° 1 - Base Aérea de Cerro Moreno,Antofagasta
 Grupo N° 7   Northrop F-5E/F
 Grupo N° 8   Hawker Hunter F.71/T.72, DH
         Vampire Trainer (Unidad-Escuela
         de Caza-Bombardeo)
 Grupo N° 9   Hawker Hunter F.71/FR.71

Ala N° 2 - BA de Quintero, Valparaiso
 Grupo N° 11 Beechcraft 99A (Unidad de Instr-
         uccion de Vuelo por Instrumentos
         y Navegación Aérea - IFR and Air
         Navigation Training Unit)

Ala N° 3 - BA General Carlos Ibáñez, Punta Arenas
 Grupo N° 6   Douglas C-47, DHC.6 Twin Otter
         (at nearby Bahía Catalina airfield)
 Grupo N° 12 Cessna A-37B

Ala N° 4 - BA de Los Cóndores (Iquique-Chacumata)
 Grupo N° 1   Cessna A-37B
 Grupo N° 4   Dassault Mirage 50
         (at Santiago-Padahuel)

Ala N° 5 - BA de El Tepual, Puerto Montt
 Grupo N° 5   DHC.6 Twin Otter, Sikorsky S.55T,
         Neiva Universal

Grupo de Helicopteros N° 3 - BA de Maquéhue, Temuco (including the *Escuela de Helicópteros*) with Bell UH-1H and Hiller UH12E/SL4; this disbanded early 1981 and the helicopters were transferred to other units.

Grupo de Transporte N° 10 - BA de Los Cerrillos, Santiago, with Douglas C-47 and DC-6, Lockheed C-130H, Beechcraft King Air, Sud SA.315B Lama and Sud SA.330 Puma (VIP) and Bell UH-1D/H.

COMANDO DE PERSONAL (Personnel Command)
DIRECCION DE INSTRUCCIÓN (Training Directorate)

Escuela de Aviación 'Capitán Avalos' at El, Bosque Santiago, with Beechcraft T-34A, Cessna T-37B/C

Escuela de Vuelo sin Motor at Las Condes Municipal Airfield, Santiago (Sailplane School), with Cessna L-19A, Standard Cirrus, LET Blanik

Escuela de Especialidades at El Bosque, Santiago (Specialists' School) with Cessna 182, 206, T-41D, Piper Dakota 236

Academia de Guerra Aérea (Air Warfare Academy) at El Bosque, Santiago; no aircraft.

Academia Politécnica Aeronáutica (Polytechnic Air Academy) at El Bosque, Santiago; no aircraft.

COMANDO LOGÍSTICO (Logistics Command)
Ala de Abastecimiento (Supply Wing), El Bosque
Ala de Mantenimiento (Maintenance Wing) at El Bosque, Santiago.

Each Ala also controls an Escuadrilla de Enlace, or base communications flight, with a mixture of Douglas C-47 and Sud SA.315B Lama, and in the case of Alas 1, 2 and 5, Sikorsky S.55T for rescue duties.

 There is also a Servicio Aerofotogramétrico (Air Photographic Survey Service) at Los Cerrillos with two DHC.6 Twin Otters, one Beechcraft King Air A100 and two Lear Jet 35.

Military Air Bases

1   Santiago (El Bosque, Los Cerrillos)
2   Valparaíso (Quintero)
2A El Belloto
3   Los Andes
4   Arica
5   Iquique (Los Cóndores)
6   Antofagasta (Cerro Moreno)
7   Vallenar
8   Coquimbo - La Serena
9   Chillán
10 Concepción
10A Temuco
11 Valdivia
12 Río Bueno
13 Puerto Montt (El Tepual)
14 Coihaiqué
15 Puerto Natales
16 Punta Arenas (Carlos Ibáñez, Bahía Catalina)

Ala Nº1 - white outer circle with dark blue edging and lettering. Mid-blue inner background with grey fist and flail with black detail and blue shading.

Ala Nº2 - yellow outer circle with grey edging and black lettering. Dark blue 'swan' with white edging, red beak; mid-blue background; turquoise sea with grey 'waves'.

Ala Nº3 - white outer circle with blue edging and lettering. Mid-blue centre, red '3' edged in dark blue; dark blue map; orange bird's head with red crest, white neck and dk blue wings.

Ala Nº4 - white outer circle with black edging and lettering. Mid-blue centre with black/grey bird with orange head and red beak.

Ala Nº5 - black outer circle with white edging and lettering. Mid-blue centre with red 'aircraft' and chain with black detail. Black lettering 'Unidos Cumpliremos'.

Grupo Nº1 - white outer circle with black edging and lettering. Mid-blue centre; white/grey bird's head and red tongue.

Grupo Nº2 - blue outer circle with white edging and lettering. Mid-blue centre with turquoise sea black submarine and ASW lettering. Yellow bird with orange feet and bill, red lifejacket, white cap with green visor, red '2' and black eye and details.

Grupo Nº3 - white outer circle with dark blue edging and lettering and pale blue '3'. Mid-blue centre, with white topped pale blue mountain. Bird's head is white with dark blue outline and eye.

Grupo Nº4 - white outer circle with black edging and lettering. Mid-blue centre with grey mailed fist and axe with black detail; white aircraft and contrails.

Grupo Nº4 (old badge) white outer circle with grey edging and black lettering; red centre, grey knife and black bat with white teeth and eyes.

Grupo Nº5 - white outer circle with dark blue edging, black lettering. Mid-blue centre with red '5' and stars, white mountain tops and stylised bird running through to of '5'.

Grupo Nº5 (old badge) - white outer circle with dark blue edging, black lettering. Mid-blue centre with black/white penguin with yellow beak & feet, green scarf, blue umbrella with red handle; red stars and lightning bolt.

Grupo N°6 - white outer circle with black edging and lettering. Mid-blue centre with black/white sealion. The segments of the globe are black-lined, antarctica is white and other continents dark blue. White stars.

Grupo N°10 - white outer circle with black edging and lettering. Mid-blue inner with black '1' and '0'/globe and red 'bird'.

Ala de Mantenimiento - dark blue outer circle edged in black and grey; mid-blue centre with grey/black propeller, gears etc.

Grupo N°7 - white outer circle with black edging and lettering. Mid-blue centre; red '7' edged in white; dark blue 'bird' edged in white. National insignia blue top, red lower half and white star all black-edged.

Grupo N°11 - white outer circle with dark blue edging and black lettering; mid-blue top and dark blue lower centre with white compass markings (three red in bottom segment), gold star.

Ala de Abastecimiento - white outer circle with black edging and lettering; mid-blue centre with white peaked grey mountains, blue scroll with black lettering 'sustimeo', gold pedestal, black bird with white head, orange beak.

Grupo N°8 - dark blue outer circle edged in black with white lettering. Yellow centre with red '8' over a black bird/bomb.

Grupo N°12 - grey outer circle with blue edging and black lettering. Mid-blue centre with yellow/black tiger, with white blazes on face and chest, red/black mouth.

Base Aérea - dark blue outer circle with grey/black edging and white lettering. Mid-blue centre with grey/white/black motif, black lettering 'MCMXXX' and yellow stars.

Grupo N°9 - black outer circle with white lettering; interior black on white.

Servicio de Busqueda y Salvamento - yellow outer circle with black edging and lettering; mid-blue centre with green/grey helicopter, red rotor and skids, white tail rotor over a black 'map'.

Regimiento de Artilleria dark blue outer circle with white edging and lettering. Mid-blue inner with yellow wings and yellow/orange/red flame, and other details in grey. Black lettering '15-Mayo-1930'.

Aircraft Review

COLOURS AND MARKINGS

The first Chilean military aircraft arrived from Britain and flew with British markings for most of their careers — the national colours of both countries were identical and British influence in Chile was considerable — but Chile had from an early date a distinctive national marking, a blue/red shield with a white star superimposed, which was based on the 1817 national flag designed by Charles Wood, a US mercenary serving in the Chilean Army, and broadly inspired by the Stars and Stripes. The blue stands for the Andes sky, red for the blood shed for liberty, white for the snow-capped Andes and the star is the 'guide star towards honour and progress'. The same motif was adopted for naval aircraft, the shield being replaced by a white outlined square.

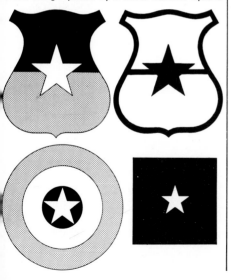

Both were superseded by a French-style red/white/blue roundel with a white star on the blue centre, which was displayed on both wings and fuselage. In all cases, the rudder was painted blue with a white star thereon. The shield marking was eventually adopted by all services, naval aircraft differing in having a white star and anchor on their blue rudders. More recently the decision to tone down FACH markings led to the adoption of two solutions: the shield was applied in black in 'ghost' form, with the camouflage showing through its outline, and the rudder star was applied in black; or the only national markings to be worn were the underwing shield and a white rudder star, plus of course the serial number (in some cases the underwing shield was even deleted).

The inscription *Fuerza Aérea de Chile* appears on most transports and helicopters. Unlike many countries which specify the use of inscriptions or numbers on the wings, the FACH applies the shield on the starboard upper and port undersides and the serial number on the port upper and starboard under surfaces — the opposite of US practice.

Political events occurring in Chile during the 1960s and 1970s determined the widespread adoption of camouflage: delivery schemes were previously retained, trainers having orange or red areas added. The US scheme of dark green/green/tan with light grey undersides was just one of several schemes, all of which are still being applied — green/brown/tan with light grey or light blue undersides, green/grey with light grey undersides, green/brown/grey with light blue undersides, brown/tan with light grey or light blue undersides, or overall glossy black. Interceptors (F-5E and Mirage 50) are painted in the US air superiority scheme of light blue with darker blue areas, and ASW-equipped Albatrosses received the dark blue scheme with white undersides initially designed for Vietnam theatre; rescue Albatrosses were dark blue with white fuselage tops. Advanced trainers, once natural metal with red areas are now white with red areas. Rescue markings consist of yellow areas and fuselage bands with black outlines and the inscription *RESCATE*. Helicopters are olive green, green/grey with light blue undersides, or overall tan or brown/tan.

SERIAL NUMBERS

Postwar serial numbers were normally allocated in blocks, with frequent re-allocations. The letter prefixes H- and J- were used for helicopters and jet aircraft respectively. Serial blocks were initially :

01 to 49	- basic trainers
50 to 99	- trainers and helicopters
100 to 199	- primary trainers
200 to 299	- basic trainers
300 to 399	- fighters
400 to 499	- communications aircraft
500 to 599	- miscellaneous types
600 to 699	- close-support aircraft
700 to 799	- fighters and fighter-bombers
800 to 899	- bombers
900 to 999	- transports

Other aircraft were operated with civil registrations in the CC-EAA to EZZ block (E denotes Estatal, or government-owned).

Aircraft known to have been operated by the FACH in postwar years include the following :

BEECHCRAFT C-45 and D-18S

The C-45 were Lend-Lease deliveries, and the D18S post-war acquisitions; all were usually referred to as C-45. The type was phased out in 1976. Known serials are : 462, 463, 464, 465, 466, 482 (w/o in 1967), 484, 485, 486, 489, 490, 493 and 496.

BEECHCRAFT AT-11 KANSAN

Ten believed delivered in 1948; withdrawn from use in 1951. Known serials are 912, 916 and 918.

BEECHCRAFT TWIN BONANZA

Five aircraft, c/ns CH.355 to CH.359. Two, with serials 478 and 479, remain in service with the Escuela de Especialidades. Five model C50, c/ns CH.355 to CH.359. Two of these, with

Beechcraft 99 305, one of nine delivered in 1970 to Grupo No.11.

Bell 47D-1 H-03, one of three helicopters of the type supplied, but no longer in use.

Bell UH-1H Iroquois H-89 photographed at Los Cerrillos in April 1977.

Cessna 182 415, delivered as long ago as 1956 with the serial 315, and still in use with the Escuela de Especialidades.

Cessna A-37B J-629 seen at Wichita before delivery on 5 March 1977.

serials 478 and 479, remain in service with the Escuela de Especialidades. Six model D50A, serialled 916 and 917, and 991 to 994.

BEECHCRAFT BARON 56TC

One only, serialled 471, c/n TG.61, delivered in January 1968, also operated by the Dirección de Aeronáutica Civil as A-2.

BEECHCRAFT KING AIR

Deliveries comprised one King Air 90 serialled 498, and one King Air A100 CC-ESA c/n B.219, equipped for photo survey and used by the Servicio Aerofotogramétrico.

BEECHCRAFT 99

Nine aircraft delivered in July-August 1970 to equip the re-activated Grupo No.11; also used as IFR trainers.

300	c/n U.137	callsign CC-EEO ex N9073Q
301	U.138	CC-EEP
302	U.139	CC-EEQ
303	U.140	CC-EER
304	U.141	CC-EES
305	U.142	CC-EET
306	U.143	CC-EEU
307	U.144	CC-EEV
308	U.145	CC-EEW

BEECHCRAFT T-34A

Thirty-six were delivered in 1953, ten in 1956, and another twenty later. Serials were 101 to 166; aircraft 117 had c/n CG.21 and 144 was c/n CG.152 ex 53-3391. All went to the Escuela de Aviación Capitán Avalos and six were later transferred to the Navy. Known crashes took place on 26.3.75 and 10.10.75.

BELL 47D-1

Three only, no longer in use :

H-01	c/n 630	
H-02	631	preserved at Museo de Aeronáutica, Santiago
H-03	655	

BELL UH-1H

Thirteen delivered, serials H-80 to H-92.

BOEING 727-22C

One aircraft serialled 901, c/n 19196 ex Western Airlines N7421U, delivered 14.1.81 for VIP use.

CASA C-101BB AVIOJET

Eight examples of this armed export version of the Spanish trainer, with eight options, are reported to be on order, to be supplied in kit form and assembled locally; up to fifty may be built to replace the T-37B/C and A-37B, and will be known as the T-36 Halcón in FACh service. The serial of the first aircraft is 401.

CESSNA 180

At least two delivered, one of which is believed to be serialled 107.

CESSNA 182

Ten aircraft delivered in September 1956 as 315 to 324 but later reserialled as 415 to 424.

415	c/n 33559	ex N5559B
416	33377	N5377B
417	33398	N5398B
418	33399	N5399B
419	33404	N5404B
420	33376	N5376B
421	33560	N5560B
422	33588	N5588B
423	33589	N5589B
424	33601	N5601B

Not all are current, but the Escuela de Especialidades operates 415, 420 and 421.

CESSNA 550 CITATION II

The Chilean Government took delivery of CC-ECN c/n 550-0104 ex N2633N, during 1980.

CESSNA L-19A

Six aircraft entered service in 1953, being allotted to Grupo 4 de Bombardeo Ligero at La Colina :

401	c/n 22880	ex US 53-2873
402	22881	53-2874
403	22882	53-2875
404	22883	53-2876
405	22884	53-2877
406	22885	53-2878

Aircraft 403, 404 and 405 remain in service with the Escuela de Vuelo sin Motor as glider tugs.

CESSNA T-37B/C

Initial deliveries included T-37B J-370 to J-373 and T-37C J-374 to J-397 :

J-370	ex 60-155	
J-371	60-156	w/o
J-372	60-157	
J-373	60-158	
J-374	62-12491	
J-375	62-12492	w/o
J-376	62-12493	
J-377	62-12494	
J-378	62-12495	w/o
J-379	63-9826	
J-380	63-9827	w/o
J-381	59-259	w/o
J-382	63-9841	
J-383	63-9842	
J-384	63-9843	
J-385	64-13429	
J-386	59-258	
J-387	59-277	
J-388	60-85	
J-389	60-132	
J-390	58-1934	
J-391	58-1885	
J-392	60-102	
J-393	59-364	
J-394	59-300	
J-395	59-359	
J-396	60-184	
J-397	59-302	

Three replacement aircraft were subsequently delivered, with duplicate serials :

J-371	58-1892
J-375	60-126
J-380	58-1966
J-381	60-79

Additionally T-37B 60-191/194 and T-37C 62-12485/12490, 63-9818/9822. 63-9845, 64-13467/13468 are also believed to have been delivered to Chile.

CESSNA A-37B

Thirty-four aircraft delivered between March 1975 and 1977 for Grupos 1, 4 and 12 :

J-600 to J-615 ex USAF 74-998 to 74-1013
J-616 to J-633   75-424 to 75-441
One was written off on 27.5.78; another on 27.11.80.

CESSNA T-41D

At least fourteen delivered: confirmed serials are 201, 203, 204, 207, 208 and 214.

CONSOLIDATED PBY-5/OA-10 CATALINA

At least twelve, serialled 400 to 411. Aircraft 400 to 405 were PBY-5, the remainder OA-10. 405 'Manutara' was rebuilt as 560 'Manutara II'.

DASSAULT MIRAGE 50

Sixteen ordered in mid-1979 for Grupo N°4, the first aircraft being delivered on 27.6.80. Serials are J-500 to J-513 (50C) and J-514 and J-515 (50DC).

DE HAVILLAND DH.115 VAMPIRE TRAINER

Five Mark T.55 were initially delivered with serials J-01 to J-05; J-01 was c/n 15798 ex G-AOXH, delivered in April 1957.
Seven ex Royal Navy Sea Vampire T.22 were delivered as J-301 to J-307 (these included XA107, 128, 166, XG769, 772 and 777), followed on 10.11.72 by three ex Royal Air Force T.11s (WZ512, XE857 and XJ774). Additional aircraft must have followed, because serials J-310 and J-322 have been confirmed. A Vampire Trainer was written off on 2.5.76, another on 24.5.79. A few remain in service with Grupo No.8.

DE HAVILLAND CANADA DHC.2 BEAVER

Eighteen were reportedly delivered and operated by Grupo de Transporte No.10, serialled 901 to 915 and 918 to 920. None remain in service. Further details of individual aircraft:

905	c/n 192	to CF-ZYE, N11252
906	194	
907	208	
908	213	
909	295	
910	316	to CF-HAN
911	353	
912	370	to CF-CQP, CF-TXG, N11257

DE HAVILLAND CANADA DHC.3 OTTER

Five were delivered in the first part of 1957 for use by the Grupo No.5 at El Tepual :

930	c/n 171	to N11250
931	176	to CF-HAS
932	190	wfu
933	193	wfu
934	195	wfu

Another nine, serialled 921 to 929 probably ex US Army, were reportedly delivered at a later date.

DE HAVILLAND CANADA DHC.5D BUFFALO

One aircraft, serialled 920, c/n 96 ex C-GTLW was delivered in November 1980.

DE HAVILLAND CANADA DHC.6 TWIN OTTER

Initial deliveries comprised eight DHC.6-100 for use by Grupo No.6; these arrived between October 1966 and March 1967 :

935	c/n 7	
936	10	
937	11	
938	16	w/o 17.11.72
939	20	to C-FQHC
940	24	
941	28	w/o 9.9.74
942	33	w/o 26.11.69

Six DHC.6-300 were delivered in May-June 1978 — note the reallocation of earlier serials :

932	583	
933	584	
934	585	
938	586	
941	589	
942	590	

Additional aircraft were obtained from the national airline LAN-Chile :

943	396	ex CC-CAE	w/o 11.7.80
944	397	CC-CBB	
945	398	CC-CBF	
946	399	CC-CBH	
947	404	CC-CBM	
948	405	CC-CBU	

DOUGLAS C-47

At least twenty-three were used, serialled 950 to 972; also 901 which became 942.
956 was c/n 4470 ex 41-18408 delivered 4.53. Aircraft withdrawn from use include 950, 954, 955, 967. 960 was written off, as was another aircraft on 31.7.75. 971 was a C-48A c/n 4148, ex N24 and 41-7684, temporarily used by the Dirección General de Aeronáutica Civil as A-1. About ten aircraft remain in service.

DOUGLAS DC-6

This transport entered service in 1966, with four ex-US civil aircraft supplied under MDAP and allocated USAF serials for delivery. The last of these, 988, was delivered in January 1968 and reportedly written off on 24.7.77. However, all four aircraft were disposed of in March 1982 to Atlas Aircraft Corp. Miami.

985	DC-6A c/n 45179	ex N93124,65-12816 to	N864TA
986	DC-6A 45177	N93122	N863TA
987	DC-6B 43522	N6522C,66-14467	N861TA
988	DC-6A 44057	N90772	N862TA

Two further aircraft are reported, ex LADECO :

989	DC-6B	CC-......
990	DC-6B	CC-......

DOUGLAS A-24B (DAUNTLESS)

At least thirteen delivered, serialled 700 to 712. They were initially used by Grupo No.4 and later Grupo No.6 and grounded through lack of spares.

Dassault Mirage 50C 504 shown at the FIDA exhibition at El Bosque early in 1982.

De Havilland Vampire T.55 J-310, wearing the Grupo 8 badge at El Bosque in March 1980.

Douglas C-47 Skytrain 951 of Grupo 10 at Los Cerrillos on 17 April 1977.

Douglas DC-6B 987 seen during a visit to Lima in 1977.

Grumman HU-16B Albatross 571 wearing the badge of Grupo 2 on the nose, was at Los Cerrillos on 17 April 1977.

Hawker Hunter FGA.71 X-001, an instructional aircraft, seen at El Bosque in March 1980.

Northrop F-5E Freedom Fighter J-806 (ex 75-0448), also at El Bosque in March 1980.

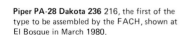

Piper PA-28 Dakota 236 216, the first of the type to be assembled by the FACH, shown at El Bosque in March 1980.

Sikorsky S.55T H-50, one of six converted from S.55C, seen here at El Bosque in March 1980.

DOUGLAS B-26 INVADER

Deliveries included four B-26B (two of which were later converted to staff transports) and thirty-four B-26C (ten in December 1954, seventeen in January 1957 and seven in March 1958). The type was declared surplus to requirements in 1975-76, though by that time many had been written off in service. Confirmed serials are 812 (w/o 16.11.62), 814, 815, 816, 817 (ex 44-34131 w/o 13.8.68), 818, 823 (w/o 21.3.64), 824, 826, 832, 835, 838 (w/o 5.62), 840, 841, 842, 843, 844 (w/o 9.4.64), 845, 846, 847, 848, 849 (ex 44-34735), 850, 851, 852, 853 and 854.

An airworthy B-26C was presented to the Confederate Air Force in March 1980, reported variously as 846 ex 44-35937 or 842 ex 43-22728. 848 is preserved at Mejillones Municipal Park, although another aircraft on display at El Bosque carries the same serial. There is also a gate-guardian at Cerro Moreno with the serial 863, though there is some likelihood that this is spurious.

FAIRCHILD PT-19 SERIES

About fifty PT-19, PT-23 and PT-26 were used until 1956. A PT-19 was serialled 73, and two PT-23 were 21 and 22.

GRUMMAN HU-16 ALBATROSS

Although there have been conflicting and persistent reports of fifteen aircraft serialled 560 to 574, it now seems that only six were delivered, probably serialled 566 to 571. In 1958 three SA-16A ex 49-097, 099 and 100 arrived, and these were followed in 1963 by three HU-16B ex 51-014, 024 and 7191. At least three of these were reconditioned to ASW standard, 571 being one of them; this was written off on 3.9.77. The type was withdrawn from use in 1979 and Grupo No.2 which had operated them was disbanded. 566, ex 49-097, was presented to the Confederate Air Force, becoming N8064N, with others passing to instructional use.

HAWKER HUNTER

A total of thirty-nine were delivered, comprising :

FGA.71 J-700/714, 721/733, 735, 737/738
FR.71A J-715/717, 734
T.72 J-718/720, 736

An FGA.71 became instructional airframe X-001. About eighteen remain operational with Grupos 8 and 9 (Black Panthers). A T.72 was written off on 26.3.80.

J-700	ex G-9-103 and Belgian AF	IF141	
J-701	G-9-104		IF106
J-702	G-9-105		IF108
J-703	G-9-106		IF44
J-704	G-9-227	R.Neth.AF	N-210
J-705	G-9-226		N-220
J-706	G-9-224		N-276
J-707	G-9-220		N-262
J-708	G-9-217		N-201
J-709	G-9-228		N-266
J-710	G-9-219		N-270
J-711	G-9-225		N-277
J-712	G-9-221		N-232
J-713	G-9-222		N-273
J-714	G-9-216	RAF	XG232
J-715	G-9-235		XK148
J-716	G-9-233		XF453
J-717	G-9-234		XJ717
J-718	G-9-232, G-APUX, (Iraq 567, Lebanon L581)		
J-719	G-9-218 and R.Neth.AF N-224		
J-720	G-9-223		N-202
J-721	G-9-296	RAF	XJ627
J-722	G-9-298		XJ713
J-723	G-9-299		XF447
J-724	G-9-312		XG199
J-725	G-9-313		XF512
J-726	G-9-318		XE561
J-727	G-9-319		XE557
J-728	G-9-322		XE644
J-729	G-9-331		XE625
J-730	G-9-332		XE580
J-731	G-9-379		WT801/7789M
J-732	G-9-380		XF323/8003M
J-733	G-9-382		XF302/7774M
J-734	G-9-383		XF317/7773M
J-735	G-9-396		WV326/7669M
J-736	G-9-397		XE704/7788M
J-737	G-9-398		WW653/7784M
J-738	G-9-391		XF982/7946M

A further six ex Royal Air Force aircraft were delivered by airfreight on 24 April 1982 :

J-	) These are thought to be,
J-	) though not respectively, ex :
J-	) XE546, XE582, XF376,
J-	) XF442, XJ686, XJ688.
J-	) all from RAF FGA.9 stocks.

HILLER UH-12E/SL4

Four UH-12E delivered June 1960; no longer in use :

H-60	c/n 2046		
H-61	2060	wfu	
H-62	2061	w/o 26.9.80	
H-63	2067	wfu	

Six UH-12E-4 (SL4) were delivered in September 1965 :

H-70	2521	to Paraguay AF
H-71	2523	
H-72	2524	
H-73	2528	
H-74	2529	
H-75	2531	to Paraguay AF

HILLER FH.1100

The Chilean Government took delivery of two, CC-ECK c/n 166 and CC-ECL c/n 170, which are no longer current.

LEAR JET 35

Two delivered in mid-1976 for the Servicio Aerofotogramétrico for photo survey work :

CC-ECO	c/n 35.050
CC-ECP	35.066

LOCKHEED F-80C

About thirty were delivered, and reportedly serialled J-321 to J-351; the following have been confirmed : J-325, 329, 330, 332, 333, 335, 336, 338, 339, 340, 341, 342, 345, 346, 347, 350 and 351. Of these 340 to 342 were ex USAF 49-454, 47-542 and 49-787 respectively. The first eighteen were delivered in January-March 1958 to Grupo No.7 de Caza-Bombardeo at Los Cerrillos, and were supplanted by Northrop F-5Es; surviving machines were then transferred to the Grupo 12 at Carlos Ibáñez, and withdrawn from use when it was disbanded in 1974. A few also saw service with Grupo 6.

LOCKHEED T-33A

The first four were delivered on 18.10.56, with four more acquired under MDAP in May 1964, and others at various unknown dates to a total of probably twenty aircraft, serialled in the J-300 range. J-315 to J-328 are confirmed, J-327 and J-328 being RT-33A. J-350, an RT-33A, and J-360 noted post-1972. A few were converted to AT-33A close support aircraft and used by Grupo No.12 pending delivery of the Cessna A-37B.

The last T-33A in service, J-314 and J-317 were withdrawn from use in 1974, the former being preserved at the Museo Aeronáutico in Santiago and the latter becoming a gateguardian at Bahia Catalina airfield. One known T-33A crash took place on 19.9.68.

LOCKHEED C-130H HERCULES

Two aircraft, model L.382C-28D, delivered to Grupo No.10 in 1972 :
995 c/n 4453
996   4496

NEIVA N.621 UNIVERSAL (T-25)

A number were obtained from Brazil — serials included 204 and 251 — and others from the Army in 1978-79 with the arrival of the Cessna R172K Hawk XPs; these later aircraft were serialled in the 310 block.

NORTH AMERICAN AT-6 TEXAN

Deliveries included twelve NA.74 (export version of the AT-6 with attack capability) and at least twenty T-6G, as well as small numbers of AT-6C and AT-6D. They were serialled in the 200 block, and confirmed serials include 209, 212, 239, 260, 261, 262, 266, 267, 269, 277, 279, 285, 287, 294, 295 and 297. A number of T-6G were armed and used by Grupo No.1 as interim equipment. No Texans remain in service, the last being withdrawn in 1978. AT-6D 200 and 201 were transferred to the Uraguay AF on 17.3.78 and serialled 378 and 379. T-6G is preserved at the Museo de Aeronáutica at Santiago with a spurious serial 200.

NORTH AMERICAN B-25J MITCHELL

Twelve aircraft delivered, serialled 800 to 811; withdrawn from use from 1954 to 1957.

NORTHROP F-5

Interest in the F-5 was first shown in 1967, but political difficulties prevented any order coming to fruition until 1976, when deliveries commenced in June of fifteen F-5E and three F-5F; they replaced Hunters with Grupo No.7.

F-5E :

J-800	c/n I-1001 ex USAF	75-442
J-801	I-1002	75-443
J-802	I-1003	75-444
J-803	I-1004	75-445
J-804	I-1005	75-446
J-805	I-1006	75-447
J-806	I-1007	75-448
J-807	I-1008	75-449
J-808	I-1009	75-450
J-809	I-1010	75-451
J-810	I-1011	75-452
J-811	I-1012	75-453
J-812	I-1013	75-454
J-813	I-1014	75-455
J-814	I-1015	75-456

F-5F :

J-815	J.1001	75-709
J-816	J.1002	75-710
J-817	J.1003	75-711

PIPER PA-28 DAKOTA 236

A number on order, to be assembled by FACH. 215 was the Piper-supplied pattern aircraft; the first to be assembled were serialled 216 to 218. Thirteen had been delivered by January 1982.

PIPER PA-28R-300XBT PILLAN (T-35)

A fully aerobatic trainer derivative of the Piper Cherokee series, using components from various models in order to keep costs as low as possible, and with a sliding canopy as its most distinguishing feature, this is to be produced by the Chilean Air Force who may acquire up to one hundred of the type. The first two aircraft were completed by Piper by mid-1981 (one was registered as N300BT), with the next three going to Chile in kit form. The type will be known as the T-35 Pillan in FACh service; first serial reported is 102.

PITTS SPECIAL

A small number of these aircraft seem to have been acquired to form an aerobatic display team; two were written off in a mid-air collision on 21.12.81.

REPUBLIC P-47D THUNDERBOLT

At least twenty were delivered under Lend-Lease during the war, equipping Grupo 1 and later Grupos 5 and 11. Another twenty-eight were delivered in 1952. The type was replaced by the Lockheed F-80 during 1958. Confirmed serials are 750, 757, 760, 762, 766 and 767, of which 750 is preserved at El Bosque.

SIKORSKY S.55/H-19

The first two S.55C were delivered in March 1957, followed by another two in May and four later; they were modified to H-19 standards, with provision for rescue equipment.

H-50	c/n 55.1059	converted to S.55T
H-51	55.1068	
H-52	55.1070	
H-53	55.1078	
H-54	55.1271	
H-55	55.1274	converted to S.55T
H-56	55.1280	
H-57	55.1281	

Another four have been converted to S.55T, and were allocated to Grupo No.2. When this was disbanded in 1979, they were passed to the SAR flights of Alas 1, 2 and 5.

SUD SA.315B LAMA

Perhaps a dozen delivered. Three are H-10 to H-12, c/ns 2514 to 2516.

SUD SA.330F PUMA

One only, H-98 c/n 1181, delivered in VIP configuration to Grupo de Transporte No.10.

VOUGHT OS2U-3 KINGFISHER

Fifteen supplied under Lend-Lease, with serials 300 to 314, ex Bu.5911 to 5925, and operated from Quintero by Grupo No.2. Aircraft 308 was the first to fly over the Chilean Antarctic Territories, and 311, since preserved, flew in the Antarctic for a period in 1949.

VULTEE BT-13

Over forty delivered, including 131, 141, 144, 145, 151, 154, 155, 156, 164, 167, 172, 177, 182, 184, 185, 186 and 189. The last aircraft were withdrawn from use in 1959.

SAILPLANES

The first Chilean military gliders of the Escuela de Planeadores (Glider School) flew without markings, but the sailplanes currently on the charge of the Escuela de Vuelo sin Motor have sequential serials prefixed V. Known examples are LET L.13 Blanik V-01, V-02, V-03, V-04, V-06 and Gron Standard Cirrus V-05. Tugs are modified Cessna L-19A.

MISCELLANEOUS

The Chilean General Directorate of Civil Aeronautics (Dirección General de Aeronáutica Civil) occasionall operates military aircraft, as a rule reserialled in a numerical sequence prefixed A. Known examples include Douglas C-47 A-1 ex FACH 971 (current with both serials on the fuselage and fin respectively), Beechcraft Baron 56TC A-2 (ex 471) and the Beechcraft D.18S A-3.
The XX- prefix is used for homebuilt aircraft, such as XX-03, a Druine D.31 Turbulent first flown in August 1967.

LET L.13 Blanik V-03 of the Escuela de Vuelo sin Motor, at Las Condes in January 1978.

Druine D.31 Turbulent XX-03, shown at El Bosque in March 1980.

Chilean Army

The 53,000 strong Ejército de Chile has a Comando de Aviación (Air Command) established on 1 October 1970, which operates a small fleet of helicopters and light transport and liaison aircraft. Its main base is Tobalaba airfield in Santiago, where the Ejército's training school is located.

Army aircraft are commonly inscribed *Ejército* or *Ejército de Chile* and their colour schemes are similar to those of the air force, though in some cases the rudder is painted red, with the star shown in white thereon.

Known Army aircraft include the following, but it should also be noted that a number of Army Flying Club aircraft with civil registrations in the CC-KIA to KIZ block, are made available for temporary Army service as required.

BELL 206A JET RANGER

Two only, 151 c/n 444 and 152 c/n 596, both later converted to 206B.

BELL UH-1H IROQUOIS

Three helicopters :

181	c/n	11399	ex 69-15110
182		11400	69-15111 w/o 3.3.75
183		11465	69-15177

CASA 212A-10 AVIOCAR

Six were ordered :

210	c/n	A-10-1-103	d/d 6.8.78
211		A-10-2-106	6.8.78
212		A-10-3-107	16.10.78
213		A-10-4-117	19.10.78
214		A-10-5-118	25.11.78
215		A-10-6-126	25.11.78

CESSNA R172K HAWK XP

Eighteen were ordered, with deliveries commencing in June 1978 with serial number 101, c/n R172-2901. The serials are 101 to 118.

CESSNA 337 SKYMASTER

Two were recently delivered with serials 205 and 207.

NEIVA N.621 UNIVERSAL (T-25)

Ten aircraft supplied by Brazil and believed serialled 101 to 110 (101 was c/n 133). No longer current; the survivors were transferred to the Chilean Air Force.

PIPER PA-32 CHEROKEE SIX 300

Two only, serialled 101 (c/n 32-40773) and 102 ; no longer in use.

PIPER PA-31 NAVAJO

Four aircraft are known to have been delivered :

201	c/n	31-517
202		31-597
203		31-600
204		

SUD SA.315B LAMA

At least sixteen helicopters, of which 159 to 161 below were allocated to the Instituto Geográfico Militar.

153	c/n	2388
154		2389
155		2390
156		2391
157		2392
158		2393
159		2487
160		2493
161		2494
162		2504
163		2553
164		2554
165		2555
166		2556
167		2557
168		2558

SUD SA.330 PUMA

Twelve SA.330F :

250		
251	c/n 1154	damaged on delivery and rebuilt using parts of c/n 1328.
252	1162	
253	1188	
254	1202	crashed 22.3.75; repaired but w/o 22.2.79
255	1208	
256	1215	
257	1234	
258	1238	
259	1242	
260	1328	w/o; parts used to rebuild 251.
261		

Three SA.330L :

262	1522	
263		
264	1527	

CASA 212A-10 Aviocar 212 seen passing through Reykjavik on delivery to the Chilean Army on 12 October 1978.

Cessna R172K Hawk XP 107, at El Bosque in March 1980.

Sud SA.330F Puma 255 at Los Cerrillos on 17 April 1977.

Cessna R172K Hawk XP 117 in low visibility markings and camouflage, contrasting with the colours of 107 shown opposite.

Sud SA.315B Lama 157, photographed at Los Cerrillos in April 1977.

Carabineros de Chile

The Carabineros, a paramilitary force which also conducts riot control and anti-terrorist duties and has a force of about 27,000 personnel, has an air unit, the Prefectura Aeropolicial, based at Tobalaba airfield, Santiago, with small detachments elsewhere. A small number of aircraft and helicopters are operated, either with civil registrations in the CC-KKA/KKZ and LLA/LLZ blocks, or serialled in a C- prefixed sequence. The inscription 'Carabineros de Chile' often appears on the fuselage sides. Aircraft known to have been used include :

C-02	Cessna 185	w/o 8.9.80
C-03	Cessna 320	w/o 11.6.79
C-4	Swearingen SA.226TC Metro	
C-5	Swearingen SA.226TC Metro	
C-06	Swearingen SA.226TC Metro	
C-7	Swearingen SA.226TC Metro	
C-8	Hiller FH.1100	
C-9	MBB Bo 105C	
C-10	MBB Bo 105C	
C-11	MBB Bo 105C	
C-12	MBB Bo 105C	c/n S.299
C-13	MBB Bo 105C	
C-14	MBB Bo 105C	c/n S.251 ex D-HDHK d/d 17.5.76.
C-15	MBB Bo 105S	c/n S.541 ex D-HDNP

Some of the unidentified Bo 105 above may well be from the following, all of which were sold to Chile on 30.4.76 : c/ns S.191 to S.195 ex D-HDEK, DEL, DEM, DEB, DDU. The Metros were ex CC-ECC (c/n TC211EEEE), CC-ECD (c/n TC212), CC-ECL (c/n TC213) and CC-ECN (c/n TC214); they all seem to have seen some service with the Navy, who were offering them for sale during 1981.

MBB Bo 105C C-12 at El Bosque in March 1980.

Swearingen SA.226TC Metro C-04, photographed at the same event.

Chilean Navy

The Chilean Naval Air Service (Servicio de Aviación Naval de Chile) came into being in 1919 at Santiago with five float biplanes of British origin — three Avro 504 powered by 130hp Clerget engines and two Sopwith Babies with 110hp Le Rhônes. Initial training was provided by the Military Aviation Service at El Bosque. A British advisory mission arrived in 1921 to organise the service, establishing a naval air base (Base Aeronaval) at Las Torpederas (it moved to Quintero, near Valparaiso, in January 1927). Additional aircraft were procured, including five Short 184 float biplanes powered by Sunbeam Maori III engines, a Felixstowe F.2B twin-engined biplane flying boat marked as *Gª Mª Zañartu* after the service's first casualty, Ensign (Guardiamarina) Guillermo Zañartu, and later (in 1926) at least eight Dornier Do J Wal flying boats (serialled 10 to 12 and 14 to 18) with Napier Lion or Rolls-Royce Eagle IX engines, to equip the 1° Grupo de Aviación Naval (1st Naval Air Group).

Four Fairey IIIF Mk.IVC float biplanes (c/ns F.976 to F.979, serials 23 to 26) were purchased for fleet co-operation duties and allocated to the 2° Grupo de Aviación Naval at Quintero, with occasional deployments to the newly-opened base at Talcahuano and the battleship *Almirante Latorre*. Other acquisitions included a Fairey IIIF Mk.IIIB (c/n F.1514 serialled 1) and two Napier Lion X-powered Fairey Seals (c/ns F.2116 and F.2117, serialled 2 and 3).

On 21 March 1930, the Servicio de Aviación Naval (under the Ministry of the Navy) was merged with the Military Aviation Service (under the Ministry for War) to create a Chilean Air Force, under the Ministry of the Interior.

A new Servicio de Aviación de la Armada de Chile (Chilean Naval Air Service) was formed in 1954, with its main base at El Belloto, near Valparaiso. Initially a small helicopter force, it has now grown to a four squadron service with an operational element — Escuadrón VP-3, equipped with EMB.111A(N) Bandeirante patrol aircraft. Its basic training unit is Escuadrón VT-4, currently flying the Pilatus PC.7 Turbo Trainer which replaced the previously used Beechcraft T-34A in 1980. Personnel strength is about five hundred all ranks. Several Chilean ships have some provision for helicopters.

Aircraft Review

COLOURS AND MARKINGS

Chilean Navy aircraft have carried markings broadly similar to those of air force aircraft, the early shield applied to air force aircraft being ousted by a white-outlined square. However, the shield later returned, and in addition naval aircraft have carried a white star and anchor on their blue-painted rudders; the star and anchor have also been painted in black on some aircraft. The inscription *NAVAL* is commonly used, and the squadron designation is sometimes presented above this, in US Navy style.

SERIAL NUMBERS

Serials are allocated in three main blocks — up to 99 for helicopters, 100 to 199 for transports, and 200 to 299 for training and patrol aircraft.

BEECHCRAFT T-34

Six aircraft ex Chilean Air Force, acquired two in 1966 and four in 1968. The type was replaced in 1980 by the Pilatus Turbo-Trainer, and the surviving aircraft transferred to the Uraguayan Navy late in that year.

201	
202	
203	w/o 23.8.76
204	
205	
206	T-34B, ex Bu.140829

BEECHCRAFT C-45 (D18S)

Three were delivered in August 1954 as A-101 to A-103 ; the A prefixes were later deleted. 102 was c/n 1019 and was passed to a civil operator. A fourth aircraft was acquired in September 1954, and A-106 is reported as ex Chilean Army E-01. A TC-45 was acquired in July 1971 from Aerosalfa.

BELL 47G/J

Fourteen helicopters of all models, including :

01	47G	c/n 1289	d/d 1954	wfu
02	47G	1290	1954	
03	47G	1291	1954	
04	47G	1687	1956	
05	47G	1688	1956	to CC-CIS
06	47G-2A	2726	9.62	to CC-CIR
07	47G-2A	2727	9.62	
13	47J-2	1842	10.61	to CC-CIQ
14	47J-2	1841	8.61	to CC-CIP
14	47J-2A	3716	8.68	replacement ; ex N8569F
HSG-1	47G-2A	2728	10.62	
HSG-2	47G-2A	2729	10.62	

01 to 05 were delivered as N-01 to N-05.

BELL 206A (ASW)

Four were delivered between February and April 1970 and designated as 'SH-57'; they are equipped for ASW and rescue duties, with provision for external torpedoes.

31	c/n 494	
32	495	
33	496	w/o
34	497	

CASA 212A-11 AVIOCAR

Four delivered in the second half of 1978 :
145 c/n A-11-1-134   d/d 5.8.78
146   A-11-2-135   5.8.78
147   A-11-3-137   6.11.78
148   A-11-4-141   6.11.78

DOUGLAS C-47

At least seven, with serials 121 to 127. One was written off on 17.9.75, and the others withdrawn from use in the late 1970s. 121 is preserved at El Belloto.

EMBRAER EMB.110C(N) BANDEIRANTE

Three aircraft replacing C-45s as executive and communications aircraft, taken on charge on 2.8.76 and based at Base Naval El Belloto.
107 c/n 110.101 ex PT-GKF
108   110.102   PT-GKG
109   110.108   PT-GKH

EMBRAER EMB.111A(N)

Six aircraft for Escuadrón VP-3 for maritime patrol, fulfilling the role which would have been taken on by four US Navy surplus Lockheed SP-2E Neptunes which were embargoed for political reasons.
261 c/n 110.147 d/d 12.77
262   110.150   12.77
263   110.154   12.77
264   110.158   12.77
265   110.162   6.79
266   110.166   9.79

GRUMMAN HU-16B ALBATROSS

Various reports of ex Air Force aircraft claim differing numbers, but it seems that there was in fact only one aircraft serial 251, which was written off at El Belloto 2.11.73.

PIPER PA-31 NAVAJO 310

One aircraft, serialled 115, c/n 31-733, was delivered in 1971.

PILATUS PC.7 TURBO-TRAINER

Ten were ordered :
210 c/n 230 d/d 7.5.80
211   231   7.5.80
212   232   7.5.80
213   233   7.5.80
214   234   21.6.80
215   235   21.6.80
216   236   21.6.80
217   237   21.6.80
218
219

SIKORSKY HSS-1N

Three helicopters, ex US Navy, delivered in 1965 :
51 ex Bu.150730   preserved at El Belloto
52   150731   instructional at El Belloto
53   150732   wfu 1977

SUD SA.319B ALOUETTE III

Ten were delivered between 30.8.77 and 1.7.78 by Aerospatiale's US subsidiary, of which three are known to have taken up serials 60, 62, 65 and 67.
C/n 2297
    2312
    2322   ex N49519
    2332   ex N49520
    2342
    2353
    2362
    2368
    2369   ex N49542
    2370

Sud SA.319B Alouette III 67 of Escuadrón HS-2, seen at the FIDA exhibition at El Bosque early in 1982.

COLOMBIA

Area	1,138,907 sq km
Population	27,200,000
Capital	Bogotá
Civil registration	HK-

The Republic of Colombia began its history as the Spanish Vice-Royalty of Nueva Granada, lost the territories now forming Ecuador and Venezuela and became the Republic of Nueva Granada in 1830, adopting the name of Colombia in May 1863. A basically agricultural country (although a substantial part of its territory remains uncultivated) Colombia is the second largest producer of coffee, produces petroleum and is rich in minerals, though at present extraction is partly in the hands of foreign concessionaires. Colombia's history has often included periods of internal strife, the most notorious being the years of *La Violencia* between 1948 and 1958, during which some one hundred thousand people lost their lives. Since General Gustavo Rojas Pinilla was overthrown in May 1957 there have been alternate periods of conservative and liberal rule, but sporadic violence remains a fact of life. There were student riots in 1965 which caused martial law to be declared, and more recently several Marxist guerilla bands with Soviet and/or Cuban backing have appeared on the political scene. Colombia was the only Latin American country to participate actively in the Korean War, with an army battalion and two light warships.

Although there was a resolution by the Ministry of the Interior calling for tenders for the establishment of an air mail service as early as April 1919, military aviation did not begin until early 1922, when an Escuela Militar de Aviación (Military Aviation School) was formed by the Ministry of War at Flandes airfield with three Caudron G.III, four Caudron G.IV and four Nieuport 17 biplanes supplied by France; the first flight was officially made in April. However, financial difficulties caused the Escuela to be closed in 1924.

It was by then an accepted fact that Colombia's strategic importance — it controls the approaches to the Panama Canal — demanded the existence of an air arm. Thus, another flying school was formed at Madrid, in Cundinamarca province in 1925 with three Wild WT biplane trainers obtained from Switzerland. The Aviación Militar's subsequent expansion was greatly helped by assistance from SCADTA

(Sociedad Colombiano-Alemana de Transportes Aéreos, or Colombian-German Air Transport Co.), an airline formed by German settlers and expatriates but later helped to some extent by the Weimar government, and staffed with veteran German pilots. Several airfields and seaplane facilities were built and jointly used by the Aviación Militar and by SCADTA's Junkers F.13, W.33 and W.34 airliners: Bogotá, Cali and Medellín amongst others, as well as Barranquilla (also a seaplane station) and seaplane facilities at Buenaventura on the Western coast, Cartagena in the North and Palanquero on the Magdalena river. The Caudron G.III and Nieuports were disposed of in 1925, but the Caudron G.IV soldiered on until 1929, by which time a Curtiss P-1 Hawk fighter and four Swiss-built Wild X observation aircraft (serialled 43 to 46) were in service; the Wild X would be struck off charge in 1933, two years after the earlier WT trainers.

During 1932 SCADTA made available to the Aviación Militar five Junkers F.13 transports, and some much-needed help came from Germany in the shape of nine Junkers W.34; these, which were shared with SCADTA, were also used in the photo-survey role and were in service until 1952. Other German aircraft received at the time included three Junkers K.43 floatplanes (One was serialled 407), and four Dornier Do 16 Wal flying boats, which were Colombia's only bomber aircraft until 1940, and were not retired until 1943; as well as two Dornier Merkur light transports which were disposed of in 1939.

Germany's commercial penetration in Latin America was soon rivalled and not long afterwards superseded by United States penetration, and Colombia was no exception.. A US Navy surplus Consolidated P2Y-1 was presented in 1932 (it was in service until 1948), and in the same year twenty-six Curtiss Hawk II biplane fighters (c/ns SH.3/6, 10/25, 30/35 serialled in the 800 block, known examples being 807, 808, 810, 814, 815 and 821) with interchangeable wheel/float undercarriages were procured, serving at Palanquero on floats until the end of the Second World War. The Escuela

Militar de Aviación was transferred to Cali and re-equipped with ten Curtiss J2 Fledgling biplane trainers in 1933 (withdrawn from use in 1950 - known serials included 22, 25) and received sixteen Consolidated PT-11C in 1934 (withdrawn from use in 1952; one was serialled 52). Curtiss also supplied thirty F8C Falcon armed reconnaissance biplanes, which were serialled 101 to 130 and were retired in 1946, and a trio of NS.1 which served until 1943. The first five Junkers Ju 52/3mce transports, again shared with SCADTA, arrived in 1933 and received the serials 621 to 625; they were followed by five more and served until 1950. These were the last of the German types to be delivered; Pan American, the 'long arm' of US economic expansion, was by now deeply penetrating Latin America, taking over the airlines established by the Germans during the early 1920s, and in fact were already in control of SCADTA, holding eighty per cent of its shares.

Since aircraft purchases were necessarily small in numbers due to financial limitations, and their serviceability was handicapped by the lack of enough skilled personnel, further aircraft had to be obtained at regular intervals. In 1934, in addition to the Consolidated PT-11C, sixteen aircraft arrived from the USA; three Ford 5-AT-C trimotor transports (including 641 and 642) which served until 1940, four Bellanca 77-140 monoplane bombers with provision for twin floats, which were withdrawn from use in 1942, and six Seversky SEV. 3MWW river patrol monoplanes (the last one was written off in 1943) as well as three modern Curtiss BT32 Condor transports (651 to 653 c/ns 54 to 56 of which 653 was written off in 1942, 651 in 1944 and 652 broken up in 1946). By then however, the meagre funds made available by the government had to be reserved for the expansion of the airline network and the maintenance of a large number of aircraft types, and no further purchases were made for years. The Escuela de Mecánicos de Aviación (Aircraft Mechanics' School) inaugurated in 1932, now became a more important establishment.

Then, in December 1941, Pearl Harbor was bomber by the Japanese, the USA entered the

Second World War and began canvassing for support from among the Latin American nations. Most made a number of bases available to the Americans; such was the case with Colombia, which thus became eligible for Lend-Lease deliveries. These began with the first of fourteen Vultee BT-15A and sixty Stearman PT-17, to re-equip the Escuela Militar de Aviación as a prelude to better things to come. Later in 1942 a few North American AT-6 Texans arrived; ninety-nine were eventually to be taken on charge. In 1943, two Lockheed C-60A Lodestars were delivered (both were retired in 1959), and a US military mission helped to re-organise the Aviación Militar, which became an autonomous service under the Ministry of War with the name Fuerza Aérea Colombiana (Colombian Air Force). Other wartime deliveries included ten Beechcraft AT-7C crew-trainers and the first Douglas C-47 in 1944, as well as six Fairchild PT-19 which were destined to have a very short life, being disposed of during 1945.

Colombia signed the Rio Pact in 1947, which was followed by further US military assistance. The Colombian Air Force received thirteen Consolidated OA-10 (PBY-5A) Catalina amphibians, two Piper L-4J Cubs, three North American B-25J Mitchell bombers, the first few Beechcraft C-45 Expeditor light transports, five Beechcraft AT-11 Kansan crew trainers, and thirty-five Republic F-47D Thunderbolt fighter-bombers; the latter, based at Palanquero, were withdrawn from use in 1956 and the survivors dumped into the Magdalena river ! The C-47 transports were used in 1948 to form an Escuadrón de Transportes Aéreos Militares (Military Air Transport Squadron), which was eventually to be expanded into a Grupo.

By 1950, the Fuerza Aérea Colombiana had a personnel strength of eleven hundred with about 210 aircraft on charge. US assistance, which had for some time been limited to administration and maintenance, was to provide more aircraft as a result of Colombia's involvement in the Korean War — the first few Beechcraft T-34A, two Cessna L-19B (withdrawn from use in 1958) and a few surplus Bell OH-13 and Hiller OH-23 light helicopters, the service's first. Colombia also procured three Rawdon T.1 trainers (120 to 122 c/ns TI.8M to TI.10M), which served between late 1952 and 1955, and twenty DHC.2 Beaver light communications aircraft. A Cessna 170 was obtained in 1954; in the same year, a single DHC.1 Chipmunk was acquired for evaluation, and although the type was not adopted for service, it continued flying until 1956. River patrol duties were entrusted to three refurbished ex US Navy Grumman J2F Ducks, procured via the USAF. The Escuela Militar de Aviación at Cali gradually re-equipped with Beechcraft T-34A.

Further aircraft arrived during 1954. Six Lockheed T-33A jet trainers were delivered in March under Reimbursable Assistance agreements and others followed in the next few years. The first Douglas C-54 Skymasters joined the Escaudrón de Transportes Aereos Militares. Canada supplied six Canadair Sabre Mk.4 in 1955; they flew from Palanquero and replaced the Thunderbolts in service. The first Douglas B-26C Invaders were also introduced into service at this time, and served until 1968. Six Aero Commander 560A were obtained in 1956/57, and at about the same time a single Beechcraft Twin Bonanza D50 was obtained as a staff transport, flying alongside a Piper Aztec 235 delivered in 1958. The Canadair Sabres were supplemented in 1963 by two ex-USAF North American F-86F Sabres, but all Sabres were grounded from 1966 onwards and gradually replaced by Dassault Mirages. The Sabres were not suited for use as fighter-bombers; the Thunderbolt replacements in this rôle were fourteen Lockheed F-80C, delivered during 1958.

At this time, the long internal struggle between political groups had caused grave damage to the nation's economy, and once again the Colombian Air Force had to wait for US aid to add to its inventory. Six Kaman HH-43B rescue helicopters, intended to supplement the OA-10 Catalinas, arrived in 1961, serving until 1968; the elderly Bells and Hillers were replaced by nine Bell UH-1N Iroquois delivered in 1963, with six UH-1H added in 1969 and a single Bell 212 in 1971. A single Helio

Courier was delivered in 1963 but retired after only two years; it was evaluated against a Pilatus PC.6/A Porter which was sold in 1966. No further STOL communications aircraft were obtained, the priorities being elsewhere.

The overall scenario has not changed since the 1960s. Most aircraft are still supplied through US assistance programmes — although there are some notable exceptions. A Fokker F.28-1000 Fellowship twin-jet airliner was purchased in 1971 as a presidential aircraft; the ageing C-47s were supplemented by Hawker-Siddeley 748s, and, due to US reluctance to supplying jet fighters in Latin America, the new Colombian fighter force was composed of French-built Dassault Mirages : eighteen Mirage 5COA fighters, 5COD operational trainers and 5COR tactical reconnaissance aircraft were acquired in 1972. The US did agree to the supply of six Northrop T-38A Talon supersonic trainers on 1 February 1978, for the use of the Escuala Militar de Aviación. Changed strategic considerations, mainly dictated by the transfer of the Panama Canal to Panamanian sovereignty, may force the US government to hand over to Colombia a number of tactical fighters, possibly F-5E Tiger II, a type which already serves with the Brazilian, Chilean and Venezuelan air arms. Ten A-37B were delivered in 1980 to begin with (these initially based at Cali) and twelve ex US Army Bell UH-1H Iroquois are to be supplied during 1982 for anti-guerilla warfare. Also expected for 1982 delivery are twelve IAI Kfir fighters.

The Fuerza Aérea Colombiana is however more than a military air arm. It incorporates SATENA (Servicio de Aeronavegación a Territorios Nacionales, or Air Navigation Service to the National Territories) a military airline which came into being in September 1962 with Catalinas and DHC.2 Beavers and was re-organised in 1966. SATENA currently flies a mixture of Douglas C-47 and C-54 and HS.748, recently supplemented by Douglas DC-6 and DC-7; their aircraft link Bogatá with the country's main population centres as well as distant jungle airstrips.

Current Organisation

The Fuerza Aérea Colombiana has a personnel of about 3,800 and comprises the following units :

Comando de Combate (Combat Command)
1º Grupo de Combate (1st Combat Group) at Base Aérea Militar (BAM) Germán Olano, Palanquero with Dassault Mirage 5CO.
2º Grupo de Combate at BAM de Apiay with Lockheed AT-33A/T-33A, perhaps to be replaced by the IAI Kfir.
Grupo de Ataque y Reconocimiento (Attack and Reconnaissance Group) at BAM Luis Gómez Niño, Barranquilla with Douglas RB-26C/B-26K.

Comando de Entrenamiento y Soporte Táctico (Training and Tactical Support Command)
Escuela Militar de Aviación at BAM Marco Fidel Suárez, Cali with Beechcraft T-34A, Cessna T-41D and T-37C and Northrop T-38A.
Grupo de Apoyo Táctico Aeronaval (Naval Air Tactical Support Group)
Academia de Aviación (Air Academy) for theoretical training.
Escuela de Helicópteros (Helicopter School) at BAM Luis F Pinto.

Reconnaissance squadron - red outer ring, medium blue background, black/white bird with orange beak and feet, red telescope.

Comando Aéreo de Transporte Militar (CATAM, Military Air Transport Command) at El Dorado International Airport, Bogotá :

Grupo de Transportes Aéreos Militares (Military Air Transport Group)
SATENA - the military airline with Douglas C-47, C-54, DC-6, DC-7 and HS.748.
Grupo de Helicópteros (Helicopter Group) at BAM Melgar, controlling small detachments all over the country with Bell UH-1B/H, SA.315B Lama, Hughes OH-6A/500C Defender.

Grupo de Bombardeo - red outer ring, medium blue background, white horse with grey shading and yellow wings with black lines.

Military Air Bases

1 Bogotá
2 Medellín
3 Bucamaranga
4 Cúcuta
5 Buenaventura
6 Cali
7 Villavicencio
8 Popayán
9 Tumaco
10 Pasto
11 Puerto Leguizamo
12 Mitú
13 Cartagena
14 Barranquilla
15 Santa Marta
16 Riomacha

Aircraft Review

COLOURS AND MARKINGS

Colombia's flag derives from that of Gran Colombia, designed by Francisco de Miranda and flown by the Libertador Simón Bolívar and comprising areas of yellow (the national wealth) and red (bloody Spain) separated by blue (the ocean and the sky). This appears as a fin flash or rudder stripes on military aircraft, which have always had a complex, segmented roundel in the national colours, at first incorporating the old eight-point Gran Colombia star, but currently with a white five-pointed star. The inscriptions Fuerza Aérea Colombiana and FAC are commonly used, and SATENA aircraft, which are commonly light grey with white fuselage tops and a blue/black cheatline, carry airline-style titling in black.

Camouflage schemes are based on US practice, although an indigenous low-visibility camouflage, consisting of dark green/dark grey upper surfaces with light grey undersides, is also in use; with this scheme, no fin or rudder markings are carried and the roundel size is very small. Non-camouflaged aircraft have the roundel in four positions, with the serial displayed on the starboard wing upper surface and port wing underside.

SERIAL NUMBERS

FAC serial numbers are allocated in blocks according to the aircraft's primary rôle :

1 to 100	trainers	
101 to 200	liaison	
201 to 300	helicopters	
301 to 500	miscellaneous	
501 to 600	light transports	
601 to 700	transports	
701 to 800	advanced trainers	
801 to 900	fighter-bombers	
901 to 1000	crew-trainers	
1001 to 1100	transports (SATENA)	
2001 to 2100	fighters and close support	
2501 to 2600	bombers	

There are of course exceptions and the odd cases of re-allocation. Some aircraft which for a number of reasons are struck off charge may be replaced by others of the same type, with the same serials, but when this happens, the suffix letter A is added to the serial of the replacement aircraft.

Aircraft used in recent years by the Fuerza Aérea Colombiana include the following :

AERO COMMANDER 560A

Six delivered 1956/57; most sold in 1966, one still in use.

550	c/n 391-71	ex N6871S	d/d 10.56	to HK-1317-W
551	430-103		12.56	
552	453-123		17.2.57	w/o 5.11.58
553	454-124		23.2.57	w/o 1.4.57
554	498-168	N6230D	4.57	to HK-1344-W
555	446-117	HK-934	1.57	to HK-1313-P

BEECHCRAFT C-45/MODEL 18

At least ten, of various versions; no longer in use. Known aircraft include D18S 515 and 516 (c/ns A.990 and A.991 respectively) delivered in December 1953; and C-45 518 and 523, the latter being converted to partial Model H18 standards.

BEECHCRAFT AT-7C NAVIGATOR

Two were delivered in 1943, and retired in 1964.

BEECHCRAFT AT-11 KANSAN

Five were delivered, serialled 900 to 904 and withdrawn in 1956. 902 was preserved at the FAC Museum.

BEECHCRAFT TWIN BONANZA D50

One only, serialled 540, c/n DH.72, delivered in May 1956.

BEECHCRAFT T-34A/B MENTOR

Forty two T-34A were delivered, serialled 301 to 342, and followed in 1978 by six ex US Navy T-34B :

301A	c/n BG.19 ex Bu.	140685
302A	BG.62	140728
306A	BG.87	140753
308A	BG.97	140763
309A	BG.135	140801
312A	BG.328	144021

About thirty Mentors remain in use with the Escuela Militar de Aviación.

BELL 47

Twenty seven helicopters, mainly ex US military; types include OH-13D, G, H and S. Known serials are 203, 204, 213, 213A, 216, 217, 222, 223 and 224. Two OH-13J (Bell 47J-2A) serialled 218 and 219 were delivered in 1954 and served until 1966. Later deliveries included Bell 47G-3B c/n 2656, 2709 to 2711 which arrived in October 1961.

BELL UH-1 IROQUOIS

Nine UH-1B were delivered in 1963, serialled 271 to 279, followed by six UH-1H in 1969, serials 291 to 296. Six of each model are believed to remain in use, and twelve more ex US Army UH-1H are expected to be delivered in 1982.

BELL 212

One only, serialled 002, c/n 30511 ex N7070J, acquired in 1971 as an executive transport.

CANADAIR SABRE Mk.4

Six were delivered in 1955 with serials 2021 to 2026 (at least one was written off), followed by a pair of North American F-86F, and possibly more later, in 1963. The first Sabres to be withdrawn from use were retired in 1966, and the type has now been completely superseded by the Dassault Mirage at BAM Germán Olano. 2023 was preserved at the FAC Museum.

CESSNA T-41D

Thirty were delivered in 1968, serialled 401 to 430, c/ns R172-0336 to 0365; the type remains in use with the Escuela Militar de Aviación.

CESSNA T-37C

Ten were delivered in 1969 for the Escuela Militar de Aviación, of which at least two have been written off. They had no previous USAF identities, having been acquired directly from the manufacturers.

2101	c/n 41176	
2102	41179	
2103	41182	
2104	41185	
2105	41190	
2106	41194	
2107	41199	
2108	41201	
2109	41203	
2110	41205	

CESSNA A-37B

Ten delivered in 1980, believed to be serialled 2151 to 2160.

CONSOLIDATED OA-10 CATALINA

Thirteen were delivered from 1946 onwards and initially based at Cartagena, Colombia's traditional naval air base. Previous USAAF serials included 44-33921, 33996 and 34013; known FAC serials are 612, 616, 619 and 621, the latter written off on 26.11.66. At least two were converted to transports and used for a time by SATENA.

Beechcraft T-34A Mentor 321, one of forty-two delivered to the FAC.

Beechcraft C-45 518 photographed at Bogota on 14 November 1969.

Douglas C-54G Skymaster 694 seen at Bogota in 1977

Dassault Mirage 5COD 3002, one of two conversion trainers delivered.

De Havilland Canada DHC.2 Beaver 120, the last of twenty, seen here in February 1977.

Douglas C-54G Skymaster 1105, the former 697, seen here in SATENA colours in December 1977.

Douglas C-47 Skytrain 686 photographed at Bogota in 1977.

Lockheed C-130B Hercules 1001 seen on a visit to Miami in February 1978.

DASSAULT MIRAGE 5CO

Fourteen Mirage 5COA fighters, two 5COR reconnaissance aircraft and two 5COD conversion trainers were procured in 1972. A Mirage 5, believed to be a 5COA, was written off on 21.8.72. Serials are :

5COA	3021 to 3034
5COD	3001 to 3002
5COR	3011 to 3012

DE HAVILLAND CANADA DHC.2 BEAVER

Twenty were delivered during the 1950s, about ten of which remain in use :

101		
102	c/n 102	ex HK-102-X
103	103	ex HK-103-X
104	149	
105	265	
106	289	
107	378	
108	408	
109	429	
110	443	
111	518	
112	523	
113	532	
114	537	
115		
116		
117		
118		w/o 5.11.77
119		
120		

DOUGLAS C-47 SKYTRAIN

Forty three C-47A, B and D were delivered, those with the A suffixes to the serial being handed over in April 1978. The type is now extensively used by SATENA. Known aircraft :

650			
651			
652			
653			
653A	c/n 14744/26189	ex 43-48928	
654			w/o 26.7.75
654A	14847/26292	43-49031	
655			
656			

657			
658			
659			
660			w/o
660A	14906/26351	43-49090	
661			w/o 21.1.72
662			w/o
662A			
663			w/o 3.5.75
664			
665			
666			
667			
668			w/o 21.2.78
669			w/o
669A	16996/34258	45-993	
670			to FAC1128
676			w/o 2.4.76
677	16802/33550	44-77218	
679			
680			
681			
682			
683			
684	15606/27051	43-49790, HK-1333	w/o 30.3.71
685			w/o 8.9.69
686			
687	9759	42-23897	to FAC1120
688			w/o 8.1.75
689	20032	43-15566	to FAC1121
691			

SATENA operated three aircraft re-serialled from the 600 series as above :

1120	ex FAC687	
1121	FAC689	
1128	FAC670	

In addition SATENA operated the following, delivered in June 1976 (mostly C-47B, but 1122 was a C-47A and 1123 a C-47D) :

1122	c/n 19606	ex 43-15140	
1123	14599/26044	43-48783	wfu 12.76
1124	15328/26773	43-49514	w/o 19.11.76
1125	14531/25976	43-48715	w/o 17.2.77
1126	16860/33608	44-77276	w/o 29.3.78
1127	16291/33038	44-76706	w/o 20.11.77

Further aircraft have been acquired more recently :

1129	
1130	
1131	w/o 13.11.80
1132	

DOUGLAS C-54 SKYMASTER

At least sixteen C-54A, B C and G were taken on charge, four of which were ex Brazilian Air Force 2400, 2402, 2407 and 2408 in 1970. DC-4-1009 serial 690 was delivered on 17.3.54 ex Scandinavian Airlines System as a presidential transport.

634				
640	C-54G	c/n 35956	ex BrazAF 2402	wfu 1976
641	C-54G	35978	BrazAF 2400	
642	C-54G		BrazAF	
643	C-54G		BrazAF	wfu
690	DC-4	42926	OY-DFY	wfu 1980
691	C-54E	27323	44-9097	d/d 8.55
692		10442	42-72337, N8343C	wfu
693				wfu 1971 ?
693A	C-54D	10813	42-72708, PortAF 7504	
694	C-54G	35980	45-527	
695	DC-4	10465	42-72360, N88908	
696	C-54G	36057	45-604	wfu
697	C-54G	36024	45-571	to FAC1105
698	C-54G	36014	45-561	w/o
698A				
699	C-54D	10853	42-72748	to FAC1106 w/o 18.12.79

Two other crashes took place on 19.2.70 and 2.6.75.

DOUGLAS DC-6

Two aircraft serialled 901 and 902 reported 1981.

DOUGLAS DC-7

One aircraft serialled 921 reported 1981.

DOUGLAS B-26 INVADER

At least seven were in service by 1954, with subsequent deliveries of three in November 1956, six in December 1956. Total deliveries are believed to have been nineteen, mostly B-26C, with a few B-26B or RB-26C (a couple of the latter are believed to remain in use), and serials believed to run from 2501 to 2519, of which the following are confirmed : 2502, 2503, 2504, 2505, 2515, 2516, 2518 and 2519 (the latter is preserved at the FAC Museum). Eight B-26K Counter-Invaders are in service, almost certainly converted from earlier aircraft.

FOKKER F.28-1000 FELLOWSHIP

One only, serialled 001, c/n 11992 ex PH-EXF, acquired in February 1971 as the presidential aircraft and still in service. An aircraft marked as PH-EXP was noted at Woensdrecht in March 1982, for the Colombian Air Force.

GRUMMAN OA-12A (J2F) DUCK

Three were delivered, ex USAF 48-1373 to 1375. Another five aircraft which were scheduled for delivery , OA-12s 48-563 to 567, were retained by the USAF.

HAWKER SIDDELEY HS.748

Four Series 260 delivered to SATENA in February/March 1972 :
1101	c/n 1702	ex G-11-1 w/o 22.8.79
1102	1703	G-11-2
1103	1704	G-11-3 w/o 9.1.74
1104	1705	G-11-4

It seems likely that further aircraft have been acquired later as two serialled 1105 and 1107 have been reported. Another new aircraft, series 371, was delivered 1.8.81 :
1108	1776	G-11-14

HELIO H.295 COURIER

One aircraft deliverd 1963 for evaluation; withdrawn from use by 1965.

HILLER UH-12/OH-23

Deliveries included three UH-12B, c/ns 670 to 672 delivered in August 1954 — one became 211, the current gate guardian at BAM General Rojas Pinilla, Melgar, and another 220, now preserved at the FAC Museum; seven UH-12E, including c/ns 2088 to 2090 delivered June 1961; and c/ns 2155, 2182 to 2184 all delivered in November 1961, of which the last three became HK-763-W to HK-765-W; and one OH-23F. Most were grounded in 1969-70, but four remain on the inventory.

HUGHES 369C/369M (OH-6A)

Deliveries included twelve 369HM :

241	c/n	480001M	d/d 4.68
242		480002M	4.68
243		480003M	4.68
244		480004M	4.68
245		490037M	4.69
246		490038M	4.69
247		490039M	4.69
248		490040M	4.69
249		490041M	5.69
250		490042M	5.69
251		490043M	5.69
252		490044M	5.69

Ten armed Model 500D Defenders followed during 1978.

IAI 201 ARAVA

Three aircraft were ordered :
951	d/d 13.3.80
952	13.3.80
953	16.3.80

IAI KFIR C.2

Twelve aircraft ordered fro delivery commencing March 1982

KAMAN HH-43B HUSKIE

Six delivered in 1961; withdrawn from use in 1968.

LOCKHEED F-80C SHOOTING STAR

Sixteen delivered, the first thirteen in 1958, and used by 10⁰ Escuadron de Caza-Bombardeo and retired by 1966. At least nine were lost in accidents. Known serials :
2057		
2058	ex 47-215	to N10DM
2061		preserved at El Dorado
2065		

LOCKHEED T-33A/AT-33A

Thirty six T-33A were delivered from 1954 onwards, and some may have been converted to AT-33A close support aircraft. Known serials include 2015 and its replacement 2015A. Four RT-33A were delivered in 1964 with serials 2071 to 2074. Another twelve T-33A were delivered in

February-April 1978 (2013A, 2031 and 2033 on 18.3.78):
2007A	ex 57-615
2013A	57-644
2014A	57-710
2025	57-720
2026	57-736
2027	57-754
2028	58-358
2029	58-564
2030	58-586
2031	58-659
2032	58-678
2033	58-706

The AT-33A were operated by the Grupo de Apuyo Tactico (Tactical Support Group) of the Training and Tactical Support Command, which became the 2⁰ Grupo de Combate in 1980.

LOCKHEED C-130B HERCULES

Three ex Canadian military aircraft were acquired via Lockheed Georgia in January 1969 for the Grupo de Transportes Aéreos Militares :
1001	c/n 3575	ex CAF 10302 and	N4653	
1002	3587	10303	N4654	w/o 26.8.69
1003	3572	10301	N6707	

NORTH AMERICAN AT-6 TEXAN

Ninety-nine AT-6B, C and D were delivered and serialled between 700 and 798. About half were eventually fitted with two 0.3 inch wing guns and racks for light bombs, for attacks against guerillas in the Villavicencio mountains. Only one survives as a staff refresher trainer; the remainder were gradually retired, beginning in 1967-68 with the last three being grounded in March 1972. AT-6D 772 was preserved at the FAC Museum; another, c/n 88-16469 was civilianised as HK-2049-P.

NORTH AMERICAN B-25J MITCHELL

Three only, withdrawn from use in 1957; no details known.

NORTHROP T-38A TALON

Six were delivered on 1 February 1978 ; details are still not known.

PILATUS PC.6/A PORTER

One aircraft, serialled 160, c/n 349 ex HB-FAY, sold in 1966 as HK-1375.

PIPER L-4J CUB

Two only, ex USAAF 45-5153 and 5180, delivered in 1947 and withdrawn from use in 1958.

PIPER PA-23 AZTEC 235

One aircraft delivered in 1958, and withdrawn from use in 1965.

REPUBLIC F-47D THUNDERBOLT

Thirty-five were delivered, serving until 1956. Known serials are 830 and 861, the latter being preserved at the FAC Museum.

STEARMAN PT-17

Sixty were delivered, including ex USAAF 41-25754/25759, 42-16495/16497, 42-16645/16647 and 42-16718/16723. The type was withdrawn in 1957, but one remains for aerobatic display work.

SUD SA.315B LAMA

Twenty-seven were reported as delivered for rescue and communications duties; no details are known.

VULTEE BT-15A

Fourteen were delivered and withdrawn from use in 1951.

Colombian Army & Navy

The Colombian Navy (Armada de la República de Colombia) with a personnel strength of about ten thousand, including two Marine battalions, operates no aircraft, nor does it have ships with provision for aircraft or helicopters. The 58,000 strong Army has no aircraft either, Army co-operation duties being performed by the FAC; it does however have a paratroop battalion.

Douglas C-47 Skytrain 659 at Bogota in early 1977.

Douglas C-47A Skytrain 1122 in SATENA colours at Bogota in February 1977.

COSTA RICA

Area	50,900 sq km
Population	2,111,000
Capital	San José
Civil registration	TI-

The Republic of Costa Rica has had a surprisingly peaceful history for a Latin-American country, largely thanks to its high degree of ethnic homogeneity, and boasts of a very low illiteracy rate. There has never been compulsory military service. The country's small army was disbanded in 1948 as a means of preventing military interference in government matters, and the constitution of November 1949 forbids its re-establishment. However, there is a Civil Guard (Guardia Civil), with paramilitary capability and a strength of about two thousand, to 'enforce the country's laws, protect private property and the lives of the citizens'. There is also a three thousand strong police force, and a number of private security organisations on the pay of wealthy landowners or the main political parties. The Customs service (Aduana) operates two patrol gunboats, an armed tug and a couple of smaller vessels, with about fifty personnel.

The Air Section (Sección Aérea) of the Public Security Ministry (Ministerio de la Seguridad Pública) has operated light aircraft for many years, ostensibly for liaison between isolated communities and casualty evacuation. Initially identified by SP (Seguridad Pública) suffixes to their numerical civil registrations, they are now registered in the TI-SPx block. Most wear roundels in the national colours of red white and blue in addition to their registrations. The inscriptions 'Ministerio de Seguridad Pública' and 'Sección Aérea' appear in white on the roundel's blue outer ring. The main base is at Aeropuerto José Santamaría, San Jose's international airport (formerly known as El Coco, opened in June 1955), although initial flying was from the capital's La Sábana airstrip. The aircraft operated are listed in the table below, from which it will be noted that most of the older types were replaced by new Piper aircraft during 1979 and 1980. The Costa Rican government also operated Cessna 170 TI-78 (written off 9.11.54) and Cessna 180 TI-233 (c/n 30891, ex N2991C, sold as TI-306G).

During a hostile incursion into Costa Rican territory by Nicaraguan-supported rebels on 16 January 1955, during which the invaders flew a Republic

P-47D Thunderbolt and two North American AT-6 Texans, the Costa Rican government was sold at a nominal price of one US dollar each, four USAF surplus North American F-51D Mustang fighters by OAS/OEA request. They were serialled 1 to 4 (ex 44-73193, 44-73339, 45-11386 and 44-74978 respectively) and flew with the Costa Rican national flag painted on the fuselage sides and wings. Serials 1 and 2 were written off on 19.1.55, and 3 on 22.1 but number 4 survived and was eventually sold to the USA as N6169U.

Costa Rica's national airline LACSA (Líneas Aéreas Costarricenses SA) was formed in December 1945 under joint government and US control, and operates both passenger and cargo services between San José and the country's main airfields, as well as to half a dozen Latin American countries and Miami, Florida.

Air Bases

1 San José
2 Santa Cruz
3 Las Cañas
4 Upala
5 Los Chiles
6 Puntarenas
7 Puerto Limón
8 Palmar

Sikorsky S-58ET TI-SPJ at San José on 24 June 1975.

Cessna U-17A TI-SPC at San Jose in June 1975; it was sold as C-GGOH in May 1980.

De Havilland Canada U-1A Otter TI-SPE also at San Jose in June 1975

De Havilland Canada U-1A Otter TI-SPG. Note the fuselage of Cessna U-17A TI-SPD at the rear.

Aircraft Review

		c/n	ex 51-		
TI-505SP	Beechcraft C-45F	AF......			Withdrawn from use
TI-506SP	Cessna 180B	50416	TI-292, N5116E		To TI-SPA. Sold as C-GGOJ **5.80**
TI-507SP	Cessna U-17A	185-0637	63-13138, N2637Z		To TI-SPB
TI-508SP	Cessna U-17A	185-0653	63-13595, N2653Z		To TI-SPC. Sold as C-GGOH **5.80**
TI-509SP	Cessna U-17A	185-0652	63-13594, N2652Z		To TI-SPD. Sold as C-GGOP **5.80**
TI-SPE	DHC. U-1A Otter	97	55-3255		Sold as C-GGOR 6.80
TI-SPF	DHC. U-1A Otter	100	55-3258		wfu
TI-SPG	DHC. U-1A Otter	225	57-6107		Sold as C-GGON 6.80
TI-SPH	Hiller FH.1100	236	TI-18		Presidential
TI-SPI	Sikorsky S.58ET	58.1050	Bu.145704		ex US Navy SH-34J. Wfu
TI-SPJ	Sikorsky S.58ET	58.1353	Bu.148957		ex US Navy SH-34J
TI-SPK	Piper Apache 235	23-1014	TI-CMA, TI-1033L, TI-1033C, CU-N629		
TI-SPL	Hughes 269C	970631			acquired 11.77
TI-SPM	Hughes 269C	970632			acquired 11.77
TI-SPN	Piper Aztec 250F	27-7954032	(N6667A)		acquired 1979
TI-SPO	Bell UH-1B	213	FAP- ?, 60-3567		wfu
TI-SPP	Bell UH-1B	426	FAP-111, 62-1906		
TI-SPQ	Piper Cherokee Six 300	32-7940111			acquired 1979
TI-SPR	Piper Cherokee Six 300	32-7940112			acquired 1979
TI-SPS	Piper Cherokee Six 300	32-7940113			acquired 1979
TI-SPT	Piper Aztec 250	27-7954069			acquired 1979
TI-SPU	Piper Seneca 200T	34-8070189			acquired 1980

CUBA

Area	114,524 sq km
Population	9,900,000
Capital	La Habana (Havana)
Civil registration	CU-

The island of Cuba was a Spanish possession from its discovery in 1492 by Columbus until December 1898, when the Republic of Cuba, after a four-year civil war during which the United States openly joined the Cuban nationalists against Spain, was recognised by the Spanish crown. Its proximity to Florida brought it under extensive US influence for most of the first half of the twentieth century; the US troops were not withdrawn from Cuba until May 1902, and between 1906 and 1909 the country was administered by provisional US governors. A treaty signed between both countries in 1903 gave the United States the right to intervene in the case of a threat to Cuban independence (this right was relinquished in 1934), and a naval base at Guantán-amo Bay.

General Fulgencio Batista y Zaldívar seized power in March 1952, and sought to obtain total control of the country; this caused growing discontent amongst some sectors of the population, which was cleverly exploited by certain political movements. Guerilla warfare began on a limited scale in 1956, under the leadership of lawyer Dr. Fidel Castro. By 1958, the guerillas, based in the mountains of Sierra Maestra, were receiving substantial US support, the American government having decided to switch sides. Dictator Fulgencio Batista resigned in January 1959 and fled, and the Castrista forces took over the country. Fidel Castro began a campaign to convert Cuba into the first Communist country in the Americas, at the same time liquidating the opposition. By 1961 Cuba was overtly a Communist country. In April of that year, large numbers of CIA-trained exiles and mercenaries attempted to land at the Bay of Pigs (Bahía de Cochinos), Las Villas province, but the operation was a complete disaster, some sources suggesting even that the invaders were 'set up'. The American government cancelled the planned air cover for the invasion forces who were left with not even the element of surprise on their side — and thus the only militant opposition to Fidel Castro's régime was annihilated. Following the October 1962 'missile crisis', the US Government agreed not to allow

Cuban exiles to use US territory as a base against Cuba, thus making the country totally safe for communism. A Cuban National Revolutionary Council in exile, and a Cuban Liberation Army still exist but limit themselves to sporadic acts of sabotage against Cuban merchant ships in US ports.

Cuba is now a member of Comecon, the Soviet Bloc economic assistance organisation. Agriculture remains the country's main resource with particular emphasis on the production of sugar, coffee and tobacco for export. and the majority of land is state-owned. The National Institute of Agrarian Reform (INRA) makes extensive use of aircraft on agricultural work. Industry still has to reach the level of many Latin American countries. Prime Minister Dr. Fidel Castro is the Commander-in-Chief of the Fuerzas Armadas Revolucionarias (Revolutionary Armed Forces) as well as First Secretary of the Communist Party of Cuba. Conscription applies for all males aged seventeen and over, and women aged between seventeen and twenty-five may volunteer for up to two years. A volunteer guerilla army was in existence between 1959 and November 1963.

The first aeronautical activities on Cuban soil began in 1912 and in March 1913 a Cuban pioneer aviator flew in Morane which he had bought from France. The first proposals for the formation of a Cuerpo de Aviación (Air Corps) under the control of the Army were presented to the government in 1915, provision being made for the creation of two air squadrons (Nos.1 and 2). A number of Cuban volunteers received flying training at Kelly Field, Texas; an airfield was opened up near Havana, and six Curtiss JN.4D biplane trainers, serialled 1 to 6, were purchased, being eventually fitted with light armament. The Escuadrilla Nº 1 of the Cuerpo de Aviación del Ejército de Cuba (Cuban Army Air Corps) was officially activated in May 1919, though the second Escuadrilla was never formed. The US government supplied a technical adviser, who in fact acted as the Cuerpo's commander. However, very little — apart from training — was done during the first five years, mainly due to the usual shortage of funds so apparent in most Latin American nations.

The need to consolidate military aviation in Cuba was finally understood in 1923, funds being voted for the purchase of aircraft — six DH.4B bombers and four Vought UO-2 observation biplanes — and to send more trainee pilots to the USA. However, in October 1926, by which time the Cuerpo had some 120 personnel (including at least twenty who were pilots), a hurricane destroyed most of the aircraft. Everything that could possibly be done was immediately undertaken with full government support, and the Cuerpo was back in operation a few months later. In May 1927, the Cuerpo was upgraded and reorganised and orders were given for the creation of a permanent flying school, and one fighter and two bomber squadrons. As usual, an American military mission arrived in Cuba to help with the reorganisation; and four Consolidated PT-3 biplane trainers were ordered to replace the surviving Curtiss Jennies.

The reorganisation finally became effective in 1934, at the time of the renewal of the US-Cuban Treaty. The Cuerpo de Aviación now comprised an Escuela de Aviación (Flying School), an Escuadron de Pelea (Fighter Squadron), and an Escuadrón de Observación y Bombardeo (Observation and Bombing Squadron). Headquarters were at Campo Teniente Brihuegas in Havana, the flying school being based at the nearby Columbia airfield. A separate Aviación de la Marina de Guerra (Naval Air Arm) was also formed, with a Howard DGA8 light transport received in 1937 and three Waco UMF3 biplanes delivered in September 1937 (c/ns 4548, 4663 and 4664 serialled 26 to 28), and during the Second World War it took delivery of two Grumman JRF-5 Goose utility transports (ex Bu. 39747 and 39748, the latter sold later as N2720A).

Cuba's political and financial situation did not permit the expansion of its air arms to anything more than a token force. Small numbers of aircraft were obtained from the USA whenever possible — four Curtiss Hawk II fighters (c/n H.19 to H.22), a similar number of Waco SH3D biplanes for use as light bombers, a couple of Bellanca Aircruiser and Howard DGA15 light transports and Curtiss-Wright

CW.19R advanced trainers, and seven Stearman A73B1 general purpose biplanes (c/ns 73072 to 73078, serialled 33 to 39 and delivered between October 1939 and March 1940). Naval aircraft, by now marked 'Marina de Guerra Constitucional' (Constitutional War Navy) had been joined by a second Howard DGA8 (serialled 54; the first one, 51 'Niña' — the young girl — was finally written off early in 1948) and a Lockheed Sirius (c/n 146 ex NC16W) which was converted to a single-seater.

Cuba was a willing ally in the pre-Pearl Harbor US neutrality policy and was thus able to receive further US aid. An Academia Nacional de Aviación Cubana - Reserva Aérea (Cuban National Air Academy - Air Reserve) was activated at Campo Teniente Brihuegas in 1941, and after Pearl Harbor Cuba became eligible for Lend-Lease deliveries which included forty-five aircraft — some Aeronca L-3 liaison aircraft, the pair of Grumman JRF-5 already mentioned, and numbers of trainers, including ten North American AT-6F (one of which later became CU-N635) and Stearman PT-13 and PT-17 biplanes (the first four were serialled 46 to 49; they may have been ex 41-25741 and 42-16274/16276 which are known to have gone to Cuba; two aircraft were disposed of as CU-N700 and CU-E837). The Cuerpo could at last expand: there were by now airfields at Havana, Camagüey, Santa Clara and San Antonio de los Baños among others, and the service was reaping the benefits of a substantial US technical assistance.

Cuba became a signatory of the Rio Pact in 1947, and subsequently received more US aircraft, this time to create a true offensive force made desirable by the Cold War: North American F-51D Mustang and B-25J Mitchell bombers, in addition to the first three Douglas C-47B (44-76391, 44-77093 plus another) for an Escuadrón de Transporte. Other aircraft followed : a few Beechcraft C-45 light transports and Consolidated PBY-5A amphibians — and later Lockheed T-33A jet trainers (at least eight armed aircraft, serials include 101, 703, 705, 707, 709, 711, 713 and 715) — arrived from the USA, a Curtiss C-46A transport (c/n 30253 ex CU-C153 and

42-96591) was temporarily impressed in 1949 with the serial 610 until sold as N3926C/YV-C-BNA. Britain supplied the service's first two helicopters, Westland Whirlwind 1 H-10 c/n WA.239 and H-11 c/n WA.240 (ex G-17-1, sold as G-AOZK). The Escuadrón de Transporte expanded to ten C-47s serialled 201 to 210 (209 was C-53D c/n 11643 ex 42-68716 and NC59410 of Pan American, delivered in February 1955). Another re-organisation took place in 1955 under Fulgencio Batista's orders, the naval air arm being absorbed into the Cuerpo de Aviación, which then became the Fuerza Aérea del Ejército de Cuba (Cuban Army Air Force).

This change of name reflected itself in the introduction of a new serialling sequence which was in the main applicable to light transports and communications aircraft and never superseded the former system, and was distinguished by the use of the prefix FAEC. Known allocations include :

Serial	Type	C/n	D/d	
FAEC-1	Piper Pacer 135	20-944	1.53	to CU-P649
FAEC-2	Piper Pacer 135	20-945	1.53	to CU-P650
FAEC-3	Piper Pacer 135	20-981	4.53	
FAEC-6	Piper Pacer 135	20-984	4.53	
FAEC-7	Piper Pacer 135	20-982	4.53	to CU-P651
FAEC-16	DHC.2 Beaver	1085	1957	
FAEC-17	DHC.2 Beaver		1957	
FAEC-18	DHC.2 Beaver	1099	1957	
FAEC-19	DHC.2 Beaver	1102	1957	
FAEC-20	Piper Super Cub 135	18-2520	3.53	
FAEC-21	Piper Super Cub 135	18-2521	3.53	
FAEC-22	Piper Super Cub 135	18-2522	3.53	
FAEC-23	Piper Super Cub 135	18-2523	3.53	
FAEC-24	Piper Super Cub 135	18-2524	3.53	
FAEC-25	Piper Tri-Pacer 150	22-3278	12.55	
FAEC-26	Piper Tri-Pacer 150	22-3356	12.55	
FAEC-27	Piper Tri-Pacer 150	22-5338	6.57	
FAEC-28	Piper Tri-Pacer 150	22-5339	6.57	
FAEC-28	Piper Apache 160	23-293	9.55	believed w/o
FAEC-29	DHC.2 Beaver	1207	1958	
FAEC-30	DHC.2 Beaver	1224	1958	
FAEC-31	DHC.2 Beaver	1228	1958	
FAEC-34	Piper Tri-Pacer 160	22-6200	5.58	
FAEC-35	Piper Tri-Pacer 160	22-6199	5.58	
FAEC-36	Piper Tri-Pacer 160	22-6201	5.58	

Note that some FAEC serials were given to aircraft which had been delivered prior to reorganisation.

Helicopters continued to be numbered in a separate sequence, with an H- prefix, including :

H-6	Bell 47J	1768	5.59
H-7	Bell 47J	1766	7.59
H-8	Bell 47J	1776	7.59
H-9	Bell 47G-2	2437	7.59
H-11	Bell 47J	1786	9.59
H-13	Bell 47G-2	2440	10.59
H-14	Bell 47G-2	2442	10.59
H-15	Bell 47G-2	2444	10.59

Britain sold fifteen Hawker Sea Fury FB.11 fighter-bombers and two Royal Navy surplus Sea Fury T.20 conversion trainers (VZ349 and VZ363) to the Cuban AAF, some of which were later used by Castro's forces. Sea Fury FB.11s serialled FAR 541 and 542 have been preserved in Castrista markings, the former at Playa Girón, and the latter at Havana's Museo de la Revolución.

Shortly before Fidel Castro's triumph, the FAEC received eighteen Douglas B-26B/C Invader attack bombers. Half a dozen were fully operational at the time of the Bay of Pigs fiasco, and the confused situation which ensued was not made any clearer when the CIA-backed invading forces flew ex US civil Invaders with faked Cuban markings ! One of these 'FAR933' survived the operation and flew back to the USA; another escaped to Guatemala and was given the FAG serial 420; and six landed in Nicaragua, their subsequent fate being anyone's guess. At least one Lockheed T-33A was reported to have been delivered. Fulgencio Batista's government was busy procuring aircraft for use against the Sierra Maestra guerilas, but the US had already decided that their former ally was expendable and embargoed aircraft exports. Affected machines were ten North American T-28A basic trainers, serialled 151 to 160, most of which remained in Miami, Florida and were eventually purchased by Aviaparts Inc., and the first of a small number of Beechcraft T-34A Mentor basic trainers, serialled 521. These were at one stage painted in full insurgent markings with serials prefixed FAR for the Fuerza Aérea Revolucionaria (Revolutionary Air Force - a name which the Cuban Air Force still uses) in case the embargo was lifted, but by then the US government had realised that Fidel Castro was not exactly a champion of the American Way of Life.

The revolutionary forces used a miscellany of light aircraft in the final stages of their struggle against the Batista régime. These included single examples of the Cessna 120, 170, 172, 180 and 310, and Piper Tri-Pacer FAR-52, and most of these were later incorporated into the regular air arm. Two aircraft deserve special mention : a Cessna 180 which defected to the USA on 22 July 1961, and Cessna 310 FAR-53 which conveniently went missing on 28 October 1959 with the revolutionary leader Camilo Cienfuegos on board.

As soon as Fidel Castro decided to present his régime openly as Moscow-inspired, there was no way to maintain his supply of aircraft and spare parts from the USA. The FAR still had a handful of F-5D Mustangs (including FAR 401, which is currently preserved at Havana's Museo de la Revolución), Sea Furies and Invaders, but they could not be expected to be kept airworthy for long. Fortunately for the FAR — although hardly surprising — the Soviet Union was more than willing to fill in the gap, and weapons poured into Cuba, while the Fidelistas were busy mopping up the opposition and stirring up popular indignation against the Yankee imperialists. Missiles were also received — hundreds of Guideline SAMs and Samlet coastal defence SSMs — which put a substantial area of the southern United States within hostile reach for the first time in modern history; this sparked off the controversial Cuban missile crisis, which in the long run helped to consolidate the Cuban government in exchange for an agreement limiting Soviet presence on the island. Some sources believe that forty-two Sandal IRBMs and thirty-six Ilyishin Il-28 tactical bombers were shipped back to the USSR, but others are rather more sceptical.

Soviet aircraft deliveries were plentiful, including the following (here it must be stressed that quantities are purely estimated) : about sixty Mikoyan MiG-15 and at least twelve MiG-15UTI conversion trainers, followed by eighty plus MiG-17 (a defecting MiG-17F was serialled 232), some forty MiG-19PF (two were 733 and 761), up to a hundred MiG-21PF, PFM and MF (including MiG-21PFMA 518) and a batch of seventeen MiG-21L delivered late in 1981 to replace earlier aircraft passed on to Nicaragua; all of these served to build up a considerable fighter force. There were thirty-three of the Ilyushin Il-28 and Il-28U bombers, which are believed to have been returned to the Soviet Union and are no longer in use, and the transport element received some twenty Ilyushin Il-14, twelve Antonov An-2 (others were registerd to government agencies) and half a dozen Antonov An-24. The helicopter force has about thirty Mil Mi-1, about twenty-four Mi-4, twenty Mi-8 and possibly some Mi-24 gunships, whilst the standard basic trainer is the Czech-built Zlin Z.326T, of which at least fifty have been received. More recently, twenty Antonov An-26 tactical transports were ferried to Cuba with Soviet civil registrations :

CCCP-47323	c/n 6603	CCCP-47333	c/n 7207
CCCP-47324	6607	CCCP-47334	7303
CCCP-47325	6610	CCCP-47335	7306
CCCP-47326	6710	CCCP-47336	7309
CCCP-47327	6803	CCCP-47337	7406
CCCP-47328	6903	CCCP-47338	7701
CCCP-47329	6904	CCCP-47339	7702
CCCP-47330	6906	CCCP-47340	7704
CCCP-47331	7006	CCCP-47324	7803
CCCP-47332	7007	CCCP-47325	7907

They were camouflaged in Cuba and given FAR serials (one became FAR 1220).

In September 1978, about twenty Mikoyan MiG-23 Flogger-E tactical fighters were delivered, giving rise to some concern in the US State Department. Later intelligence reports indicate that fifteen MiG-27 Flogger-F ground-attack fighters and at least two MiG-23U Flogger-C conversion trainers have also been delivered. The Floggers are based at San Julián and the Havana suburban airfield of Guines, although the interceptor Escuadrones normally operate from Camagüey, Santa Clara and San Antonio de los Baños. The latest US State Department estimates put the strength of the Fuerza Aerea Revolucionaria at about 450 aircraft, including 190

fighters, 100 transports, and 90 helicopters; of the fighters, about ninety are MiG-21s, thirty MiG-23s (two squadrons of fifteen), and a hundred MiG-19s and MiG-17s.

Soviet military aircraft are of course regular visitors to Havana's José Martí International Airport and in fact there is a semi-permanent detachment of Soviet military Tupolev Tu-20 (Bear) electronic reconnaissance/maritime patrol bombers at San Antonio de los Banos. Soviet aircraft have also been reported on the small Isla de la Juventud (Island of Youth), known in pre-revolutionary days as Isla de los Pinos (Pinetree Island), where there are a number of prison camps for dissidents.

Cuba's new rôle in the Soviet global strategy, that of providing expeditionary troops for intervention elsewhere, has been added to its former assignment in communist expansionism, that of training guerilla forces for operation all over Latin America. Cuban troops have been active in Africa since the time of Angola's independence, and are acting as indispensable support for Angola's badly consolidated Marxist regime. FAR pilots fly the Angolan MiG-17, 19 and 21, mainly on ground-attack missions against pro-Western UNITA guerilla forces. Soviet and Cubana airliners are used for long-distance support and ferry flights.

There is of course no information available from official Cuban sources as to the FAR's organisation or strength. However, it is known that the FAR maintains a naval co-operation element, and that the navy itself operates no aircraft, although it controls a number of Samlet anti-shipping missile sites (some sources suggest that these are operated by FAR personnel). The Navy also has over a hundred small vessels, including some twenty missile armed patrol boats, but no ships have provision for aircraft. Cuba follows the Soviet model of close integration of all branches of the armed forces, and thus there is no separate army aviation either, but the Army has a small number of Frog-4 SSMs. The Cuban Army has about 130,000 all ranks (plus 90,000 reserve troops) and is assisted as necessary by the Peoples Militia of up to 200,000. Other

paramilitary and youth organisations total some 15,000; a similar number of State Security Troops, modelled on Soviet lines, also exist.

The FAR is believed to have about twenty fighter and fighter-bomber Escuadrones, at least two Escuadrones de Transporte, plus a basic training school and an operational conversion unit. The Escuela Nacional de Aviación Civil (National Civil Aviation School) provides crew training on ex FAR Ilyushin Il-14 transports. The missile force comprises about two dozen V750VK Guideline SAM sites, plus numbers of SA-3 Goa and SA-7 Grail anti-aircraft batteries.

The United States still hold a Naval Air Station at Guantánamo Bay, which provides gunnery training and target towing facilities for Atlantic Fleet units. US Naval Composite Squadron VC-10 is the resident unit, and there is a two-aircraft base flight.

COLOURS AND MARKINGS

Designed by the national poet Miguel Teurbe Tolon in 1849 and first carried by General Narcisco Lopez, the Cuban national flag was inspired by the United States flag, and was officially adopted in 1902. The three blue stripes represent the country's three original provinces; red stands for the blood shed by the patriots, and white for the purity of their cause. The triangle symbolises the revolutionary principles of Liberty, Equality and Fraternity. This flag has always been painted on Cuban military aircraft as a rudder flash. The roundel, which appears on the wings and (optionally) fuselage sides, reproduces the flag's main motifs.

The tradition in favour of these markings was so strong that the FAR's interim marking, a red-outlined white star flanked by blue bars (applied on the wings and fuselage), was soon abandoned. During the 1970s camouflage schemes based on East German and Soviet practice and consisting of disruptive areas of brown and green, have been used on some tactical aircraft.

Military Air Bases

1 La Habana - *transport base*
2 San Antonio de los Baños - *fighter, bomber and transport base*
3 Cienfuegos - *transport base*
4 Santa Clara - *fighter base*
5 Camagüey - *fighter base*
6 Santiago de Cuba - *transport base*
7 Guantánamo - *US base, NAS Guantanamo Bay*

DOMINICAN REPUBLIC

Area	48,442 sq km
Population	5,600,000
Capital	Santo Domingo
Civil registration	HI-

The Dominican Republic occupies the eastern part of the island of Hispaniola, discovered by Christopher Columbus on 5 December 1492; Santo Domingo founded by the discoverer's brother Bartholomew in 1496 is the oldest city in the Americas. The western part of the island is the Republic of Haiti, which shares a 193-mile border but has little in common with its neighbour, being a black nation speaking a French dialect and suffering from a substantially lower standard of living. This has long reflected itself in illegal immigration into the Dominican Republic, which remains a serious problem and has caused occasional border incidents; the two nations have been hostile several times in their history, and in fact the island was unified under the Haitians between 1822 and 1844, when the Dominican Republic was founded. The main source of wealth is agriculture, the principal exports being sugar, cocoa and coffee.

In 1941 the Dominican Army formed an Aviation Company (Compañía de Aviación del Ejército Dominicano) to provide a more effective defence of the frontier with Haiti, under instructions from the president, General Rafael Trujillo Molina; the headquarters were at General Andrews Airport, Ciudad Trujillo (now Santo Domingo), and the first aircraft were obtained from those already on the civil register -- including a Ford 4-AT trimotor (ex HI-2), a 5-AT-C (ex HI-5) and two Piper J.5A Cub Cruisers (ex HI-1 and HI-4, believed later sold as HI-86 and HI-110).

Following the United States involvement in the Second World War, the Dominican Government received additional machines from the USA in exchange for defence facilities; Aeronca L-3B liaison aircraft, Curtiss CW.19R and North American AT-6A Texan advanced trainers, Piper AE-1 Cub ambulances, a trio of Stearman PT-17 primary training biplanes and Vultee BT-13 basic trainers. A CW.19R named 'Colón' (Columbus) and which is currently preserved at Santo Domingo, was acquired in 1937 by the Dominican Government and successfully completed a pan-American flight in November-December of that year.

No further aircraft were required for a number of years and flying was limited by a tight budget. In time however, it became obvious that an effective air arm had to be formed. This led in 1948 to the reorganisation of the Compañía de Aviación, which became the Cuerpo de Aviación Militar Dominicana (Dominican Military Aviation Corps), its headquarters moving to Base Aérea Presidente Trujillo, in the capital's suburb of San Isidoro. At the same time, a re-equipment programme was initiated, orders being placed in the United States and Britain for more modern aircraft. From Britain came five Fairey-refurbished de Havilland Mosquito FB.VI fighter-bombers delivered in August-September 1948, and ten Bristol Beaufighter TF.X converted to Mk.VIF standards. The United States provided twenty-five Republic F-47D Thunderbolts for an Escuadrón de Caza-Bombardeo (Fighter-Bomber Squadron) and a single Boeing B-17G. The first Escuadrón de Caza was formed in October 1952 with some of the thirty-two ex Swedish Air Force North American F-51D Mustangs, later augmented by at least ten ex USAF Cavalier-converted F-51D. The Mustangs eventually formed the Grupo de Caza Ramfis, named after the dictator's son, Ramfis Trujillo. Sweden also supplied an initial batch of eight de Havilland Vampire FB.50 jet fighter-bombers, at least another thirty-three FB.50 and F.1 following. The Vampires, fitted with underwing bomb racks, served alongside the Thunderbolts until 1958, when they were relegated to advanced training, and then provided the country's first-line air defence, a few remaining in use to this date.

By 1958, the service was known as the Fuerza Aérea Dominicana (Dominican Air Force), was commanded by the Head of State through a State Secretary for the Armed Forces (previously the State Secretary for War, Navy and Aviation) and operated from a number of airfields and airstrips, including Dajabón, Montecristi and Puerto Plata in the north, Descubierta, La Vega, San Juan and Santiago in the centre, and Azau, Barahona, La Romana, Neiba, Pedernales and El Seibo in the south.

The Dominican Republic's internal stability was badly shaken following the assassination of General Trujillo in May 1961; although he had left office in 1952, the Trujillo family remained in power through Héctor Trujillo Molina until 1960 and was still very influential thereafter. With Trujillo dead, the usual free elections were held and Dr. Joaquin Balaguer elected as president, followed in February 1963 by Prof. Juan Bosch who was deposed in September of that year. A civil war followed between April and September of 1965, during which the FAD saw limited action. Order was restored by an OAS/OEA-appointed Inter-American Peace Force, made up of Brazilian, Costa Rican and Paraguayan forces as well as US Army and Marine units; an interim president was appointed, and new elections took place in June 1966. All this unrest made the re-organisation of the FAD an urgent matter. Small numbers of aircraft were handed over by the USA, including North American T-6G Texans, Beechcraft AT-11 crew trainers, a pair of Sikorsky UH-19 transport helicopters, two Beechcraft C-45 light transports and some Douglas B-26C Invaders. Other aircraft included two ex-Naval Catalinas, two Hiller UH12C light helicopters, three North American T-28A basic trainers (six armed T-28D arrived later for border patrol duties), and eight Cessna T-41D primary trainers. It was intended to replace the aged Vampires with surplus Hawker Hunters, but financial difficulties caused this plan to be shelved.

The Fuerza Aérea Dominicana, which has lately placed some emphasis on anti-guerilla operations, has its headquarters at San Isidoro, Santo Domingo, has a personnel strength of about 3,500, and receives technical assistance from a Santo Domingo based US Military Aid Advisory Group (MAAG).

Current Organisation

The FAD's current flying units are :

Escuadrón de Caza with twelve North American/Cavalier F-51D.

Escuadrón de Caza-Bombardeo with three Douglas B-26K and eight dH Vampire FB.50.

Escuadrón de Apoyo Táctico with six North American T-28D.

Escuadrón de Transporte Aéreo with six Douglas C-47 and five Curtiss C-46.

Escuadrón de Comunicaciones with three DHC.2 Beavers.

Escuadrón de Helicópteros with two Bell 205A-1, two Hiller UH12, six Hughes OH-6A, and Sud Alouette II/III.

Escuela de Aviación Militar with six North American T-6G,

Escuela de Aviación Militar with six North American T-6G, two Beechcraft AT-11, eight Cessna T-41D and two Lockheed T-33A.

Escuadrilla Presidencial with one SNIAS AS.365 Dauphin 2 helicopter.

Additionally, the government owns the presidential aircraft, Boeing 727-2J1 c/n 21036, but this is operated in civil marks as HI-242.

Escuadron de Caza-Bombardeo - blue/white/red outer rings with white indentations. Yellow background; red insect with grey wings and bomb, red shield, white propwash. Roundels on wings.

Grupo de Caza Ramfis - red outer ring, orange background, green dragon with purple wings and claws, red eye and flames; black lettering, white stars.

Military Air Bases

1 Santo Domingo (San Isidoro)
2 Montecristi
3 Puerto Plata
4 Santiago
5 La Vega
6 Pedernales
7 Barahona
8 Azua
9 San Cristóbal
10 La Romana

Aircraft Review

COLOURS AND MARKINGS

The Dominican roundel is based on the national flag designed in 1844 by Juan Pablo Duarte, the leader of the Threefold (La Trinitaria) Movement, thus named because of its struggle for God, Country and Liberty. Red stands for the blood shed for independence, white for the people's sacrifices and blue for liberty. The flag appears as a rudder or fin flash (omitted on camouflaged aircraft) and again in roundel form, although the latter incorporates a Celtic cross. Transports are usually marked *Fuerza Aérea Dominicana* and most aircraft have FAD applied on the fin. Some operational types fly in a distinctive camouflage scheme, basically dark green with large dark brown blotches; these have small-size roundels and no tail markings apart from FAD and the serial number.

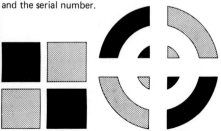

SERIAL NUMBERS

The FAD differs from many Latin American air arms in having an extremely clear serialling system. Aircraft are given a four digit serial in one of three blocks : 1000 for fighters and advanced trainers; 2000 for bombers and fighter-bombers; 3000 other types, with the first two digits signifying the aircraft type, as follows:

10	North American AT-6 Texan
11	Republic F-47D Thunderbolt
15	various communications types
16	North American T-28D
19	North American F-51D Mustang
23	Boeing B-17G Fortress
25	North American B-25H Mitchell
27	de Havilland Vampire
28	North American T-28
29	Consolidated PBY-5A Catalina
30	various helicopters
31	Curtiss C-46 Commando
32	Douglas B-26 Invader
33	Lockheed T-33A
34	Douglas C-47 Skytrain

Aircraft known to have been used by the FAD:

AERO COMMANDER 520

One only, serialled 1507, c/n 8, ex HI-27 and N1504.

AERONCA L-3B

Four believed delivered. Two were civilianised in 1950 as HI-10 (c/n 11883) and HI-11 respectively.

BEECHCRAFT C-45

Possibly two, of which one was serialled 1510.

BELL 205A-1

Two helicopters serialled 3018 and 3019.

BOEING B-17G FORTRESS

2301 only, used as a transport.

BRISTOL BEAUFIGHTER VIF

Ten aircraft ex Royal Air Force stocks in late 1948, converted from TF.X standards and serialled 306 to 315. Aircraft 309 was ex RD432.

CESSNA T-41D

Eight delivered, ex USAF 71-1059 to 1062, 74-2093 to 2096, five of which remain in service. Two were serialled as 1505 and 1508 (not communications serials !).

CONSOLIDATED PBY-5A CATALINA

Serial 2901 is confirmed; Coast Guard GC-17 presumably later became 2902. Two were reported to be in use until recently.

CURTISS C-46A COMMANDO

At least six, five of which are believed to be still on charge :

3101	c/n 30437	ex 42-96775, Bu39560	
3102			
3103			
3104	26755	42-3622	to N9070 5.70
3105			
3106			

DE HAVILLAND MOSQUITO FB.VI

Five aircraft :

301	ex RAF	TE612	d/d 18.8.48
302		TE909	18.8.48
303		TE822	3.9.48
304		TE873	29.9.48
305		RF939	29.9.48

DE HAVILLAND VAMPIRE F.1/FB.50

Forty two aircraft were obtained from Sweden, F.1s 2701

Aero Commander 520 1507, the sole example operated by the FAD, at San Isidoro 20.6.72.

Morane-Saulnier MS.893A Commodore 180 1506, again at San Isidoro in June 1972.

De Havilland Vampire FB.50 2726 at San Isidoro in June 1972.

Douglas C-47 Skytrain 3404 at the same location and time; seven C-47s were supplied.

to 2725 (converted to fighter-bombers) and FB.50s 2726 to 2742. Nine are believed to be in service.

DE HAVILLAND CANADA DHC.2 BEAVER

One only, 1504, c/n 136, sold as HI-23.

DOUGLAS C-47 SKYTRAIN

At least seven were taken on charge with serials 3401 to 3407; five are said to remain in use.

DOUGLAS B-26C INVADER

In January 1963 four B-26s were known to be operated under MAP (though one was for spares use), but five more, supposedly sold to Chile for aerial survey work, were later added to the fleet. Five surviving aircraft were offered for sale in December 1967, including FAD 3203, 3206 and 3207, of which 3206 had been converted for transport duties. Most of the others were converted for counter-insurgency duties, and three are said to be still in use.

HILLER UH12

Two were procured :
3001 UH12A c/n 128   ex N8128H
3002 UH12C   813   HI-38

HUGHES OH-6A

Seven helicopters acquired; one was written off on 22.3.76.

LOCKHEED T-33A

At least six serialled 3301 to 3306, of which at least two are said to be still in service.

MORANE-SAULNIER MS.893A COMMODORE

One Rallye Commodore 180 only, serialled 1506, c/n 11450 still in service.

NORTH AMERICAN B-25H MITCHELL

Two aircraft serialled 2501 and 2502; the latter was sold as N3970C.

NORTH AMERICAN F-51D MUSTANG

Thirty-two were obtained from Sweden, followed by at least another eleven ; most if not all were refurbished by Cavalier. The serials appear to have been 1900 to 1942 inclusive, and twenty-nine of the ex-Swedish aircraft are identified :

44-13917	ex Swedish 26004
44-63511	26169
44-63688	26161
44-63701	26015
44-63739	26070
44-63759	26067
44-63762	26129
44-63791	26086
44-63818	26147
44-63819	26150
44-63830	26125
44-64091	26111
44-64152	26110
44-72033	26099
44-72051	26026
44-72074	26008
44-72075	26126
44-72086	26009
44-72107	26070
44-72123	26092
44-72126	26012
44-72151	26028
44-72164	26143
44-72177	26014
44-72188	26103
44-72202	26112
44-72406	26094
44-72438	26131
44-72449	26124

NORTH AMERICAN T-28A/D

Three T-28A were delivered, ex USAF 49-1513, 1543 and 1665, becoming 2801 to 2803 though not necessarily in the same order; they were sold as HI-315, HI-283 and HI-282 respectively. The Escuadrón de Apoyo Táctico (Tactical Support Squadron) still uses six T-28D serialled 2804 to 2809, and two more T-28Ds have been noted in camouflage colours, serialled 1603 and 1610.

NORTH AMERICAN AT-6 TEXAN

About a dozen AT-6A were delivered under Lend-Lease, followed by some forty machines of later models, including T-6G. Confirmed serials are 1001 to 1040, 1051 and 1058.

REPUBLIC F-47D THUNDERBOLT

Twenty-five were delivered, serialled 1101 to 1125. They were relegated to advanced training duties in 1958 and then retired in 1964.

SIKORSKY S.55C

Two only, no longer in service :
3003   c/n 55.1156
3004   55.1174

SNIAS AS.365 DAUPHIN 2

One helicopter delivered to the Escuadrilla Presidencial in 1978, c/n 5003 ex F-WTNL.

STEARMAN PT-17

Three aircraft, ex USAAF 42-16648 to 42-16650.

SUD ALOUETTE II

Two SE.3130 Alouette II were :
3005 c/n 1245
3006   1281
Another SE.3130 serial was 1520 (this later sold as HI-54); an unidentified SE.3130 was sold as HI-195. There were also two SE.3180 Alouette II Astazou :
3007   2141   to HI-234
3008   2195

SUD SA.316 ALOUETTE III

One is in service :
3009   c/n 1442

Army & Gendarmeria

The mid-1950s saw the formation of a small artillery spotting element within the Dominican Army (Ejército Dominicano), flying three Cessna 170 from 1959 onwards; no replacements are known to have been acquired. The Army itself is quite small, with a total strength of 11,000 in four infantry brigades and two artillery regiments (one of them anti-aircraft). The 10,000-man Gendarmería does not operate any aircraft.

Coast Guard & Navy

The Guardia-Costas, operating under the control of the 4,200-strong Dominican Navy (Marina de Guerra Dominicana) used to have two Consolidated PBY-5A Catalina amphibians, one of which had the serial GC-17, alongside half a dozen patrol vessels. At least one Catalina survived and may have become FAD 2902. The Navy itself operates no aircraft, and no ships have provision for helicopters. The main naval bases are at Las Calderas, west of the capital, and San Pedro de Macorís, between Santo Domingo and La Romana.

North American T-6G Texan 1051 , a camouflaged example at San Isidoro in June 1972.

North American T-6G Texan 1058 in natural metal finish at the same location and date.

ECUADOR

Area	455,502 sq km
Population	7,814,000
Capital	Quito
Civil registration	HC-

The Republic of Ecuador, once a Spanish colony and later a part of the Greater Colombia Federation became independent on 13 May 1830. A predominantly agricultural country, Ecuador is one of the relatively few independent nations to have part of their boundaries not yet delimited — the 1942 Treaty which gave Peru part of the Amazonian territories was unilaterally denounced in 1961 and the Galápagos Islands (officially known as the Archipélago de Colón) are temporarily administered by the Ministry of National Defence.

Military service is compulsory for all males aged twenty and over, for a period of twelve months, but actual conscription is limited by current needs and budgetary planning. The Head of State is also the Commander-in-Chief of the Armed Forces. There is a 5,800-strong national police force, the Policía Civil Nacional, normally controlled by the Ministry of Internal Affairs, which comes under the Ministry of National Defence in case of war. Ecuador is divided into four Army defence regions with headquarters at Quito, Guayaquil, Cuenca and Pastaza respectively.

Although plans were in existence in 1919 to invite a United States military mission into Ecuador and to acquire a few Royal Air Force surplus aircraft, Ecuadorian military flying began in 1920, when an Italian air mission established a flying school at Eloy Alfaro, facing Guayaquil, on the opposite bank of the Guayas river, with five SAML Aviatiks plus a few Ansaldo SVA and Savoia biplanes and an Italian commanding officer. The school was officially named as the Escuela de Aviación Militar (Military Flying School) and became the nucleus of the Cuerpo de Aviadores Militares del Ejército Ecuatoriano (Ecuadorian Army Military Aviators' Corps). A number of Ecuadorian officer pilots were brought up to wings standards by Italian instructors and in time a second airfield was opened up at Quito. The Escuela subsequently re-equipped with ten Italian-supplied Gabardini training biplanes but the Cuerpo's development was handicapped by financial problems, and military flying was reduced progressively, although a re-organisation took place in the early 1930s allowing for the formation of an operational element within the renamed Fuerza Aérea del Ejército Ecuatoriano (Ecuadorian Army Air Force). The Escuela de Aviación Militar was moved to Simón Bolívar airfield in Guayaquil and an air ambulance service inaugurated with a Ford 5-AT-CS trimotor acquired in 1931.

By 1935 the decision was taken to re-organise the service in depth along US lines. The Escuela was placed under the command of a US instructor, a few selected Ecuadorian pilots were sent to the United States to receive advanced training, and the first modern biplanes were acquired — a single Curtiss-Wright CW.14R Osprey observation aircraft and six CW.16E basic trainers. These were followed in 1938 by a small number of CW.19R advanced trainers, although Italy was not forgotten, a couple of IMAM Ro 37bis reconnaissance biplanes being procured. Little else was accomplished for some time, apart from the inauguration of six new airfields - Manta in the north, Latacunga and Riobamba in the centre, and Cuenca, Loja and Salinas in the south. In January 1941, in return for the concession of facilities for the construction of an airfield at Punta Salinas as part of the Panama Canal defence network, the US government sent an air mission to re-organise once again the Ecuadorian air arm; the deal included a handful of Fairchild PT-19 and North American AT-6 trainers, and the establishment of a basic training school at Salinas airfield.

1941 was a difficult year for Ecuador; its Amazonian territories were occupied by Peru and their greater part was surrendered to Peru by the January 1942 Rio de Janeiro arbitration protocol. Then, after Pearl Harbor in 1941, the US government began pressuring Ecuador to take over the national airline, Sociedad Ecuatoriana de Transportes Aéreos (SETA, Ecuadorian Air Transport Company) which had been founded, and was still being run by the Germans. This at least had a positive result as far as the Ecuadorian AAF was concerned — the airline's Junkers Ju 52/3m were impressed into military service. US aid followed; half a dozen obsolete

Seversky P-35 fighters were delivered to equip Ecuador's first Escuadrilla de Caza, followed by three Ryan PT-22 trainers (ex USAAF 41-15174 to 15176) for the Escuela de Aviacion Militar. It was not much, but it had to do until the end of the Second World War, by which time the Escuela had re-equipped with forty-seven Ryan STM series trainers.

The Ecuadorian AAF entered the second half of the 1940s as a diminutive force, controlled by the Ministry of Defence through a Comandancia de Aeronáutica (Air Command). Things began to change for the better after Ecuador signed the 1947 Rio Pact; an extensive re-organisation took place, the service being renamed as the Fuerza Aérea Ecuatoriana (Ecuadorian Air Force) as a consequence of its new autonomy. Small numbers of North American AT-6 trainers, Consolidated PBY-5A amphibians and Beechcraft C-45 light transports were taken on charge, as were a few Douglas C-47 which were to become the initial equipment of an expanded transport force, the Transportes Aéreos Militares Ecuatorianos (TAME, Ecuadorian Military Air Transport). The Catalinas, which were also placed under TAME control, equipped a patrol Escuadrilla which also flew transport missions from the Ecuadorian mainland to the Galápagos Islands. Some twenty Republic F-47D Thunderbolt fighter-bombers equipped a fighter Grupo and remained in service until 1964.

Modernisation plans were surprisingly far-reaching for such a peaceful country with a disastrous military tradition; an order was placed in May 1954 for six English Electric Canberra B.6 bombers and twelve Gloster Meteor FR.9 reconnaissance/fighters, making Ecuador the second South American nation to have a tactical jet force. Although the Meteors are no longer in service, three of the Canberras were still very much active in 1979-80. A relatively effective close-support unit, the Escuadrón de Caza-Bombardeo 2112 was also formed in June 1958 with the first of sixteen US-supplied Lockheed F-80C Shooting Stars.

From then on, the Ecuadorian Air Force has

tried hard to maintain its post-war image of an up-to-date efficient force. Although a small degree of United States aid has been received, Ecuador maintained trade links with Great Britain, orders being placed in more recent years for sixteen BAC Strikemaster Mk.89A close-support aircraft and twelve BAC Jaguar tactical fighter-bombers (two of these being conversion trainers); other aircraft were obtained from US, French or Canadian manufacturers, or from the national airline Ecuatoriana. There was an urgent need for a fighter type; initial plans to obtain twelve ex-Belgian Air Force Hawker Hunter F.6 and a single T.7 fell through for political reasons, and an order for twenty-four IAI Kfir C2 from Israel was not taken up due to US restrictions on the export of powerplants, but in 1977 sixteen Dassault Mirage F1JE and two F1JB were ordered, all having been delivered by mid-1980.

Current Organisation

The present day Fuerza Aérea Ecuatoriana has a personnel of about 4,800, and comprises the following units :

Ala de Combate 21 (Combat Wing 21) at Taura, made up of three Escuadrones -
Escuadrón de Combate 2111 'Aguilas' with BAC Jaguar International.
Escuadrón de Combate 2112 with Cessna A-37B
Escuadrón de Combate 2113 with BAC Strikemaster 89A.

Escuadrón de Bombardeo with English Electric Canberra B.6

Grupo de Transportes Aéreos Militares (Military Air Transport Group) incorporating TAME- Transportes Aéreos Militares Ecuatorianos, with Douglas C-47 and DC-6, DHC.5D Buffalo, DHC.6 Twin Otter, HS.748, Lockheed C-130H Hercules and L.188 Electra, Boeing 707, 720, 727 and 737. These aircraft usually operate from Mariscal Sucre Airport, Quito, and some are shared with Ecuatoriana.

Escuela de Aviación Militar at Guayaquil with Cessna T-41 and A150, Beechcraft T-34C, Lockheed T-33A and SIAI Marchetti SF.260C.

There are also a number of liaison and rescue Escuadrillas using the Beechcraft King Air 90, Piper Navajo, Sud SA.315B Lama, SA.330 Puma and SA.316 Alouette III.

Ala de Combate 21 - white/black with all lettering and aircraft silhouettes in red, landscape green and star blue.

Escuadrón 2111 - yellow and black with white Meteor silhouette; 'Aguilas' and '2111' are black on white.

Escuadrón 2112 - yellow background, green landscape; green and black dragon with red nose/nostrils, white wings and tail.

Escuadrón 2113 - white/black outer rings; inner disc is light blue; white bird with yellow beak; red lightning bolt.

TAME - blue disc with white edging, and a black bird.

Military Air Bases

1 Guayaquil
2 Punta Salinas
3 Eloy Alfaro
4 Quito
5 Latacunga
6 Riobamba
7 Cuenca
8 Loja

Aircraft Review

COLOURS AND MARKINGS

Like Colombia's, Ecuador's flag is based on the Gran Colombia flag and its colours are said to symbolise the country's natural resources (yellow), the sky and the sea (blue) and the blood shed by the patriots (red). It appears on military aircraft as a fin flash or rudder stripes, and the roundels, often applied on the wings only, have the same colours in proportions directly related to those of the flag. The inscriptions *FAE* and *Fuerza Aérea Ecuatoriana* appear on air force aircraft.

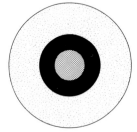

Although the usual US camouflage schemes are used, the FAE had adopted its own brown/tan disruptive scheme with reduced-size markings; in some cases, the fin markings have been omitted.

SERIAL NUMBERS

Most current FAE aircraft use their constructors numbers as serial numbers, with the prefix 'FAE'. The use of 'Buzz-number' type codes with prefixes denoting the aircraft's primary role, is common on first-line aircraft and trainers.

Aircraft known to have been used by the Fuerza Aérea Ecuatoriana in recent years include :

BAC 167 STRIKEMASTER Mk.89A

Sixteen were delivered between 1972 and 1976 and allocated to Escuadrón de Combate 2113.

243	c/n 311	ex G-27-207
244	312	G-27-208, G-AZXL
245	313	G-27-209
246	314	G-27-210
247	315	G-27-211
248	316	G-27-212
249	317	G-27-213
250	318	G-27-214
251	337	G-27-235
252	338	G-27-236
253	339	G-27-237
254	340	G-27-238
255	347	G-27-246
256	348	G-27-247
257	349	G-27-248
258	350	G-27-249

BAC JAGUAR INTERNATIONAL

Deliveries to Escuadrón de Combate 2111 were made during 1977. The serials correspond with SEPECAT build numbers. Ten Jaguar A single-seaters :

289	c/n 172	ex G-27-268
302	181	G-27-269
309	188	G-27-270
318	191	G-27-271
327	197	G-27-272
329	199	G-27-273
339	206	G-27-274
340	207	G-27-275
348	214	G-27-276
349	215	G-27-277

Two Jaguar B two-seaters :

283	168	G-27-266
305	183	G-27-267

BEECHCRAFT C-45 EXPEDITOR

Ten believed to have been delivered, of which six were still in use in 1976, but now presumed to have been withdrawn.

BEECHCRAFT T-34 MENTOR

T-34A TH-334 and TH-344 are confirmed, the latter being

on display at Quito-Mariscal Sucre. Subsequent orders were placed for twenty turbine-powered T-34C, delivered in 1978 with serials including 0014 and 0018 to 0030.

BEECHCRAFT KING AIR E90

One only, HC-DAC c/n LW.178 used for navaid calibration by the Dirección de Aviación Civil (Directorate of Civil Aviation).

BEECHCRAFT SUPER KING AIR 200

One aircraft, HC-BHG c/n BB.723 delivered in 1981 for use as a VIP transport, but written off on 24.5.81.

BELL 47G

Three were used; no details known.

BELL UH-1D IROQUOIS

At least two delivered, serialled 820 and 823.

BELL 212

An unspecified number delivered in 1979.

BOEING 707-321B

Four aircraft, all originally Pan Am, delivered 1976-1981, and shared with Ecuatoriana :

19265/HC-BCT	c/n 19265	ex N420PA
19273/HC-BGP	19273	N451RN
19277/HC-BFC	19277	N424PA
20033/HC-BHY	20033	N896PA

BOEING 720-023B

Three aircraft retaining Ecuatoriana livery and shared with the airline :

18033/HC-BDP	c/n 18033	ex N7547A, HC-AZO
18036/HC-AZP	18036	N7550A
18037/HC-AZQ	18037	N7551A

BOEING 727-2T3

One only, delivered to TAME 30.9.80, named 'Colopaxi'. 22078/HC-BHM   c/n 22078 ex N1293E,(N710EV)

BOEING 737 -2V2

One new aircraft delivered 5.10.81 : 22607/HC-BIG   c/n 22607   ex N8283V

CESSNA 172F

Eight aircraft delivered in April 1965 :

835	c/n 52835
836	52836
837	52837
838	52838
840	52840
841	52841
845	52845
847	52847

CESSNA 180

A few delivered; details unknown.

CESSNA 320

At least one; details not known.

CESSNA 337D

One only 1159/HC-QYA, c/n 337-1159, formerly HC-GYA of the Dirección de Aviación Civil (Directorate of Civil Aviation).

CESSNA A-37B

Twelve were delivered for use by the Escuadrón de Combate 2112, the first arriving in April 1976 :

374	c/n 43528	exUSAF 75-374
375	43529	75-375
376	43530	75-376

De Havilland Canada DHC.5D Buffalo 064, one of two delivered in April 1976 for TAME use.

Beechcraft T-34C Turbo-Mentor 0020 and others seen at Wichita prior to delivery.

Cessna T-41D 0436, one of twelve for the Escuela de Aviacion Militar.

Douglas C-47B Skytrain 77164/HC-AUT at Quito in July 1978.

Douglas DC-3 1969/HC-AUV in TAME colours at Quito on 18 April 1972.

377	43531	75-377
378	43532	75-378
379	43533	75-379
380	43534	75-380
381	43535	75-381
382	43536	75-382
383	43537	75-383
384	43538	75-384
385	43539	75-385

CESSNA T-41D

Twelve were delivered to the Escuela de Aviación Militar in 1970 :

433	c/n	R172-0433
434		R172-0434
435		R172-0435
436		R172-0436
437		R172-0437
438		R172-0438
439		R172-0439
440		R172-0440
441		R172-0441
442		R172-0442
443		R172-0443
444		R172-0444

CONSOLIDATED PBY-5A CATALINA

Three were used, of which one, 53602 is preserved at Quito Mariscal Sucre airport.

CURTISS C-46 COMMANDO

One was operated with the serial 810; this may have been C-46D c/n 33206 ex 44-77810 and Peruvian AF 61-324.

DASSAULT MIRAGE F1J

Sixteen F1JE single-seaters serialled 801 to 816 and two F1JB two-seaters serialled 830 and 831 were ordered in 1977, with deliveries completed in 1980. 805 was written off on 25.6.80.

DE HAVILLAND CANADA DHC.5D BUFFALO

Two delivered in April 1976 for TAME use :
HC-BFG/063 c/n 63
HC-BFH/064   64
A third aircraft was ordered in December 1980.

DHC.6 TWIN OTTER 300

Three aircraft delivered on 28 April 1975:
446/HC-BCG   c/n 446
453/HC-BAV   453   w/o 2.9.80
457/HC-BAX   457   w/o 21.5.81
A fourth was acquired in the USA in October 1977 :
440/HC-   440   ex N547N

DOUGLAS C-47/DC-3

Fourteen plus were taken on charge, most being given dual serials/registrations in addition to 'buzz-numbers' - for example CA-164 for 77164/HC-AUT, CA-448 for 76448/HC-AUQ. Of the following identified aircraft, 1969 was a DC-3-209 delivered with USAF funds; 4341 was a C-47; 11747 and 11775 C-53D; 49785, 49789, 76448 and 77164 C-47B and the remainder C-47A. About six remain in service.

1969/HC-AUV	c/n 1969	ex N17323	
4341/HC-AUZ	4341	41-7842,PP-ANP	
11747/HC-AUY	11747	42-68820, PP-AKI	
11775/HC-AVD	11775	42-68848,N9321R	
15677/HC-AUR	20143	43-15677	
20120/HC-A....	20120	43-15654, N16774	
20179/HC-AUK	20179	43-15713, PP-YPJ	
			w/o 12.9.71
23926/HC-A....	9788	43-23926	w/o 1971
49785/HC-AUP	15601/27046	43-49785	
49789/HC-AUS	15605/27050	43-49789	
76448/HC-AUQ	16032/32780	44-76448	
77164/HC-AUT	16748/33496	44-77164	preserved at Quito
92066/HC-AVC	11825	42-92066	

DOUGLAS DC-6B

Six aircraft; the first two were acquired in September 1964 and summer of 1965, the rest in 1970/71.
43266/HC-ATK   c/n 43266   ex N90754   To N9429 in 1973
43564/HC-A....   43564   N90767   wfu 1975

44691/HC-AVH	44691	CC-CCE	Preserved at Quito
45063/HC-AVI	45063	CC-CCG	wfu 1978
45133/HC-AXS	45133	N37581	
45535/HC-AVG	45535	CC-CDN	

ENGLISH ELECTRIC CANBERRA B.6

Six aircraft ordered in May 1954 and delivered 801 to 806, but later given BE prefixes to their serials; they were renumbered early in 1963 :
BE-801 became 71390/BE-390
BE-802   71391/BE-391
BE-803   71402/BE-402
BE-804   71405/BE-405
BE-805   71411/BE-411
BE-806   71509/BE-509
71509/BE-509 (as such early in 1974) later became 71409 correcting an earlier administrative error.

GLOSTER METEOR FR.9

Twelve were delivered in 1954 to Escuadrón de Combate 2111 :

701	ex-RAF VZ597	d/d 9.7.54
702	WH547	14.7.54
703	VW366	16.8.54
704	WB136	23.8.54
705	VZ610	13.9.54
706	WH540	15.9.54
707	WH543	29.9.54
708	WH549	23.9.54
709	WH550	7.10.54
710	WH553	20.10.54
711	WH554	29.10.54
712	WH555	19.11.54

They were all re-numbered, the new serials including FF-116 FF-119 and FF-123, the latter being preserved at the Museo Aéreo de la FAE at Quito. A Meteor was written off 3.3.75.

HAWKER SIDDELEY HS.748 Srs.2

Five aircraft: two Series 246, one Series 267 which became the Presidential aircraft and two Series 285 freighters with a large loading door on the port side of the fuselage :

682/HC-AUD	c/n 1682	d/d 3.10.70	
683/HC-AUF	1683	23.10.70	w/o 20.1.76
684/HC-AUK	1684	21.11.70	to FAE 001
738/HC-BAZ	1738	21.11.75	
739/HC-BEY	1739	10.4.76	

HILLER FH.1100

One only, c/n 71, delivered in October 1967 but no longer in service.

LOCKHEED L.188 ELECTRA

Six aircraft obtained for use by TAME: two L-188A-08-11 c/ns 1002 and 1004; two L.188A-08-08 c/ns 1040 and 1052, one L-188A-08-10 c/n 1050 and one L.188C-08-06 c/n 2004.

1002/HC-AMS	c/n 1002	ex VR-HFN	d/d 3.75	wfu
1004/HC-ANQ	1004	VR-HFO	3.75	wfu
1040/HC-AZT	1040	N9701C	27.2.75	
1050/HC-AZL	1050	N278AC	3.11.74	
1052/HC-AZY	1052	N9702C	6.75	
2004/HC-AZJ	2004	N385AC	6.8.74	

Aircraft were named 1040 'Azuay'; 1050 'Guayas'; 1052 'Galápagos'; 2004 'Pichincha'.

LOCKHEED C-130H HERCULES

Two model L.382C-74D were delivered :

743	c/n 4743	d/d 12.7.77	(HC-BEF)
748	4748	9.8.77	w/o 12.7.78

The crashed aircraft was replaced by an L.382C-87D :

812	4812	4.79	

Another w/o 29.4.82 near Quito.

LOCKHEED F-80C SHOOTING STAR

Sixteen were delivered between 1957 and 1960, of which six were returned to the USA in July 1965. They were used by the Escuadrón de Caza-Bombardeo 2112. Known aircraft are :

TF-184	ex 47-184	
TF-394	48-394	
TF-769	49-769	
TF-808	49-1808	
TF-809	49-1809	
TF-810	49-1810	
TF-851	49-851	†
TF-867	49-867	
TF-872	49-1872	†
TF-884	49-884	†

† These three aircraft became ground targets at the US Navy's China Lake NAWC gunnery range.

LOCKHEED T-33A

At least twelve delivered, including :

AT-707	ex 52-9707	d/d 1962
AT-799	52-9799	d/d 1962
AT-919	53-5919	d/d 1962
	52-9502	
	52-9589	
	52-9607	
	53-4910	

Another T-33A, on Ala de Combate 21 charge, was 52-9945 which flew as TD-945, and is preserved at the Museo Aéreo de la FAE, Quito.

NORTH AMERICAN AT-6 TEXAN

Some thirty believed delivered, mainly AT-6, AT-6A and AT-6D. None remains in service. Three were :

20310/TB-310	at Parque Aeronáutico Mariscal Sucre, Quito
43233	ex 41-33233 ?; at Museo Aéreo de la FAE
86058/TB-058	ex 42-86058 at Colegio Técnico Aeronáutico, Quito.

NORTH AMERICAN B-25J MITCHELL

One is in the Museo Aéreo de la FAE in Ecuadorian Air Force markings with the serial B-N9069Z, an adapted US civil registration; it was originally 44-86866; no further details of its acquisition or service, if any, are known.

NORTH AMERICAN T-28A

About twenty T-28A were delivered, half of which were eventually modified to T-28D standards as interim close-support aircraft (one was 0-91647 of Escuadrón de Combate 2113; this has been preserved). Eight or nine are believed to remain in service. The T-28D conversions equipped Escuadrones de Combate 2112 and 2113 until 1977-78. Known aircraft include :

49-1545	ex 49-1545	
0-91647	49-1647 (T-28D)	
91686	49-1686	
00211	50-211	
50243	50-243	
51-3572/TB-572	51-3572	

PIPER PA.31 NAVAJO

Two aircraft only :

31-571/HC-ARB	c/n 31-571	
31-572/HC-ARC	31-572	w/o 7.3.80

REPUBLIC F-47D THUNDERBOLT

About twenty delivered; withdrawn from use in 1964.

SIAI-MARCHETTI SF.260C

Twelve reportedly delivered in 1978; no further details.

SIKORSKY UH-19B

One was 527536 (ex 52-7536) and another flew as '54'.

SUD SA.315B LAMA

Four helicopters, used mainly for rescue duties.

SUD SA.316 ALOUETTE III

Six were delivered, including :

967	c/n 1967	
969	1969	
971	1971	
975	1975	w/o 4.6.77
982	1982	w/o 10.3.77

SUD SA.330C PUMA

Two only, delivered in 1974 :

226	c/n 1226	ex F-WKQD
227	1227	ex F-ZKBL. W/o 24.12.76, but sold back as F-WIPC, later SA.330J I-EHPD.

English Electric Canberra B.6 805 — an early shot.

Douglas DC-6B 43266/HC-AJF, one of the TAME transport fleet.

Hawker Siddeley HS.748 Srs.285 738/HC-BAZ is one of two with a large loading door to port.

Lockheed C-130H Hercules 748 photographed in July 1978, shortly prior to being written off.

Hawker Siddeley HS.748 Srs.267 FAE 001 /HC-AUK, the Presidential aircraft, photographed in February 1977.

Ecuadorian Army

The Servicio de Aviación del Ejército Ecuatoriano (SAE) is the flying branch of the Ecuadorian Army (which has a strength of 27,500 all ranks), and it undertakes artillery observation and communications duties for the ground forces, as well as having a small training element. SAE aircraft are either based at Quito, where the Military Academy and Officers' School operate, or are detached to any of a number of airfields and airstrips around the country, in support of the eleven infantry battalions, ten independent infantry companies and three artillery regiments of the Ecuadorian Army.

Army aircraft carry national markings similar to those of the air force, and carry the inscriptions *SAE* or *Ejercito*. An SA.315B Lama flew in a distinctive overall camouflage of brown, light green and slate grey.

Aircraft serial numbers are prefixed according to rôle; examples include AE for Artillería y Escuela (artillery and training), E for Escuela (training), T for Transporte (transport). The IGM prefix is used on aircraft operated by the Army's Instituto Geográfico Militar (Military Geographic Institute), which is in charge of photo survey and weather reconnaissance. Aircraft known to have been used by the Servicio de Aviación del Ejército include :

BEECHCRAFT QUEEN AIR 80

Two aircraft operated by the Instituto Geográfico Militar, the first a model 80, the second a model A80 :
LD230 'Cóndor I' c/n LD.230 ex HC-AKI
IGM-240   LD.240

BEECHCRAFT SUPER KING AIR 200

One aircraft serialled AEE-001, delivered early 1981.

CESSNA T-41D

At least two : one is E-150.

CESSNA 172G

One, delivered in November 1965, was SAE-R-1520, c/n 53868.

CESSNA 185D

Two were delivered in February 1965 :
SAE-R-1525 c/n 185-0839
SAE-R-1530   185-0858

CESSNA TU.206D

One aircraft, IGM-371 c/n 01371 delivered as HC-IGM.

DE HAVILLAND CANADA DHC.5 BUFFALO

Four were due for 1981 delivery, but only one, AEE-501 c/n 104 appears to have been delivered so far. AEE-502 is allocated to c/n 107; the others should be AEE-503/504.

HILLER UH12E

Two are believed to have been delivered.

IAI 201 ARAVA

Five aircraft :
T-201	c/n 0010	ex 4X-IAH
T-202	0011	4X-IAJ
T-203	0012	4X-IAK
T-204	0019	4X-IAR
T-205	0023	4X-IAV

LEAR JET 24D

One only, equipped for photo-survey :
IGM-401 c/n 24.312

PILATUS PC.6/B TURBO-PORTER

Three were delivered; one is T-185 c/n 307L.

SHORT SKYVAN 3M-400-6

One only, T-100/HC-AXH, c/n SH.1868 ex G-AXNV and G-14-40, delivered on 27.4.71 and initially based at Teniente Coronel Colón Grijalva airfield, Rio Amazonas. It was sold as N5592Y in March 1980.

SUD SA.315B LAMA

At least two :
IGM-313 c/n 2313
?   2576

SUD SA.316 ALOUETTE III

Two are known to have been used by the IGM :
IGM-229 c/n 2229
IGM-275   2275 w/o 27.3.79

Beechcraft Queen Air 80 LD-230 of the Instituto Geografico Militar, at Quito in 1977.

IAI 201 Arava T-203 seen here passing through Prestwick on delivery.

Lear Jet 24D IGM401 equipped for photo-survey work, at Quito in 1977.

Cessna T.337F AN-211 of the Ecuadorian Navy.

Cessna TU.206D IGM-371 was delivered to the IGM as HC-IGM. It is seen at Quito in 1969.

Ecuadorian Navy

The Ecuadorian Navy, which has a personnel of about 3,800 including 700 Marines, formed an Aviación Naval del Ecuador in 1967 with a Cessna 320E communications aircraft, and has since used a miscellany of light aircraft and helicopters, which are marked 'NAVAL'. Ecuadorian Navy vessels have no onboard provision for aircraft or helicopters. Known ANE aircraft include :

BEECHCRAFT T-34C-1

Three were delivered in April 1980.

BEECHCRAFT SUPER KING AIR 200

One aircraft ANE-231 c/n BB.771 delivered early in 1981.

CESSNA 177

One was delivered in July 1968, AN-201 c/n 177-01158; it is believed no longer current.

CESSNA 320E

AN-101 only, c/n 320E-0086 ex HC-AMX, delivered 1967.

CESSNA T-41D

Two were delivered in 1973 and another in April 1974 :
AN-205   c/n R172-0546
AN-206   R172-0560
ANE-107

CESSNA 337

A number have been acquired, including :
ANE-206 T.337G c/n 0089   d/d 24.4.73
AN-211   T.337F   01395   10.71
AN-212   T.337F   01396   10.71
ANE-202 is also reported; no details known.

IAI 201 ARAVA

Two aircraft :
ANE-234   c/n 0044   ex 4X-IBR d/d 27.5.77
ANE-402   0020   4X-IAS   10.8.75
One was written off on 29.4.79, and the other was then re-serialled as ANE-202.

CESSNA 500 CITATION

One aircraft only :
ANE-201 c/n 500-0389   ex N471H/N3202M

SUD SA.316 ALOUETTE III

Two were delivered in April 1974 :
ANE-301 c/n 2067
ANE-303   2074

IAI 201 Arava ANE-234 seen at Prestwick in May 1977 whilst on delivery.

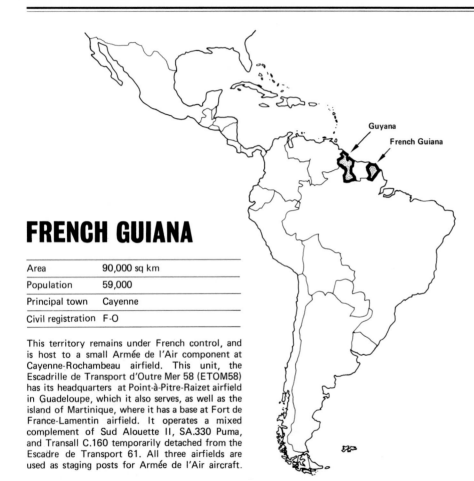

Guyana

French Guiana

FRENCH GUIANA

Area	90,000 sq km
Population	59,000
Principal town	Cayenne
Civil registration	F-O

This territory remains under French control, and is host to a small Armée de l'Air component at Cayenne-Rochambeau airfield. This unit, the Escadrille de Transport d'Outre Mer 58 (ETOM58) has its headquarters at Point-à-Pitre-Raizet airfield in Guadeloupe, which it also serves, as well as the island of Martinique, where it has a base at Fort de France-Lamentin airfield. It operates a mixed complement of Sud Alouette II, SA.330 Puma, and Transall C.160 temporarily detached from the Escadre de Transport 61. All three airfields are used as staging posts for Armée de l'Air aircraft.

GUYANA

Area	214,969 sq km
Population	830,000
Capital	Georgetown
Civil registration	8R-

Guyana, formerly British Guiana, is situated on the north eastern coast of South America between Surinam and Venezuela. It was initially a Dutch colony but was captured by the British in 1796; it became independent on 26 May 1966 and the left-wing policies of its government led to its becoming a 'Co-operative Republic' on 23 February 1970. Tourism, agriculture and mining provide most of the national revenue.

The Guyana Defence Force of about six and a half thousand personnel, formed the Defence Force Air Wing in 1968 (renamed Air Command in 1973) with headquarters at Timehri Airport, near Georgetown. This airfield had been built by the Americans during the Second World War as Atkinson Field, and was renamed as Timehri on 1 May 1969. Air Command aircraft operate with civil registrations, their only distinctive markings being the initials G.D.F. and the national flag, or its colours of red, yellow and green as an overall trim. Aircraft known to have been registered to the Guyana Defence Force Air Command are shown in the table.

Aircraft Review

Reg'n	Type	C/n	Ex	D/d	Remarks
8R-GCJ	Helio H.295 Courier	1233	VP-GCJ	4.67	Withdrawn from use 1971
8R-GCU	Helio H.295 Courier	1282	VP-GCU	9.67	Withdrawn from use 1971
8R-GCV	Helio H.295 Courier	1285	VP-GCV	9.67	Written off 13.7.69
8R-GDN	Britten-Norman BN.2A-6 Islander	230	G-51-230	2.71	
8R-GDQ	Britten-Norman BN.2A-6 Islander	231	G-51-231	2.71	
8R-GEE	Britten-Norman BN.2A-27 Islander	720	G-BCHO	10.74	
8R-GEL	Sud SA.319B Alouette III	2228		7.75	Withdrawn from use
8R-GEM	Sud SA.319B Alouette III	2233	F-WXFE	9.75	Withdrawn from use
8R-GEN	Cessna U206F	206-03083		10.75	
8R-GEO	Bell 212	30758	N49751	4.76	
8R-GEQ	Bell 212	30760	N49753	4.76	
8R-GER	Britten-Norman BN.2A-27 Islander	478	G-BDJX	12.75	
8R-GES	Britten-Norman BN.2A-27 Islander	482	G-BDKY	12.75	
8R-GET	Britten-Norman BN.2A-27 Islander	484	G-BDLG	3.76	
8R-GEX	Bell 206B Jet Ranger	2077		1.77	
8R-GEY	Bell 206B Jet Ranger	2085		1.77	
8R-GEZ	Bell 212	30808		12.76	Sold as N80704
8R-GFB	Beechcraft Super King Air 200	BB.82		9.75	
8R-GFF	Short Skyvan Srs.3M	SH.1966	G-BGWB	1979	Written off 22.1.81

Britten-Norman BN.2A-27 Islander 8R-GEE seen at Bembridge in October 1974.

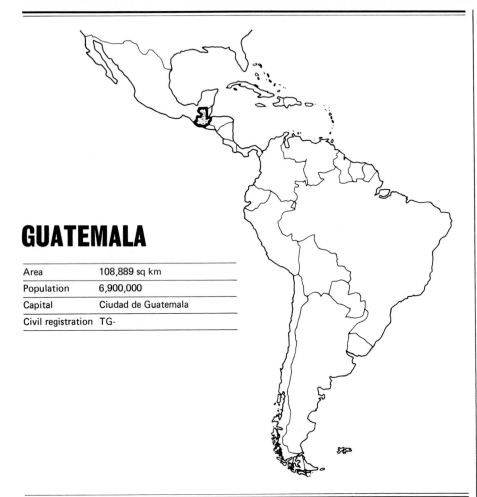

GUATEMALA

Area	108,889 sq km
Population	6,900,000
Capital	Ciudad de Guatemala
Civil registration	TG-

The Republic of Guatemala, which was once a Spanish captaincy-general, and gained independence in 1821, is the most northerly state of Central America. It has a rather eventful history, largely as a consequence of its heavily mixed population (over forty-five per cent of Indian origin, most of the remainder — the ruling classes — being of mixed Spanish and Indian blood). The country's economy has an agricultural basis, its soil being very fertile; large areas were exploited by the United Fruit Company until the 1953 Agrarian Reform expropriations, and bananas remain to this day an important export, second only to coffee.

The President is also Commander-in-Chief of the Armed Forces, through a Defence Ministry (Ministerio de la Defensa); two-year military service is compulsory for males between the ages of eighteen and fifty. The Army, organised in eight battalions, including one of Paracaidistas (parachutists), numbers 13,500, and is complemented by the Policía Nacional or National Police Force of 3,000. There is also a Security Police, specially trained in counter-guerilla tactics against Cuban-backed insurgent bands. A small naval force was formed in January 1959 for river patrol and anti-smuggling duties with about a dozen patrol craft, a few auxiliary boats and 450 personnel, including 200 Fusileros Navales (Naval Riflemen) or marines. Neither the Army nor the Navy operate aircraft.

Military aviation in Guatemala started in 1920 with the arrival of a French air mission and a handful of surplus French aircraft, but progress was slow. A bloodless revolution of 1921 had no aviation intervention, as the French instructors did not want to become involved in local politics and there were no Guatemalan pilots at that time. The Guatemalan Military Aviation Corps (Cuerpo de Aviación Militar de Guatemala) was formed in 1929 under Army control, consisting of a flying school (Escuela de Aeronáutica Militar) at Campo de La Aurora, Ciudad de Guatemala, and a complement of a few obsolete French machines, a pair of Avro 504K and single examples of the Morane-Saulnier MS.35 primary trainer and the Nieuport 28 fighter.

Little else — apart from maintenance — was done until 1934 when two Waco BSO (c/ns 3564/3565) were acquired. Funds were made available for a much-needed modernisation, which began with the purchase of four Waco UMF3 (c/n 3937/3940) in May 1934, followed by six Waco VPF7 (c/n 4651/4656, delivered in July 1937 and serialled 14/19) and seven ex-USAAC Boeing P-26A formerly based in the Panama Canal Zone (these were finally retired in the late 1950s, after a few years' use as fighter-trainers, and two were sold in the USA — 0672 ex 33-123 and 0816 ex 33-135). Twelve Ryan STM.2 primary trainers were also bought: six (c/n 192/197 serialled 21 to 26) were delivered unarmed in July-August 1938, but were later fitted with two 0.3 inch wing guns, and six (c/n 301/306, serialled 27 to 32) were completed with armament.

In early 1942, facilities were granted to the USA for the establishment of defence bases in Guatemala in exchange for Lend-Lease credits. This move brought in Stearman PT-17, Vultee BT-15 and North American AT-6 trainers, Douglas C-47 transports and at least one Cessna UC-78 Bobcat light transport (c/n 5286, ex 43-7766, later sold as TG-CEQ). By the end of the war, the Cuerpo de Aviación Militar had over forty aircraft on charge, including six Boeing P-26A, two Stearman PT-17, ten Ryan STM.2, nine Waco UMF3 and VPF7, three North American AT-6, five Vultee BT-15 and a handful of Douglas C-47 transports and Beechcraft AT-11 crew trainers. There were some twenty airfields and seventy personnel, including thirty pilots who also flew for the state-owned Compañía Guatemalteca de Aviación SA, the country's internal airline.

An American military mission was sent to Guatemala in the middle of 1945 to re-organise the service, which in 1948 was renamed as the Fuerza Aérea Guatemalteca (Guatemalan Air Force). Additional aircraft were gradually taken on charge as the tiny air arm began to expand — half a dozen Cessna 170A and 170B, two Aero Commanders, two Hiller UH12A and a Bell 47B (the service's first helicopters), and numbers of North American AT-6 Texans and F-51D Mustangs, the latter superseding the ancient Boeing P-26A still in active use. The transport force was expanded with more C-47, a pair of Douglas C-54 Skymasters and a former Olympic Airways Douglas DC-6B.

The FAG's first jet type was the Lockheed T-33A trainer and it was intended at the time to form an operational jet unit, probably with F-80C fighters, although the idea had to be shelved due to changes in US foreign policy. In the event thirteen Cessna A-37B close-support aircraft were obtained between 1971 and 1975, but a request for six Northrop F-5E Tiger II tactical fighters in early 1978 was turned down.

There were one or two colourful moments in the FAG's history. A Douglas B-26B Invader flown by CIA crews during the 1961 Bay of Pigs invasion of Cuba escaped to Guatemala and was promptly forgotten by the US authorities; it was finally painted in FAG colours — it would be a waste to let it rot away in the open — and given the serial 420, and is believed to be still extant.

The FAG is currently replacing some of its more obsolete aircraft. Light transports were obtained in the USA, and ten IAI Aravas from Israel, following the successful evaluation of an Israeli demonstration aircraft. The US reluctance in making military aircraft available to Latin American countries led to purchases elsewhere, including twelve Pilatus PC.7 Turbo-Trainers from Switzerland. An order was also placed for SIAI-Marchetti SF.260W Warrior close-support trainers, but delivery was embargoed by the Italian government before the first two, which had been painted as 371 and 372 left the factory. A change in the US political stance has however allowed the delivery during 1980/81 of three Bell 212 and six Bell 412 helicopters, and for a refurbishment programme in the USA for the A-37Bs.

Current Organisation

The Fuerza Aérea Guatemalteca has a personnel of about 450, and headquarters at Los Cipresales, Ciudad de Guatemala, where most of the flying units are also based; the exceptions are the transport force which operates from the capital's La Aurora International Airport, and the fighter-bombers which are now based at San José. The main units are the following :

Escuadrón de Caza-Bombardeo (Fighter-Bomber Squadron) with two Lockheed T-33A, eight Cessna A-37B.

Escuadrón de Transporte (Transport Squadron) with eight Douglas C-47, one C-54, one DC-6B and ten IAI Arava.

Escuela de Aviación Militar (Military Aviation School) with three Cessna T-37C, seven North American T-6G, twelve Pilatus Turbo-Trainers and two Cessna 172K.

There is also a Presidential Flight with a Beechcraft Super King Air 200, and communications units with four Cessna 170B, three Cessna 180, two Cessna U206C, and various helicopters.

Military Air Bases

1   Ciudad de Guatemala
    (Los Cipresales and
    La Aurora)
2   Champerico
3   Quezaltenango
4   Escuintla
5   Iztapa
6   San José
7   Cobán
8   Izabal
9   Livingston
10 Puerto Barrios
11 La Libertad
12 Flores

Ground attack unit -
white disc outlined in black; black bird with white eyes, yellow beak and legs; black and white axe.

Aircraft Review

COLOURS AND MARKINGS

The United Provinces flag inspired that of Guatemala whose blue/white/blue stripes appear as a fin flash or rudder stripes on military aircraft. Wing roundels

consisted of a white six-pointed star within a blue disc, with a blue centre, but a five-pointed star became standard by 1939. The shade of blue used for both roundels and rudder stripes became darker after the creation of the Guatemalan Air Force in 1948 and remains as such to this day. There is an extensive use of the inscription *FAG*, or *Fuerza Aérea Guatemalteca* on some transports.

The use of camouflage did not become current until the late 1960s, although some fighters in the 1940s had olive green wing and tailplane upper surfaces. US-style schemes are standard, but some aircraft have been seen in an overall olive green or dark green livery.

SERIAL NUMBERS

FAG aircraft are identified by a three-digit serial, and quite often these serials fall into a pattern for each type, such that the last two digits are multiples of the first digit, or failing this, successive aircraft of each type are serialled so that the 'last two' are allocated at arithmetical intervals determined by the first digit; reference to the listings which follow will hopefully make this clear — see for example the Aravas.

Aircraft known to have been used since the last war are the following :

AERO COMMANDER 680/690

One Aero Commander 680 :
545 c/n 504-174 ex N6236D Sold as TG-HMV
One Aero Commander 690 :
565 11005 TG-JAC Returned to TG-JAC

BEECHCRAFT AT-11 KANSAN

Two believed delivered; no further details.

BEECHCRAFT SUPER KING AIR 200

One aircraft serialled 001, c/n BB.125, for the Presidential Flight , delivered 1976.

BELL 47B

One was delivered in February 1949, c/n 23 ex NC103B.

BELL UH-1D IROQUOIS

Nine believed to have been delivered, of which six remain in service from La Aurora. One is serialled 160.

BELL 206B JET RANGER

One serialled 165, c/n 3168, delivered 1981.

BELL 212

Three delivered 1980/81.

BELL 412

Six delivered 1980/81.

CESSNA 170

Two Cessna 170A delivered in March 1952 :
473 c/n 20215 ex N1772D
581 20213 N1770D
Four Cessna 170B :
275 26966 N3423D Sold as TG-JEC 2.75
363 26965 N3422D
547 26968 N3425D
731 26967 N3424D Sold as TG-JUA

CESSNA 172K

Six reported as delivered; two in current service. One is :
612 c/n 59026 ex N7326G

CESSNA 182C

One only, delivered in June 1960 :
624 c/n 52869 ex N8969T

CESSNA 180

One 180 delivered in January 1955 :
0469 c/n 31321
Three Cessna 180H :
642 51512 ex N2712X d/d 2.65
648 51593 N2793X 7.65
654 51591 N2791X 7.65

CESSNA 185C

One aircraft delivered in November 1963 :
636 c/n 185-0666 ex N2666Z

CESSNA U206C

Two aircraft delivered in April 1968 :
690 c/n 206-1065 ex N29092
696 206-1081 N29111

CESSNA A-37B

Eight were delivered between 1971 and 1975 :
432 ex USAF 73-1651
436 73-1652
440 73-1653
444 73-1654
448 73-1655
452 73-1656
456 73-1657
460 73-1658
Other aircraft seem to have followed at a later date, including 416 and 428, both of which were being refurbished in the USA in November 1981. One believed dbr 20.11.81.

DOUGLAS C-47 SKYTRAIN

About twenty were delivered; one of the early aircraft was Los Cipresales-based 0749. Another was marked 'Ejecutivo' and used as a presidential aircraft with the serial 321. Other confirmed aircraft are :
500
505 wfu
510 wfu
515

520
525 wfu
530
535 wfu
540
545 wfu
550 c/n 14841/26286 ex 43-49025
555 33499
560
565 wfu
570
575 wfu
580
590
One was written off 29.2.80; several remain in service.

DOUGLAS C-54 SKYMASTER

Two aircraft serialled 798 and 800, the latter delivered on 28.5.75 and written off on 29.2.80.

DOUGLAS DC-6B

One only, acquired 1972, and current with the Escuadron de Transporte :
926 c/n 45539 ex SX-DAD, N111AD

DOUGLAS B-26 INVADER

Eight aircraft (though some reports say ten) delivered from 1960 onwards and serialled 400, 404, 408, 412, 416, 420, 424 and 428, all B-26B except for 424 which was a B-26C. 420 is said to be a former CIA aircraft abandoned in Guatemala after the Bay of Pigs fiasco. Five survived in September 1968 and were assigned to the Special Air Warfare Strike/Reconnaissance unit, four to operate as unarmed bombers and the fifth armed with machine guns for reconnaissance use; the other three aircraft were used for spares. The type was little used and replaced by the Cessna A-37B.

HILLER UH12/OH-23

Two UH12A were delivered, one of which was c/n 127 ex N8127H and arrived in October 1949. Later, an ex US Army OH-23G was taken on charge.

IAI 201 ARAVA

Ten aircraft :
808 c/n 0022 ex 4X-IAU d/d 3.10.75
816 0025 4X-IAX 12.11.75
824 0030 4X-IBC 10.1.76
832 0028 4X-IBA 5.2.76
840 0029 4X-IBB 14.2.76
848 0033 4X-IBF 16.3.76
856 0035 4X-IBH 11.5.76
864 0045 4X-IBR 10.7.76
872 0047 4X-IBT 28.9.76
880 0048 4X-IBU 30.10.76

LOCKHEED T-33A

Six believed delivered, of which five understood to be still in use. Serials include 721 (preserved), 728, 735, 742, 749.

NORTH AMERICAN AT-6 TEXAN

About twelve AT-6 were delivered under Lend-Lease and after the war. Twelve T-6G followed in the 1950s; of these one (ex 49-3528) was sold as TG-JOM, three others as TG-GES, TG-HOV and TG-HUT, and seven remain in service.

NORTH AMERICAN F-51D MUSTANG

Six F-51D and one TF-51D were supplied in 1955 and had the serials 24 to 30; others - at least another six - were later taken on charge. An F-51D ex 44-74430 and N8673E was civilianised as TG-REI. The last surviving aircraft were replaced in 1976 by Cessna A-37Bs, and one, serialled 360, became a gate-guardian at Los Cipresales. Other identified aircraft are :
345 ex 44-84660 to N88828 (TF-51D)
351 44-74391 N38229
354 44-63663 N41749
366 44-73452 N74190
? 44-72907 N41748
? 44-74902 N38227
Three F-51D performing aerobatics collided in mid-air and crashed on 12.1.72.

POTEZ CM.170R MAGISTER

Three aircraft delivered from France, serials 509 to 511.

PILATUS PC.7 TURBO-TRAINER

Twelve aircraft :

211	c/n 226	ex HB-HDF	d/d 3.4.80		
215	1132	HB-HCV	11.8.79		
218	130	HB-HCZ	11.8.79		
			(reverted to HB-HCZ from 11.79 to		
220	133	HB-HCW	12.10.79		4.80)
229	134	HB-HCX	12.10.79		
267	131	HB-HCU	9.79		
274	135	HB-HCY	12.10.79		
278	225	HB-HDE	3.4.80		
284	224	HB-HDD	3.4.80		
?	227	HB-HDG	3.4.80		
?	228	HB-HDH	16.4.80		
?	229	HB-HDI	16.4.80		

The three missing serials are believed to be , not necessarily in order, 240, 248 and 253.

SIAI-MARCHETTI SF.260W WARRIOR

An order for twelve was cancelled after an Italian govern-ment embargo was applied in 1981; the first two had been painted at the factory with serials 371 and 372.

SIKORSKY UH-19

Three machines serialled 110, 120 and 130; no longer in use.

STEARMAN PT-17

About six delivered. One was c/n 754538 ex 42-16375; another was c/n 754539 ex 42-16376 serialled 34 and later sold as TG-CEU-42. Another was serialled 21, still extant in 1979.

> **Douglas C-47 Skytrain** 550 photographed at McDill, Florida in April 1974.
>
> **IAI 201 Arava** 808 at Prestwick during its delivery flight in October 1975.

HAITI

Area	27,750 sq km
Population	5,500,000
Capital	Port-au-Prince
Civil registration	HH-

The Haitian Republic is not strictly speaking a Latin American country, but rather a French-speaking Black nation (most people speak the French dialect known as Créole); however it is included in this book because Haiti occupies the western third of the island of Santo Domingo (Hispaniola), the remaining two thirds being the Dominican Republic. Haiti became independent from French rule on 1 January 1804 and has had emperors, kings and presidents-for-life in succession; it was united with the Dominican Republic from 1822 to 1844 and was under United States occupation from 1915 to 1934. Haiti is a mainly agricultural country of a rather low economic level, its main income deriving from the export of coffee, sugar and sisal. Voodoo, a national religion, remains influential in political life.

The Haitian Armed Forces (Forces Armées d' Haïti) comprise the Army, Navy and Air Force; officers are appointed by the President-for-Life, who is also their Commander in Chief. The Army (Garde d'Haïti) with an approximate personnel of six thousand, is responsible for internal security and border patrol duties — illegal emigration to the Dominican Republic, which has a higher standard of living, is a major problem which has even caused some border clashes. The Garde comprises nine Military Departments, three of which are based at Port-au-Prince (one being the Police) and includes the 260-man Presidential bodyguard and the Léopards commando unit; no aircraft are known to be used. There is a 6,000 strong civilian militia known as the Volontaires de la Sécurité Nationale (National Security Volunteers), which now incorporates the notorious security police ('Tonton Macoute' or bogeymen) organised by former dictator François Duvalier. The Navy is limited to a coast guard force (Garde Côtière) with half a dozen patrol vessels and about three hundred men.

The first military aviation in Haiti was during the US occupation when the First US Marine Brigade was based at Port-au-Prince; its attached flying component was an observation squadron VO-2M which was renumbered as VO-9M on 1 July 1927.

The Haitian Air Corps (Corps d'Aviation d'Haïti) with a personnel strength of about two hundred and fifty, was formed in 1943, mainly for transport and communications duties, with headquarters at Bowen Field, Port-au-Prince, a former US Marine Corps airfield. Transport duties are currently shared with the national airline Air Haiti which was formed in December 1959 with United States assistance. There is a small operational element, although purely combat types (the close-support North American AT-28D) were disposed of during 1978 on the instructions of the country's strong-man, Jean-Claude Duvalier, son of the late dictator.

The Air Corps' first combat aircraft were six North American F-51D-15-NA Mustangs (ex USAF 44-15650/15655, flown as 15650 to 15655); F-51D 44-73129 ex N5480V was also used until sold to the USA as N515L in December 1974. These Mustangs were superseded in October 1973 by ten North American AT-28D, which were in fact ex-Armée de l'Air Sud Aviation Fennecs refurbished by a US firm on a Haitian Government contract. They were disposed of in March 1978 and were :

1236	c/n 174-398	ex 51-7545	Fennec No. 119	to N14113
1237	174-386	51-7533	116	N14144
1238	174-164	51-3626	96	N14121
1239	174-	51-		N
1240	174-364	51-7511	120	N14110
1241	174-	51-		N
1242	174-395	51-7542	124	N14112
1243	174-	51-		N
1244	174-158	51-3620	60	N14104
1245	174-289	51-3751	147	N14108

Another two aircraft were

?	174-108	51-3570	98	N14103
?	174-471	51-7618	128	N14108

The current Air Corps counter-insurgency force consists of six Cessna 337, converted by Summit Aviation before delivery with four underwing pylons for machine guns and light bombs and unofficially referred to as 'O-2-337'.

The Air Corps' first transport aircraft were a Lockheed C-60 Lodestar 3111 and a Boeing S307 2003. The latter (c/n 2003 ex NC19903) was delivered in 1954 and operated by the Compagnie Haitienne de Transports Aériens as a presidential transport before being sold in 1957 as N9307R. These aircraft were supplemented by a pair of Beechcraft C-45, one of which is still in service; three DHC.2 Beavers (including ex US Army U-6A HH-1267 and 1268 delivered in 1977), a Cessna 402 and a Beechcraft Baron 58 (serialled 1251, c/n TH.531) all of which are current; and a few Douglas C-47, three of which survive (two were ex Piedmont Airlines machines). C-47s known to have been used:

3681	C-47A-DK	c/n 13681	ex 42-93736
4262	C-47-DL	4262	41-7775, N54327
4265	C-47-DL	4265	41-7777
5878	C-47B-DK	16881/34137	45-878
9175	C-47A-DK	9175	42-23313, N147A

Two unidentified machines in current use are serialled 1233 and 1235, to which the HH- prefix is added when they are operated by Air Haiti.

The first trainers to be received were three Stearman PT-17 and three Fairchild PT-19, later supplemented by a pair of Vultee BT-13A, three North American T-6G and Beechcraft AT-11 3516 (perhaps ex 42-37238, known to have been delivered in April 1948) which was later converted to a transport with a 'solid' nose. None of these remains in use, the current trainer fleet consisting of three Cessna 150, one Cessna 172, One Cessna 310 and a Beechcraft Bonanza 35, the last two also serving on communications duties.

The six Sikorsky S.55 helicopters delivered with serials H-1 to H-6 have now been disposed of and replaced by a similar number of S.58/CH-34C converted by Orlando Helicopter Airways; at least two of these have been converted to turbine power as S.58T. Known S.58 serials include H-1 to H-4, and H-8 which was delivered in July 1978. Helicopter training is provided by two Hughes 269C and two Hughes 369C; one of the latter is serialled 1245, which duplicates an AT-28D serial.

Additional re-equipment is not expected to take place within the next few years unless there is an unforseen change in requirements - such as a political upheaval in the neighbouring Dominican Republic. The Air Corps' efficiency depends heavily on US assistance, which at the time of writing seems set to continue for as long as necessary.

For an air arm of such a diminutive size, the existence of a serialling system is by no means a necessity, and for many years constructors numbers doubled as serial numbers. However, in 1976 it became the rule to number military aircraft in the HH-1200 to HH-1299 block, with the HH- civil registration prefix usually omitted. Known allocations in this series are :

1233	Douglas C-47	current
1235	Douglas C-47	current
1236-1245	North American AT-28D	disposed of in 1978
1245	Hughes 369C	current
1246-1250	Cessna O-2-337	current
1251	Beechcraft Baron 58	current
1260-1265	North American F-51D	reported as such but 1265 apparently is duplicated by a Cessna O-2-337.
1267-1268	DHC U-6A Beaver	

Note that a number of Haitian military aircraft have their serials prefixed FAA (Force Aérienne, Avion) or FAH (Force Aérienne, Hélicoptères). Transports may instead have the civilian prefix HH-.

COLOURS AND MARKINGS

The Haitian national flag has had a remarkable flexibility in its layout throughout the country's history, although for most of the air force's history its colours have been blue and red, vertically (or horizontally) separated. The Corps d'Aviation marking incorporated a blue/red disc within a US-style white outline.

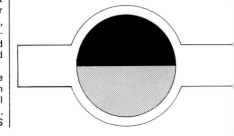

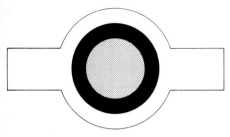

When the blue portion of the flag became black in June 1964 (the black standing for the Black Haitians, and the red for the mulattoes), the disc became black and red. More recently, the white outline was given a black border, and the central disc became red with a thick black or very dark blue border. Variations are known to exist.

Sikorsky S.58T H-8 at Sanford, Florida awaiting delivery after conversion by Orlando Helicopter Airways in July 1978. It is overall light grey.

North American AT-28D (Sud Fennec) 1240 at Tucson after disposal in 1978.

HONDURAS

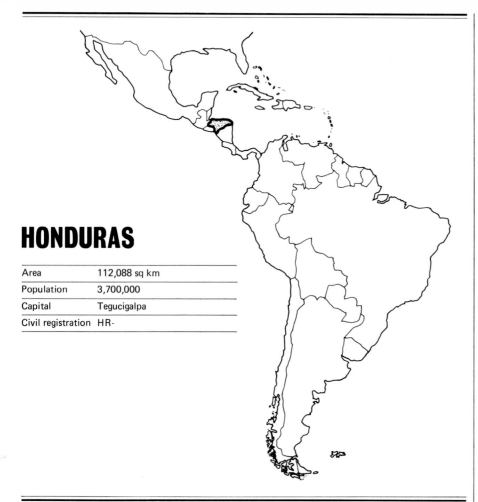

Area	112,088 sq km
Population	3,700,000
Capital	Tegucigalpa
Civil registration	HR-

The Republic of Honduras, the largest of the Central American countries, seceded from Spain in 1821 and became independent from the Federation of Central America on 5 November 1838. It is mainly an agricultural, largely unexplored country; forty five per cent of its territory is covered by forests. Its population consists of a minority of white and mixed-race and a majority of Indian stock and some aboriginal tribes still speak no Spanish. Honduras has been involved in boundary disputes with Guatemala, Nicaragua and El Salvador, and in fact there was a brief shooting war with El Salvador in 1969-70; on the other hand, internal security problems are of a minor nature, the three underground guerilla bands known to exist being largely ineffective. The Chief of State is the Commander-in-Chief of the armed forces through a Ministry (Departamento de las Fuerzas Armadas) and every male citizen aged between eighteen and fifty-five is liable for military service for a period of eighteen months.

The Honduran armed forces have always been severely limited by available funds, but the first steps towards the formation of an air arm were taken fairly early. During 1921, the government acquired a pair of old, khaki-painted Bristol F.2b Fighter biplanes from an ex Royal Flying Corps Canadian, Ivan D Lamb, who was given the rank of General and the official post of Director General of Aviation, controlling all military and civil flying in Honduras. Later on, an Escuela Nacional de Aviación (National Aviation School) was inaugurated at Tegucigalpa under the supervision of an Italian national, Luigi Vendetti, for military and commercial pilot training; but the two old biplanes remained the only military machines until the early 1930s, and during the 1933 revolution, air power materialised in the form of a couple of hurriedly converted Stinson airliners from the Honduran branch of TACA (Transportes Aéreos Centro-Americanos), a joint Central American airline.

This incident did at least enhance the importance of military aviation in the country and later in 1933 the Aviación Militar Hondureña (Honduran Military

Aviation) was officially formed, incorporating an Escuela de Aviación Militar (Military Flying School) under the command of US mercenary, Colonel William C Brooks, with a trio of ex-TACA Stinson airliners. Tegucigalpa's civil airport, Tocontín, became the first military airfield. Other early aircraft included five Stinson Model O parasol monoplanes used for armed reconnaissance and four Boeing 95 mailplanes purchased from United Air Lines and converted to bombers (two of these were c/n 1052 ex NC189E and 1068 ex NC424E). A small number of Waco UPF7 were obtained in 1935 (two UEC, c/n 3576 ex NC12440 and 3640 ex NC12474 had been obtained in 1933-34) and served until as late as 1947, and in mid-1936 a single Curtiss T32 Condor biplane transport (c/n 35 ex NC12374) was acquired for use by the Directorate General of Aviation, although remaining under Aviación Militar control; it eventually disappeared on an internal flight.

Apart from single examples of the Beechcraft B17L (c/n 9 ex NC12591) and C17R (c/n 77 ex NC15835), the service's first modern aircraft were three North American NA.16 — the ancestors of the AT-6 Texan — acquired in December 1937; two were armed NA.16-2A (NA.42 c/n 42-691 and 692) and the third a more powerful NA.16-2H (c/n 2 ex NC16025), a former company demonstrator which had previously been earmarked for delivery to the Chinese Air Force. Three Ryan STM monoplanes serialled R23 to R25 arrived in 1938 for use as fighter-trainers, with light armament fitted, there being plans to form a modern operational force over the next few years.

However, these plans suffered a setback with Pearl Harbor and the United States declaration of war on Germany and Japan, as no aircraft were available to neutral countries. It was not until the Hondurans joined the Allied side in December 1944, and even then this was just a bureaucratic exercise, that the country became eligible for US military aid, which in the event comprised small numbers of Stearman PT-13 and PT-17, Vultee BT-13 and Beechcraft AT-11 trainers for the Escuela de Avia-

ción Militar, and Beechcraft UC-43 and Noorduyn UC-64 Norseman light transports to help establish an air transport force to connect the capital with a number of newly-opened airfields such as Gracias a Dios, San Pedro Sula and Trujillo. To these were later added a few Douglas C-47 and a single Lockheed UC-26A (Model 10A Electra). The United States also provided a Laister-Kauffman TG-4 training glider which remained in service until the early 1950s, and at least two Fairchild PT-23.

Such was the equipment of the Honduran air arm until the country's signature of the Rio Pact in 1947. Further US aid followed, including a handful of relatively modern fighters which equipped the first combat unit: five Bell P-63E-1-BE Kingcobras and seven Lockheed P-38L-5-LO Lightnings. At the same time, the command of the service was, for the first time in its history, given to a Honduran officer, Lt.Col.Hermán Acosta Mejía, who was killed in 1955 when his P-38L crashed in Tegucigalpa. Other aircraft received were additional Douglas C-47, a single Martin B-26C Marauder (later sold in the USA as N1502) and small numbers of North American T-6G trainers and Beechcraft C-45 transports.

Replacement aircraft were not procured until after the early 1957 conflict with Nicaragua. The Kingcobras and Lightnings were replaced by a mixture of Vought F4U-4, -5 and -5N Corsairs, twenty being delivered between 1956 and 1961 and based at Tocontín. Three Convair P4Y-2 Privateer bombers converted to transports were also purchased which, together with a single Curtiss C-46 and at least two Fairchild C-82A Packets, considerably expanded the transport fleet.

The service was re-organised in 1954 as the Fuerza Aérea Hondureña (Honduran Air Force), a mainly independent air arm which maintained close links with the Army high command via a Jefatura de las Fuerzas Armadas (Armed Forces Command) and included a quasi-civil airline element, Rutas Aéreas Nacionales SA or RANSA, flying military transports, sometimes with both serial numbers and civil registrations.

Subsequent aircraft procurements depended

mainly on US assistance schemes, although a few light aircraft were obtained directly from the manufacturers. Other machines came from assorted sources; a notable example was a single Douglas B-26C Invader acquired in 1971, which was brought into Honduras from Costa Rica during the July 1969 'football war' with El Salvador. This, one of the silliest conflicts in history, was caused by a disputed World Cup football match which degenerated into a riot and then an all-out war. Honduran F4U Corsairs engaged Salvadorean Air Force Corsairs and Mustangs in air combat, and it is believed that about eight Honduran aircraft of all types were brought down during the war — twice as many as were lost by El Salvador.

More recently, in late 1975, six Cessna A-37B close support aircraft were supplied by the United States, but State Department reluctance in providing aircraft to Latin American countries made Honduras turn to Israel, which provided twelve Dassault Super Mystère B2 jet fighters, two IAI Arava light transports and an IAI Westwind 1123 executive jet; additional fighters, this time North American F-86K Sabres, came from Venezuela. It is however likely that following recent developments in Central America and a change in United States policy, renewed assistance from the USA will be forthcoming.

Current Organisation

The Fuerza Aérea Hondureña has a personnel of about 1,200 all ranks, though a few hundred civilians are employed, mainly for maintenance work under temporary contract, and consists of the following units at the three principal bases:

Base Aérea Coronel Héctor Caracciolo, Moncada, La Ceiba :
Escuadrilla de Caza with Dassault Super Mystère B2
Escuadrilla de Caza-Bombardeo with North American F-86K/Canadair F-86E-M

Escuadrilla de Ataque with Cessna A-37B
Escuadrilla de Reconocimiento with Lockheed T-33A/RT-33A.

Base Aerea Coronel Armando Escalón Espiñal, San Pedro Sula :
Escuadrilla de Transporte with Douglas C-47, C-54, C-118A, IAI Arava and Lockheed 188A Electra.

Base Aerea Teniente-Coronel Hermán Acosta Mejía, Tegucigalpa :
Escuela de Aviación Militar with Cessna T-41D
Escuadrilla de Comunicaciones with Cessna 180/185 and Sikorsky UH-19.

Military Air Bases

1 Tegucigalpa (Tocontín)
2 Puerto Cortes
3 San Pedro Sula
4 Trujillo
5 Cataraca

COLOURS AND MARKINGS

The first Honduran military aircraft had the national coat of arms painted on the fuselage sides. Later, a blue/white/blue roundel (on wings only) and rudder stripes based on the Honduran flag (itself based on that of the United Provinces) came into regular use but the wing roundels were soon replaced by blue/white/blue wingtips, a blue star being placed on the white wing and rudder stripes. More recently, the wing roundels have been occasionally used again.

Colour schemes displayed by aircraft taken on charge are normally retained in service, with transports having white fuselage tops and blue cheat lines. The inscription *Fuerza Aérea Hondureña* often appears on transport aircraft and helicopters.

Aircraft Review

Aircraft known to have been used by the Fuerza Aérea Hondureña in recent years are as follows :

BEECHCRAFT C-45 EXPEDITOR

A dozen believed delivered, of which about six remain in use. One was serialled 105.

BELL P-63E-1-BE KINGCOBRA

Five were delivered in 1948 and retired in 1960 :
400	ex 43-11727
401	
402	
403	
404	43-11731

CESSNA T-41D

Five aircraft serialled 217 to 221, delivered in 1973 and still in use.

CESSNA A-37B

Six aircraft serialled 1001 to 1006, although 1001 to 1006 were re-numbered as 1007 and 1008 respectively :
1003	ex 74-1718	w/o
1004	74-1719	
1005	74-1720	
1006	74-1721	
1007	74-1722, 1001	
1008	74-1723, 1002	

CESSNA 180 and 185

Four aircraft were reported; details are unknown, but a 180 was serialled 113.

CONVAIR P4Y-2 PRIVATEER

At least three, converted as transports and serialled 792, 794 and 796; no longer in use. Two were ex Bu.59742 and 59763, which became HR-195-P and N7237C respectively.

CURTISS C-46 COMMANDO

One only, withdrawn from use; no further details known.

DASSAULT SUPER MYSTÈRE B2

Twelve ex Israeli DF/AF aircraft, re-engined with Pratt & Whitney J52 turbojets: six were delivered in 1976 and six more in 1978-79.

DOUGLAS C-47 SKYTRAIN

At least sixteen were acquired between 1945 and 1958 and allocated to the Escuadrilla de Transporte. Four are said to remain in service, one having been written off on 25.7.77. Aircraft 302 (later 321) was a C-53D, the others were C-47A or C-47B.
	c/n		
300	12786	ex 42-92931	w/o 5.5.57
301	6096	41-18690, N54075	d/d 4.9.58
302	11696	42-68769, N86593	reserialled 321
303			
304	12962	42-93089	
305	19426	42-100963	

```
306
307    16795/33543  44-77211
308
309
310
311
312
313
314
315
```

DOUGLAS C-54 SKYMASTER

Four are reported to have been delivered, including :
```
612
795  C-54B  c/n 18382  ex 43-17182, N95413  d/d 1960
                                              wfu 1971
798  C-54E      27318   44-9092, AN-BAE  d/d 1971
                                        to N22504 in 4.78
```

DOUGLAS C-118A

One aircraft only :
```
800  c/n 44642  ex 53-3271
```

DOUGLAS B-26C INVADER

Costa Rican civil Invader TI-1040P, c/n 29197 ex 44-35918 was obtained in 1969 and registered as HR-276, being transferred to the Honduran Air Force in 1971 with the serial 276 - a quick repainting job ! It later became FAH 510.

FAIRCHILD C-82A PACKET

At least two were delivered, serialled 793 and 1011; they are no longer in service.

FOUGA MAGISTER

Four aircraft, presumably ex Armee de l'Air, were reported at Bordeaux-Merignac in September 1981 prior to delivery.

IAI WESTWIND 1123/1124

One Westwind 1123 delivered 24.4.76 :
```
318  c/n 183  ex 4X-CKG    reserialled HR-001 in 1981
```

One Westwind 1124 delivered in 1981 :
```
HR-002   333     4X-CTA
```

IAI 201 ARAVA

Two aircraft only :
```
316  c/n 0031  ex 4X-IBD  d/d 21.2.76
317      0034     4X-IBG      20.3.76
```

LOCKHEED UC-36A ELECTRA

One aircraft only :
```
104  c/n 1011  ex 42-56638, NC14260  Sold as N4963C
```

LOCKHEED 188A ELECTRA

One model 188A-08-10 acquired in July 1979 :
```
555  c/n 1028  ex N6106A
```

LOCKHEED P-38L LIGHTNING

Seven P-38L-5-LO delivered in 1948. One crashed in 1955 killing Lt.Col Acosta Mejía, and those remaining in use were replaced by F4U Corsairs in 1958-59, the last four being sold in the USA in 1961; one went to the USAF Museum.
```
500
501
502
503  ex 44-53097
504     44-26961
505     44-53232
506     44-53095
```

LOCKHEED T-33A/RT-33A

At least three delivered and believed to be current. One was serialled 200, and another, 222 was re-serialled as 1200.

NORTH AMERICAN AT-6 TEXAN

Twelve AT-6 and T-6G were reported as delivered, including T-6G 49-2944, 2998, 3031 and 3476 which were taken on charge in 1956. Serials were 200 et seq. Six remained in use in 1978-79.

NORTH AMERICAN T-28A (SUD FENNEC)

Eight Sud Aviation Fennecs (converted T-28A) were obtained from the Moroccan Air Force late in 1978, but impounded in the USA because of financial problems. They remained in open storage at Tucson for a long time, but US civil marks have now been allocated, which may indicate their further disposal. Note the combined serial/ferry registrations :

```
HR226A  ex 51-7632/Fennec No.01
HR227A     51-7844         08
HR228A     52-1226         23  to N8522X
HR229A     51-3557         43     N8522B
HR230A     51-3530         49     N8528A
HR231A     51-3528         52     N8523B
HR232A     51-3565         56     N85222
HR233A     51-3627         64     N8539A
```
About half a dozen ex-USAF T-28A had previously been taken on charge during the early 1960s; no details to hand.

NORTH AMERICAN F-86 SABRE

Four ex Venezuelan Air Force F-86K were delivered with serials 1100 to 1103, but saw very limited service. Half a dozen ex Jugoslav Air Force F-86E-M were also delivered (they were crated to Florida where they were re-assembled and converted prior to delivery) of which serials 3001 to 3005 are confirmed, and in June 1977 an ex USAF F-86F was taken on charge with the serial 3009.

PIPER PA-12 SUPER CRUISER

One only, M-109, c/n 12-102, ex XH-103.

PIPER PA-23 APACHE 235

One only delivered in January 1965 :
```
112  c/n 27-606  Sold as HR-233
```

SIKORSKY S.52-2

At least one, serialled 814, used for communications and rescue work, but no longer in service.

SIKORSKY UH-19 (S.55)

Three at least, believed to be in current use; no details known.

Lockheed **T-33A** 222 at San Pedro de Sula in May 1975.

IAI 201 Arava 317, the second of two delivered early in 1976.

North American **F-86E Sabre** 3001 at Key West, Florida in July 1976, in a colour scheme of pale blue overall with dark blue trim.

North American **F-86K Sabre** 1101 in natural metal finish with a red and white sharkmouth.

SIKORSKY S-76

One helicopter FAH-001 c/n 760061, delivered c.1981.

VOUGHT F4U CORSAIR

A total of twenty F4U-4, -5 and -5NL were acquired for use by the FAH and serialled 600 to 619. The first three were delivered in March 1956, followed by another seven in June; later acquisitions comprised three in February 1960, one in March, four in December 1961 and a final pair at a later date. They operated from Tocontín, with secondary bases at La Mesa airfield, San Pedro Sula and Puerto Cortés. remained operational as late as 1976-77, but have since been replaced by ex Israeli Air Force Super Mystères. The following were sold during 1979-80 :

F4U-4	ex Bu. 96995	to N4908M
	97280	N49092
	97288	N4907M (w/o 7.6.81)
F4U-5	122179	N4903M
	122184	N49051
	124486	N49068
	124560	N4901W
	124724	N4901E

Four aircraft were noted in a yard at Jacksonville, Florida during 1981, serials 610 (ex Bu.97338), 611, 617 and 692. The latter, with its out-of-sequence serial also carried its previous US Navy unit marks and was probably acquired by the FAH for spares use only.

VULTEE BT-13A

About twelve used; eight were still in service in 1963 but were grounded in 1966-67.

Army/Coast Guard Civil Guard

Honduras also has a 13,000 strong Army (ten battalions) and a Coast Guard (one hundred personnel and ten small ships) as well as a Civil Guard of some 3,000, but none of these services operates aircraft.

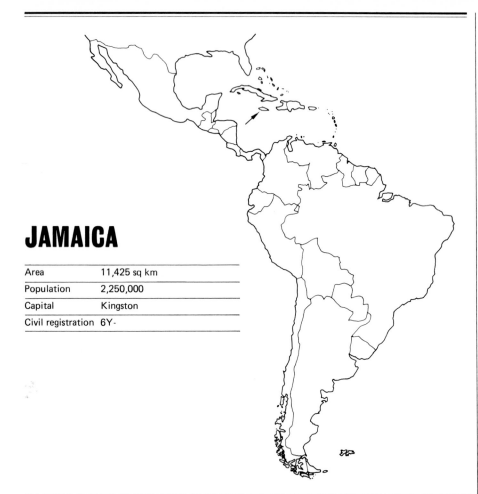

JAMAICA

Area	11,425 sq km
Population	2,250,000
Capital	Kingston
Civil registration	6Y-

A Spanish colony until 1655, Jamaica was captured by the English, who ruled the island until 6 August 1962 when independence was granted. The Jamaica Defence Force, which has a personnel of about four thousand, created an Air Wing in July 1963 with British Army support and later Canadian Armed Forces advisers. The Air Wing, which currently has some 250 men, has no offensive capability, but concentrates on communications, photo survey and recue duties. It also flies reconnaissance missions for the Defence Force Coast Guard when requested. There are two main airfields : Up-Park Camp at Kingston, and Montego Bay.

Air Wing aircraft are serialled within three main sequences — JDFA for auxiliary (liaison) aircraft, JDFH for helicopters and JDFT for transports. The aircraft which have been operated are listed in the table below, though it should be noted that there are also at least two Sud SE.3130 Alouette II in service, and that the Jet Rangers have been brought up to Bell 206B standards.

The Jamaica Constabulary Force has 5,500 personnel, and there are other paramilitary units of about 3,200, but the Air Wing is the only organisation to operate aircraft.

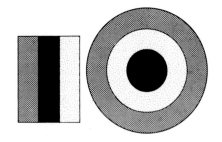

COLOURS AND MARKINGS

The Jamaican flag, comprising a yellow St.Andrews cross separating two black (horizontal) and green (vertical) triangles contrasts with the simplicity of the military markings — a green/yellow/black roundel and a green/black/yellow fin flash. Green stands for agriculture, black for the natives and their burdens and yellow for the country's sunshine and natural resources. Delivery colour schemes are retained in service, and the inscription *Jamaica Defence Force* is often applied.

Aircraft Review

Serial	Type	C/n	Ex	D/d	Remarks
JDFA-1	Cessna 185	185-	N........	7.63	Written off
JDFA-2	Cessna 185	185-	N........	7.63	wfu
JDFA-3	Cessna 185	185-	N........	7.63	wfu
JDFA-4	Cessna 185	185-	N........	7.63	wfu
JDFH-1	Bell 47G-3B-1	2901		10.63	Withdrawn from use
JDFH-2	Bell 47G-3B-1	2907		3.64	Sold as N83779 6.77
JDFH-3	Bell 206A Jet Ranger	657	N4738R	6.71	
JDFH-4	Bell 206A Jet Ranger				
JDFH-5	Bell 206A Jet Ranger				
JDFH-6	Bell 212			1975	
JDFH-7	Bell 212			1975	
JDFH-8	Bell 212			1975	
JDFH-14	Bell 206A Jet Ranger				
JDFH-15	Bell 206A Jet Ranger				
JDFT-1	De Havilland DHC.6 Twin Otter 100	60		9.67	Sold as C-GIAW 7.77
JDFT-2	Britten-Norman BN.2A-8 Islander	699	G-BAYE	4.74	
JDFT-3	Beechcraft King Air 90	LJ......		1975	
JDFT-4	Beechcraft Duke 60			1975	
JDFT-5	Britten-Norman BN.2A-21	796	G-BDTH	1.77	
JDFT-6	De Havilland DHC.6 Twin Otter 300	531		5.77	

Cessna 185 JDFA-3 photographed at Up Park Camp in April 1975.

MEXICO

Area	1,972,355 sq km
Population	71,500,000
Capital	Ciudad de México (Mexico City)
Civil registration	XA-, XB-, XC-

The United States of Mexico, which comprises 31 states and a federal district, and is the only Latin American country in North America, has had a troubled history. The Aztecs - who, incidentally, were the founders of Mexico City - defeated the aboriginal Olmecs, and were in turn overrun by Hernando Cortés's conquistadores. After about three centuries of Spanish rule, independence was proclaimed in 1810, but the new country's first strong ruler, who proclaimed himself emperor, was executed in 1824. Internal order was little more than theoretical, particularly north of the Rio Grande, an area which was lost after the secession of Texas and the 1846-48 war with the United States of America. France imposed an emperor on Mexico in 1864, but he was overthrown and executed three years later. More unrest followed, although some order was established during the two dictatorships of Porfirio Díaz, the last one ending in 1911. A constitution, based on a previous draft dated 1857, was approved in February 1917 and has since been frequently amended. Mexico is still mainly agricultural, although industrialisation is constantly being expanded; mineral resources are also vast. Mexico has recently reduced the imports of most manufactured goods to a minimum; exports mainly to the USA, include coffee, bananas and sisal - Mexico is the world's main sisal producer. Natural gas and oil production have also increased dramatically, to such an extent that it is now the fourth largest oil producer in the world, and it is expected that Mexico will become a world power in the next few decades, provided, of course, that there is political stability.

It was exactly the permanent semi-anarchy of the nineteenth century that made Mexico conscious of the importance of air power. The country was one of the first to employ aircraft on offensive operations; during the 1911 troubles, a US mercenary pilot, Hector Worden, was hired by the Francisco Madero faction and undertook a number of reconnaissance and ground-attack missions — the latter with the use of dynamite sticks — achieving some results. This was only a year after playboy

Alberto Braniff made the first powered flight in Mexico (also the first to take place in a Spanish-speaking country), in January 1910. Also in 1911, the French pilot Roland Garros, who was to achieve fame during the First World War, demonstrated to President Porfirio Díaz how ground-attack tactics could be developed, flying a Blériot XI monoplane. The first three trainee pilots to receive instruction in the USA left Mexico in 1912. Early in the following years, a Deperdussin monoplane was successfully demonstrated as a light bomber before the War Secretary, but plans to send thirty-one Army officers to a French flying school were cancelled due to the outbreak of the First World War. Two officers already in France decided to volunteer for Armée de l'Air service as a means of gaining operational experience.

Two token Escuadrillas were already in existence in Mexico — in fact, since 1913. The Escuadrilla del Noreste (Northeast Flight) had two Morane-Saulnier monoplanes, and the Escuadrilla del Pacífico (Pacific Flight) a couple of Glenn Martin pusher biplanes. A third unit, the Escuadrilla del Norte (Northern Flight), which was to have five Wright L biplanes, was never formed, because its aircraft were captured by 'the other side' during the perpetual civil wars and probably destroyed. A proper air arm, however, did not exist.

President Venustiano Carranza, at the instance of his nephew Major Alberto Salinas, created an air arm in 1915 with five assorted aircraft, a US mercenary commander and half a dozen personnel. The new force was immediately expanded; a flying school and a repair establishment, the Talleres Nacionales de Construcciones Aeronáuticas (TNCA, National Aircraft Manufacturing Workshops) were inaugurated at Balbuena, Mexico City in November 1915, and — which can be seen as almost miraculous — production of a Mexican-designed aircraft began in the following year ! The first type to be built was the TNCA Serie A, a tandem two-seat biplane powered by a Mexican-designed Aztatl six cylinder aircooled radial driving a Mexican-developed airscrew, designed by TNCA's Italian director

Francesco Santarini. Incidentally, a Serie A, No.9, with an Anzani-Aztatl engine was used in July 1917 for the country's first airmail service.

Other types were put into limited production in 1918-19 out of necessity as no foreign aircraft were available: the improved Serie B, the Serie C Microplano single-seat lightweight scout, a couple of Blériot-based monoplane designs and the two seat Serie H parasol monoplane, designed by Santarini with the collaboration of Mexican engineer Juan Gillermo Villasana, fifteen of which were built and flown with machine guns and bomb racks.

By 1920 the Mexican air arm, or Arma Aérea de las Fuerzas Constitucionales (Constitutional Forces' Air Arm) had some fifty TNCA aircraft. Then President Carranza was overthrown and another civil war followed, absorbing the pilot output of the Escuela Militar de Aplicación (Military Aviation Trining School). The new president appointed Lt. Ralph O'Neil, a US Army fighter ace to act as adviser, and he assumed command of the Army's air component in 1922. During this civil war, a few aircraft were purchased from foreign sources — a handful of US-built DH.4B 'Liberty Planes' in 1924, four Lincoln-Standard biplanes, three Farman bombers, a single Sopwith 1½ Strutter and a dozen Bristol 93A Beaver two-seat general-purpose biplanes, the latter being joined by two examples of the Beaver's reconnaissance version, the Type 93B Boarhound II (c/n 7232/7233). A more modern observation biplane, the Douglas O-2, was adopted by the Mexicans in 1926. An initial order was placed for eight O-2C, similar to the US version (c/n 358/365). Nine improved machines, designated O-2M and based on the USAAC O-32, were ordered in 1929 (c/n 608/616), followed by another three with detail changes as O-2M-2 (c/n 925/926, 946).

Amazingly enough, the TNCA still kept making their own designs, this time developed by Ángel Lascurain y Osio: Toloche parasol fighters with Gnôme rotary engines, Sonora two-seat low-wing monoplane trainers, México parasol trainers, and Quetzalcoatl general purpose aircraft. The TNCA also built under licence a version of the Avro 504K

with a 504N-type undercarriage as the Avro Anahuac, which was the Escuela Militar de Aplicación's standard equipment until 1930-31 (two ex-RAF Avro 504K, one ex E9441, were also operated). Other foreign-built aircraft were gradually procured: ten surplus Bristol F.2b Fighters, a Bristol 84 Bloodhound, and twelve Vought UO Corsair biplanes used by US-trained pilots to suppress insurgents in the April 1929 revolution. The latter type was subsequently built under licence by the Fábrica de Aviones Azcarate (Azcarate Aircraft Factory), 32 being completed in 1932 and serving well into the Second World War as 'Corsarios Azcarate'. This same factory had in 1928 built numbers of Azcarate Modelo E sesquiplane trainers, the intended replacement for the Avro Anahuac.

Early in 1930 the Mexican air arm comprised the Escuela, renamed as the Escuela de Aeronáutica Militar del Ejército, and the 1. Regimiento de Aviación (Air Regiment), with three ten-aircraft squadrons (Escuadrón de Bristols with Bristol Fighters, Escuadrón de Corsarios with Vought Corsairs, and Escuadrón de Douglas with Douglas O-2M), plus ten liaison/observation aircraft and a staff machine, all based at Balbuena, and a personnel strength of 650. A three-squadron 2. Regimiento de Aviación was established in March 1931, but actually formed in 1932 using the licence-built Corsairs. There were airfields at Chihuáhua, Ciudad Juárez, Culiacán, Guadalajara, Laredo, Mazatlán, Mérida, Mexicali, Monterrey, Morelia, Oaxaca, Páchuca, Puebla, Queretaro, San Luis Potosí, Tampico, Torreón and Veracruz. In fact the Fuerza Aérea Mexicana was far too large for the newly-found peace, and its efforts were turned to the development of an airline network and the expansion of the air mail service. Goodwill flights were made; a naval air arm was formed; and older aircraft were quietly retired. New purchases, made in the USA for financial and political reasons, were few and far between. During the 1930s and until early 1942, procurements were limited to a small number of Consolidated PT-3 and Fleet 21 primary trainers, six Ryan STM advanced training monoplanes (one of which, No.3

c/n 184 was later sold in the USA as N7828C), a few Waco D6 general purpose biplanes, and Spartan Zeus tandem-seat light bombers, which were a cheap export variant of the Executive cabin monoplane. The TNCA continued to design prototypes, which failed to enter production due to budgetary restrictions. Between May 1938 and January 1939 the FAM helped to suppress a revolution led by Gen. Saturnino Cedillo.

An agreement signed on 1 April 1941 between the Mexican and US governments gave both parties the right to use certain bases on a reciprocal basis, in exchange for US technical assistance. After Pearl Harbor, a joint US-Mexican Defense Commission was formed; Mexico declared war on the Axis powers on 29 May 1942 following the sinking of Mexican shipping in the Gulf of Mexico by U-boats, and Mexican bases were placed at the disposal of the USA for the protection of the Gulf. At the same time, the service was re-organised with substantial US assistance; two additional flying schools were created and Lend-Lease deliveries commenced. In addition a small number of RCAF surplus Fleet Finch primary training biplanes were acquired. In March 1944 seven FAM pilots were assigned to San Diego NAS for conversion to the Dauntless dive-bomber in preparation for the delivery of the shore-based A-24B version to Escuadrón Aéreo de Pelea 200. More Mexican flying and ground crews underwent conversion training in Texas in 1944, forming Escuadrón de Pelea 201 (201st Combat Squadron) in early 1945 with 25 Republic P-47D Thunderbolts. The Escuadrón reached Clark Field, in the Philippine island of Luzon, in April, and was attached to the USAAF's 58th Fighter Group, at the time the only Fifth Air Force unit flying the P-47D. The Mexicans of the Fuerza Aérea Expedicionaria (Expeditionary Air Force) flew a total of 785 ground-attack sorties until Japan's surrender, seven pilots being lost in action. The TNCA was still in operation during the war, and though it had been given orders in 1942 for 45 of its own design , the Tezuitlán primary trainer, only five were completed, its role being fulfilled by US-provided aircraft.

During the course of World War Two, the FAM had received under Lend-Lease 72 North-American AT-6, 52 Fairchild PT-19, 24 Beechcraft AT-11, 18 Vultee BT-13, 19 Vultee BT-15 and two Beechcraft AT-7 trainers. Transport and utility types consisted of four Lockheed C-60, two Beechcraft UC-45 and three Fairchild UC-61, whilst the combat types were the 25 P-47D Thunderbolts, 26 A-24B Dauntless and five OS2U-1 Kingfishers. The post-war rundown was however rapid and by 1947 so few aircraft remained airworthy that the FAM Commander Gen.Antonio Cardenas Rodriguez pleaded for some action, and for the air force to be given autonomy. Although this was not granted, a small number of new aircraft were introduced to alleviate the crisis; three B-25J Mitchells for Escuadrón Aereo 206, and Douglas C-47 transports and PT-17 Kaydet trainers from US surplus stocks. The combat element was rationalised to a single P-47D unit, Escuadrón Aéreo 201, and several counter-insurgency/close-support Escuadrones with T-6s. Although many of the more obsolete machines — including most of the TNCA aircraft — were retired, progress was slow and indeed much of the equipment still in use in the 1960s consisted of wartime aircraft. During the 1950s there were huge problems caused by inadequate maintenance, and a scandal involving corruption amongst high-ranking officers.

The FAM was established under the control of the Ministry of National Defence (as was, and still is, the Army, but not the Navy, which has a separate ministry) with discrete operations and administration organisations. Eight air bases (Base Aérea Militar)were given a first-rank status, a ninth being added later :

No.1 El Saltillo, Santa Lucia, México state
No.2 Ixtepec, Oaxaca state
No.3 El Ciprés, Ensenada, Baja California Norte
No.4 Cozumel, Quintana Roo state
No.5 Zapopán, Jalisco state
No.6 Puebla, Puebla state
No.7 Pié de Cuesta, Acapulco, Guerrero state
No.8 Mérida, Yucatán state
No.9 La Paz, Baja California Sur state

During 1958-9, 55 ex-USAF T-28A Trojan trainers were acquired, and modified for use in the COIN and CAS roles, thus releasing T-6s which were re-assigned to the newly-created Colegio del Aire (Air College) formed at Zapopán on 29 August 1959, and which also comprised the Escuela de Meteorologia (Meteorological School).

A measure of internal stability and the safety of the borders with the USA in the North and Belize and Guatemala in the South, coupled with budgetary considerations meant that there was little urgency to acquire many new aircraft. The FAM, in comparison with other Latin American air forces, was relatively late in entering the jet age, and fifteen ex-RCAF de Havilland Vampire F.3 jet fighters and two two-seat T.11 trainers were obtained for Escuadrón Jet de Pelea 200, and a similar quantity of ex-USAF Lockheed T-33As provided the equipment for Escuadrón Jet de Pelea 202. The transport force was built up with Douglas C-47, C-54, DC-6 and DC-7, some of which remain in service, and smaller types have been purchased worldwide, including from the USA twenty Beech Musketeer III trainers and twenty Bonanza F.33Cs; from Israel ten IAI Aravas; from Britain Short Skyvans and Britten-Norman Islanders; from France Sud Alouette II and III, and from Switzerland Pilatus PC-7 Turbo-Trainers.

The Mexican aeronautical industry was not forgotten: thirty-two Lockheed-Azcarate LASA.60 utility aircraft were completed, although the type, initially intended for production in Argentina, was to achieve much greater success in Italy where it was built as the Macchi AL.60 in a number of versions. The TNCA has been modernised, and currently specialise in maintenance, though there is a chance that licence manufacture (possibly of Embraer types) will be resumed in the future.

Particularly since the withdrawal of the Vampires in 1967, the role of the FAM has been that of a policing force, with a severely restricted combat capability, but the development of natural resources has made the country perhaps more susceptible to outside aggression, and the southern borders may no longer be considered safe, due to communist infiltration throughout Central America; even to the North, there have been diplomatic clashes with the US government over the millions of illegal immigrants pouring from Mexico into the southern and western United States. Efforts to obtain thirty-six Northrop F-5E Tiger II from the USA in 1980 failed for political reasons, and after that there were negotiations with Israel for the supply of at least twenty-four IAI Kfir fighter-bombers, but this deal failed for both political and economic reasons. However, a new order was placed in 1981 for ten F-5E and two F-5F Tiger II for immediate delivery to equip Escuadrón de Defensa 401. When all fifty-five aircraft on order have been delivered, the PC.7 Turbo-Trainer will become the most proliferous type in the inventory; initially in 1978 they were ordered for the Colegio del Aire, but additional orders were later placed to re-equip T-28A units in both the training and CAS/COIN roles. Further F-5 orders are expected, perhaps to equip up to four Escuadrones, and a modernisation of the transport fleet may be anticipated, particularly the replacement of the Douglas C-47s, and the addition of an aircraft of the Lockheed Hercules type.

Current Organisation

The organisation of the FAM basically comprises nine Grupos Aereo, which, assigned to the Bases Aerea Militar, each supposedly consist of two Escuadrones and their support elements. Personnel strength is around 4,500.

1º Grupo Aéreo

Escuadrón Aéreo 208, based at Santa Lucia with IAI 201 Arava.

Escuadrón Aéreo 209, based at Santa Lucia with Bell 205A, Bell 206B, Bell 47G, Alouette III, and Puma. Helicopters are deployed to other bases.

Escuadrón Mixto de Entrenamiento Táctico (EMET, Tactical Training Squadron) based at Zapopán with North American T-28A.

2º Grupo Aéreo

Escuadron Aereo de Pelea 206 based at Puebla with Pilatus PC.7.

Escuadron Aereo de Pelea 207 based at Ixtepec with Pilatus PC.7.

3º Grupo Aéreo

Escuadrón Aéreo de Pelea 203, based at La Paz with Pilatus PC.7.

Escuadrón Aéreo de Pelea 204, based at El Ciprés with Pilatus PC.7.

4º Grupo Aéreo

Escuadrón Aéreo de Pelea 201, based at Cozumel with North-American T-28, expected to convert to Pilatus PC.7.

Escuadrón Aéreo de Pelea 205, based at Mérida with North-American T-28, expected to convert to Pilatus PC.7.

5º Grupo Aéreo

Escuadrón Aéreo 101, based at Santa Lucia with Aero Commander 500.

Escuadrón Aéreo de Reconocimiento Fotográfico (EARF, Photo-reconnaissance squadron) based at Santa Lucia with Aero Commander 500S.

6º Grupo Aéreo

Escuadrón Aéreo de Transporte Pesado (EATP) 301, based at Santa Lucia with Douglas DC-6/7.

Escuadrón Aéreo de Transporte Pesado 302, based at Santa Lucia with Douglas C-54.

7º Grupo Aéreo

Escuadrón Jet de Pelea 202, based at Santa Lucia with Lockheed AT-33A.

Escuadrón Jet de Pelea 200, with Vampires was disbanded in 1967. Newly forming is *Escuadrón de Defensa 401* with F-5E/F Tiger IIs.

8º Grupo Aéreo

Escuadrón Transporte Ejecutivo operates and maintains civil-registered, government-owned executive Douglas C-47/DC-3, based in the military area of Mexico City International Airport.

Escuadrón Aéreo de Transporte Presidencial (Presidential Air Transport Squadron) based at

Mexico City International Airport with a mixed fleet including Boeing 727, 737, Bell 212, Fairchild F.27, HS.125, Lockheed 188 Electra, Rockwell Sabre and Sud Puma. *NOTE* that the inscription *UTAPEF* seen on some of the presidential aircraft is believed to stand for 'Unidad de Transporte Aéreo Presidencial del Estado' (Presidential Air Transport Unit of the Federal State).

9º Grupo Aéreo

Escuadrón Aéreo de Transporte Mediano (EATM) 311, based at Santa Lucia with Douglas C-47.

Escuadrón Aéreo de Transporte Mediano 312, based at Santa Lucia with Douglas C-47.

Escuela Militar de Aviación at Zapopán, consists of two elements : the *Colegio del Aire (Air College)* which operates Beechcraft Musketeer and Bonanza, North American T-6 and Pilatus PC.7, and the *Escuela Militar de Especialistas de la Fuerza Aérea (EMEFA, Military School of Air Force Specialists)* at Zapopán, a non-flying unit. The EMA is controlled by the Dirección General de Educación Militar, or Directorate General of Military Education.

Escuadrón Aereo 205 - outer ring blue with black inscription. Inner green field, dark green tufts, light grey sky, dark grey cloud, yellow lightning, brown mountain: white helmet, green visor. Orange/black tiger, tan belly claws, and paws. Black/white compass.

Escuadrón de Pelea 201 - white disc, black border and lettering; green and maroon bird with black face and yellow beak, yellow spurs and green pistols. The bird is called 'Pancho Pistolas'.

Escuadrón Aéreo 207 - outer ring orange with black inscription. Inside, light blue background, pink indian's face with black/white eyes, black hair, red warpaint, brown headband, white horns, red/white feather. Face has black mouth contours.

Escuadrón de Bombardeo - white outer circle with black edges and lettering. Inner disc orange with black/white face/eagle's head.

Military Air Bases

1	Ciudad Juárez		
2	Mazatlán		
3	Monterrey		
4	Guadalajara	13	Vera Cruz
5	San Luís Potosí	14	Acapulco
6	Tampico	15	Ixtepec
7	Querétaro	16	Tehuantepec
8	Morelia	17	Tapachula
9	Balbuena	18	Ciudad del Carmen
10	Ciudad de Mexico	19	Campeche
10A	Santa Lucia	20	Mérida
11	Pachuca	21	Cozumel
12	Puebla	22	Chetumal

Aircraft Review

COLOURS AND MARKINGS

The Mexican tricolour flag, adopted in its present form with the proclamation of the Republic in 1823, symbolises independence and hope (green), peace (white) and unity (red). These colours appeared on the wings of the earliest Mexican military aircraft within a shield, the colours being diagonally presented as a memento of the so-called Flag of the Three Guarantees of 1821. In 1925, the familiar tricolour triangle was adopted. Green/white/red rudder stripes were then, as now, mandatory.

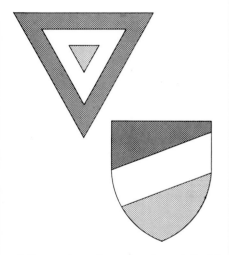

Delivery colour schemes have been retained in service and no specific camouflage schemes have ever been introduced. Expeditionary Thunderbolts in the Pacific during the war had both USAAF and Mexican markings. The inscription FAM is worn by most aircraft.

SERIAL NUMBERS

Mexican serial numbers are normally allotted in apparently random blocks, prefixes being used as a rule. These can be just FAM, the air force's initials, or may denote the aircraft's unit or primary role, and are often changed when the aircraft is transferred to another unit. Re-serialling may also occur. Prefixes include the following :

AP	Avión Presidencial (presidential aircraft)
BHB	Bombardero-Habilitación Beechcraft (AT-11 - Beechcraft Bomber Trainer)
BID	Bombardero Intermedio Douglas (A-26 — Douglas Medium Bomber)
BIN	Bombardero Intermedio North American (B-25 — North American Medium Bomber)
BMM	Bombardero Mediano Mitchell (B-25 — Mitchell Medium Bomber)
BR	Búsqueda y Rescate (Search and Rescue)
BRE	Búsqueda, Reconocimiento y Escuela (Search, reconnaissance and training)
BRL	Búsqueda y Rescate LASA (LASA Search and Rescue)
DN	Defensa Nacional (National Defence)
EAN	Entrenador Avanzado North-American (T-6 -- North-American Advanced Trainer)
EAP	Entrenador Avanzado Pilatus (PC.7 — Pilatus Advanced Trainer)
EBA	Entrenador Beechcraft Avanzado (Bonanza — Beechcraft Advanced Trainer)
EBP	Entrenador Beechcraft Primario (Musketeer — Beechcraft Primary Trainer)
EFL	Enlace y Fotográfico LASA (LASA-60 — LASA Photographic & liaison)
EPF	Entrenador Primario Fairchild (PT-19 — Fairchild Primary Trainer)
EPS	Entrenador Primario Stearman (PT-13 — Stearman Primary Trainer)
ETL	Escuadrón de Transporte Ligero (Light Transport Squadron)
ETM	Escuadrón de Transporte Mediano (Medium Transport Squadron)
ETP	Escuadrón de Transporte Pesado (Heavy Transport Squadron)

FAM	Fuerza Aérea Mexicana (Mexican Air Force)
HBRA	Helicóptero de Búsqueda y Rescate Alouette (Alouette Search and Rescue Helicopter)
HBRB	Helicóptero de Búsqueda y Rescate Bell (Bell 212 — Bell Search & Rescue helicopter)
HOP	Helicóptero de Observación y Policía (Observation and Policing Helicopter)
HRA	Helicóptero de Reconocimiento Alouette (Alouette Reconnaissance Helicopter)
JE	Jet Entrenador (Jet Trainer)
JP	Jet de Pelea (Jet Fighter)
JS	Jet de Soporte (Support Jet)
MU	Mitsubishi Utilitario (Utility Mitsubishi)
PZT	Pelea de Zona Thunderbolt (P-47D — Thunderbolt Point Defence Interceptor)
TEB	Transporte Ejecutivo Beechcraft (Beechcraft Executive Transport)
TED	Transporte Ejecutivo Douglas (Douglas Executive Transport)
TEP	Transporte Ejecutivo Piper (Piper Executive Transport)
TP	Transporte Presidencial (Presidential Transport)
TPH	Transporte Presidencial Helicóptero (Presidential Transport Helicopter)
TTD	Transporte de Tropas Douglas (Douglas Troop Transport)

During 1979, presidential and executive aircraft were given a Government registration in the range XC-UAA to UZZ in addition to their serials.

Some VIP aircraft have additional DN- prefixed serials, e.g. Boeing 727 TP-02/ĐN-01, indicating use by the Ministry of National Defence (Defensa Nacional).

AERO COMMANDER 500S

Twenty were delivered in 1974 and operated by various Escuadrones for communications, but all now operate with 5° Grupo.
ETL-1251 c/n 3211

ETL-1252	3212
ETL-1253	3213
ETL-1254	3214
ETL-1255	3215
ETL-1256	3216
ETL-1257	3217
ETL-1258	3218
ETL-1259	3219
ETL-1260	3220
ETL-1261	3240
ETL-1262	3241
ETL-1263	3242
ETL-1264	3243
ETL-1265	3244
ETL-1266	3245
ETL-1267	3246
ETL-1268	3247
ETL-1269	3248
ETL-1270	3249

BAC ONE-ELEVEN 201AC

One only, TP-0201, c/n 005, ex-XB-MUO for the Escuadrón Aéreo de Transporte Presidencial; reverted to XB-MUO in mid-1977.

BEECHCRAFT T-34A MENTOR

At least four received; transferred to the Mexican Navy.

BEECHCRAFT MUSKETEER SPORT 23

Twenty aircraft delivered new in 1970 for the Colegio del Aire, serialled EBP-301 to EBP-320.

BEECHCRAFT BONANZA F.33C

Twenty aircraft delivered new in 1975 for the Colegio del Aire, serialled EBA-401 to EBA-420.

BEECHCRAFT C-45 EXPEDITOR

At lease ten believed delivered, all now withdrawn from use. One was 44-87256, delivered in January 1951. Two other known aircraft are TEB-5500 (broken up 10.76) and TEB-5501, ex TEB-500 and TEB-501 respectively.

BEECHCRAFT AT-11 KANSAN

About twenty, including ex-USAAF 41-27353, 27409, 27493, 42-36969, 37029, 37054, 37064, 37091, 37097, 37138, 37647, 37687, 43-10396, used by Escuadrón Aéreo 101 and Escuadrón Aéreo de Reconocimiento Fotográfico but all now withdrawn from use. Known examples are BHB-1512, BHB-1518, BHB-1530, 1531 and 1533.

BEECHCRAFT 95-55 BARON

One noted December 1981 as FAM-1305.

BEECHCRAFT KING AIR 90

One aircraft, TP-208/XC-UTG.

BEECHCRAFT SUPER KING AIR 200

One aircraft first noted 12.81, TP-209/XC-SLP.

BELL 47G

Eighteen reported at have been delivered, of which fourteen were still in use in 1980. No serial details known, but most are believed to be ex US Army OH-13.

BELL 205A IROQUOIS (UH-1H)

At least five delivered, currently on charge of Escuadrón Aéreo 209 :

1151	c/n	30118
1152		30122
1153		30126
1154		30125
1155		30124

BELL 206B JET RANGER

Initially five helicopters serialled 1001 to 1005, though reports indicate re-serialling as EBRE-1161 to 1165; the EBRE- prefix has now been dropped.

BELL 212

Two were delivered in July 1971 :
TPH-01 c/n 30517 ex N7946J
TPH-02 30521 N7947J
A Bell 212 previously registered to the Mexican Attorney General (211/XC-BEB c/n 30734) was reported to be in use by the FAM in 1977, and three further helicopters were reported in 1981 as HBRB-1181, 1186 and 1188.

BOEING 727

Two Boeing 727-51 acquired from Northwest Orient in September 1977 as presidential transports, and named as 'Quetzalcoatl I' and 'Quetzalcoatl II' respectively :
TP-01/XC-UJA c/n 19123 ex N477US
TP-02/XC-UJB 19121 N475US
Five further aircraft (727-14 model) acquired May and September 1981 from Mexicana:

10501/XC-	18912	XA-SEP
10502/XC-	19427	XA-SEM
10503	18908	XA-SER
10504	18909	XA-SEU
10505	18911	XA-SEA

BOEING 737

A Boeing 737-247, B-12001, later re-serialled as TP-03, c/n 20127 ex N4523W was acquired from Western Airlines on 27 June 1980. A second aircraft, model 737-112, TP-04, c/n 19772 ex N48AF was acquired in 1981 from Air Florida.

BRITTEN-NORMAN BN.2A-7R ISLANDER

Six aircraft were delivered between May and September 1971 and later diverted to various government agencies (XC-FIK to the Presidential General Staff, XC-GOQ to the National Institute of Nuclear Energy):

TP-0207	c/n 250 ex	N47JA	
TP-0208	252	N48JA	
TP-0209	255	N49JA to	XC-FIK(1)
TP-0210	293	N35JA	XC-FIY
TP-0211	294	N39JA	XC-FOJ
TP-0212	286	N52JA	XC-GOQ

Another aircraft, c/n 420 ex N23JA was bought by the Mexican government in 1975, and appears to be operated by the air force on behalf of the Governor del Estado de Chiapas at Tuxtla as XC-FIK(2)

Boeing 727-51 TP-01 'Quetzalcoatl I' seen at Shannon in May 1978.

Bell 212 TPH-02, another presidential transport delivered in 1971.

CESSNA 182

One aircraft noted 12.81 as FAM-1311.

CESSNA TU.206E

At least two aircraft :
600 c/n 206-01507 ex (N9107M)
606   206-01506   (N9106M)

CESSNA 310R

One aircraft at least, TP-0218 used by the Escuadrón Aéreo de Transporte Presidencial.

CURTISS C-46D COMMANDO

An ex-Israeli Commando c/n 33271, ex 44-77875 and 4X-ALB was operated briefly in the mid 1950s as X-T-1, before disposal as N10012.

DE HAVILLAND CANADA DHC.5D BUFFALO

An aircraft was delivered for evaluation, and seems to have resulted in orders, as TP-215 c/n 98 and TP-216, probably c/n 100, were seen at the manufacturers in 1980 prior to delivery.

DOUGLAS A-24 (DAUNTLESS)

About ten delivered. A few were based at Pié de la Cuesta, near Acapulco, in 1959-60; one of these was serialled 2525. One aircraft was civilianised as XB-ZAH.

DOUGLAS B-26B INVADER

Ten believed supplied. One was converted to VIP configuration with the serial 1300, and used during 1971-72; it was derelict at Mexico City in November 1975. Two, also converted to VIP transports, were presented to the French Air Force in 1953: Z001 'El Fantasma' in April (yellow overall), and Z002 'El Indio' in May (red overall). B-26B 1302 was converted by On Mark to executive aircraft and civilianised as XB-SIJ.

DOUGLAS C-47 SKYTRAIN

About forty were obtained in all, including ex-USAAF 42-23390, 92867, 93816, 44-77255, and 45-1017 which was sold in Brazil as PP-AXY. About a dozen remain in use with EATM311 and 312. Known examples include :

AP-0201	'Revolucionario'
TP-0202	'Mexicano' preserved at Mexico City
TP-0203	
TP-304/XC-UPD	
ETM-2118	
TED-6006	'Plan de Ayuda'
TED-6007 ex TP-6007	'Galiana'
TTD-6010 ex TTD-610	
TTD-6016	
TP-6017	
TTD-6020	
TTD-6021	
TTD-6023	'Antonio Cordemus R'
	to TP-6023 then TED-6023
TED-6024 ex TTD-6024	wfu
ETM-6025	
TP-6026	
TTD-6028	
TED-6035	wfu 1978
TED-6036	
TED-6037	wfu 1978
TED-6040	

DOUGLAS C-54D SKYMASTER

Five aircraft for Escuadrón Aéreo de Transporte Pesado 302, serialled FAM-7001 to 7005, later ETP-7001 to 7005. Four were still in use in 1979.

DOUGLAS DC-6

About twenty have seen service, most of them DC-6B, though TP-0203 and a couple of others were DC-6. The first few were delivered early in 1966, and the last pair (ex-French Air Force) in 1978-9. A number may well be ex-USAF C-118A, and are in fact referred to as C-118A. An unidentified aircraft crashed early in November 1979.

TP-0203	c/n 43129	ex XA-MUB 'Francisco Zarco'; d/d 2.66; to TP-03 then TP-203, and w/o 6.12.78.
TP-0204		
ETP-10001	44059	XC-MEX; to N88975 8.77
ETP-10002		

ETP-10003	43134	XA-MUM d/d 3.66
ETP-10004		
ETP-10005		
ETP-10006		
ETP-10007		
ETP-10008		
ETP-10009		
ETP-10010		
ETP-10011		
ETP-10012		
ETP-10013		
ETP-10014		
ETP-10018	45226	N72539, French AF named 'Tlacaelel I'
ETP-10019		French AF; 'Tlacaelel II'

DOUGLAS DC-7B

Three aircraft, believed acquired for EATP301 :
ETP-10101
ETP-10102
ETP-10103 c/n 45407 ex N365AA and AP-01, d/d 1.64

FAIRCHILD PT-19

Quite a few of the original fifty-two aircraft survived the war and remained in use until the early 1960s. One was EPF-54.

FAIRCHILD F-27 FRIENDSHIP

Five aircraft of which the first two were acquired early 60s, the others late 70s :

AP-0203	F-27A	c/n 30 ex	XC-CAT. 'Insurgente'. Sold as N2815J 21.5.65.
AP-0204	F-27F	90	N2719R; temporarily to XC-COX, restored as TP-204/XC-UTC.
TP-0205	F-27	26	N555AU. To Navy as MT-0745
AP-0206			
AP-0207			

An aircraft TP-203/XC-UTC was noted in 1981, possibly a new acquisition taking up previously used marks.

HAWKER-SIDDELEY HS.125-400A

One aircraft TP-0206, c/n 25216/NA743 ex XC-GOB, later re-serialled TP-108/XC-UJH, then sold as N125JW in 1981.

HILLER UH-12E

One aircraft reported on charge late 1980.

IAI 201 ARAVA

Five aircraft were delivered in 1973-74, with a further five in 1976. All serve with Escuadrón Aéreo 208 for transport and SAR, but are equipped to carry machine gun and rocket pods for their secondary counter-insurgency and close air support roles. All were delivered with civil registrations, and later re-serialled 2001-2010.

XC-GAW/BRE-01 to	2001	c/n 0005	ex	4X-IAC
XC-GAX/BRE-02	2002	0006		4X-IAD
XC-GEB/BRE-03	2003	0008		4X-IAF
XC-GEC/BRE-04	2004	0009		4X-IAG
XC-GED/BRE-05	2005	0010		4X-IAH

(2005 reported 1981 as 'BRE-208)

XC-BIW	2006	0036	4X-IBI
XC-BIX	2007	0039	4X-IBL
XC-BIY	2008	0035	4X-IBH
XC-BIZ	2009	0037	4X-IBJ
XC-BOA	2010	0040	4X-IBM

LOCKHEED T-33A

Fifteen aircraft were delivered in 1961 as JE-001 to JE-015, of which JE-015 was written off on 17.7.78. A dozen were converted to AT-33A for use by Escuadrón Aéreo 202, and eight remained on charge in late 1980. There have been reports of further deliveries, but there seems little evidence of this except perhaps the report of an aircraft marked JE-016 at Miami in May 1981. In particular, seven ex Netherlands Air Force machines were reportedly procured (two on 16.3.72 and five on 7.4.72) via the US firm Consolidated Aero Exports, and allocated US ferry registrations as follows :

N646	c/n	6608	ex 51-8824 and M-56
N647		5544	51-8760	M-53
N648		6285	51-6953	M-52
N649		5863	51-6531	M-55
N650		5860	51-6528	M-51
N651		5223	50-370	M-49
N652		5034	49-884	M-48

However, they were apparently never delivered; all but N650 and N651 were registered to US owners by January 1977, and the lot remained in open storage at Tucson in September of that year. Seven aircraft remain in use, the following having been written off : JE-001 (3.12.81), JE-003, JE-005 to 008, JE-012, JE-014 and JE-015.

LOCKHEED 1329 JETSTAR 8

One only, used by the Ministerio de la Defensa Nacional : JS-10201 c/n 5144 ex N5508L, re-serialled DN-01.

LOCKHEED L-188AF-08-15 ELECTRA

One aircraft only, TP-04 'Morelos', c/n 1104, ex N284F, obtained in 1978, became TP-0201 on 3.2.79 and later TP-201/XC-UTA.

LOCKHEED-AZCARATE LASA 60

About forty LASA 60 were completed, eighteen of which entered service with the FAM. Known serials included :

1018	later BRL-1018	c/n 1018
1024		1024
1028	EFL-1028	1028
1036		1036

Other machines included c/n 1001 XC-PEZ, 1005 XB-LAG, 1012 XB-LEQ, 1013 which was to have become HR-185-P but is believed to have served with the FAM, 1017 N144U, and 1022 XB-LUT.

MITSUBISHI MU.2B-35

One aircraft only, MU-1550 c/n 566 ex N210MA, delivered in February 1973, and also used by the Mexican Army High Command. Withdrawn from use.

NORTH AMERICAN B-25J MITCHELL

About ten believed delivered, including 44-86712, 86717, and serialled in the 3500 block; 3501 and 3503 confirmed.

NORTH AMERICAN T-6 TEXAN

Eighty-two AT-6 were delivered during the war (six AT-6B, 47 AT-6C including 41-32768, 42-4181, 42-44143, 48940, 49001, and twenty-nine AT-6D); another forty-five followed in 1950. Over twenty remained in use with the Colegio del Aire by 1980/81. Known serials include :

EAN-702	
EAN-704	
705	
708	
EAN-711	
EAN-712	
EAN-735	
749	
EAN-757	preserved at Zapopán air base
EAN-759	
EAN-761	
EAN-763	
774	
781	
782	
783	
787	
788	
796	
801	
802	
804	
808	
EAN-812	
814	
EAN-825	
828	

NORTH AMERICAN T-28A TROJAN

Eighty believed delivered, over thirty of which remain in use with Escuadrones Aéreos 201, 205, 206, 207 and the EMET. The type is being replaced by the Pilatus PC-7. Known serials include 904, 910, 912, 915, 916, 918, 920, 924, 927, 930, 934, 939, 940, 945, 946, 949, 952, 961, 972, 975 and 980. T-912 and T-980 have also been reported, although serial presentation was usually T-28-904 etc. and the T-28 prefix was later discontinued.

NORTHROP F-5E/F TIGER II

Twelve aircraft ordered 1981 (ten F-5E and two F-5F) for Escuadrón de Defensa 401. The first two aircraft were noted at the factory prior to delivery in October 1981.

PILATUS PC-7 TURBO-TRAINER

Twelve aircraft ordered in 1978 were delivered in 1979, and subsequent orders for twenty-six in 1980 and seventeen in 1981 are in the course of delivery. It is believed the first eight aircraft were c/ns 122 to 129, and the next thirty c/ns 194 to 223. The first fifty-eight aircraft are believed to

Douglas C-47 Skytrain TP-0202, at one time a presidential aircraft, now preserved at Mexico City.

Douglas C-54D Skymaster ETP-7005, one of five for the Escuadrón Aéreo de Transporte Pesado 302.

Beechcraft Bonanza F.33C EBA-401 to EBA-405 in a pre-delivery line-up at Wichita.

Lockheed T-33A JE-002 photographed at Miami in September 1977.

Britten-Norman BN.2A-7R Islander TP-0207, the first of six delivered in 1971.

Douglas DC-6 ETP-10014, which may in fact be an ex-USAF C-118A.

IAI 201 Arava BRE-03/XC-GEB on delivery at Prestwick in August 1973; it later became 2003.

Short SC.7 Skyvan 3M-100 TP-0213 was delivered in January 1974; three others followed in 1977.

be serialled 501 to 558, with EAP- prefixes added for those aircraft operated by the Escuela Militar de Aviacion. Further deliveries have been made by airfreight through Amsterdam in early 1982; c/ns 271 to 275 have been noted.

PIPER PA-23 AZTEC 250F

At least one aircraft, serialled TEP-1303.

PIPER PA-32 CHEROKEE SIX

At least one aircraft, BR-1050.

REPUBLIC P-47D THUNDERBOLT

Twenty-five were delivered to the newly-formed Escuadrón de Pelea 201, and flew with USAAF serial numbers, Mexican and US insignia, and Mexican sequence numbers - examples included 44-33523 '6' , 44-33710, and 44-33721 '18'. Escuadrón de Pelea 201 still had a few as late as 1962, but with FAM serials: one was PZT-1003.

ROCKWELL SABRE

Five aircraft delivered as executive transports :

TP-103/XC-UJC	Sabre 75A c/n	380-67	ex N2528E
TP-104/XC-UJD	Sabre 75A	380-68	N2538E
TP-105/XC-UJE	Sabre 60	306-139	N650C
TP-106/XC-UJF	Sabre 60	306-144	N2519E
TP-107/XC-UJG	Sabre 40A	282-130	XC-SRA

The single Sabre 40A was formerly operated by the Secretariat for Agrarian Reform.

SHORT SC.7 SKYVAN 3M-100

Four aircraft were delivered :

TP-0213 c/n SH.1920 ex G-BBPL	d/d	22.1.74
TP-0215	SH.1951	G-BEHZ	30.1.77
TP-0216	SH.1952	G-BELY	13.3.77
TP-0217	SH.1953	G-BELZ	20.5.77

Two became TP-210/XC-UTI and TP-211/XC-UTJ.

STEARMAN PT-13 KAYDET

A number of these biplane trainers were delivered under

Lend-Lease, and a dozen rebuilt machines were delivered to the Colegio del Aire in 1967 ! Half a dozen of these were still on charge in 1980, and four noted as instructional airframes in 1981.

SUD SA.318 ALOUETTE II

Two taken on charge :
HBRA-1101 c/n 1894 Sold as N88019
HBRA-1102 1895
Another Alouette II, c/n 1742, ex French military, was on loan to the Mexican Air Force between August 1962 and September 1963, but returned to France.

SUD SA.316 ALOUETTE III

Reportedly nine delivered, including :
HRA-111
HOP-210 c/n 1134
HOP-211 1135 ex F-WJDF
HOP-212 1142
The remaining aircraft are reported as 1131 to 1135, having discarded earlier HBRA- prefixes.

SUD SA.330 PUMA

Four aircraft reported to have been delivered, including :
TPH-01/XC-UHA
TPH-02, crashed 22.5.79 but rebuilt and sold as N2261M.

Mexican Army & Police

The Mexican Army, which has a peacetime strength of about 70,000, but in wartime would have about 72,000 regular and 250,000 conscripted personnel, has no air arm of its own, but comprises a two-battalion parachute brigade (Brigada de Fusilieros Paracaidistas), and maintains close co-operation with the FAM. The police forces, with a total personnel of about 60,000 including the 'Rurales' or rural constabulary, operate aircraft on contract as needed, with their civil registrations retained, but do not maintain an air arm.

Mexican Navy

Although Mexican naval aviation can trace its origins as far back as 1917, when an Army TNCA Serie A was successfully converted and flown as a sea-plane, and several naval officers trained as pilots during the late 1920s and early 1930s, the Servicio de Aviación de la Armada de Mexico was not formed until 1940, with less than a dozen pilots and two aircraft handed over by the Army — a Fairchild KR.34 and an Azcarate Modelo E. Following Mexico's declaration of war on Germany, coastal patrols were flown by the air force, as the Navy had neither the aircraft nor the crews, but the situation gradually changed. The 1er Escuadrón Aeronaval (1st Naval Air Squadron) was formed on 4 May 1943 at Vera Cruz with half-a-dozen Lend-Lease Vought OS2U-3 Kingfishers (serialled MB-01 to MB-06), which flew for some time on wheels from Tampico. On 5 October 1943, an Escuela de Aviación Naval (Naval Aviation School) was formed, also at Veracruz, with about a dozen aircraft transferred from Army stocks — six Fairchild PT-19, a few Consolidated 21C biplanes and a single Beechcraft AT-7 crew-trainer. Previously, flying training was undertaken at the army school.

Two Grumman J2F-6 Duck utility biplanes (MV-07 and MV-08) were acquired in 1947, serving until 1951, when the survivor MV-08, was returned to the USA. Other aircraft obtained at the time were a few Stearman PT-17 and five Consolidated PBY-5A Catalina amphibians.

The first Naval helicopters, four Bell 47J delivered in November 1958, formed the 2° Escuadrón Aeronaval (Búsqueda y Salvamento), a specialised search and rescue unit. A 3° Escuadrón Aeronaval was formed with six Beechcraft C-45, eventually re-equipping with the Grumman HU-16 Albatross.

The Escuela de Aviación Naval eventually grounded its old equipment including a couple of OS2U-3 Kingfishers — one was MB-03 which was presented to the US Navy for restoration and is currently on display on the preserved *USS Alabama* — and re-equipped with four Beechcraft T-34A Mentors initially allocated to the FAM.

The Aviación de la Armada began an expansion programme in the 1960s, with some aircraft transferred from the FAM and a miscellany of light aircraft and helicopters of US and French origin. It now comprises, in addition to the Escuela, small maritime patrol, transport and SAR Escuadrones, and a personnel strength of about 350. The overall strength of the Navy is about 18,500 personnel, with about eighty medium and small ships, none of which has provision for aircraft or helicopters.

Aircraft Review

COLOURS AND MARKINGS

Naval aircraft carry insignia similar to those of the air force, and use the inscriptions *Marina, Armada* or *Armada de Mexico.*

SERIAL NUMBERS

Serials are of up to three digits, with a distinctive prefix as follows :

HMR	Helicóptero Marina Rescate (Naval Rescue Helicopter)
ME	Marina Entrenador (Naval Trainer)
MP	Marina Patrullero (Naval Patrol)
MT	Marina Transporte (Naval Transport)
MTX	Marina Transporte Experimental (Experimental Naval Transport)
MU	Marina Utilitario (Naval Utility)
MV	Marina Vigilancia (Naval Surveillance)

BEECHCRAFT BONANZA F.33C

Six aircraft, including :
ME-014
ME-015
ME-016
ME-017 c/n CJ.108

BEECHCRAFT T-34A MENTOR

Four aircraft, ex FAM, serialled ME-010 to ME-013.

BEECHCRAFT C-45 EXPEDITOR

Six aircraft, probably ex FAM, have been confirmed :
ME-14
MT-55
MP-82
MP-84
MT-255
MP-380

BEECHCRAFT BARON B.55

Two only, ME-051 and ME-052.

BELL 47G/J

Six, perhaps more, were used, the first four Bell 47J being delivered in November 1958.

HMR-27	47J	c/n 1754
HMR-29	47J	
HMR-30	47G	'24387'
HMR-128	47J	
HMR-131	47G-3B-2	6711 d/d 11.68

BELL UH-1H IROQUOIS

HMR-140 reported 1981.

CESSNA 150J

Three aircraft only, probably delivered 1969 :
ME-001 c/n 70937
ME-002
ME-003

CESSNA 180

Three aircraft known :

MU-02	180	c/n 30677	ex N2377C
ME-20	180A	32803	N9506B
ME-21	180A	32817	N9520B

CESSNA 310

Three serials are known : ME-056, MT-56 (possibly the same aircraft ?) and MT-211.

CESSNA 337G

MT-104 c/n 337-01479 ex (N1879M) delivered mid-1970s. Another aircraft serialled MT-422 was reported in 1981.

CESSNA 402

Two aircraft only, MT-103 c/n 402-0333, and MT-212.

CONSOLIDATED PBY-5A CATALINA

Five were acquired in 1947. At least one was converted to a transport - MT-03 'El Marinero'. None remain in service.

DH CANADA DHC.5D BUFFALO

One aircraft delivered in October 1980 : MT-220

DOUGLAS C-47

Known aircraft include :
MT-101
MT-201
MT-202 in storage by 9.76
MT-203
MT-204

FAIRCHILD F-27 FRIENDSHIP

Two were acquired as C-47 replacements :

| MT-205 | c/n 25 | ex N4305F | d/d 6.7.76 |
| MT-206 | 3 | N27WA | 19.9.78 |

A third aircraft was obtained from the FAM in 1978 :

| MT-0745 | 26 | TP-0205 |

An aircraft serialled MT-125 was reported during 1981.

Stearman PT-17 ME-10 in overall yellow colours at Vera Cruz in March 1968.

Cessna 150J ME-003 one of three delivered around 1969.

Bell 47J HMR-128 also yellow overall at Vera Cruz in March 1968.

Beechcraft T-34A Mentor ME-011 in yellow training colours at Vera Cruz in March 1968.

Beechcraft C-45 Expeditor MP-380 in overall silver with dayglo tips at Vera Cruz in March 1968.

GRUMMAN HU-16 ALBATROSS

Four HU-16A/B were initially obtained from the RCAF; four US machines followed in 1977. It is also known that civil Albatross N9387 (ex RCAF 9306) was cancelled 11.6.76 as exported to Mexico, and that on 7.4.76 eight HU-16D were released from storage for sale to the Mexican Navy (ex Bu.137913, 137914, 137917, 137920, 141273, 141274, 141280 and 141283) - these may be the ones delivered early in 1979. Eight are believed to be in current use with the 3° Escuadron Aeronaval, operating in two detachments from La Paz, Baja California del Sur, and Ensenada, Baja California del Norte - the latter being an FAM base. Known serials are MP-101, MP-103, MP-201, MP-202, MP-203, MP-301, MP-305, MP-306, MP-401, MP-403, MP-404 and MP-405.

HUGHES 269A

Two were obtained from government agencies, but disposed of early in 1980 :
c/n 720113 ex XC-CUO to N5598T
c/n 1010018 XC-DED N........

LEAR JET 24D

One aircraft delivered in 1975 : MTX-01 c/n 24.313.

NORTH AMERICAN AT-6 TEXAN

At least one aircraft, ex FAM, serial unknown.

STEARMAN PT-17

About four believed delivered in the late 1940s. Two still exist, ME-08 and ME-10.

SUD SA.313 ALOUETTE II

Five were delivered, of which four remain in use. No more details known.

SUD SA.319B ALOUETTE III

At least five :
HMR-132 c/n 2049 ex F-WTNH
HMR- ?   2050   F-WTNF
HMR- ?   2156
HMR- ?   2157
HMR- ?   2279

Lear Jet 24D MTX-01, a single example of the type delivered in 1975.

NICARAGUA

Area	148,005 sq km
Population	2,395,000
Capital	Managua
Civil registration	YN- (AN- until September 1979)

Nicaragua rejected Spanish rule in 1821 and became an independent republic in 1838 after a period of joint national and Mexican rule and a time with the United Provinces of Central America. Its strategic importance was quickly understood by the United States, whose influence in Nicaragua started in 1912; a treaty was signed in August 1914 giving the USA facilities for the establishment of military bases. In January 1927 a 600-man US Marine Expeditionary Force was sent to Nicaragua to protect US interests; it included Observation Squadron VO-4M (which became VO-7M on 1 July 1927), to which VO-6M (later VJ-6M) was added in June 1928 to form the 2nd Marine Brigade. The Marine Expeditionary Force left Nicaragua in February 1933 and the 1914 treaty was eventually abrogated in July 1970.

Military flying began in 1920 when the United States presented the newly-formed Guardia Nacional (National Guard) with four Curtiss JN.4 and seven DH.4 in return for assistance in peace-keeping operations in the Panama Canal Zone. These aircraft were based at Managua airfield but were seldom used. After the US Marine occupation of the country, the Guardia Nacional acquired three Swallow biplanes from the Checker Cab Co of San Francisco, for use against the guerilla forces led by Augusto Sandino. Flown by two ex US Army pilots, and maintained by fifteen Nicaraguan ground crew, the Swallows were used for reconnoitring the combat areas and dropping light bombs on guerilla formations, achieving some success. They were extensively supported by US Marine aircraft operating from the country's numerous rivers and lakes with some Loening OL amphibians and Vought O2U Corsair float biplanes and flying casualty evacuation missions as well. Four O2U Corsairs made one of the first recorded aircraft attacks against a fortified position without ground forces' support, when during the 1927 campaign they successfully cleared a 1,500-strong guerilla fort at Chipote without loss. The US Marine force was based at Archibald Field near Managua, where in 1929 a weather station was established — a second station was later opened at León, north of the Managua lake.

For a number of years, apart from the off anti-guerilla patrol, little flying was undertaken. USMC supplies and troops were regularly ferried to Managua on board Pan American Airways Fokkers flying to South America. When the US Marines withdrew, they transferred the control of the Guardia Nacional to General Anastasio Somoza García, who later took over the country as the only Nicaraguan qualified to rule. The Guardia Nacional, a regular army as well as a police force, continued to receive United States assistance and was eventually enlarged to include a small Guardia Costera (Coast Guard) of some two hundred personnel and half a dozen patrol craft. By 1979, the Guardia Nacional had some 7,100 personnel, of which 1,500 were attached to the Air Force.

A regular Fuerza Aérea de la Guardia Nacional de Nicaragua (Nicaraguan National Guard Air Force) was formed on 9 June 1938 under the Ministry for War Navy and Aviation, with a small number of aircraft including a couple of Waco D light reconnaissance bomber versions of the two-seat SH3D biplane and an ex Royal Canadian Air Force, CCF-built Grumman GE.23 Goblin two-seat biplane fighter serialled GN-3. An Escuela del Aire (Aviation School) was established with US assistance, and from 1942 onwards received small numbers of Lend-Lease Stearman PT-13A, Fairchild PT-19 and North American AT-6; instructors were provided by the US Government. Additional trainers and a few Lockheed P-38 were subsequently received, but the Fuerza Aérea was never more than a token force; by the end of the Second World War it had no more than thirty officers and forty other ranks, plus about two dozen aircraft, including two directly-purchased Taylorcraft 65 : BC65 c/n 3374 and DC65 c/n 4176, delivered early in 1942.

Nicaragua's signing of the Rio Pact in 1947 gave a new life to the Fuerza Aérea de Nicaragua, as it was now known. Twelve Republic F-47D Thunderbolt fighter-bombers were supplied (six F-47N were later added) and remained in service until 1964; other US deliveries included small numbers of Beechcraft C-45 and Douglas C-47 transports and twenty-six F-51D Mustangs were received from Sweden, later to be supplemented by additional aircraft from USAF stocks. The FAN's expansion also dictated the transfer of some military flying to Managua's Las Mercedes airport.

An unexpected delivery took place during the aborted Bay of Pigs raid against Fidel Castro's communist régime in Cuba. Four Douglas B-26B and B-26C Invaders flown by rebel crews landed in Nicaragua and were impressed into the FAN which had operated another B-26 from 1958 onwards; they were supplemented by another two aircraft in 1963. The Invaders equipped a combat squadron until the mid-1970s, when they were grounded due to rear fuselage and tailplane spar fatigue. Most new FAN aircraft, however, were delivered in a more orthodox way !

The mid-1970s also saw the rebirth of the so-called Frente Sandinista de Libertación Nacional (Sandinista National Liberation Front), extensively trained and supplied by Cuba, and having nothing in common with Augusto Sandino's guerillas except for its name. The Sandinistas began operations in Nicaragua's eastern regions, where the Indian and Negro minorities live (most of the half-caste three-quarters of the population, as well as the white minority, live in the western areas); apart from the usual harassment of the Guardia Nacional, they tried to exploit the population's grievances against the government, such as the economic difficulties caused by the December 1972 earthquake which nearly destroyed Managua. Costa Rica became a sanctuary for the Sandinistas, which caused a serious international incident on 14 October 1977: two Nicaraguan Aviocars opened fire against an unidentified ship on the Rio Frio believed to be carrying arms for the Sandinistas, but on board was Costa Rica's Minister of Public Security and his party including other government officials and newsmen; only a diplomatic intervention by the OAS/OEA prevented an armed conflict. The first full-scale guerilla operations took place in August 1978, aiming to start a civil war as a means of deposing President Anastasio Somoza Debayle.

Although they failed, additional backing from Cuba and Nicaragua's traditional adversary Costa Rica, as well as the termination of United States support of the Somoza regime, caused a destructive civil war to begin in June 1979. President Somoza was defeated in July, largely due to the exhaustion of fuel and ammunition and the difficulty in obtaining military supplies which had to be ordered from such faraway countries as Portugal. The Sandinista transitional government was at pains to present itself as democratic and moderate, but changes did take place at once (one of the less important ones was the renaming of Las Mercedes as Sandino International Airport). Little is known about the current situation of the Guardia Nacional except for the purges which it has suffered, and with avowed Marxists in key places it is unlikely that detailed information will become available in the near future.

Before the civil war, the Fuerza Aérea de Nicaragua consisted of an Escuadrón de Combate at Las Mercedes with nine Cessna 337D (five of which were operational), six North American T-28D and two Lockheed AT-33A; an Escuadrón de Transporte also at Las Mercedes with three Douglas C-47, four Beechcraft C-45 and 'eight' IAI Aravas, with other C-47s and a couple of CASA 212 Aviocars in reserve:

Military Air Bases

1 Managua (Las Mercedes)
2 Granada
3 Chinandega
4 León
5 Boaco
6 Somoto
7 Jícaro
8 Santa Cruz
9 Puerto Cabezas
10 Las Perlas
11 Bluefields
12 Acoyapa

the Escuela del Aire with four North American T-6G, three Piper Super Cubs and six Cessna 172s: a communications element with ten Cessna 180 and 185, and a helicopter force with Hughes 269A and B, four Hughes OH-6A and two surviving Sikorsky S.58 converted with racks for two five hundred pound bombs. About twenty of these aircraft are believed to remain airworthy after the war, and there is no indication that the FAN's organisation was radically changed. The main bases in current use are Managua-Sandino, Puerto Cabezas, Siuma and Los Brasiles.

The Nicaraguan armed forces were disbanded in mid-1979 and temporarily replaced by Sandinista guerilla formations pending a nationwide political purge. Steps were taken in mid-1980 to re-form them with Cuban and Soviet assistance and the new Fuerza Aérea Sandinista is now believed to operate five Douglas C-47, two or three Lockheed T-33A, a couple of North American T-28D, a CASA 212A Aviocar and two Sikorsky CH-34A, flown by Cuban mercenaries as well as Sandinistas. A number of MiG-21s were supplied by Cuba during 1981, with pilot training being carried out in Bulgaria, and it is also reported that two Alouette III helicopters are being supplied by France during 1982 as part of a $17 million deal including two fast patrol boats and army equipment. A handful of the FAN aircraft were flown to Honduras by Guardia Nacional personnel loyal to President Somoza at the end of the civil war, but their fate is unknown. The crew of a Nicaraguan aircraft defecting to Honduras in March 1982 reported the delivery to the FAS of six Soviet transport aircraft and two helicopters; these are known to be Mil Mi-8.

Aircraft Review

COLOURS AND MARKINGS

The Nicaraguan markings are unique in that they have never really been standardised, several roundel designs being used, together with US-style rudder stripes. The national flag, based on that of the United Provinces, is blue and white, but FAN markings used blue, white, red and yellow. The country's first marking was the coat of arms, painted on the fuselage sides. The inscription *Fuerza Aérea de Nicaragua* was applied on some transports, and the use of camouflage, though to no specific rules, was also introduced before the Sandinista takeover. Since that takeover, a new FAS logo has been introduced, as illustrated below; there is a white outline to black FAS lettering, with a red and black flash.

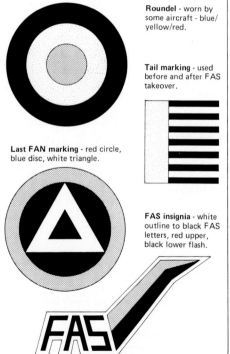

Last FAN marking - red circle, blue disc, white triangle.

Roundel - worn by some aircraft - blue/yellow/red.

Tail marking - used before and after FAS takeover.

FAS insignia - white outline to black FAS letters, red upper, black lower flash.

Red outer ring, dark blue background with white lettering 'Nicaragua' and black 'FAN'. Yellow wings, red circle, blue centre, white triangle. This badge often appeared on aircraft.

The aircraft below are those known to have been operated by the FAN. Naturally there is a shortage of information on post-civil war re-seriallings, but it does appear that most of the aircraft which are now in use have been renumbered, and they carry 'Fuerza Aérea Sandinista' inscriptions .

AERO COMMANDER 500/680/690

Three 500U were temporarily used — they were registered to the Ministry of National Defence; the first two were handed over to the Nicaraguan National Bank.

AN-BFU	c/n 1765-49	ex AN-ASD (2)
AN-BIH	3052	AN-ASD (3)
AN-MDN	3112	N9158N

One model 680F L :

321	1822-151	HK-852-P

One model 690A on loan :

AN-ASD	11222

BEECHCRAFT C-45

At least seven were supplied in 1947-48, ex USAF 43-35764 35858; 44-47116, 47298, 47355, 87114, 87188. Others were delivered later. Four were still in use in 1978.

BEECHCRAFT BONANZA A35

One only, delivered 5.77 :
1017 c/n D.1674 ex N673B

CASA 212A-7 AVIOCAR

Five aircraft delivered between June 1977 and June 1978 with delivery registrations in the AN-BSx block. By June 1979 only two were reported serviceable, 421 and 424. Following the Sandinista takeover, two aircraft have been reported in new marks and re-serialled 221 and 222; these are frequently reported as ex 420 and 422 respectively, though this would seem to conflict with the information above and known write-offs.

420	c/n A7-1-80	ex AN-BSV	d/d 18.6.77	
421	A7-3-90	AN-BSX	17.9.77	
422	A7-4-91	AN-BSY	4.4.78	w/o 29.1.79
423	A7-5-95	AN-BSZ	11.5.78	w/o 5.1.79
424	A7-2-97	AN-BSW	16.6.78	

CESSNA 172

Six aircraft, mostly model 172I and 172K, bought second-hand from the USA :

20	c/n 57081	ex N46162	d/d 24.3.77
21	57382	N46611	24.3.77
22	57626	N78462	24.3.77
23	56513	N8313L	
24	58579	N84689	
25	57359	N46572	

CESSNA 180

At least eight aircraft :

1000				
1001	180E	c/n 51102	ex AN-AOB, N2602Y	
1002		30480	AN-ASV	
1003		30228	AN-ANY, N1528C	
1004	180F	51247	AN-AQC, N2147Z	
1005		47115		w/o 14.5.76
1006	180C	50875	AN-AMV, N9375T	
1007				

CESSNA 185/U-17B

At least one 185C :
1010 c/n 185-1243
Two U-17B (model A185E) :

1008	185-02026	ex 72-1357
1009	185-02027	72-1358

CESSNA 337D

Ten aircraft with provision for light armament; the first five were delivered on 5.6.76.

311	c/n 337-01703	ex N53563	w/o 22.12.78
312	337-01704	N53564	
313	337-01705	N53566	
314	337-01706	N53567	
315	337-01707	N53569	
316	337-01710	N53572	
317	337-01714	N53576	w/o 1.77
318	337-01715	N53577	
319	337-01717	N53579	
320	337-01723	N53585	

DE HAVILLAND CANADA DHC.3 OTTER (U-1A)

Six were delivered, all ex US Army :

1011	w/o 7.9.76
1012	
1013	
1014	
1015	w/o 10.76
1016	wfu

DOUGLAS C-47 SKYTRAIN

At least twelve were taken on charge. One serialled 208 was a C-47D. Other known serials are 410, 411, 414, 416, 417, and 418, the latter two delivered from the USA on 19.5.76. Two C-47 were transferred to the Government as AN-ASP (C-47-DL c/n 4519 ex 41-18457, N69040, N321HA) and AN-AWT. At least one was an AC-47D gunship. An unidentified C-47 was shot down by Sandinista guerillas in April of 1979. One post-war serial is known - 203.

DOUGLAS B-26 INVADER

A single B-26 was obtained from an unspecified source in 1958. Four B-26B and B-26C used in the Bay of Pigs invasion were impressed, and another two were obtained in 1963 in a deal where Mustangs, C-45s and Thunderbolts were traded in; six further aircraft are reported supplied under MAP in 1966, and one was acquired for spares in 1963. Confirmed serials were 400 to 404, 420 and 422. All surviving aircraft

were later re-serialled in the 600 block. 601 and 603 were reported as current in 1979, and 602 was still at Managua even though it had been registered as N99422 in March 1977 to Military Aircraft Restoration Corp. as part of a reported trade-in deal against new Cessna aircraft. 604 was also reported as being delivered from the USA in April of 1977. Three aircraft, all A-26B, were registered in the USA as part of the trade-in deal :

N99420	c/n 7220	ex 41-39507
N99422	7136	41-39423
N99425	6875	41-39162

HAWKER SIDDELEY HS.125-600B

One only, AN-BPR, c/n 256037, allocated to the Ministerio de la Defensa as presidential aircraft and used by President Somoza to leave the country in July 1979, became YN-BPR.

HUGHES 269

Two Hughes 269A :

AN-ARO	c/n 630236
AN-ASX	930294

One 269B :

AN-ASY	540093

HUGHES OH-6A

Seven or eight were delivered, but only four remained in service at the time of the civil war. Known examples are :

511	ex 66-17750	w/o 24.3.71
512	66-7939	
513		w/o
514		w/o
515	66-17212	w/o
516	66-17213	w/o 20.8.75
517	66-17214	w/o 3.2.72

HUGHES 369HS

Four helicopters reported :

528		d/d 11.77
529	c/n 106-0872S	11.77
530	106-0873S	
531		

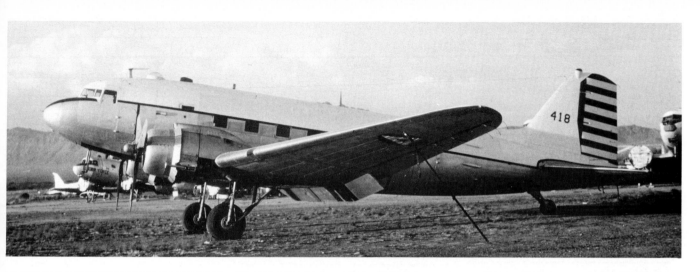

Douglas C-47 418 photographed at Tucson in May 1976.

CASA 212A-7 Aviocar 421, the second of five aircraft delivered 1977-78.

IAI 201 ARAVA

Eight were reported to have been delivered, but there seems no evidence to support the arrival of any more than one aircraft, AN-BIR c/n 005 ex 4X-IAC of the Ministerio de la Defensa, which was apparently serialled 419, and is almost certainly the aircraft which has appeared in FAS service with the new serial 223.

LOCKHEED T-33A

Ten were delivered; confirmed serials were 304, 306, 307 (ex Bu.131745, 52-9700), 308, 309, 310. Five, perhaps more, were converted to AT-33A armed trainers; 310 was preserved as a gate-guardian. Post-war serials include 172, 174 and 175.

MIKOYAN-GUREVICH MiG-21PFM

Several aircraft are reported to have been supplied in 1981 by Cuba's Fuerza Aérea Revolucionaria.

MIL Mi-8

Two helicopters presented by the Soviet Union during 1981.

NORTH AMERICAN F-51D MUSTANG

Twenty-six ex Swedish Air Force aircraft were obtained and initially flew with GN- prefixed serials, such as GN-15 and GN-91) They were :

44-63552	ex Swedish 26049	
44-63634	26121	to N6149U
44-63649	26137	N6162U
44-63675	26152	N5452V
44-63691	26068	
44-63705	26148	
44-63865	26018	N6163U
44-63880	26156	
44-64071	26082	
44-64122	26130	N150U
44-72031	26021	N6152U
44-72059	26142	N6150U/Bolivian AF
44-72066	26007	
44-72090	26038	
44-72093	26010	
44-72105	26043	
44-72219	26054	
44-72272	26056	
44-72291	26055	N6140U/Bolivian AF
44-72320	26066	
44-72331	26085	
44-72359	26097	
44-72389	26083	
44-72416	26101	
44-72446	26139	N6164U
44-72483	26087	N13410/Salvador AF

Another twelve were delivered from USAF stocks in 1954: 44-72440, 73106, 73235, 73352, 73844, 73969, 74210, 74326, 74585, 74728, 74866 and 84877.
Eight were obtained from miscellaneous sources; two were sold as N6153U and N6170U and the other six were :

44-63668	to N6161U
44-63766	N6166U
44-63775	N6167U
44-63788	N6165U
44-74978	N6169U
44-84864	Nicaraguan AF 126 and N4223A

NORTH AMERICAN T-28D TROJAN

Six were delivered, the surviving aircraft being included in the 1977 trade-in deal for new aircraft.
213 c/n 109-009 ex 40-9999 to N99. . . 2.78
215
216
217 c/n 159-52 ex 49-1540   N99395 3.77
218   159-157   49-1645   N99394 3.77
219   N99. . . 2.78
Three US civil identities for ex-Nicaraguan aircraft for which the serial tie-ups are not known are :
N99393 c/n 174-389 ex 51-7536
N99412   '122'
N99414   '222'
Another aircraft was reported to be serialled 413 (a rather surprising out-of-sequence allocation), and to have crashed.

PIPER PA-18 SUPER CUB

Three aircraft believed in use, including one serialled 27.

PIPER PA.23 AZTEC 250

One only serialled 1018, c/n 27-499 ex AN-AOA, w/o 1.81.

PIPER PA-34 SENECA 200

One only, ex Colombian civil HK-1795 c/n 34-7652099, impounded in November 1976.

REPUBLIC F-47 THUNDERBOLT

Twelve F-47D were supplied in 1947-48, later to be supplemented by six F-47N (ex USAF 44-88974, 89131, 89259, 89265, 89400, 89439) one of which became FAN 71. The type was withdrawn in 1964.

SNIAS SA.316 ALOUETTE III

Two ordered for early 1982 supply from France.

SIKORSKY CH-34A

Twelve were delivered; the serial 519 was allocated twice, the second time to a presidential S.58T which was delivered in December 1976. Two CH-34As were used during the civil war with racks for light bombs; a couple are believed to be still in use.

517	ex 56-4321	w/o 7.9.76
518	56-4312	Converted to S.58T in 1979
519	57-1700	w/o
519		(S-58T) w/o 17.11.78
520	57-1699	Converted to S.58T
521	57-1699	Converted to S.58T
522	56-4313	Converted to S.58T
523		
524		
525		d/d 3.77
526		d/d 1977
527		d/d 6.77

One helicopter was ex 57-1694. One became 51 in FAS service, possibly ex 518.

VULTEE BT-15A

One was delivered in July 1945 under Lend-Lease; it was ex USAAF 42-41898.

PANAMA

Area	75,648 sq km
Population	1,826,000
Capital	Ciudad de Panamá (Panama City)
Civil registration	HP-

The Republic of Panama came into being on 3 November 1903 as a result of a US-inspired separation of part of Colombian territory; the United States recognised the new country on the thirteenth of that month and on the eighteenth Panama authorised the construction by the USA of a canal to connect the Atlantic and Pacific Oceans — a project that had previously been vetoed by Colombia ! Thus it is not surprising that links between Panama and the United States have until recently been very close; in fact, Panama depended almost completely on Washington for its security.

Early in 1933, the decision was taken to replace Panama's small navy with an air force — a step unprecedented anywhere in the world — and this was established under Guardia Nacional (National Guard) control as the Guardia Nacional del Aire (Air National Guard), with a Keystone Commuter biplane and two lightly-armed Travel Air Speedwing biplanes. These aircraft were intended for coastal surveillance and internal policing duties, under the command of US-trained Capitán Marco Gelabert, a former Cuban Air Force officer. Little military flying took place until Pearl Harbor, mainly because the USAAC and US Navy units based in the Canal Zone fulfilled more than adequately the necessary requirements.

Panama granted special rights to the USA in 1941 for the establishment of military bases in the country, ostensibly for the defence of the Canal. The US forces were based at France Field in the Canal Zone, under the command of the Sixth Air Force, which was to expand into the future Caribbean Air Command. Some re-organisation took place within the Guardia Nacional del Aire, which became the Fuerza Aérea de la Guardia Nacional and was finally disbanded in 1945. No military flying was undertaken for a number of years, the coastal defence being entrusted to the Guardia Costas (Coast Guard) and its paid of armed patrol boats, with twenty-five personnel under Guardia Nacional Control.

The first steps towards the rebirth of Panama's air arm took place during the early 1960s when a

De Havilland Canada DHC.6 Twin Otter 300
FAP-205 at Downsview in July 1973.

Cessna 402B FAP-209 seen at Panama City in
January 1977.

Piper PA.31 Navajo FAP-200

Bell UH-1H Iroquois FAP-101 at Tocumen on
20 June 1973.

Douglas C-47A Skytrain FAP-201 at Tocumen
on the same date.

Cessna 185 GN-001 was taken on charge of the Guardia Nacional's Destacamento Aéreo No.1 (No.1 Air Detachment). This evolved early in 1969 into the Fuerza Aérea Panameña (Panamanian Air Force), still subordinated to the Guardia Nacional, with US assistance, partly as a result of the October 1968 military coup which overthrew the newly-elected Arnulfo Arias cabinet and established a provisional government. Two US Navy Martin PBM-5 Mariner flying boats and three Bell 47G helicopters were borrowed as interim equipment (although the Mariners proved unsuitable), and a Ministry of Agricultural and Livestock Development DHC.2 Beaver HP-757 was temporarily operated on loan before aircraft procurement began in early 1969. The first FAP aircraft were two Douglas C-47, a few Cessna U-17B and two ex-police Hiller FH.1100 helicopters (a third was later obtained from Helicópteros de Panamá SA).

The Fuerza Aérea Panameña currently has no combat aircraft although a few may be obtained as soon as Panama is given control of the Canal. Some twenty-five aircraft and helicopters perform transport, communications and policing duties, and are based at Ciudad de Panamá's two main airfields, Paitilla and Tocumén, as well as one in the town of David. Balboa airfield in the Canal Zone is shared by the USAF and FAP. Fourteen former US bases in Panama were turned over to Panama in October 1979, and most of these are still in use.

Although Panama has abundant resources, these are largely unexplored and only about fifteen per cent of the land is cultivated; foreign investments are limited by the Leftist leanings of the country's strong man Omar Torrijos, and the resulting economic difficulties have restricted the acquisition of new aircraft, although a small number have been purchased from American and Canadian manufacturers. Negotiations took place in 1977 for the purchase of a few Embraer Bandeirante light transports, intended to replace the Otters and C-47s, but fell through for lack of finance. On the other hand, United States assistance is not likely to pour in, considering Panama's recent involvement in left-wing politics in Latin America; in June 1980 for example, an Aero Commander twin with an FAP crew was running ammunition for Marxist guerillas in El Salvador when it crashed due to engine failure, causing a minor international incident.

Military Air Bases

1 Ciudad de Panama (Tocumen, Paitilla)
2 Bocas del Toro
3 David   5 Chitre
4 Santiago   6 La Palma

Aircraft Review

COLOURS AND MARKINGS

The red white and blue quartered Panama flag, representing the two main political parties (blue and red), peace (white) and loyalty and strength (the two stars), was designed by President Manuel Amador Guerrero and appears on the wings of FAP aircraft in the US-style circle and bars shape. A simplified fin flash — or more commonly rudder

stripes — is also used. Prewar aircraft were inscribed RDeP or RDePGN.

The standard finish of FAP aircraft is light grey with white fuselage top, and the inscription *Fuerza Aérea Panameña*.

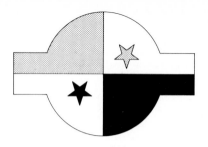

AIRCRAFT SERIALS

FAP aircraft are allocated three-digit serial numbers, usually prefixed FAP, within five blocks :
001 to 099   communications (inc.helicopters)
100 to 199   helicopters
200 to 299   twin-engined transports
300 to 399   single-engined transports
400 to 499   multi-engined transports

Aircraft known to have been used by the Fuerza Aérea Panameña are :

BELL UH-1 IROQUOIS

Twelve UH-1B were delivered, seven in 1976 and five in 1977. These included :

	c/n	ex
111	c/n 426	ex 62-1906
112	1200	64-14076
113	1174	64-14050
114	1197	64-14073
115	1224	64-14100
116	415	62-1895
117	844	63-8622

Another UH-1B c/n 455 ex 62-1935 was sold as HP-999 in mid-1980.
Ten UH-1H were also delivered, serials 101 to 110, and five UH-1N arrived in 1976 - serials 001 to 004 and 100.

BRITTEN-NORMAN BN.2A ISLANDER

Two aircraft :
207 BN.2A-26 c/n 722 ex HP-709, G-BCGZ
208 BN.2A-6R   256   N50JA   to HP-786 in 1980

CASA 212 AVIOCAR

One aircraft delivered 4.82, with two more reported to be due to follow :
215 c/n 212A-31-1-237 d/d 4.82
220
225

CESSNA 180

Six believed delivered, including 002, 003, 004 and 006.

CESSNA 185/U-17A

A Cessna 185C c/n 185-0701 ex HP-10 and N5801T, was delivered as GN-001 and later became FAP 001. Four U-17B were reported to have been delivered under MAP agreements.

CESSNA 402B

One aircraft, serialled 209. An aircraft serialled 211 was seen in 1981 and said to be the only example of its type, having been confiscated from drug smugglers in 1977; it is almost certain that 209 has been re-serialled.

CESSNA T-41D

One was reported with the serial 007.

DE HAVILLAND DHC.6 TWIN OTTER 300

At least three aircraft :
205 c/n 284 ex HP-101 d/d 5.70   w/o 2.8.81
206   HP-
210   448   HP-710   2.75

DE HAVILLAND CANADA DHC.3 OTTER

Six were delivered in 1972 with serials 301 to 306; two of these remain in use.

DOUGLAS C-47A SKYTRAIN

Four aircraft. The first two were taken on charge in 1969; one was ex HP-11 and one of the two , c/n 6068 ex 43-30637 and HP-496, was sold to COPA Airlines as HP-665. Another two were supplied by the USA on 17.1.70.
201
202
203 c/n 20336 ex 43-15970
204   10267   42-24405

DOUGLAS DC-6BF

One was delivered in January 1971 and serialled 401, c/n 43521 ex LV-IEN. It was transferred to a government agency in 1975 as HP-641.

HILLER FH.1100

Three helicopters, the first two of which were previously on the civil register owned by the Guardia Nacional; the third came from Helicópteros de Panamá SA in November 1969.
101 c/n 91 ex HP-15, N591FH
102   119   HP-16, N380FH
103   132   HP-495, N429FH

LOCKHEED 188C ELECTRA

One model L.188C-08-17 delivered on 13.2.74 :
400 c/n 2022 ex N322CA

PIPER PA-31 NAVAJO

Three aircraft at least, the first delivered on 1.10.78 :
200 c/n 31-7812099 ?
201   31-7812101 ?
209   31-7812113

SHORT SKYVAN Srs.3

One aircraft delivered on 13.9.78 :
300 c/n SH.1959   ex G-BFUI

PRESIDENTIAL TRANSPORTS

The Government of Panama operates a presidential aircraft. The first was an unidentified, unserialled Douglas C-47 marked 'Presidencia de la República', which was retired on the arrival of IAI Westwind 1123 HP-1A, c/n 180 ex 4X-CKD which was delivered on 24.3.75 and sold as N1019K in May 1979. This was replaced by another HP-1A, Dassault Falcon 20F c/n 382 ex N138F, which is currently in use.

The Canal Zone

The Canal Zone which bisects Panama was transferred to United States sovereignty under the terms of the November 1903 Hay-Bunau-Varilla Treaty 'in perpetuity'; in return the USA agreed to purchase the various lands from their original owners, to pay an annuity to the Panama Government and to guarantee Panama's independence. The treaty was revised in 1936, with an increase in the annuity and the cessation of the guarantee of independence and subsequently further revisions have taken place. However, Panama's current leader and Guardia Nacional Commander, Brigadier General Omar Torrijos gradually introduced a programme of radical Cuban-inspired internal changes and finally demanded a change in the Canal Zone status. This was achieved with the election of Jimmy Carter to the US presidency; he successfully had Congress give approval to a bill to transfer the control of the Zone to Panama by stages, from December 1979 to December 1999. Such a decision, of enormous strategic importance since it will change the balance of power in the Americas, was bitterly attacked in the United States and it is quite possible that later political changes in the White House and in Central America may cause its reversal.

The Canal Zone covers some 1,432 sq.km. and has an approximate population of 38,000, the majority being US citizens. It includes the head-quarters of the US Southern Command , which oversees United States defence interests in Latin America, including the administration of local Military Assistance Programs. The United States Air Force Southern Air Division, which replaced the former Caribbean Air Command, is based at Howard Air Force Base, north of Balboa, which is also the base of Tactical Air Command's 24th Composite Wing which operates Cessna O-2A and Bell UH-1 Iroquois. Allbrook Air Force Base, to the north of Panama City is home of the Inter-American Air Forces Academy, also a Tactical Air Command unit operating Cessna A-37Bs, and the Air Rescue Co-ordinating Center, and is the centre for the training of Latin American flying and maintenance personnel.

If the transfer of sovereignty does take place as scheduled, it is likely that some of the US military facilities will be taken over by Panama, although the USA will retain the right to defend the Canal and maintain its neutrality.

Hiller FH.1100 FAP-103, one of three acquired from the civil register, also at Tocumen in 1973.

Lockheed L.188C Electra FAP-400, the sole example, delivered in 1974.

PARAGUAY

Area	406,750 sq km
Population	3,200,000
Capital	Asunción
Civil registration	ZP-

A predominantly agricultural country, Paraguay became independent on 14 May 1811 and has had some notable successes in preserving its sovereignty. Argentina, Brazil and Uraguay formed a Triple Alliance in 1864 and declared war on Paraguay, which despite numerical inferiority and its ultimate defeat in 1870 with very heavy losses, fought with determination and survived. More recently, a conflict with Bolivia led to the Gran Chaco War (1932-1935), Paraguay achieving an undoubted victory and some territorial gains which were confirmed by the 1938 peace treaty. The country's troubles did not end there; there were recurring social disturbances for many years, which ended only when General Alfredo Stroessner, Commander in Chief of the Armed Forces, came to power in July 1954 and imposed peace at the cost of the loss of some civil liberties. Exile groups based in neighbouring countries have since attempted to stage a coup d'etat but without success.

Military service is compulsory for males aged from eighteen to twenty and lasts for eighteen months, followed by up to nine years in the reserves. The Army, one of the last in the world to have a first-line horsed cavalry force, has, 12,500 personnel, most of them conscripts, plus up to 60,000 in the reserves in case of war; the Navy has about 2,000 on strength (including five hundred Marines and the Coast Guard) and the Air Force about two thousand. There are also about eight thousand police with a paramilitary capability.

The Paraguayan National Army Air Forces (Fuerzas Aéreas del Ejército Nacional Paraguayo) were formed in 1927, with headquarters and a flying school at Campo Grande airfield, near the capital, Asunción. Organisation work was performed by a French military mission which had arrived in Paraguay in 1926 and the first aircraft to be flown were French surplus machines — three Morane-Saulnier MS.139 primary trainers and three Hanriot HD.1 fighters, which were intended as advanced trainers. The first operational aircraft were fourteen Potez 25 A2 reconnaissance bombers powered by 450hp Lorraine-Dietrich engines and serialled 1 to

14, which arrived at the time of the worsening of the relations with Bolivia over the possession of the Gran Chaco area; they were allotted to the 2° Escuadrón de Reconocimiento y Bombardeo (2nd Reconnaissance and Bombing Squadron) at Isla Poi in June 1933. When the Gran Chaco dispute evolved into a shooting war, most of the Paraguayan pilots were foreign mercenaries and it soon became obvious that some improvements were overdue. An Italian military mission was given the task of re-organising the service, which re-equipped with Italian aircraft — small numbers of Breda Ba 25 basic trainers, Caproni AP.1 two-seat ground-attack aircraft (some of which were AP.1Idro floatplanes), Caproni Ca 101 three-engined bomber transports and two Ca 309, Breda Ba 44 light transports (one was T-15) and five Fiat CR.20bis and five CR.32 biplane fighters, the latter equipping a fighter squadron, the Escuadrón de Caza *Los Indios (The Indians.*

Although there were occasional dogfights between Paraguayan and Bolivian aircraft, most of the missions flown were bombing and/or reconnaissance. Paraguay's material inferiority was compensated by superior leadership and training which secured the country's victory, although economically Paraguay was left in a very poor state.

Consequently, very few changes took place in the next few years. Argentina presented Paraguay with three surplus FMA-built Dewoitine D.21 fighters in 1937; a few Breda Ba 65 were received from Italy in 1938, and 1939 saw the arrival of a number of Wibault 73 C1 fighters for the 1° Escuadrón de Caza (1st Fighter Squadron). However, little operational flying was undertaken, the meagre budget which was available being used for an expansion of the training programme and maintenance of the existing aircraft.

1939-40 and the war in Europe required the acquisition of a few Brazilian-built Muniz M9 primary trainers for the Campo Grande flying school. A subsequent agreement with the United States led to the delivery of small numbers of Beechcraft C-45 and Douglas C-47 transports. Fairchild PT-19,

Vultee BT-13 and North American AT-6 trainers, and Piper L-4 observation aircraft. Ten Stearman PT-17 primary trainers were also delivered.

Until 1946 the Fuerzas Aéreas del Ejército were a branch of the Paraguayan Army under the Ministerio de la Guerra y Marina (Ministry for War and the Navy). In that year, however, an independent service was formed, the Fuerza Aerea del Paraguay, which remains to this day basically a transport and communications force with a small operational element. Re-equipment took place gradually, with Brazil being a primary source as a result of a mutual co-operation agreement. Eleven Fábrica do Galeão-built Fairchild PT-19 (Model 3FG) were supplied to supplement the US-built machines at Campo Grande, followed by eight Brazilian-built Fokker S 11, fourteen armed North American T-6G Texans and small numbers of other types. Argentina supplied a single DH.104 Dove 1 light transport and the Ministry of Defence (as the former Ministry for War and the Navy had been renamed) took delivery of a Beechcraft Bonanza P35 in July 1963; the type was already in FAP service, a pair of Bonanza H35 having been delivered in May 1957. An important development had taken place in 1954: Transporte Aéreo Militar (TAM) was formed to operate flights to remote areas of the country, playing a valuable part in the development of the country.

Plans existed for a re-equipment programme in the mid-1970s. Late in 1976, six IAI 201 Arava light transports were ordered from Israel, but the order had to be cancelled just before deliveries were due to begin because of financial difficulties (one of the aircraft was 4X-ICG c/n 0060). Late in 1977 interest was shown in the Embraer EMB.326GB Xavante as a possible replacement for the Escuadrón de Caza's armed T-6G Texans, but six Cessna A-37B were offered instead by the USA and the idea was shelved. In the event, the A-37B were never delivered and nine Xavantes were finally ordered in April 1979.

Eight Aerotec Uirapurus were obtained from Brazil. Argentina presented a pair of FMA-built MS.760A Paris jet communications/trainers, one

of which was subsequently fitted with light armament. Transport aircraft were procured from several sources; two Douglas C-54 and additional C-47 arrived from the USA, and three Douglas DC-6B came from Brazil, retaining the Brazilian Air Force designation 'C-118'. Single examples of the DHC.3 Otter and DHC.6 Twin Otter were also operated.

Military Air Bases

1 Asunción (Campo Grande)
2 Mariscal Estigarribia
3 Bahía Negra
4 Fuerte Olimpo
5 Concepción
6 Pilar
7 San Ignacio
8 Villarrica
9 San Pedro

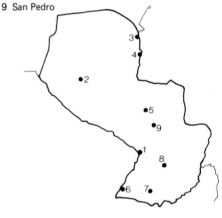

Current Organisation

The Fuerza Aérea del Paraguay, with headquarters at Asunción-Campo Grande, currently comprises the following units:

Escuadrón de Caza at Campo Grande with six Cessna A-37B and two armed T-6G Texans

Grupo Aereo Táctico (Tactical Air Group) at Campo Grande with Embraer EMB.326GB Xavantes.

Transporte Aéreo Militar the military air transport unit at Campo Grande with twelve Douglas C-47, two Douglas C-54, three Douglas DC-6B, a Convair C-131D and single examples of the DHC.3 Otter and DHC.6 Twin Otter. Most of these TAM aircraft are kept at the Aeropuerto Internacional Presidente General Stroessner, Asunción.

Escuela del Aire at Campo Grande with eight Aerotec A122A Uirapurus and eight Fokker S 11; this also incorporates the **GET, Grupo de Entrenamiento Táctico (Tactical Training Group)** with ten armed T-6G Texans and an MS.760A Paris, re-equipping with Embraer Xavantes.

There is also a communications element with fourteen Bell 47G/OH-13 and five Cessna 185, which are occasionally shared with the Army.

Aircraft Review

COLOURS AND MARKINGS

Paraguayan military aircraft were always given red/white/blue roundels and horizontal red/white/blue rudder stripes, a yellow 'Star of May' appearing on the fuselage sides and on the white rudder stripe. The fuselage star has since been replaced by roundels

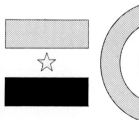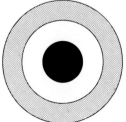

and the rudder stripes appear as fin flashes on camouflaged aircraft, which follow the US tactical scheme. The inscription *Fuerza Aérea Paraguaya* is sometimes used.

AIRCRAFT SERIALS

Aircraft known to have been used by the Fuerza Aérea del Paraguay include :

AEROTEC A122A UIRAPURU

Eight were delivered in 1975 to the Escuela del Aire :

0041	c/n 095
0043	096
0045	097
0047	098
0049	099
0051	100
0053	104
0055	105

A Uirapuru has been reported as 0079, which may indicate that further aircraft have been delivered.

BEECHCRAFT BONANZA 35

Two Bonanza H35 delivered in May 1957 :

T-11	c/n D.5122
T-15	D.5126

A Bonanza P35 went to the Ministerio de la Defensa Nacional in July 1963 :

T-5B	D.7257

BELL 47G/OH-13

About twenty believed delivered, fourteen of which remain in use. A VIP machine was serialled H-001 but is no longer in service. Two Bell 47G were transferred to the Navy.

CESSNA 185/U-17A

Five aircraft, of which one is serialled T-03.

CESSNA 337

At least one, serialled 0019.

CESSNA 402

At least one serialled T-0021 later 0221.

CONSOLIDATED PBY-5A CATALINA

One, used as a transport, was serialled T-29. It was used in 1955 by Peron to leave Argentina for exile in Paraguay.

CONVAIR 240/C-131D

Three model 240-6 were used briefly :

ZP-CDN	c/n 50	ex LV-ADN	'Carlos Antonio López'
ZP-CDO	62	LV-ADO	'General Bernardino Caballero'
ZP-CDP	72	LV-ADP	'José Gaspar Rodríguez de Franco'; w/o 26.5.67 when in airline service with LAP.

One C-131D (commercial model 440-79) ex USAF :

T-93	321	55-294

This was named 'Carlos Antonio López' and reportedly was withdrawn from use in December 1974, but it remains in service and has been reserialled as 2001.

DE HAVILLAND DH.104 DOVE 1

One aircraft only presented to President Alfredo Stroessner by the Argentine Government; withdrawn from use.

T-73	c/n 04202	ex Argentine AF T-73

DE HAVILLAND CANADA DHC.3 OTTER

One aircraft presented by the Argentine Government on 9 November 1971 :

T-05	ex Argentine AF P-11

DE HAVILLAND CANADA DHC.6 TWIN OTTER

One series 200 delivered in July 1968 as a presidential transport, c/n 137, and flown as ZP-GAS (for General Alfredo Stroessner).

Two further aircraft were seen at Downsview in 1981 prior to delivery, TAM-2027 c/n 744 and TAM-2029 probably c/n 747. They were not delivered, and c/ns 744 and 747 became 5A-DJG and 5A-DJH instead in July 1981.

DOUGLAS C-47 SKYTRAIN

About thirty were taken on charge, of which probably more than twelve remain in service. Re-numbering in the 2000 block took place during 1980, known examples including 2001 to 2010, 2016, 2019, 2021 and 2033.

T-21			
T-23			
T-27	c/n 13621	ex 42-93682/Argentine AF T-27	
T-31			
T-35			
T-37			
T-39			
T-41			
T-43	9517	42-23655	
T-45			to 2004
T-47			
T-51			
T-53			
T-55			
T-57			
T-59			
T-61			
T-63			
T-65			2007
T-69			2016
T-71			
T-73			
T-75			
T-77			2003
T-79			
T-81			
T-83			
T-85			

DOUGLAS DC-6B

Three aircraft ex Brazilian Air Force 'C-118s', all still in use and reserialled in the 4000 block during 1980 :

T-87	c/n 43822	ex FAB 2415	to 4001
T-89	43824	2416	4002
T-91	44166	2412	4003

EMBRAER EMB.326GB XAVANTE

Nine were ordered in April 1979, with serials 1001 to 1009 The first seven were delivered on 7 May 1980. 1002 has the c/n 79160403. A tenth and final aircraft serialled 1010 was delivered on 8.1.82.

DOUGLAS C-54 SKYMASTER

Two were obtained from the USA are are still in use.

FAIRCHILD PT-19

About a dozen were supplied under Lend-Lease, and then there were eleven ex Brazilian Air Force aircraft (FAB serials 0323, 0351, 0369, 0421, 0422, 0424, 0433, 0436, 0465, 0535, 0550). All have been withdrawn from use; known Paraguayan serials are 011, 015, 017, 019, 021 and 023.

FOKKER S.11-4

Eight ex Brazilian Air Force aircraft, flown as T-27-0025, 0027, 0029, 0031, 0033, 0035, 0037, 0039 (later FA-025, 027 etc.).

MORANE-SAULNIER MS.760A PARIS

Two obtained from Argentina; one was armed and remains in service with the GET.

NORTH AMERICAN T-6 TEXAN

Twenty of all models believed delivered. Twelve armed aircraft still in use; one serialled 0101 was ex USAAF 42-85344 and Brazilian Air Force 1633. The armed Texans are of, or were brought up to T-6G standard. Another confirmed serial is 0143.

STEARMAN PT-17

Ten delivered under Lend-Lease, ex USAAF 41-25732 to 25736 and 41-25749 to 25753.

De Havilland Canada DHC.6 Twin Otter 200 ZP-GAS, acquired in 1968 as a presidential transport.

Embraer EMB.326GB Xavante 1004; nine were delivered in 1980.

Paraguayan Navy

The Servicio de Aeronáutica de la Marina (Naval Air Service) was originally formed in 1927 by the French at Campo Grande, but was short-lived, which is understandable as Paraguay has no direct access to the sea except through the Argentine-controlled Paraná-Paraguay river system. The service initially shared the Army's MS.139 primary trainers and later received from Italy an SAML-Aviatik A3 basic trainer and two flying boats, a Cant 10ter and a Savoia-Marchetti S.59 which flew until the service was absorbed into the Army Air Force. After the Second World War, a few aircraft were obtained from Argentina — a few ex-Argentine Navy Grumman F6F-5 Hellcats, Grumman JRF-4 0128 c/n 1100 (ex Argentine Navy 0186) and two JRF-5 0126 c/n B.53 and 0127 c/n B.29 (both ex-Argentine Navy. JRFs 0126 to 0128 were eventually sold in the USA as N3284, N3283 and N3282 respectively. However, it was not until the mid-1960s that naval flying became fully established. Though the Navy is small, with about 2,000 personnel and twenty light ships, it now controls a Servicio Aeronaval de la Armada del Paraguay (Paraguayan Naval Air Service).

COLOURS AND MARKINGS

Paraguayan naval aircraft carry markings similar to those of the air force, with the exception of the fin flash, which is superimposed on an anchor marking.

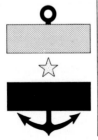

AIRCRAFT SERIALS

The service is known to have operated the following:

BELL 47G

Two machines, ex Paraguayan Air Force, usually deployed aboard a helicopter lighter.

CESSNA 150M

Four used as primary trainers and light communications aircraft; serials are 121 to 124.

CESSNA U206

Two U206A delivered in August 1966 :
130 c/n 206-0648 ex N4948F
131   206-0649   N4949F
Two U206C delivered circa 1968 :
132   206-1159   N29197
133   206-1223   N71912

CESSNA 210

One known example, serialled 136

DOUGLAS C-47 SKYTRAIN

One only, delivered in 1979, ex Argentine Navy 0278/5-T-26, and serialled T-26.

NORTH AMERICAN T-6G TEXAN

At least two armed examples, ex Paraguayan Air Force, serials 400 and 446, for river patrol duties.

Paraguayan Army

The Arma Aérea del Ejército Paraguayo (Paraguayan Army Air Arm) operates three Hiller UH12E on artillery spotting duties; they include two UH12E-4 c/ns 2521 and 2531 presented by the Chilean Air Force in July 1980. The previous equipment was three Brazilian supplied Neiva 56B Paulistinha liaison aircraft serialled E-01, E-03 and E-05. The Cessna 185s operated by the Air Force are also sometimes used by the Army.

PERU

Area	1,285,215 sq km
Population	17,300,000
Capital	Lima
Civil registration	OB-

The Republic of Peru, once the centre of the powerful Inca empire, became the most important of the Spanish Viceroyalties after conquistador Francisco Pizarro executed the last of the Incas, Atahuallpa, in 1533. Peru declared its independence on 28 July 1821 after the Argentine liberator General San Martín expelled the Spanish, but this independence was not recognised until 1824. The country has had a fair share of political instability — not to mention border disputes with Ecuador (the latest of a series began in January 1981) and Chile — which continues to this day but does not seem to affect the Peruvian's friendliness to foreigners. In October 1968 the democratically-elected president Fernando Belaúnde Terry was overthrown by a military junta headed by General Juan Velasco Alvardo, who initiated a revolutionary programme of sweeping social reforms. Velasco's régime had to cope with some opposition, both internal and external, and came to depend more and more on Soviet support. The first Soviet military advisers arrived in 1973 — the first time they were established in South America — and substantial quantities of Soviet hardware have since been supplied, including 250 T55 tanks, more than a dozen small ships, and quite a few aircraft, especially since the late 1976 and early 1978 agreements between the two countries.

The Soviets also undertook to build up a radar network along the border with Chile and supply SAM-2 Guideline, SAM-3 Goa and SAM-7 Grail missiles. Peruvian pilots were to be trained in Cuba and ground crews in Peru by Soviet instructors. Although Velasco was deposed in August 1975 and replaced by the more moderate General Francisco Morales Bermúdez, Peru's current stand has not changed much, although internal policies have been restrained by the need to achieve some economic stability, which was badly affected by land reform laws and the formation of collective farms.

Peru has the potential to be a wealthy country, containing oilfields, substantial mineral deposits and an important fishing industry, but many of the resources are still unexploited and agriculture is still the basis for the economy, about half of the population being connected with this.

Despite Peru's extreme altitudes, or perhaps because of them, there has always been a keen interest in aeronautical matters. Balloon flights took place from the early 1860s, and in 1902 the Peruvian consul in Paris, Pedro Paulet Mostajo, designed a rocket-propelled aircraft which although never built was a remarkable pioneering effort in its field and is now internationally recognised as such. Basic courses on aviation existed since 1910 at the Army Transport School, parallelled by the activities of the Aero Club Peruano (Peruvian Aero Club). Initial provisions for the systematic training of flying and ground crews were taken in 1912 when a French military adviser was signed on and an Avro 503 float biplane ordered from Britain. However, plans to establish an air arm were delayed by the First World War and the Avro was never delivered, eventually being impressed into Royal Naval Air Service use with the serial 889. Until the end of the war nothing much could be done apart from sending trainee pilots to the El Palomar school in Argentina (from 1917 to 1919) and acquiring a limited amount of flying experience on Aero Club aircraft.

The Servicio de Aviación Militar del Ejército del Peru (Peruvian Army Air Service) was formed in January 1919. A French air mission arrived in November bringing along four Morane-Saulnier parasol trainers, a small number of Salmson 2 A2 observation biplanes and Caudron G.III trainers and four flying boats — a Lévy-Lepen and three Schreck-FBA. By this time, there was a Centro de Aviación Militar de Lima (Lima Military Aviation Centre) at Maranga, near Callao (Lima's port). Other available aircraft included a Morane-Saulnier LA fighter, to which two SPAD VII C1 fighters and a Curtiss JN.4 Jenny trainer were later added.

A regular air mail service was operated by the Army from 1920. In 1921 the French air mission was replaced by a British one, surplus Royal Air Force aircraft being made available : three Bristol F.2b Fighters, a single Blackburn RT.1 Kangaroo bomber biplane (ex RAF B9972 and G-EAKQ) and at least twelve Avro 504K (four in 1920, four in 1921 and four - ex E372, E391, E395 and E399 - in early 1922). An air base was inaugurated at Las Palmas in July 1922 and later became the service's most important establishment, housing the Escuela de Aviación Militar Jorge Chávez (Jorge Chávez Military Aviation School) since its activation in 1923.

A United States air mission arrived in 1924 and initiated a long period of US influence on Peruvian military aviation. In due course, the earlier observation types were replaced by four different versions of the ubiquitous Vought Corsair biplane : the UO-2, the O2U-1E and the export models V.65 and V.80P, the latter being based on the armed SU-1 scout version. In 1927, by which time there were new airstrips at Bellavista, Cerro de Pisco, Cuzco, Puno and Iquitos and the service had over three hundred personnel, the Las Palmas base commanding officer became Peru's first parachutist. A few Avro 504R had entered service.

The military and naval air arms merged on 20 May 1929 to form the Cuerpo de Aeronáutica del Peru (Peruvian Air Corps) under the unified Ministry for the Navy and Aviation, which also controlled civil flying. There were five small training units at three bases - Las Palmas, Ancón and Iquitos, a fighter element, the 1er Escuadrón de Reconocimiento (1st Reconnaissance Squadron) with Vought Corsairs, and the newly-formed 1er Escuadrón de Transporte (1st Transport Squadron) with three Stearman C3R — seven, numbered 4E1 to 4E7, had been procured mainly for training — a Travel Air biplane, a second-hand Boeing 40B-4 and a former US Air Mail Douglas M4 floatplane which doubled as a bomber. Small numbers of Nieuport 121 C1 fighters, Hanriot 240 utility aircraft and Potez 39 A2 army co-operation biplanes showed that the early links with France had not been severed, but United States influence grew steadily and ten Curtiss Falcon (Model 37F) attack biplanes were procured in addition to six Douglas O-38P (c/ns 1141 to 1146) purchased in 1932.

The Cuerpo de Aeronáutica was involved in the 1933 border conflict with Colombia, the Curtiss Falcons being used against ground targets and the Vought Corsairs for river patrol and anti-shipping duties. A need for more advanced aircraft was soon recognised but the Peruvians were upset to note that the Americans were selling aircraft to both sides; alternative sources were sought and twelve machines purchased from Fairey in Britain — six Fox II float biplanes (c/n F.1965 to 1970) and six Seal general purpose biplanes (c/ns F.1934 to 1939). In 1939 however, Italy's ambitions to become a major world power led to her seeking links with Latin American countries. Peru was more than willing to accept Italy's assistance as a way to limit the dreaded Yankee expansionism and an Italian air mission was invited to visit the country. An agreement with Caproni gave Peru a ten-year monopoly in the construction and overhaul of Caproni types and plans to re-equip the Cuerpo with these Capronis got under way. Small numbers of Ca 100 primary trainers, Ca 311 transports (Nicknamed 'Panchos'), Ca 114 fighters, Ca 135 medium bombers and Ca 310 general purpose aircraft were ordered. Unfortunately they were not particularly suitable to Peru's difficult operating conditions and substandard maintenance and licence production was therefore limited (only twelve out of twenty-five Ca 100 were ever completed, at a substantial loss) although valuable experience was gained. The Ca 135 bombers (Ca 135 Tipo Peru), the Cuerpo's most impressive type, comprised six Italian-built aircraft to be followed by thirty-two locally-built examples with uprated Isotta-Fraschini radials, but only twenty-six are believed to have been completed.

As a result of this disappointing exercise, the Peruvian Government was forced to turn again to the USA, which at least made economic and technical sense. The Cuerpo had previously flown American aircraft, and a Ford 4-AT trimotor had just been bought second-hand; ground-crews were also used to the characteristics and constructional methods of US aircraft. The first orders were placed during 1938 and one of the first aircraft to arrive (in July 1939) was a Barkley-Grow T8P.1 twin-engined light transport which flew for a short time as OB-GGK and was later assigned to the 2° Escuadrón de Comando (2nd Staff Squadron) until it was written off in 1945. Seven North American NA.50A fighters, based on the AT-6 Texan, arrived in 1939 (c/ns 50-948 to 954; one serialled 251 was preserved), followed by small numbers of Curtiss-Wright CW.22 fighters, Grumman G.21A amphibious transports, Vultee 54 trainers and ten Douglas 8A-3P attack bombers (c/ns 412 to 421). The latter, based on the Douglas 8A-2 version of the Northrop A-17 which had been adopted by Argentina, had a long service life, the last few survivors being withdrawn from use in the late 1950s.

Mention must be made of a typically Peruvian single-engined high-wing light transport, the Stinson-Faucett F.19 eight-seater which was built and operated by Compañía de Aviación Faucett SA, an internal airline; a small number were built and a few were passed on to the Cuerpo de Aeronáutica. So close were the links between military and civil aviation in Peru that civil aircraft sported Peruvian rudder stripes and the Certificate of Airworthiness number — which in emergency doubled as a serial number — on the fin in addition to the civil registration. This practice continued until the adoption of numerical registrations in the 1960s.

When the Second World War began in September 1939 the Cuerpo was — on paper at least — a sizeable force. Four Air Regions (Regiones Aéreas) existed : RA del Norte (Northern) with two bomber and one fighter squadrons and an army co-operation group, RA del Sur (Southern) with a similar number of units, RA del Oeste (Western) with an attack and a transport squadron and an observation group, and RA del Centro (Central) with five training and one naval co-operation squadrons. Due to financial restrictions, most of these units were below strength some having no more than a couple of aircraft, but the infrastructure on which expansion could be based was there. New tactics were constantly developed; the first mass paradrop took place in September 1940. Additional aircraft were obtained as funds permitted; two to be bought were Curtiss CT.32 Condor airliners c/n 59 ex OB-IIA and 61 ex OB-IIC, another two being lost in civilian service.

In 1941 the Cuerpo was fully involved in a massive invasion of Ecuador caused by another border dispute, which almost reached Guayaquil. Ecuadorian air opposition was negligible, due not only to the diminutive size of its air arm but also to the shortage of pilots caused by internal political purges. Despite their unpopularity, the Caproni types were used to good effect and the Cuerpo's losses were limited to a pair of NA.50A fighters.

The United States were by then fully into their 'armed neutrality' policy, which was just short of open belligerency and additional efforts were made to secure co-operation from the Latin American governments in case of an involvement in the war. Peru was sent a US Marine Colonel to act as Inspector General of Aviation and Peruvian pilots were sent to the USA for advanced training. The Cuerpo was re-organised, with a more realistic order of battle :

Escuadrón de Aviacion Nº.1 at Chiclayo
Escuadrón de Aviacion Nº.4 at Ancón
Escuadrón de Aviacion Nº.5 at Iquitos
Escuadrilla de Transportes Nº.6 at San Ramón-Montaña.
Escuela Central de Aeronáutica Jorge Chávez at Las Palmas.
Escuela de Hidroaviación at Ancón
Parque Central de Aeronáutica at Las Palmas

The Aero Club provided a reserve pilot training scheme (Cuerpo de Aviadores de Reserva) at Limatambo, which was subsequently expanded under a National Air League with the arrival of ten Taylorcraft Cubs, and moved to Collique airfield in Lima. A separate Ministry of Aviation came into being in January 1942 and during the same year a Servicio de Aerofotografía (Photo Survey Service) and a Servicio de Meteorología (Weather Service) were created.

Peru was not particularly benefitted by the Lend-Lease scheme, no more than sixty-seven aircraft being delivered; these included twenty-eight Curtiss P-36G (serialled 301 to 328 ex USAAF 42-108995 to 109006), a handful of Bell P-63A Kingcobras

and at least one Lockheed C-60 Lodestar. Large-scale deliveries did not take place until after Peru signed the 1947 Rio Pact; the operational element received twenty Republic F-47D Thunderbolts and an equal number of North American B-25J Mitchell bombers; Douglas C-47 and Curtiss C-46 equipped three Escuadrones de Transporte; a few Lockheed PV-2 Harpoon patrol bombers were also delivered, as were numbers of Stearman PT-17, Fairchild PT-26, North American AT-6 and Beechcraft AT-11 trainers and a couple of Consolidated PBY-5A Catalina amphibians for the Servicio de Reconocimiento Marítimo y Búsqueda y Rescate (Maritime Reconnaissance and Search and Rescue Service).

By 1948-49, the Cuerpo had some four thousand personnel, and the following order of battle :

Grupo de Aviación Nº 1
Escuadrón de Caza Nº 11
Escuadrón de Ataque Nº 13
Escuadrón de Transporte Nº 14
Escuadrón de Reconocimiento Nº 15

Grupo de Aviación Nº 2
Escuadrón de Caza Nº 21
Escuadrón de Ataque Nº 23
Escuadrón de Transporte Nº 24
Escuadrón de Reconocimiento Nº 26
Escuadrón de Comunicaciones Nº 29

Grupo de Aviación Nº 3
Escuadrón de Ataque Nº 33

Grupo de Aviación Nº 4
inactive

Grupo de Aviación Nº 5
Escuadrón de Transporte Nº 54
Escuadrón de Observación Nº 57

The attack squadrons operated a mixture of armed AT-6 Texans and Douglas 8A-3P.

Three de Havilland Canada DHC.2 Beavers were obtained in 1949 for the Escuadrón de Comunicaciones. A re-organisation was by then already in progress and in July of the following year the air arm was renamed as the Fuerza Aérea Peruana.

MDAP deliveries eventually led to a modernisation of the FAP by 1955, with its first jet fighters, North American F-86F Sabres, beginning to replace the obsolescent F-47D Thunderbolts of Escuadron de Caza N° 12; half a dozen Lockheed T-33A trainers were also delivered, as were eight Douglas B-26C Invader attack bombers. However, the last Thunderbolts were not withdrawn from use until 1958-59.

Orders were placed in Britain in October 1955 for eight English Electric Canberra B.Mk.8 tactical jet bombers and sixteen Hawker Hunter F.Mk.52 fighters (the export version of the Royal Air Force F.Mk.4). At the same time, obsolete aircraft were scrapped in 1955-56; one was the Curtiss CT.32 Condor c/n 59.

Another re-organisation took place in 1957, mainly to rationalise the FAP's operational procedures. Four Grupos were established :

Grupo de Caza N° 12 - F-86F, Hunter and T-33A squadrons.
Grupo de Caza N° 13 - two squadrons of F-47D.
Grupo de Bombardeo N° 21 - B-25J, B-26C and Canberra squadrons.
Grupo de Transporte N° 41 - C-46 and C-47 units.

There was also an Academia del Aire (Air Academy) at Las Palmas with PT-17, PT-26, AT-6 and AT-11, a patrol unit with PV-2 Harpoons, and the SAR unit with two Catalinas, G.21A Geese and the first helicopters - two Hiller UH12B and a Sud SE.3130 Alouette II. The jungle communications service, activated in May 1928 as the Servicio Aéreo a la Montaña (Mountain Air Service) as part of the Escuela de Hidroaviación at Ancón, became the TANS or Transportes Aéreos Nacionales de la Selva (literally, National Air Transport to the Jungle - 'selva' being the Amazon Basin area).

The 1960s were predictable enough as far as aircraft procurement was concerned; repeat orders were placed for Royal Air Force surplus Canberras, US assistance included the delivery of Cessna T-37B trainers and (later) A-37B close-support aircraft, Lockheed C-130E Hercules and Beechcraft C-45 transports, not to mention the aircraft obtained directly from the American manufacturers such as Bell 47G and 212 helicopters and Beechcraft Queen Air light transports; and small numbers of aircraft came from European sources : Pilatus PC.6/B Turbo-Porter light transports from Switzerland and (much to the surprise of some observers) twelve Dassault Mirage 5P and two 5DP from France, to form an up-to-date interceptor force. Mirages were subsequently adopted by other Latin American countries.

The political changes brought about by Velasco's revolutionary régime reflected themselves in the delivery of fairly large numbers of Soviet-built aircraft on very favourable credit terms: thirty-six Sukhoi Su-22 and Su-22U variable-geometry strike fighters were the most obvious acquisition at the low cost of 250 million US dollars, but at least forty-eight Mil Mi-8 and eight Mi-6 transport helicopters and more recently sixteen Antonov An-26 tactical transports were also delivered. The Soviet aircraft were reportedly disappointingly unreliable and costly to operate, although some of their troubles may have been caused by poor maintenance; in any case, another sixteen Su-22 were ordered in the early part of 1980 and the aircraft in service were retrofitted with some basic US avionics in an effort to improve their efficiency.

However, not all recent new procurements have been from the USSR. There have been further deliveries of Lockheed Hercules transports and the transport fleet was augmented at the end of 1981 by the purchase of two second-hand Douglas DC-8 from Swiss airlines. The most noteworthy overseas procurements are however a batch of Macchi MB.339AP from Italy as T-37B replacements; after delivery of the first fourteen aircraft, production is to commence in 1983 in Peru at a new Indaer-Peru factory being built with Macchi assistance; it is reported that sixty-six aircraft will be built over a six-year period.

Current Organisation

The Fuerza Aérea del Peru has a current strength of about 9,500 and is under the direction of the Ministry of Aviation, the Minister acting as its Commander-in-Chief, and comprises the following:

Grupo de Caza 12 at Limatambo, made up of Escuadrones de Caza 11 and 13 with Sukhoi Su-22.

Grupo de Caza-Bombardeo 13 at Chiclayo with two squadrons of Dassault Mirage 5P/5DP and one of Cessna A-37B

Grupo de Bombardeo 21 at Limatambo with two squadrons of Canberras (often operating from Lima-Jorge Chavez) and a squadron of Cessna A-37B normally deployed at Chiclayo, being replaced by Macchi MB.339AP.

Grupo 31 (Servicio de Reconocimiento Marítimo y Búsqueda y Rescate) at Callao with a squadron of Grumman HU-16B Albatross

Grupo de Transporte 41 at Lima-Jorge Chávez :
Escuadrón 1 - C-130 Hercules
Escuadrón 2 - DHC.5 Buffalo
Escuadrón 3 - Antonov An-26, Douglas C-47, C-54, DC-6 and DC-8, Curtiss C-46

Grupo 42 (TANS, Transportes Aéreos Nacionales de la Selva) at Iquitos with Douglas C-47, DHC.6 Twin Otters and Pilatus PC.6/B Turbo-Porters.

Grupo de Helicópteros 3 at Callao with Bell 47G, 206B and 212, Mil Mi-6 and Mi-8, Sud Alouette III.

Grupo de Comunicaciones 8 at Callao with two squadrons of Beech Queen Air, King Air and 99.

Escuadrilla Presidencial at Lima-Jorge Chávez with Fokker F.28 Fellowship and Bell 212.

Academia del Aire at Las Palmas with Beechcraft T-34A, Cessna T-37B/C, T-41A and 150, North American AT-6 Texan and Pitts S.2A.

Servicio Aerofotográfico Nacional (National Air Photographic Service) at Lima-Jorge Chávez with a pair of Lear Jets

Military Air Bases

1 Limatambo
2 Ancón
3 Callao
4 Talara
5 Piura
6 Iquitos
7 Chiclayo
8 Cajamarca
9 Trujillo
10 Huánuco
11 San Ramón
12 Ayacucho
13 Cuzco
14 Puerto Maldonado
15 Pisco
16 Arequipa

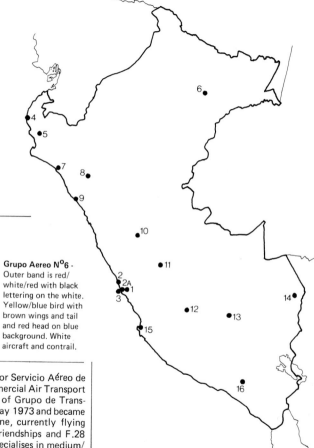

Grupo Aereo N°6 -
Outer band is red/white/red with black lettering on the white. Yellow/blue bird with brown wings and tail and red head on blue background. White aircraft and contrail.

Peru's military airline, SATCO or Servicio Aéreo de Transportes Comerciales (Commercial Air Transport Service), once an integral part of Grupo de Transporte 41, was re-organised in May 1973 and became the purely civil AeroPeru airline, currently flying civil-registered Fokker F.27 Friendships and F.28 Fellowships. Grupo 41 now specialises in medium/heavy military transport, with Grupo 42 (TANS) flying regular feeder services to remote settlements in the Amazon Basin.

Aircraft Review

COLOURS AND MARKINGS

When the Peruvian liberator General José de San Martin arrived in Peru in September 1820, he was so impressed by a welcoming flock of flamingoes — with red wings and white breasts — that red and white became the country's colours and appear in roundel form and rudder stripes on Peruvian military aircraft. The inscription *Fuerza Aérea del Peru* is commonly used.

Colour schemes are as a rule those in which the aircraft were delivered. Transports are either left in natural metal, or light grey with white fuselage tops and a dark blue cheat line.

AIRCRAFT SERIALS

The Fuerza Aérea del Peru has a distinctive serialling system, introduced in 1950 to replace the complex prewar and wartime squadron/role codes. Three-digit serials were allocated within seven blocks (100 for fighters, 200 bombers and fighter-bombers, 300 transports, 400 trainers, 500 miscellaneous, 600 helicopters and 700 communications), sequential allocations being normally adhered to; re-allocations were — and still are — very frequent and took place when a serial became vacant through disposal or cancellation of a given aircraft. An extensive renumbering took place in 1960; at the same time, a USAF-type two-digit prefix indicating the year of procurement was added to the basic serial, but this prefix has now fallen into disuse.

Aircraft known to have been used by the FAP since the Second World War are :

ANTONOV AN-26

Sixteen delivered in 1977-78 for use by Grupo de Transporte 41; four more were expected to follow.

362	c/n 5405	d/d	6.11.77
363	5408		6.11.77
366	5409		6.11.77
367	5410		6.11.77
374	5502		7.1.78
375	5506		21.5.78
376	5509		7.1.78
377	5601		7.1.78
378	5602		21.5.78
379	5610		23.5.78
386	5701		21.5.78
387	5703		7.1.78
388	5704		23.5.78
389	5802		23.5.78
391	5803		23.5.78
392	5805		21.5.78

BEECHCRAFT AT-7C NAVIGATOR

At least two, ex USAAF 43-33478 and 33531.

BEECHCRAFT AT-11 KANSAN

At least five were delivered, ex USAAF 42-37485, 37656, 43-10332, 10469, 10485. Known FAP serials are 441, 442, 494 and 495.

BEECHCRAFT C-45G/H EXPEDITOR

About thirty believed to have been delivered, including :

691	c/n AF.769	ex 52-10839	
708			
709	AF.84	51-11527	
711	AF.202	51-11645	to OB-T-856
714	AF.421	51-11864	OB-I-822
720	AF.574	52-10644	OB-I-823
721	AF.526	52-10596	OB-T-855
722	AF.874	52-10944	OB-I-824
724	AF.801	52-10871	OB-I-825
725	AF.653	52-10723	OB-T-854
726	AF.155	51-11598	OB-I-826

Another C-45G c/n AF.464 ex 51-11907 became OB-I-922. The OB-I- registered aircraft were operated by the Dirección de Aviación Civil (Directorate of Civil Aviation) at Collique.

BEECHCRAFT T-34A MENTOR

At least six delivered, of which four were reported to be in use by the Academia del Aire in 1979-80.

BEECHCRAFT QUEEN AIR A80

Eighteen were delivered to Grupo de Comunicaciones 8 :

729	c/n LD.245	d/d	9.65
730	LD.251		9.65
731	LD.254		9.65
732	LD.247		9.65
733	LD.248		9.65
734	LD.252		9.65
735	LD.253		9.65
736	LD.258		10.65
737	LD.259		11.65
738	LD.260		11.65
739	LD.261		11.65
740	LD.262		11.65
741	LD.264		1.66
742	LD.265		1.66
743	LD.266		1.66
744	LD.267		1.66
745	LD.268		1.66
746	LD.269		1.66

Another three were completed with photo survey equipment for government use and delivered in 1966 :

OB-F-790	c/n LD.272
OB-F-791	LD.274
OB-F-792	LD.276

BEECHCRAFT KING AIR C90

Five delivered to Grupo de Comunicaciones 8, of which three are serialled 747, 748 and 750.

BELL 47G

About thirty taken on charge, of which about fifteen remain in service; eight were transferred to the Peruvian Army. The known machines are :

611	47G	c/n 1325	
617	47G-3B-1	6520	
618	47G-3B-1	6521	
619	47G-3B-1	6522	
620	47G-3B-1	6523	
621	47G-3B-1	6524	wfu
622	47G-3B-1	6525	
624	OH-13S		wfu
647	47G-5A	25054 d/d 12.71	
648	47G-5A	25055	4.72 wfu
649	47G-5A	25056	4.72
650	47G-5A	25057	4.72
651	47G-5A	25058	4.72 wfu
652	47G-5A	25063	1.72
653	47G-5A	25064	4.72 w/o 13.9.72
654	47G-5A	25065	4.72
655	47G-5A	25066	4.72 w/o 5.3.73
656	47G-5A	25067	4.72 w/o 23.1.73
657	47G-4A	7508	w/o 13.3.74
659	47G-3B-2A		
660	47G-3B-2A		wfu
661	47G-3B-2A		
662	47G-3B-2A		
663	47G-3B-2A		
664	47G-3B-2A		
665	47G-3B-2A		
666	47G-3B-2A		

Fiscal year prefixes were used for a time; for example 653 was 72-653 at the time of its crash.

BELL 206B JET RANGER

Ten machines for Grupo de Helicópteros 3 :

667	
668	
669	
670	
671	
672	
673	w/o 2.11.75
674	
675	
676	

BELL UH-1D/H IROQUOIS

Known UH-1D are :

600		
625		
629	c/n 4549	ex 64-13842
632	4809	65-9765

One UH-1H :
685

BELL 212

At least fifteen helicopters :

602	c/n 30611		
603	30614		
604	30619		
605		w/o 16.5.74	
608		w/o 6.10.74	
610	30637		
612			
615			
617			
618			
619			
644	30530	d/d 4.72	w/o 26.6.74
645	30531	4.72	
646	30541	4.72	w/o 11.9.74
686		1980 ?	

Another w/o 23.10.78

CESSNA 150F

Three have been reported, serials 411, 510 and 511.

CESSNA 185A

Nine aircraft delivered in January 1962, of which four are believed to remain on charge :

335	c/n 185-0304	ex N4104Y	w/o
336	185-0311	N4111Y	
337	185-0308	N4108Y	
338	185-0320	N4120Y	w/o
339	185-0309	N4109Y	w/o
340	185-0321	N4121Y	w/o
341	185-0310	N4110Y	w/o
342	185-0322	N4122Y	
343	185-0323	N4123Y	

CESSNA T-41A (172G)

Twenty aircraft for the Academia del Aire :

422	c/n 54405
423	54406
424	54407
425	54421
426	54423
427	54432
428	54434
429	54443
430	54445
431	54454
432	54456
433	54465
434	54467
435	54476
436	54478
437	54478
438	54489
439	54498
440	54500
443	54509

Also a batch for the Escuela de Aviación Civil at Collique :

OB-I-793	c/n 54511
OB-I-794	54520
OB-I-795	54522
OB-I-796	54531
OB-I-797	54533
OB-I-798	54542
OB-I-799	54544

CESSNA T-37B/C

Peru was the first Latin American country to receive the T-37, with twenty T-37B and twelve T-37C reported to have been acquired. The first fifteen T-37B were :

61-459	ex N5428E	
61-460	N5429E	
61-461	N5430E	
61-462	N5431E	
61-463	N5432E	
61-464	N5427E	
61-465	N5433E	
61-466	N5434E	
61-467	N5435E	
61-468	N5436E	w/o
61-469	N5437E	
61-470	N5438E	
61-471	N5439E	
61-472	N5440E	
61-473	N5441E	w/o

Note that the above serials were Peruvian, not USAF. The remaining five T-37B were ex USAF 60-164 to 168. The T-37C, ex USAF 63-9823, 66-13611/13621, were also serialled within the same block. Unidentified T-37 serials include 447, 474, 475 and 482.

CESSNA A-37B

Thirty six were delivered in 1975 to Grupos 13 and 21, following a successful evaluation against the BAC Strike-master :

115	ex 74-1694	
116	74-1695	
117	74-1696	
118	74-1697	
119	74-1698	
120	74-1699	
121	74-1700	
122	74-1701	
123	74-1702	
124	74-1703	
125	74-1704	
126	74-1705	
127	74-1706	
128	74-1707	
129	74-1708	
130	74-1709	
131	74-1710	
133	74-1711	
134	74-1712	
136	74-1713	
137	74-1714	
139	74-1715	
141	74-1716	
144	74-1717	
145	75-669	
146	75-670	
147	75-671	
148	75-672	
149	75-673	
150	75-674	
151	75-675	
152	75-676	
153	75-677	
154	75-678	
155	75-679	
156	75-680	

One was written off on 27.3.80; three crashed during a formation flight on 31.1.79.

CESSNA 320

Two only :

344	c/n 320-0094	ex N5794X
345	320-0095	N5795X

CONSOLIDATED PBY-5A CATALINA

Three PBY-5A are known to have been used including 379

and 380; the latter was reported as ex RCAF Canso 11040. Three OA-10A were also taken on charge (ex USAAF 44-33965, 33991 and 34020). A PBY-5A was written off on 23.12.67.

CURTISS C-46 COMMANDO

Twelve C-46D (321/332) and five C-46F (650/652 d/d 6.57, 653 d/d 6.58 and 385 d/d 1966) were taken on charge. C-46D 321 to 324 were brought up to C-46F standards. One crashed on 20.1.71, others were withdrawn from use, and two are believed to be still current.

61-321	c/n 33724	ex 44-78328	to OB-XAL-577 5.61
61-322	32865	44-77469	to OB-XAM-578 5.61
61-323	33104	44-77708	to OB-XAN-579 5.61
61-324	33206	44-77810	to OB-XAO-580 5.61
61-325	33268	44-77872	
61-326	32867	44-77471	to OB-R-804 7.65
61-327			
61-328	33720	44-78324	to OB-R-808 7.65
61-329	32823	44-77427	to OB-R-806 7.65
61-330	22222	44-78399	to OB-R-948
61-331	32961	44-77565	
61-332	33083	44-77687	
65-385	22405	44-78582,N5076N	to N5076N '66
650	22546	44-78723	to FAP 57-308, N67994 OB-XAH-541 1960
651	22593	44-78770	to FAP 57-309, N67993 OB-XAI-542 1960
652	22559	44-78736	w/o 1958 N67991
653	22568	44-78745	to FAP 57-310, N67986 OB-XAJ-543 1960, restored as FAP 310 in 1973 and current.

DASSAULT MIRAGE 5P/5DP

Twelve Mirage 5P (181 to 192) and two 5DP two-seaters (197 and 198) were delivered in 1968. A further eight Mirage 5P (101 to 108) followed in 1974, and a third 5DP (199) in March 1976. Another six Mirage 5P (to be 109 to 114) were ordered in 1980. A Mirage 5P was written off on 8.3.71.

DE HAVILLAND CANADA DHC.2 BEAVER

The first three were ordered in 1949 :

c/n104	ex CF-GQR	d/d 2.51
108	CF-GQS	3.51
111	CF-GQT	3.51

Three more were delivered in 1964 :

64-374	1580	sold as CF-QQD
64-375	1582	sold as CF-QQE
64-376	1584	wfu

A final trio followed in 1966 :

382	1667	sold as CF-QQF
383	1675	sold as CF-QQG
384	1676	sold as CF-QQH

DE HAVILLAND CANADA DHC.5 BUFFALO

Sixteen were delivered in 1971-72 for use by Grupo 41, although 328 was on Grupo 8 charge for a time. One was written off on 22.12.79.

321	c/n 44	
322	45	wfu by 1978
323	46	
324	47	
325	48	
326	49	
327	50	
328	51	
329	52	
346	53	
347	54	
348	55	
349	56	
350	57	
351	58	
352	59	

DE HAVILLAND CANADA DHC.6 TWIN OTTER

Three Twin Otter 100 were delivered in November 1967 and disposed of during the second half of 1971 :

67-390	c/n 73	to CF-PPD
67-391	75	to CF-CSF
67-392	82	to CF-SCF

These were followed by eighteen Twin Otter 300 for use by TANS : 300, 303, 304, 307, 312, 313, 317 and 318 between May and October 1971, initially with '71-' prefixes to their serials; 302, 306, 309 and 311 in September-October 1973, initially with '73-' prefixes; 333 in July 1974; the second 303 in May 1976; and 376, 378, 381 and 386 later.

300	314	w/o 2.2.76, rebuilt as C-GKBD
302	378	
303	315	w/o 10.7.74; replaced by a second aircraft
303	483	d/d 5.76, flown initially as '483'
304	316	
306	379	

307	317	
309	384	
311	385	w/o
312	322	
313	323	w/o
317	324	
318	325	
333	418	
376	6....	
378	6....	
381	6....	
386	6....	

DOUGLAS B-26B/C INVADER

The first eight of sixteen B-26B/C and one RB-26C were delivered in 1955; previous USAF identities included 43-22530, 22564, 22588, 22629, 22666, 22674. FAP serials were 214 to 230, though the first aircraft were originally serialled 572 to 579. The type was withdrawn from use in 1966-67.

DOUGLAS C-47 SKYTRAIN/DC-3

Over thirty were taken on charge and operated by SATCO, TANS and Grupo de Comunicaciones 8. Six were still in use in 1977 (301, 315, 356, 361, 369 and 373) and of these at least four remained in 1979-80. Fiscal year prefixes were used for a number of years; those known are 55-304, 61-320 and 62-357 and 358. Known aircraft are :

301				
304	DC-3A-414	c/n 4177	ex FAP487	
311	C-47B	17102/ 34369	45-1099	to OB-XAT-653
315	C-47			wfu 1978
316				
320	C-47A	15238/ 26683	PP-YQH	to OB-XAK-568
321				
326	C-47B			to OB-R-804
355				
356				
357	C-47A	13828/ 25273	43-48012	
358	C-47A	13897/ 25342	43-38081	
359				
361				
364				
365				

Helio H.395 Super Courier 1573 at Yarinacocha
in November 1969.

Douglas C-47 Skytrain 371 photographed at Lima
in September 1969.

English Electric Canberra B(I).68 257 as G-52-12 at Cambridge prior to delivery in June 1978.

Bell 212 603 in overall red at Dallas-Love Field in July 1978.

Cessna A-37B 151 seen prior to delivery in 1977 at Wichita.

Beech Queen Air A80 737 at Arequipa in October 1969; eighteen were delivered to Grupo 8.

De Havilland Canada DHC.2 Beaver 383 at Yarinacocha in November 1969.

Dassault Mirage 5P 185, one of twelve delivered in 1968.

De Havilland Canada DHC.5 Buffalo 322 and 325 prior to delivery in 1971.

De Havilland Canada DHC.6 Twin Otter 300 302 acquired for TANS use.

367	C-47A	19749	43-15283	w/o 4.6.66
368				
369				
371				
372				
373				
385				
483	C-47B	17007/ 34270	45-1004	to OB-XAF-539
484	C-47A	9920	42-24058	to OB-XAE-538
485	C-53D	11718	N19913	to OB-XAA-534
486	C-47A	20057	43-15591	to OB-XAG-540
487	DC-3A-414	4177	N30008	to FAP 55-304
488	DC-3A-279B	4800	N28334	to OB-XAC-536
489	DC-3A-279A	2192	N25652	to OB-XAD-537
696	C-53	4830	N54311	to OB-XAP-581
?	C-47B	17006/ 34269	45-1003	
?	C-47B	17008/ 34271	45-1005	

The OB-XAA/XAZ block was reserved for SATCO aircraft in June 1960 when SATCO became semi-independent from Transportes Aéreos Militares although still under FAP control. With the demise of SATCO, a few C-47 and C-53 remained on the civil register (such as OB-R-534, 536, 537 and 568) but others returned to the FAP with new serials :

OB-XAC-536	ex 488	to FAP 49-305	
OB-XAD-537	489	50-306	
OB-XAP-581	696	60-314	

DOUGLAS C-54 SKYMASTER

Nine were delivered (386 to 388 late in 1966, initially as 66-386 etc.) and operated by Grupos 8 and 41 (SATCO). Three were still on Grupo 41 charge in 1979.

361	C-54A	c/n 10334	ex 42-72229, N88921	
362	C-54B	10476	42-72371, N88897	
363	C-54B	10435	42-72330, N88898	
386	C-54D		42-	
387	C-54D	10731	42-72626	to OB-R-949
388	C-54D	10830	42-72725	to OB-R-862
393	C-54			
394	C-54			
395	C-54			

DOUGLAS DC-6

Four aircraft were taken on charge. The first was an ex Scandinavian Airlines System DC-6 :
377 c/n 43116 ex OY-AOH d/d 3.64, wfu

The other three were DC-6B probably ex-USAF C-118As, and were serialled 379 to 381.
The FAP also operated a civil-registered DC-6AF, OB-R-611 of APSA (Aerovias Peruanas SA).

DOUGLAS DC-8-62F

Two ex Swiss civil aircraft obtained at the end of 1981 :

370	c/n 46078	ex HB-IDK	d/d 27.12.81
371	45984	HB-IDH	29.12.81

ENGLISH ELECTRIC CANBERRA

The first Canberras to be delivered, between May 1956 and February 1957, were eight B(I)Mk.8 :

474		
475		
476		w/o 23.9.56
478		
479		
480		
481		
482		

An unidentified aircraft was written off on 11.6.59, and the six survivors renumbered in 1960 as 206, 207 and 209 to 212. A replacement aircraft was delivered on 18.11.60 and took up the 'missing' serial 208. Two aircraft crashed : 207 on 8.2.72 and 210 on 8.4.63.
Six B.Mk.2, ex Royal Air Force, were delivered in 1966 :

233	ex RAF WJ974,	G-27-76
234	WJ976,	G-27-77
235	WK112	
236	WH726	
237	WH868	
238	WE120	

Two T.Mk.4 were delivered in 1966 :

231	WH659
232	WJ860

.... and a third in 1973 :

246	W . . . ., G-27-224

Seven B.Mk.56 were delivered in 1969 :

239	WT208,	G-27-96
240		G-27-97
241		G-27-98
242		G-27-99
243		G-27-100
244		G-27-101
245	WT344,	G-27-145

Ten B(I)Mk.68 followed in 1975 :

247	WT368,	G-52-2
248	XK951,	G-52-3
249	WT342,	G-52-4
250	WT364,	G-52-5
251	WT340,	G-52-6
252	XH234,	G-52-7
253	XM273,	G-52-8
254	XM936,	G-52-9
255	XM263,	G-52-10
256	XM276,	G-52-11

An eleventh aircraft arrived on 5.7.78 :

257	XM278,	G-52-12

Unidentified crashes took place on 30.6.72 and 7.10.71.

FOKKER F.28-1000 FELLOWSHIP

One is currently the presidential aircraft :
390 c/n 11100 ex PH-EXY d/d 30.3.76
SATCO also used three Fellowships, obtained in the early part of 1973, which were re-registered on transfer to AeroPeru.

OB-397	c/n 11059	to OB-R-1020
OB-R-398	11065	OB-R-1018
OB-R-399	11066	OB-R-1019

GRUMMAN G.21A GOOSE

The four aircraft obtained in 1940, c/ns 1050 to 1053, were serialled 2TP-1H to 2TP-4H. The H suffix indicated hidro-avión (seaplane) and the 2TP part showed that they were operated by the Escuadrón de Transporte Nº2. 2TP-2H and -4H became FAP 323 and 324 respectively and were later sold in the United States as N327 and N328. The FAP also used at least one JRF-5, which has been preserved with the serial 164.

GRUMMAN HU-16B ALBATROSS

Five were delivered and allocated to Grupo 31; four remain in service :

517	
518	w/o
519	
520	
521	

HAWKER HUNTER

Sixteen Hunter F.52 were delivered in 1956 to equip a new unit, Escuadrón de Caza Nº14 which was activated on 30.5.56 and was absorbed by Grupo de Caza 12 in 1957. Hunters were occasionally deployed to the northern airfield of Talara near the border with Ecuador. The type was not replaced in service until early 1980.

630	ex RAF	WT717
631		WT776
632		WW662
633		WT758
634		WT803
635		WT766
636		WT800
637		WT774
638		WT734
639		WT756
640		WT796
641		WT768
642		WT759
643		WT779
644		WT773
645		WT765

A single Hunter T.62 two-seat conversion trainer, 681 ex RAF WT706 was delivered in 1960.

HELIO H.395 SUPER COURIER

Five were delivered, with interchangeable wheel/twin-float undercarriage, and shared with the Army. Three were 1572, 1573 and 1574.

HILLER UH12B

Two only, c/ns 858 and 866, delivered in August 1957 for SAR duties.

LEAR JET 25B

Two aircraft used by the Servicio Aerofotográfico Nacional :

522	c/n 25.159	ex N66JD
523	25.164	

LOCKHEED PV-2 HARPOON

Six believed delivered; one was 421.

LOCKHEED F-80C SHOOTING STAR

The first three of sixteen aircraft were delivered in March 1958. Initially with serials in the 660 block (660 to 666 are confirmed), the F-80C were re-numbered in the 150 block (known serials are 152, 153, 156, 163, 166). Most were used by Grupo de Caza-Bombardeo 13 until the type was withdrawn from use in 1973.

LOCKHEED T-33A

Sixteen believed delivered, initially with serials in the 590 block (one was 591) and used by Grupo de Caza 12 and the Academia del Aire. Re-numbered aircraft included 480, 481, 482, 484, 487, 488, 490, 494 and 495. A few were converted to AT-33A close-support aircraft, eight of which were reportedly in service in 1979.

LOCKHEED C-130 HERCULES

The first Peruvian Hercules were two ex-civil model L.382E-26C delivered in April 1973 to Grupo de Transporte 41 :

394	c/n 4358	ex N60FW	(noted 4.81 with dual markings as FAP394/OB-R-1188)
395	4364	N70FW	to OB-R-1004, w/o 19.2.78

A third machine, a model L.382E-27C was transferred from the national airline SATCO -

396	4450	OB-R-956	

Three L.100-20 (L.382E-37C), generally similar to the C-130H, were delivered between November 1976 and January 1977 :

382	4706
383	4708
384	4715

Two further L.100-20 (L.382E-47C) were delivered 3.81 :

397	4850	
398	4853	ex N4119M

MACCHI MB.339AP

Fourteen were ordered in mid-1980 as Cessna T-37B replacements, of which the following were seen prior to delivery in 1981 : 452, 456, 467, 468, 473, 477, 479 to 482. Sixty-six more are to be built from 1983 over a six year period by Indaer-Peru at a new factory being constructed with Aermacchi assistance.

MIKOYAN MiG-21F

Twelve Cuban Air Force 'Fishbed-C' were allocated to the FAP for conversion training of future Su-22 pilots. Details are unknown, and there are suggestions that these aircraft were retained in Cuba, where the training programme may take place.

MIL Mi-6

Eight are reported to have been delivered to Grupo de Helicópteros 3, including serials 679 to 684.

MIL Mi-8

Most Mi-8 were allocated to the Army, but at least eight were taken on FAP charge, including 630, 631, 634, 677, 678 and 679, and six remained in service in 1979-80. One was operated in FAP markings with the civil registration OB-E-996. Two crash dates known are 5.11.76 and 20.2.81.

MORANE-SAULNIER MS.760A PARIS

Two aircraft believed ex Brazilian Air Force; no details.

NORTH-AMERICAN AT-6/SNJ TEXAN

At least thirty AT-6C/D, T-6G, SNJ and BC-1A were delivered to the FAP, about a dozen remaining on Academia del Aire charge. Previous USAAF identities included AT-6C 41-32445, 32985, 42-44263, 44300 and AT-6D 42-84408, 84568, 84611, 84612, 84701, 86141, 86447, 44-81160, 81174. The following were delivered in May 1954 :

559	SNJ-2	ex Bu2564	
560	BC-1A	39-820	
561	SNJ-2	Bu2556	
562	SNJ-2	Bu2572	

.....and the following in June 1954 :

565	SNJ-2	Bu2563	preserved
566	BC-1A	39-854	
567	SNJ-2	Bu2019	
568	SNJ-2	Bu2024	
569	SNJ-2	Bu2033	
570	SNJ-2	Bu2012	

Surviving machines were renumbered in the 400 block (one was 422).

Fokker F.28-1000 Fellowship 390, the current presidential aircraft.

Lear Jet 25B 522, one of two used by the Servicio Aerofotográfico Nacional.

Mil Mi-8 FAP-634 at Lima in 1971 in a basically Aeroflot colour scheme.

Lockheed C-130E Hercules 396 was formerly with SATCO and is seen here at Zurich in April 1975.

Pilatus PC.6/B1-H2 Turbo-Porter 336 on floats with TANS.

NORTH AMERICAN B-25J MITCHELL

Twenty were delivered in 1947, including ex USAAF 44-29912, 30296, 30360, 30361, 30384, 30398, 30403, 30418, and eventually equipped two squadrons of Grupo de Bombardeo 21 until replaced by Canberras. Known serials are 472, 473, 474 and 475.

NORTH AMERICAN F-86F SABRE

Fifteen were supplied between June and September 1955, ex USAF 51-13227, 13249, 13255, 13491, 13494, 13495, 13499, 13501 to 13503, 13505, 52-5286, 5289,5295, 5296, and used by Grupo de Caza 12 until replaced by the Sukhoi Su-22 during 1979-80. Early serials included 591 and 595; post-1960 serials included 130, 131, 171 and 179.

PIAGGIO P.136-L2 (TRECKER GULL)

At least two aircraft :
312 c/n 237 ex N40038
313   238   N40039   broken up at Iquitos 1965
A third serialled 314 has also been reported.

PILATUS PC.6/B1-H2 TURBO-PORTER

Seventeen were delivered in 1975-76 in a distinctive orange white and black livery for use by TAMS on either wheels or twin floats; ten were still operational in 1980. Known aircraft are :
313
314   w/o 17.3.75
316   w/o 13.9.74
334
335
336
337
338
339 c/n 743 w/o 16.3.77
340   744
341   745
342
343
344
345
374
376

PITTS S-2A SPECIAL

Six were procured for use by the FAP's aerobatic team but they may double as aerobatic trainers at the Academia del Aire.

REPUBLIC F-47D THUNDERBOLT

Twenty were delivered in 1948; subsequent deliveries made up a grand total of fifty-seven, ex USAAF 44-90293, 90298, 90332, 90399, 90402, 90413, 90425, 90442, 90444, 90455, 90456, 90459, 90471, 90477, 90479, 90483, 45-49113, 49125, 49133, 49156, 49167, 49169, 49176, 49181, 49187, 49191, 49192, 49204, 49205, 49224, 49304, 49308, 49326, 49335, 49349, 49404, 49408, 49424, 49426, 49427, 49434, 49437, 49451, 49452, 49458, 49461, 49465, 49469, 49476, 49478, 49486, 49492, 49493, 49494, 49501, 49529, 49552. Initial serials included 422, 442, 542 and 544; later serials were 114, 115, 116, 119, 122, 123, 124, 125, 126, 127. The type was withdrawn from use during 1959 and six aircraft were eventually sold in the United States :
114 ex 44-90471 to N47DA
115   45-49131 ?   N47DB
116   45-49167   N47DC
119   45-49192   N47DD
122   45-49205   N47DE
127   45-49335   N47DF

STEARMAN PT-17

About twelve delivered, known serials including 400 and 404. Aircraft 400 was used as the prototype SEMAN conversion with a Lycoming IO-470-F engine and detail refinements.

SUD SE.3130 ALOUETTE II

A first batch of five were delivered in 1960 :
60-601 c/n 1421 wfu
60-602   1438 w/o 20.5.64
60-603   1439 w/o 16.6.62
60-604   1485 w/o 30.5.62
60-605   1486 to OB-XAW-656
A sixth, ex French military machine was also procured :
610   1074 w/o 20.2.67
It is believed that another two Alouette II were also taken on charge.

SUD SE.3160 ALOUETTE III

Four were delivered initially :
616 c/n 1024
636   1025
641   1031   temporarily to OB-XAV-655
642   1032   w/o 18.12.73
Later deliveries include c/n 1486, and the following batch of eight :
636   1999
637   2002   to OB-E-974
638   2006
639   2007
640   2018
641   2019
642   2027   to OB-E-976
643   2028
One of this batch became OB-E-970; ten Alouette III are said to be still in use.

SUKHOI Su-22

Thirty-six of the 'Fitter-F' were ordered in 1976, including at least four Su-22U two-seat operational trainers, and all had been delivered by early 1978; another sixteen aircraft were ordered in the early part of 1980. One of the first batch was written off in an accident and replaced by a new Soviet-supplied aircraft. The only known serial is 017; some illustrations of these aircraft appeared in the April 1981 editions of 'Air International' and 'AirFan'.

NOTE : There is at Callao a preserved Grumman J2F Duck in FAP markings with the serial '164'. This was never operated by the FAP, and the 'serial' is the C of A number of its former civil registration OB-KAA-164.

Peruvian Army

The Peruvian Army (Ejército Peruano) comprises some sixty thousand personnel in twelve brigades and a number of independent battalions; military service is compulsory for all males aged twenty to twenty-five, but annual conscription is limited by existing vacancies and requirements. A Servicio de Aviación del Ejército del Peru was formed in 1971 using five Peruvian Air Force Helio Super Courier liaison aircraft on loan and has since been considerably expanded, lately with the assistance of Soviet advisers. It currently consists of a sizeable force of helicopters with a small fixed-wing element, and its main base is Callao.

No less than forty-two Mil Mi-8 transport helicopters were supplied to the Army by the Soviet Union but these have had a poor serviceability record and are now mostly relegated to storage or awaiting repair. Further aircraft procurement is limited by budgetary restrictions caused by a decline in the Peruvian economy, although unconfirmed reports suggest that two GAF N22 Nomad twin-engined light transports have been ordered from Australia.

Aircraft Review

Peruvian Army aircraft carry a modified roundel, with a red triangle in the middle. The inscription *Ejército Peruano* is commonly used. Aircraft known to have been used by the Army are :

BELL 47G

Eight helicopters, ex Peruvian Air Force.

BEECHCRAFT QUEEN AIR A65

One VIP aircraft, EP751 c/n LC-233, ex OB-M-848.

CESSNA 185

Five reported in service.

MIL Mi-6

Known serials are EP-626, 627, 630 to 636, 643, 677 to 684. EP-626 was written off 28.2.75 and EP-633 on 11.10.74.

MIL Mi-8

Forty-two supplied, of which known serials are EP-501, 502, 504, 507, 510, 511, 516, 517, 518, 519, 522, 526, 531, 532, 534, 537, 541, 542, 546, 547, 549, 561, 564, 567, 571, 576, 577, 581, 583, 584, 586. EP-507 was written off on 17.5.78.

SUD SA.318C ALOUETTE II

Eight helicopters :

EP-312	c/n 2344	ex F-WKQD
EP-315	2345	F-WKQD
EP-318	2350	
EP-321	2351	
EP-329	2356	
EP-334	2357	
EP-337	2358	
EP-341	2362	w/o 1.3.76

National Police & Civil Guard

The National Police Force has a paramilitary department, the Guardia Civil with a personnel of about 25,000, controlled by the Ministry for Internal Affairs and Police, but does not operate aircraft on a regular basis.

Peruvian Navy

A Cuerpo de Aviadores de la Armada Nacional (Corps of Aviators of the National Navy) was set up in 1920 by a United States Naval mission which also helped to establish a seaplane base at Ancón, near Callao and supplied nine Curtiss Seagull flying boats (model 18, a rebuilt version of the wartime MF). Another mission arrived in 1924 to establish a training programme, also forming naval bases at Maranga, Trujillo and Tumbez. The Cuerpo was then renamed as the Servicio de Hidroaviación de la Marina del Peru (Peruvian Navy Hydroaviation Service) under a US Naval officer and a few additional aircraft were obtained from surplus stocks, including a handful of Curtiss F.5L flying boats and twelve ex Royal Air Force Avro 504K training biplanes (including E372, E391, E395 and E399).

Small as it was, the Servicio tried hard to be effective, and it was thus that the first Peruvian first-line military aircraft unit was a naval squadron, the 1er Escuadrón de Reconocimiento, formed in 1928 with six Airco DH.9 reconnaissance bombers. During the same year, four Douglas DTB torpedo biplanes (c/ns 253, 254, 384, 385) were acquired.

The Servicio had 175 personnel by 20 May 1929 on which date it merged with the Army air service to form the Cuerpo de Aeronáutica del Peru under the Ministry for the Navy and Aviation. Despite this merger, naval aircraft did retain some individuality — such as distinctive markings — until as late as 1940, and it was the Navy which ran a twice-weekly airline service between San Ramón and Iquitos with Keystone and Stearman three-seat biplanes and at least one Hamilton float monoplane. Ancon, twenty miles north of Lima, remained the main naval air base and flying school.

A new Servicio de Aviación de la Armada del Peru — eventually renamed the Servicio Aeronaval de la Marina Peruana — was established in the late 1950s with headquarters at Callao, where all flying training and transport was and is concentrated. The

Servicio currently flies transport, communications and anti-submarine aircraft, marked *ARMADA* or *NAVAL*. The Navy which has a personnel strength of about ten thousand has four cruisers which have provision for helicopters : the *Capitán Quiñones* (ex, *Almirante Grau* and *HMS Newfoundland* transferred 30.12.59), the *Coronel Bolognesi* (ex *HMS Ceylon*, transferred 9.2.60), the *Almirante Grau* (ex *HrMs De Ruyter* transferred 1973) and the *Aguirre* (ex *HrMs De Zeven Provincien* transferred in 1973).

Aircraft Review

COLOURS AND MARKINGS

Peruvian Navy aircraft carry markings similar to those of the Air Force, except that there is an insignia blue anchor superimposed on the roundel. The inscriptions *Armada* or *Naval* are used.

AIRCRAFT SERIALS

These are allotted in the 400 & 500 blocks with rôle prefixes as follows:

AA	Armada Antisubmarinos	Naval ASW
AE	Armada Exploración	Naval reconnaissance
AI	Armada Instrucción	Naval training
AT	Armada Transporte	Naval transport
HA	Helicóptero Antisubmarinos	ASW helicopter
HC	Helicóptero Carga	Transport helicopter
HE	Helicóptero Exploración	Reconnaissance helicopter

Aircraft known to have been used by the Navy are:

AGUSTA-BELL 212AS

Six aircraft for operation from the two ex Dutch Navy cruisers and the Lupo-class frigates ordered from Italy :
HE-470 c/n 016 d/d 21.2.78
HE-471   4.78
HE-472
HE-473
HE-474
HE-475

AGUSTA-SIKORSKY S.61D (SH-3D)

Four helicopters serialled HA-430 to HA-433; HQ-490 and HQ-491 have also been observed.

BELL 47G

Five helicopters; details not known.

BELL UH-1 IROQUOIS

At least six UH-1D and UH-1H; one is UH-1D HC-410.

BELL 206A/B JET RANGER

Ten helicopters; details unknown.

BEECHCRAFT T-34 MENTOR

At least two T-34A serialled AI-501 and AI-504, and six T-34C-1 serialled AI-510 to AI-515.

CESSNA 310

At least one serialled 515, now withdrawn from use.

DOUGLAS C-47 SKYTRAIN

Eleven are known, serials AT-502/503, 510/513, 520/524. The serials were originally unprefixed. AT-502 is a C-47A c/n 9980 ex 42-24118, OB-R-246 d/d 6.10.66.

FOKKER F.27 FRIENDSHIP 400 MPA

Two maritime patrol aircraft :
AE-560 c/n 10548 ex PH-EXD d/d 17.9.77
AE-561   10549   PH-EXE   25.2.78
The latter was temporarily leased back to Fokker for use as a demonstrator with the registration PH-MPA.

GRUMMAN S-2E TRACKER

Nine aircraft based at Lima-Jorge Chávez :
AA-540	ex Bu152831
AA-541	
AA-542	
AA-543	152340
AA-544	
AA-545	152357
AA-546	152332
AA-547	
AA-548	152369

NORTH AMERICAN T-28 TROJAN

At least one serialled 400.

PIPER PA-23 AZTEC 250C

One only, serial 501, c/n 27-2760 delivered in January 1965.

SUD SA.316 ALOUETTE III

Three aircraft originally delivered as :
N-410	c/n 1945 ex F-OCCR
N-411	2012
N-412	2013

They were later re-serialled as HAS-410 to 412, and then again as HAS-420 to 422. HAS-421 crashed on 4.9.76. Note the anomaly of the HAS prefix rather than HA.

Beechcraft T-34C-1 Turbo-Mentor AI-510, first of six.

Douglas C-47 Skytrain AT-510 at Lima in Sept.1969.

Agusta-Sikorsky S.61D (SH-3D) HA-431 seen at Cascina Costa prior to delivery in March 1978.

PUERTO RICO

Area	8,897 sq km
Population	3,319,000
Capital	San Juan
Civil registration	N

The only Latin-American country under Anglo-Saxon rule, Puerto Rico was discovered by Columbus in November 1493, annexed by Spain in 1509 and occupied by the United States of America in 1898 during the Spanish-American War. On 10 December of that year, Spain agreed to transfer its sovereignty over Puerto Rico to the United States. Several moves have been made since the end of the Second World War towards greater autonomy — additional electoral powers in 1947, the right to draft its own constitution in 1950, and the reclassification of Puerto Rico as a Free Commonwealth associated to the USA — but today opinions are divided between statehood and total independence. There is an underground separatist movement, with some support among the poorer, mixed-race classes, which operates through bombing and other acts of violence; as recently as 12 January 1981, eight Puerto Rico Air National Guard A-7D Corsair were destroyed in a terrorist attack at Muniz ANGB with a ninth aircraft badly damaged; even the gate-guard F-104G was destroyed. Puerto Rico's income is derived from textile and chemical industries as well as agriculture, but emigration continues at an ever increasing rate, there being over seven hundred thousand Puerto Ricans in New York City alone. However, the island's importance is largely caused by its strategically vital position near to some major shipping routes.

Puerto Rico, as a part of the USA, has no air force of its own. However, there is a Puerto Rico Air National Guard, often referred to by its initials (PRANG !), whose title appears in full on its transport aircraft in both English and Spanish as 'Guardia Nacional Aérea de Puerto Rico'. Its current operational unit is the 198th Tactical Fighter Squadron on the 156th Tactical Fighter Group, based at Muniz Air National Guard Base and flying Vought A-7D Corsair II, which replaced the Lockheed F-104C and D Starfighters flown until mid-1975. PRANG aircraft may have a small representation of the red, white and blue Puerto Rican flag — similar in design to that of Cuba but with the colours reversed — displayed on their tail surfaces.

EL SALVADOR

Area	20,865 sq km
Population	4,700,000
Capital	San Salvador
Civil registration	YS-

The Republic of El Salvador, the smallest yet most densely populated of the Central American countries seceded from the Central American Federation in 1839 and formally became independent in 1841. Its history has been characterised by constant periods of violence, leading to military intervention in politics to restore a degree of public order; in fact most of the country's governments have been controlled by the military.

El Salvador's only potential enemy is the neighbouring republic of Honduras, border clashes being not infrequent (there was even a state of war in mid-1969). The main security problem is of a largely internal nature, deriving from a high rate of population increase, coupled with an unstable, coffee-based economy which depends on foreign market demands. Social inequalities are exploited by radical groups which in turn bring police and right-wing retaliation, and a measure of guerilla activity which had been apparent escalated to such a pitch prior to the March 1982 elections (which usurped President Duarte in favour of a right-wing coalition) that a state of civil war was nearly reached. Military service is compulsory for all males aged between eighteen and fifty, but the actual yearly intake is dependent on National Assembly resolutions and available funds.

The Salvadorean Army has a personnel strength of approximately six thousand, plus Territorial Service reserves, and in the event of a national emergency takes over the control of the three thousand strong Guardia Nacional, a paramilitary security force. It also controls a paratroop battalion which is currently at a mere company strength. The tiny navy has about 130 personnel and half a dozen lightly-armed patrol boats.

The Servicio de Aviación Militar de El Salvador (El Salvador Military Aviation Service) was formed in 1922 with five SAML-Aviatik biplane trainers acquired in Italy, which were allocated to an Escuela de Aviación Militar (Military Flying School) established at Ilopango near San Salvador. Ilopango also housed the Escuela de Especialistas (Specialists' School) which trained ground crews The country's economy did not allow for the expansion of the air arm and the next few years were mainly spent in opening up a number of airfields : Ahuachapán, Chalatenango, San Miguel, San Vicente, Sonsonate, Usulután and Zacatecoluca. Aircraft procurement was almost non-existent, and it was not until the mid-1930s that efforts were made to expand the Servicio, The Escuela de Aviación Militar received a small number of Fleet 10 biplane trainers, and two operational Escuadrillas were formed, the Escuadrilla de Caza (Fighter Flight) with Curtiss-Wright Osprey biplane fighters and the Escuadrilla de Reconocimiento (Reconnaissance Flight) with Waco F2 biplanes. Each had three aircraft plus a fourth in reserve.

Four Caproni AP.1 single-seat attack monoplanes were obtained from Italy just before the Second World War, but the ever growing United States influence in Latin America caused a switch to the American types. Subsequent bilateral defence agreements brought small numbers of Lend-Lease aircraft from 1943 onwards — Fairchild PT-19 and Stearman PT-13A trainers and Vultee BT-13A basic trainers, followed by some Beechcraft AT-11 twin-engined crew-trainers shortly after the war (these later doubled as light transports).

When El Salvador signed the 1947 Rio Pact, a United States air mission was sent to reorganise the Servicio, which became the Fuerza Aérea Salvadoreña (Salvedorean Air Force) and re-equipped with Douglas C-47 transports, North American AT-6 Texan trainers (later supplemented by Beechcraft T-34A Mentors), and Vought F4U-5 and FG-1D Corsairs, the latter being allocated to the Escuadrilla de Caza.

Subsequent deliveries took place from time to time. For example, the Corsairs were supplemented (and finally replaced) in 1968-69 by thirteen Cavalier-refurbished North American F-51D and one TF-51D, one of which was lost to enemy ground fire during the short 'soccer' war with Honduras. Numbers of assorted transport and liaison types were also obtained. In 1975, as a result of United States reluctance in supporting conservative regimes in Latin America, El Salvador requested Israeli assistance in modernising the FAS. This was granted and Israel supplied redundant Dassault Ouragan jet fighters and IAI-built Potez CM.170 Magister armed jet trainers; favourable terms were also given for the purchase of four IAI 201 Arava light transports. Early in 1978 the FAS bought three refurbished ex French Air Force CM.170 Magisters from Aérospatiale, and Israel supplied four Dassault Super Mystère B.2 jet fighters in February 1979, with more following later, probably to a total of eighteen. Also entering service during 1980-81 was the Bell UH-1H Iroquois helicopter, these probably from US military sources and acquired particularly for anti-guerilla operations, alongside some Hughes 500 light helicopters.

Early in 1982, before the large-scale unrest, the Fuerza Aérea Salvadoreña had a personnel strength of just under a thousand, and was organised in the following units :

Escuadrilla de Caza at San Miguel with seventeen Dassault Ouragan and probably eighteen Dassault Super Mystere B.2.

Escuadrilla de Ataque at Ilopango with nine CM. 170 Magisters.

Escuadrilla de Transporte at Ilopango with sixteen Douglas C-47, two DC-6, four IAI 201 Arava.

Escuela de Aviación Militar at Ilopango with ten North American T-6, three Beechcraft T-34A, one Beechcraft AT-11, six Cessna T-41A/C.

Helicopter element - three Sud SA.315B Lama, two SA.316 Alouette III, one Hiller FH.1100, Bell UH-1H Iroquois and Hughes 500s.

A guerilla attack on the Ilopango airfield on 27 January 1982 resulted in the destruction or damage to many FAS aircraft : six UH-1Hs were destroyed though another may be repairable, three C-47s were destroyed and two more seriously damaged, five Ouragans destroyed and one badly damaged (and the repair of such an obsolete type is open to question), and one Magister damaged. Immediately after the attack, the United States announced a large aid package, probably to include up to twelve more UH-1H, three or four Fairchild C-123 transports, about eight Cessna A-37B and four Cessna O-2A, all expected to come from US military stocks. It is also likely that four further Super Mystère B.2 will be supplied by Israel.

Military Air Bases

1 San Salvador (Ilopango)
2 Ahuachapan
3 Santa Ana
4 Sonsonate
5 San Vicente
6 San Miguel
7 La Union

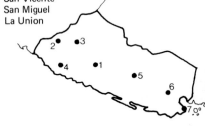

Aircraft Review

COLOURS AND MARKINGS

The blue/white/blue of the United Provinces flag appears on military aircraft as wing roundels and horizontal rudder stripes or fin flash. Transport aircraft often carry the inscription *Fuerza Aérea Salvadoreña*, whilst other types commonly carry *FAS*, often as a prefix to the aircraft serial number.

AIRCRAFT SERIALS

Aircraft known to have been used by the Fuerza Aérea Salvadoreña include the following :

BEECHCRAFT T-34A MENTOR

Perhaps six; three were serialled 64 to 66 and used by the Escuela de Aviación Militar.

BEECHCRAFT AT-11 KANSAN

At least three, one of which remains in use.

BELL UH-1H IROQUOIS

This type is known to have entered service during 1980/81, presumably from US military sources, with fourteen reported delivered in Ferbruary 1981. One is serialled 254, and another '49', presumably 249. One was written off 11.5.81, and six destroyed in the Ilopango raid on 27.1.82. Up to twelve more are expected from the USA during 1982.

CANADAIR C4 NORTH STAR

One example of this Canadian version of the Douglas DC-4 was taken on charge in 1968. It was serialled 300, c/n 114 ex YS-27C of the national airline TACA and was withdrawn from use in 1972.

CESSNA 180

At least seven aircraft :
```
63
67   c/n 32593   ex N7696A
68       32615      N7718A
69       32614      N7717A
80
83
84
```

CESSNA 182

One only, serialled 70, c/n 33714 ex N5714B

CESSNA 185

At least one aircraft, serialled 82

CESSNA T-41

Six T-41A believed delivered, including :
```
90
91   ex  65-5256
92       65-5132
93
```
At least one T-41C was also delivered, c/n R172-0283, ex 68-7892/N7892N.

DASSAULT OURAGAN

At least eighteen aircraft, serialled 700 to 717 were delivered in 1975 from IDF/AF stocks to the Escuadrilla de Caza. It was reported that seventeen remained in service until the Ilopango raid on 27.1.82 when five were destroyed and one seriously damaged.

DASSAULT SUPER MYSTÈRE B.2

Four delivered initially in 1979 ex IDF/AF, but believed to have been supplemented by later deliveries to a total of eighteen used by the Escuadrilla de Caza.

DOUGLAS C-47 SKYTRAIN

Sixteen were in service with the Escuadron de Transporte. Serial allocation may be 100 to 115, as aircraft 101, 103, 104, 105, 106, 107, 108, 109, 110, 111, 112, 113, 114 are confirmed. Three were destroyed and two damaged in the attack at Ilopango on 27.1.82.

DOUGLAS DC-6

At least two ex TACA aircraft :
```
301  DC-6A  c/n 45323  ex YS-35C   w/o 2.5.76
302  DC-6B      45078     YS-32C
```
A third aircraft, serialled 303, has also been reported.

DOUGLAS B-26 INVADER

Five aircraft seem to have been used for counter-insurgency work. The known serials are 600, 602, 603 and 604 (all B-26B), whilst the sole B-26C operated in light grey overall with no markings or serial and may have been 601. 600 was sold in the USA in November 1974

HILLER FH.1100

One helicopter, c/n 185, sold in the USA in December 1979.

HUGHES 500

At least one, serialled 35, noted late 1981.

IAI 201 ARAVA

Four aircraft for the Escuadrón de Transporte :
```
801  c/n 0013  ex 4X-IAL  d/d 17.12.74
802      0014     4X-IAM       16.1.75
803      0017     4X-IAP       22.4.75
804      0018     4X-IAQ        9.6.75
```

NORTH AMERICAN AT-6 TEXAN

Known serials are 72 to 78; over a dozen were delivered including five SNJ-5, and ten remained in service recently. Two were civilianised as YS-172P and YS-183P.

NORTH AMERICAN F-51D MUSTANG

At least thirteen Cavalier-refurbished F-51D and a two-seat TF-51D were delivered, including five in mid-1968. Previous serials included :
```
P-51D   44-11153   to N34FF 12.74
        44-13253   to N35FF 10.74
        44-72483   to N13410
        44-73350   ex N6176C; to N33FF 12.74
        44-73458   ex N554T; to N36FF 10.74
        44-73656   ex N5073K
        44-73693   ex N6357T
        44-73973   ex N6325T
        44-74960
        45-11559   ex N6451D; to N30FF 10.74
```

P-51K   44-11353
          44-12473   to N32FF 12.74

A known early FAS serial was 23, and a later one 402. Two P-51C, ex USAAF 44-10753, 10755, were also reported as delivered, possibly for spares.

POTEZ CM.170 MAGISTER

Six IAI-built aircraft, serialled 500 to 505 were delivered in 1975, and three French-built were acquired from Aérospatiale late in 1978 - serials 509 to 511. One was damaged at Ilopango 27.1.82.

STEARMAN PT-13A

A small number were delivered under Lend-Lease during the Second World War. It is believed that another five Stearmans purchased in the USA in 1953-54 were also taken on charge:

N5474N	c/n 758260
N50490	752708
N52108	753596
N54652	751632
N64931	756817

SUD SA.315B LAMA

Three reportedly delivered for search and rescue duties.

SUD SA.316 ALOUETTE III

At least two; one is serialled '23', and one is c/n 1888.

VOUGHT FG-1D CORSAIR

Twenty FG-1D (the Goodyear-built version of the F4U Corsair) were delivered during the second half of 1957 with the serials 201 to 220 (201 was ex Bu.92460). Four F4U Corsairs were obtained in October 1959 as a source of spares. The FG-1D were not successful in FAS service, suffering from a high degree of unserviceability. The Escuadrilla de Caza was as a rule unable to keep more than eight or nine flying at a time, and by 1968 only four were operational (a fifth machine was repaired and put back into service later). The FG-1D was finally retired after the July 1969 'Soccer War' against Honduras and replaced by the F-51D Mustangs.

Douglas C-47 Skytrain 108 at Howard AFB in June 1975.

North-American F-51D Mustang 402 in a camouflage colour scheme

IAI 201 Arava 803 at Brussels in April 1975, on delivery for the Escuadrón de Transporte.

Douglas DC-6A 301 during a visit to Miami in November 1976.

SURINAM

Area	163,820 sq km
Population	448,000
Capital	Paramaribo
Civil registration	PZ-

Surinam is situated in South America between Guyana and French Guiana and was until November 1975 a Dutch colony with a substantial white population, now rather diminished due to migration to the Netherlands. Although by no means a Latin-American country, with a mixed population of whites of Dutch extraction, aboriginal Indians, negroes and mestizos, Surinam is phasing in the use of Spanish as its main working language. Current official languages are Dutch and English, and the Surinamese dialect is employed mainly in rural areas.

Dutch forces are regularly deployed to Surinam and supplemented by local compulsory recruiting. Although mainly consisting of infantry and support units, Koninklijke Luchtmacht (Royal Netherlands Air Force) maritime patrol and transport aircraft often operate from Paramaribo-Zanderij. The two Fokker F.27-400MPA M-1 and M-2 which have recently been delivered to the Dutch air force's 320 Squadron at Hato in the Netherlands Antilles are expected to be deployed to Paramaribo on occasions.

Surinam has a token army of about six hundred, and up to now has had no air force. However, early in 1982 steps were taken to form an air arm and four Pilatus Britten-Norman BN-2A-21 Defenders ordered :

SAF001	c/n 916	ex G-BIUA	d/d 25.2.82
SAF002	2108	G-BIXE	25.3.82
SAF003	2116	G-BJEA	
SAF004			

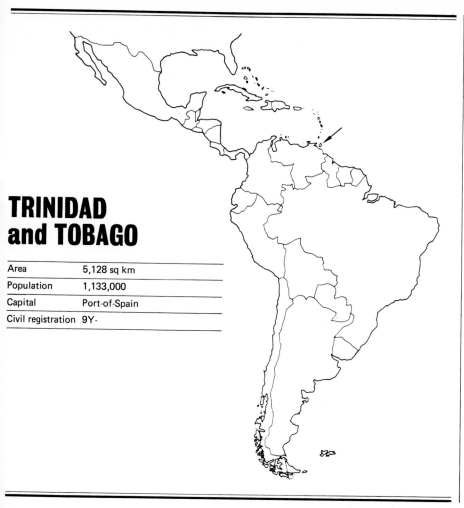

TRINIDAD and TOBAGO

Area	5,128 sq km
Population	1,133,000
Capital	Port-of-Spain
Civil registration	9Y-

The island of Trinidad (Trinity) was colonised by the Spaniards and occupied by the British in 1797; it was joined with the smaller Tobago in 1889. Independence was granted on 31 August 1962.

The country's economy, largely based on tourism but with the production of oil and asphalte becoming increasingly important, does not permit an expansion of its defence forces. In any case, the population, mostly of African and Amerindian origin, is peaceful enough, and the 2,500-strong police force is adequate for the country's needs.

There exists a one thousand strong Trinidad and Tobago Defence Force which started air operations in June 1966 with a Cessna 337A c/n 337-0441 ex N5341S, serialled TTDF-1 and inscribed *Trinidad and Tobago Coast Guard* — a remarkable example of inter-ministerial co-operation as the TTDF is directly controlled by the Prime Minister and the Coast Guard by the Ministry of Home Affairs; the Cessna was later sold as N74184. Two Sud SA.341G Gazelles were obtained in April 1973 (TTDF-2 c/n 1029 ex F-WTNS and 'NS-1' and TTDF-3 c/n 1044 ex 'NS-2'); they went to the Ministry of National Security as 9Y-TFO and 9Y-TFN in February 1977. More helicopters were acquired later, one being written off on 21 July 1979 and another being SA.341G Gazelle 9Y-TGU c/n 1566 ex N9003A. A Cessna 402 TTDF-1 was noted early 1982 re-using the earlier Cessna 337 marks. Two new Sikorsky S.76s are 9Y-TGW and TGX, c/ns 760176/760185.

TTDF aircraft and helicopters are marked with the national flag (red with a black diagonal band edged in white — the colours representing vitality - red, purity - white and strength - black) and with optional red/white/black rudder stripes or fin flash (red leading). The main airfield is Piarco on Trinidad, a former Fleet Air Arm station, and Crown Point on Tobago; there are several airstrips on Trinidad.

US/British agreements in April 1941 gave the US a ninety-nine year lease on bases in Trinidad, but this was given up in 1960, and there remains only a small US satellite tracking station, although the Port of Spain and Chaguaramas naval bases would be made available in an emergency.

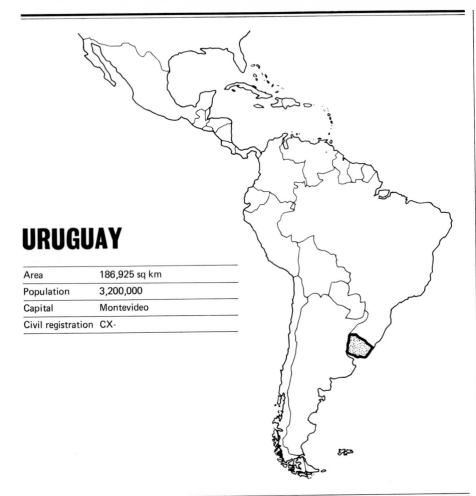

URUGUAY

Area	186,925 sq km
Population	3,200,000
Capital	Montevideo
Civil registration	CX-

The Oriental Republic of Uruguay, once a Spanish possession and for a time a Brazilian province, was granted independence on 25 August 1825 and still remains a primarily agricultural and cattle-raising country. Although it has a generally higher standard of living for peasants than most other Latin-American countries, its political history has been moderately uneventful, with periodical revisions of the constitution and in more recent years a fair degree of urban guerilla warfare by such groups as the Cuban-backed Tupamaros and Montaneros. Despite this background, military service is voluntary, defence spending is low and the police force has a strength of only 2,200 personnel (half of whom are engaged in anti-guerilla operations).

There has been an interest in aeronautical matters in Uruguay since the 1850s, which never disappeared in spite of financial difficulties The first public flights by a heavier-than-air craft took place in 1911-12, the pilot being an Italian, Bartolomeo Cattaneo; but military aviation did not come into being until 1912, when a Naval officer, Alférez de Navio (ensign) Atilio Frigerio, completed flying training in Italy and presented the Uruguayan government with plans for the formation of a flying school. In March 1913, the Minister for War and Navy issued a request for military aviators, to be trained at Los Cerrillos on a Farman biplane (named *El Águila - the eagle*) by an experienced Frenchman, Marcel Paillette, under government contract (financial constraints restricted his contract to three months). Two Army officers were sent to Argentina where they received their wings in 1915; another two were trained at Los Cerrillos in Chile.

On 20 November 1916, an Escuela Militar de Aviación (Military Aviation School) was formed at Paso de Mendoza, near Montevideo under the command of Chilean-trained Capitán Juan Manuel Boiso Lanza. Its initial equipment consisted of five Castaibert monoplanes, four two-seat 913-IV and a 914-V three-seater, designed and built in Argentina by French-born Pablo Castaibert, who was later to organise the Uruguayan military aviation workshops. Capitan Boiso Lanza later joined the French Air

Force as a volunteer pilot and died in a crash in France in August 1918, his name eventually being given to the Paso de Mendoza base.

The Castaiberts, occasionally referred to as Morane-Castaiberts because of superficial similarities with contemporary Morane-Saulnier monoplane designs, were joined in 1917 by two Henry Farmans built in Argentina, the first of which, named *El Águila* in memory of the similarly-named 1913 machine which flew at Los Cerrillos, was delivered in July. At about the same time, Castaibert built a 'Penguin' ground trainer — an aircraft with a low-powered engine and short-span wings, which could be taxied but not flown — which remained in use at the Escuela Militar de Aviación until 1921 when training procedures fully conformed with international standards. Britain supplied four surplus Avro 504K trainers in September 1919, one of which crashed on 2 October due to the inexperience of its crew; another twelve were later obtained, and an additional machine was built by the Escuela Militar de Aviación workshops in 1921. As was customary in those days, they were numbered in sequence; this confusing system, which meant that there were for example a Breguet 14 A2 N° 1 and an Avro 504K N° 1 flying at the same time, was not discarded until after the Second World War.

1921 was the year of French assistance, which had begun in December of the previous year with the delivery of the first of eight SPAD XIII fighters. France handed over six Breguet 14 A2 bombers and two 14T ambulances (a more modern 14Tbis arrived in 1928), and six Nieuport 83 trainers were promised, arriving in the following year. A single Airco DH.9 bomber was received from Britain. In 1923, partly due to the fact that Uruguay had a substantial Italian colony, Italy delivered four Ansaldo biplanes, one an A.1 Balilla , two SVA.5 fighters and an SVA.10 reconnaissance bomber. On 15 January 1924, the first operational unit, an Ecuadrilla de Caza (Fighter Squadron) was officially formed with a pair of SPAD XIII. An Italian-built Schreck-FBA flying-boat, named *Zambra* was donated to the service in 1924, and Britain supplied a single

Martinsyde F.4 Buzzard biplane fighter for evaluation. With all the limitations imposed by Uruguay's precarious financial situation, the service was slowly expanding and the country was more air-minded than ever before. In 1925, Paso de Mendoza (Camino Mendoza according to some documents) became a staging post for the Latécoère airliners flying between Rio de Janeiro in Brazil and Buenos Aires in Argentina. A Uruguayan airline, Aeroposta Uruguaya, was also formed, although it never had any aircraft and its only airfield, Pando, was sold to the government for military use. An attempt to cross the South Atlantic by four Uruguayan officers, on an Italian-built Dornier Super Wal named *Uruguay* ended in tragedy in February 1927, but other endurance flights were successfully accomplished. A few SPAD XII two-seat biplanes and more Breguets were taken on charge as were seven Breguet 19 A2 general purpose biplanes and no less than twenty-four Nieuport 27 single-seat fighters. Two modified Breguets, powered by the 450hp Lorraine-Dietrich 12Eb and referred to as Breguet Montevideos, were built locally in 1928, one of them flying on floats for a period; the other crashed in Colombia whilst en route from Montevideo to New York. At that time the service had sixty-four aircraft on charge.

Seven Potez 25TOE two-seat general purpose aircraft were procured in France in 1929, serving until 1942 under a variety of conditions without a single fatal crash. In January 1935, they were used for ground-attack duties against anti-government rebels with considerable success; the uprising was put down in a matter of weeks, largely because of the skilled use of air power. By that time, several new airfields were in use — Salto and Tacuarembó in the north, Cerro Largo and Treinta y Tres (thus named as a tribute to the 'Immortal thirty-three' heroes of independence) in the east, Durazno in the centre, Paysandú in the west and Rocha and Maldonado in the south.

A medical evacuation branch (Aviación Sanitaria) was formed in 1930 with two Breguet 14Tbis, under Ministry of Public Health control; these were

little used and were supplanted in 1933 by a Farman 190 and later by a de Havilland DH.89 Dragon Rapide CX-ABU c/n 6333. Replacement Potez 25TOE arrived by sea an October 1932 but the desperate need for new aircraft for the Escuela de Aviación Militar could not be met at the time. A limited re-organisation took place in 1934, the Potez 25TOE being allocated to four Patrullas (Flights); at the same time twenty-five aircraft were struck off charge as unserviceable — seven Breguet 14 A2, seventeen Avro 504K and a Morane-Saulnier MS.35. More far-reaching changes took place in 1935: on 31 December, the service was renamed as the Aeronáutica Militar Uruguaya, controlling two air bases, the training school now known as the Escuela Militar de Aeronáutica, repair and storage facilities, and the whole of civil flying in the country. Limited funds were made available for aircraft procurement, a Hanriot 431 Trainer being obtained in 1936; in October of the same year, the Farman 190 ambulance was extensively overhauled and restored to service (it eventually became CX-ABH). In 1937 the Escuela re-equipped with eighteen de Havilland DH.82A Tiger Moths (serials E.1 to E.18, c/ns 3288, 3310/3313, 3499, 3503/3505, 3612/3620) and moved in November to Pando airfield, by then named Aeródromo Militar General Artigas. Six IMAM Ro 37bis reconnaissance biplanes were purchased in Italy and a Stinson SR.7B Reliant (Serial S-1, later 500) in the United States, the latter being allotted for the personal use of the Commander-in-Chief.

Ten two-seat Waco JHD general purpose biplanes, based on the commercial SH3D were purchased directly from the manufacturers and operated for many years with a fair degree of reliability; the first six had c/ns 4710 to 4715. A Breda Ba 64 transport came from Italy.

In 1939 the Aeronáutica Militar was under Army control, and comprised five Divisiones:

1ª División - Headquarters, staff and airstrips.

2ª División - Base Aeronáutica N° 1 Capitán Boiso Lanza, Camino Mendoza;
Base Aeronáutica N° 2 Teniente 2°

Mario Walter Parallada, Durazno.

3ª *División* - Escuela Militar de Aeronáutica, Aeródromo Militar General Artigas, Pando.

4ª *División* - Workshops, stores and supply services at Base Aeronáutica Nº 1

5ª *División* - Dirección General de la Aeronáutica Civil (Directorate General of Civil Aeronautics)

In March 1940, the Order of Battle was as follows:

Base Aeronáutica Nº 1
Escuadrilla de Información (Reconnaissance Squadron) with three Waco JHD, plus a base flight with a Hanriot biplane trainer with provision for a survey camera and Tiger Moth E-15.

Base Aeronáutica Nº 2
Escuadrilla de Información with three Ro 37bis and two Potez 25 (detached to it but independently controlled) and a base flight with Tiger Moths E-16 and E-17.

Grupo de Reserva General (General Reserve Group)
Escuadrilla de Informacion and Escuadrilla de Bombardeo, each with three Potez 25TOE, and a base flight with Tiger Moth E-4.

Escuela Militar de Aeronáutica
Nine Tiger Moths, two Potez 25TOE and a DH.89 Dragon Rapide ambulance

División de Talleres, Almacenes Generales y Servicios (Workshop, Stores and Services Department)
Farman 190 ambulance, the executive Stinson Reliant and a communications Tiger Moth.

In June 1940 Uruguay agreed to place a number of air bases at the disposal of the United States government in case of an emergency and later became eligible for Lend-Lease deliveries. The first batch arrived in mid-December 1941, days after the Pearl Harbor attack and comprised some much-needed modern equipment: the first few North American AT-6 Texan advanced trainers and seven Curtiss SNC-1 basic trainers. Fifty Fairchild PT-19 and PT-26 were delivered in 1942 to replace the Tiger

Moths, followed by the first of ten Beechcraft AT-11 crew trainers. 1943 deliveries were limited to single examples of the Beechcraft UC-43 and UC-45 which were allocated to the Escuela Militar de Aeronáutica, and three Piper AE-1 Cub ambulances and a Beechcraft AT-10 were delivered in 1944.

An American air mission arrived in January 1947 to reorganise the Uruguayan Air Force and did not take long before the need was understood to create a transport force as well as an effective operational element. A Grupo de Aviación de Bombardeo was formed (on paper only) in April at Aeródromo Militar General Artigas, and seven AT-6 Texans and five AT-11 Kansans were delivered in November, being officially taken on charge in May 1948. The first two Douglas C-47 transports arrived in 1947, theoretical training procedures were modernised in 1948-49, and the bomber group, renamed as the Grupo de Aviación Nº 3 was transferred (still on paper only) to Base Aeronáutica Nº 1. Other aircraft including three Ryan L-17B Navion light transports were eventually delivered and a civil airline, PLUNA (Primeras Líneas Uruguayas de Navegación Aérea - First Uruguayan Air Navigation Routes) was established under military control, although for the time being on paper only.

Eleven North American B-25J Mitchell medium bombers arrived in June 1950 to equip Grupo de Aviación Nº 1, the first unit of an operational Brigada; another three B-25J and a B-25H were taken on charge later. The Brigada also comprised Grupo de Aviación Nº 2 with twenty-five North American F-51D Mustang fighters delivered in November and December 1950. The much-needed transport unit, Grupo de Aviación Nº 4, was formed at Carrasco in March 1951 with five Douglas C-47 and a Beechcraft UC-45; in May, Grupo 2 was declared operational, and PLUNA was finally established in the November. Finally the Aeronáutica Militar Uruguaya became the Fuerza Aérea Uruguaya on 4 December 1953, with complete autonomy from the Army and controlled by the Ministry of National Defence. In October of the following year, ten additional

T-6 Texans were supplied by the USA, and in January 1955 nine de Havilland Canada DHC.1 Chipmunk primary trainers were taken on charge.

But this was not all. The first Bell H-13G helicopters arrived in July 1955 and in August the Grupo de Aviación Nº 1 was provisionally moved to Durazno as a tactical reconnaissance unit. The inscription *Fuerza Aérea Uruguaya* became mandatory on transports in May 1956 — an indication of the new pride in the service, which was enhanced with the arrival of four Lockheed T-33A in late October. These were Uruguay's first jet aircraft and were allocated to Grupo de Aviacion Nº 2 in preparation for the delivery of F-80C fighters. The first five F-80C Shooting Stars arrived in April 1958 and were based at Carrasco (Montevideo) which was then the only airfield capable of accepting jet aircraft. Grupo 2 had totally converted to the new type in 1960 and four of the surviving Mustangs, no longer needed, were transferred to the Bolivian Air Force. The Mustang was declared obsolete in June 1960.

A military airline, Transporte Aéreo Militar Uruguayo (TAMU), was formed in August 1961, serving a number of routes within the country and later to Argentina, Brazil and Paraguay; Bolivia was added to the network in December. A Servicio de Comunicaciones y Electrónica (Electronics and Communications Service) was activated in March 1963, and in August of the same year the last B-25J Mitchells were declared surplus to requirements. A SAR Group (Grupo de Búsqueda y Rescate) was established at Base Aeronáutica Nº 1 in December 1963. The three Air Commands (Comandos Aéreos) currently extant were formed in July 1965. In 1969 Grupo de Aviación Nº 1 changed its rôle from tactical reconnaissance to advanced training.

The F-80C Shooting Stars were withdrawn from service as the US-supplied Cessna A-37B became available, and the Escuela took delivery of seven Cessna T-41D. Twelve ex-Argentine Air Force North American F-86F Sabres which were to have been supplied in late 1976, were vetoed by the United States government in one of the State Department's periodic changes of foreign policy. The most recent acquisitions have been a Fokker F.27-100 Friendship donated by the Netherlands Government, a VIP Lear Jet 35A, a couple of Bell 212 for SAR duties, and a batch of variously-equipped CASA 212s in the process of delivery from Spain.

Military Air Bases

1   Montevideo (Carrasco, Capitan Boiso Lanza)
2   Salto
3   Paysandú
4   Mercedes
5   Colonía del Sacramento
6   Tacuarembó
7   Durazno (Santa Bernardina)
8   Melo
9   Treinta y Tres
10   Pando
11   Canelones (General Artigas)
12   Laguna del Sauce
13   Rocha

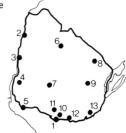

Current Organisation

The Fuerza Aérea Uruguaya presently has about three thousand personnel, and is organised as follows.

Comando Aero-Táctico (CAT, Tactical Air Command)
Brigada Aérea Nº 1 at Base Aeronáutica Nº 1 Capitán Boiso Lanza, Carrasco :

  Grupo de Aviación Nº 2 (Caza)   Cessna A-37B, Lockheed T-33A
  Grupo de Aviación Nº 3 (Transporte)   Douglas C-47, CASA 212 Aviocar
  Grupo de Aviación Nº 4 (Transporte)   Fokker F.27/Fairchild FH.227D, Beech Queen Air 80
  Grupo de Aviación Nº 5 (Búsqueda y Rescate) Bell UH-1B/H, 212, Hiller OH-23F, Cessna U-17A
  Grupo de Aviación Nº 6 (Transporte)   Embraer EMB.110 Bandeirante

Brigada Aérea Nº 2 at Base Aeronáutica Nº 2 Teniente Segundo Mario Walter Parallada, Santa Bernardina Airport, Durazno :

  Grupo de Aviación Nº 1 (Instrucción y Entrenamiento)   Beechcraft T-34A/B, North American T-6
  Escuadrilla de Enlaces -   Cessna 182 and Piper Super Cub

Comando Aéreo de Entrenamiento (CADE, Air Training Command)
Escuela Militar de Aeronáutica at Aeropuerto Militar General Artigas, Pando - Cessna T-41D, Beechcraft
                                      T-34B and North American T-28/Sud Fennec.
Escuela Técnica de Aeronáutica (Air Technical School) -non-flying unit
Escuela de Comando y Estado-Mayor (Command and General Staff School) - non-flying unit

Comando Aéreo de Material (CAM, Air Material Command)
Brigada de Mantenimiento y Abastecimiento (Maintenance and supply brigade) - non-flying unit
Brigada de Comunicaciones y Electrónica (Communications and electronics brigade) - non-flying unit
Dirección de Aeródromos (Directorate of Airfields) - non-flying unit

The *Dirección General de Aeropuertos Nacionales (DIGAN, Directorate-General of National Airports)* is also under FAU control.

The transport Grupos form Transporte Aéreo Militar Uruguayo (TAMU) which shares its aircraft with PLUNA (since that airline's re-organisation in 1974) on its domestic routes; these aircraft carry both FAU serials and civil registrations.

Mention must be made of a FAU airfield of some importance, although without resident units; the Aeródromo Ángel S Adami at Melilla.

Grupo 2 - sky blue disc with a thin black outline; black and white cat with white outlined whiskers, red mouth, black claws; grey and black mouse; yellow lightning flash.

Grupo de Caza Nº 2 - an air force blue shield edged in yellow; white aircraft with a red trail from a brown ball. The scroll is blue with yellow lettering.

Aircraft Review

COLOURS AND MARKINGS

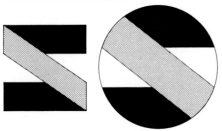

The first Uruguayan military aircraft were marked with the flag of the independence hero General José Gervasio Artigas — horizontal blue/white/blue stripes with a diagonal red band — on their rudders and this design was subsequently used as the basis for the Uruguayan roundel. Delivery colour schemes are retained in service, and the inscription *Fuerza Aérea Uruguaya* appears on some transport aircraft.

AIRCRAFT SERIALS

FAU serials follow a simple system introduced after the Second World War, and are allocated within the following blocks:

001 to 099	helicopters
100 to 199	bombers and crew trainers
200 to 299	fighters and advanced trainers
300 to 399	advanced and basic trainers
400 to 499	(reserved)
500 to 599	transports
600 to 699	primary trainers
700 to 799	communications
800 to 899	miscellaneous types

Prefixes to serial numbers were at one time used extensively, consisting of B for Base Aeronáutica or G for Grupo de Aviación followed by the respective Base or Grupo number. However, these have been discontinued, and the only prefix in current use is T for transport, and even this is sometimes dropped.

Aircraft known to have been used by the Fuerza Aérea Uruguaya since 1945 are :

BEECHCRAFT UC-43

One only, serialled 501

BEECHCRAFT AT-11 KANSAN

Ten aircraft serialled 100 to 109. Prefixed serials included B2-100, B2-101, G3-107. At least one AT-11 was converted for photo-survey and operated by Grupo de Aviación N°3. Aircraft 101 was preserved at the Museo Nacional de Aviación; another two were converted to partial C-45 standards.

BEECHCRAFT C-45 EXPEDITOR

An early UC-45 was delivered in 1943 and seven C-45F after the war. Known serials are 501 to 506 (ex G4-501 to G4-506) and 540. Two AT-11 converted to partial C-45 standards were also serialled 503 and 504. No longer in use.

BEECHCRAFT T-34 MENTOR

Over forty T-34A and T-34B believed delivered, including 25 T-34B during 1977-78. Known serials are T-34A 650 and T-34B 660 to 684.

BEECHCRAFT QUEEN AIR A65

Two delivered to Grupo de Aviacion N°4 :

T-540	c/n LC....	w/o 1972
T-541/CX-BKP	LC.326	

Five more delivered in November 1978 :

T-542/CX-BKU	LC.317
T-543/CX-BKQ	LC.266
T-544/CX-BKR	LC.279
T-545/CX-BKS	LC.294
T-546	

BELL OH-13G

Two were delivered in April 1955 to Grupo de Aviación N°5

BR-001	c/n 1253	ex 53-3805
BR-002	1254	53-3806

The BR- prefix (Búsqueda y Rescate) was probably used to avoid confusion with two similarly-serialled naval helicopters

BELL UH-1B/H IROQUOIS

Used by Grupo de Aviación N°5. Known machines are UH-1B 060 to 065 (ex US Army 60-3565, 61-703, 61-713, 62-2105, 63-8711, 63-8735, but not necessarily in that order), and UH-1H 050 to 055, of which 053 has been written off.

BELL 212

Two acquired in 1981 for SAR duties.

BELL 222

One serialled 071, c/n 47036.

CASA 212 AVIOCAR

Deliveries of this Spanish twin transport began in July 1981. They are operated by Grupo de Aviacion N°3. 534 is a long-nosed maritime/SAR version.

530/CX-BOF	c/n CC28-1-186	d/d 7.81
531/CX-BOG	CC28-2-187	7.81
532	A28-1-189	8.81
533	A28-2-198	11.81
534	AS28-1-229	1.82

CESSNA 182D

Two aircraft are known :

523	c/n 53548	became 740
524	53549	741

A Cessna 182A serialled 742 has also been reported.

CESSNA 310L

One only, serialled 542, ex CX-ARA, written off 1977.

CESSNA T-41D

At least seven aircraft :
```
601   c/n R172-0392   ex 69-7675
602       R172-0393      69-7676
603       R172-0394      69-7677
604       R172-0395      69-7678
605       R172-0396      69-7679   w/o 10.75
606       R172-0452      70-2027
607       R172-0494      70-2456
```

CESSNA U-17A

Ten aircraft delivered mid-sixties, serialled 750 to 759. At least 755 and one other are equipped for SAR duties.

CESSNA A-37B

Eight aircraft were delivered to Grupo de Aviación Nº2, to replace F-80C Shooting Stars :
```
270   ex USAF 75-410
271           75-411
272           75-412
273           75-413
274           75-414
275           75-415
276           75-416
277           75-417
```

CURTISS SNC-1 FALCON

Seven were delivered in December 1941 and later serialled G2-201 to G2-207. Aircraft G2-205 was preserved in the Museo Nacional de Aviación.

DE HAVILLAND CANADA DHC.1 CHIPMUNK

Ten Canadian-built aircraft were supplied as E-600 to E-609 (prefix later dropped). They had a short career in the FAU and were handed over to civilian flying clubs. The Museo Nacional de Aviación has aircraft 608.

DE HAVILLAND CANADA DHC.2 BEAVER

One only, serialled 852, c/n 252 ex N1547V, delivered in 1952 and disposed of as N9LB.

DOUGLAS C-47 SKYTRAIN

At least eighteen have been taken on charge, the first two (507 and 508) in 1947-48; other deliveries were 515 on 11.12.61, 516 and 517 (ex Dutch X-15, X-17) on 31.8.62, 518/521 ex USAF in 1962, 522 ex USAF on 10.3.69, and 523/524 ex PLUNA in 5.72. Ten remain in service. Prefixes were used temporarily; for instance G4-507 and G4-510 became 507 and 510, and the latter was eventually flown as T-510.

```
507   C-47A c/n 13823/25268  ex 43-48007
508   C-47A     13744            42-93793  c/s CX-BJD
509   C-47A     13946/25391      43-48130      CX-BHO
510   C-47A     19021            42-100558     CX-BJG
511   C-47A     19301            42-100838     CX-BJH
                                             w/o 12.2.78
512   C-47A     13947/25392      43-48131
513   C-47A     19617            43-15151
514   C-47A     20604            43-16138      CX-BKH
515   TC-47B    16022/32770      44-76438
516   C-47A     14163/25608      43-48347      CX-BHP
517   C-47B     16663/33411      44-77079
518   C-47B     14538/25983      43-48722
519   C-47B     16683/33431      44-77099      CX-BHQ
520   C-47B     15178/26623      43-49362      wfu
521   C-47A     19231            42-100768     CX-BHR
522   C-47B     14288/25733      43-48472
T-523 C-47A     9226             42-23364,CX-AQC
T-524 C-47      4471             41-18409,CX-AIJ
```

EMBRAER EMB.110 BANDEIRANTE

Five EMB.110C transports were delivered in September and October of 1975 for joint use by TAMU and PLUNA; the T-prefix was at first not used.
```
T-580/CX-BJJ  c/n 110.076  ex PT-GJI
T-581/CX-BJK      110.079     PT-GJJ
T-582/CX-BJB      110.081     PT-GJK
T-583/CX-BJC      110.082     PT-GJL
T-584/CX-BJE      110.083     PT-GJM  w/o 22.6.77
```
A single EMB.110B1 with photo-survey capability was obtained in August 1978 :
```
T-585/CX-BKF      110.187
```

FAIRCHILD PT-19/PT-26

At least sixty PT-19 and PT-26 were delivered; known serials are PT-19 630 to 639 and PT-26/PT-19 640 to 689. Serials with prefixes included B1-674 and 'SC-753'. A PT-26 was

transferred to the Navy; others became CX-AXC, CX-AVG (c/n T42-3109) and CX-AYD (c/n T42-1732). Another, c/n T43-5512 is derelict at Montevideo's Ángel S Adami airfield and PT-19 634 is preserved in the Museo Nacional de Aviación.

FAIRCHILD FH.227D

Three aircraft operated by TAMU and PLUNA :
```
T-570/CX-BHX  c/n 571  ex N2744R  d/d 19.7.71
T-571/CX-BHY      572     N2745R     8.71 w/o 13.10.72
T-572/CX-BIM      574     N2785R     24.8.73
```
The T-prefix was not used initially.

FMA IA.58 PUCARA

Six were ordered in November 1980 for delivery in April of 1981.

FOKKER F.27 FRIENDSHIP 100

Two aircraft, initially with unprefixed serials, delivered to TAMU on 10.12.70 and 11.3.70 respectively :
```
T-560/CX-BHV  c/n 10199  ex LN-SUW/PH-FDN
T-561/CX-BHW      10202     PH-FDR
```

HILLER OH-23F

Four were delivered to Grupo de Aviación Nº5, two in 1964 and two in 1966 :
```
026   c/n 2297  ex 64-14850
027       2298     64-14851
028       5115     67-14867
029       5116     67-14868  reported sold as VH-FFT
```
One crashed in 1967.

LEAR JET 35A

One VIP aircraft acquired in 1981, serial 500 c/n 35A-378.

LOCKHEED T-33A

Eight aircraft serialled 201 to 208 plus a spare airframe (209) were delivered to Grupo de Aviación Nº2 and three remain in service as AT-33A.

Beechcraft Queen Air A65 540, the first of seven delivered, was written off in 1972.

Cessna A-37B 272 at Wichita in November 1976 before delivery to Grupo de Aviación N°2.

Fairchild FH.227D T-570/CX-BHX, one of five Friendships delivered to TAMU.

Beechcraft C-45 Expeditor 504, in fact an AT-11 converted to approximate C-45 standards.

Cessna U-17A 755, one of ten delivered in the mid sixties.

Lockheed T-33A 205 at Montevideo-Carrasco in December 1976.

North American T-6G Texan 370.

LOCKHEED F-80C SHOOTING STAR

At least seventeen aircraft, serialled 210 to 226 and used by Grupo de Aviación N°2 until withdrawn from use in 1971. Identified aircraft are 210 ex 47-202 and 218 ex 49-432, the latter delivered on 17.6.58. Aircraft 213 has been preserved at the Museo Nacional de Aviación at Montevideo.

NORTH AMERICAN T-6 TEXAN

The first few aircraft arrived in December 1941; the next seven in November 1947. Subsequent deliveries brought the total to about fifty, with serials between 330 and 379. Prefixes used were B2, G1 and S. Six of the aircraft delivered in 1947 were ex USAAF 42-3903, 43960, 44014, 44393, 49045 and 84375. The last two to be acquired were given the re-allocated serials 378 and 379, and were AT-6D presented by Chile on 17.3.78, having formerly been FACh 200 and 201. Known aircraft include :

AT-6B	330, 331, 332, 333, 334, 335, 336
AT-6C	341, 342, 343, 344
AT-6D	337, 339, 352
T-6G	354, 356, 366, 369, 370, 371, 372, 373, 374, 375, 376 (preserved), 377, 378, 379.

NORTH AMERICAN B-25 MITCHELL

Eleven B-25J were delivered in June 1950 with serials G3-150 to G3-160; previous USAF serials (not in order) : 44-30269, 30273, 30461, 30593, 30604, 30723, 30729, 30735, 30743, 30878 and 31190. Another three B-25J, G3-161 to G3-163 and a B-25H G3-164 were delivered in 1952. The prefix was later deleted (note the use of G3- instead of the correct G1-). Aircraft G3-158 was preserved at the Museo Nacional de Aviación.

NORTH AMERICAN F-51D MUSTANG

Twenty-five were delivered to Grupo de Aviación N°2 as G2-251 to G2-275 (prefixes later omitted). G2-262 was ex USAF 44-63559; the others (not in order) were ex 44-63392, 63476, 63478, 63485, 63492, 63508, 63517, 63518, 63530, 63535, 63549, 63557, 63575, 63577, 63593, 63594, 63611, 63613, 63615, 63618, 63750, 63807 plus one other. They were declared surplus in June 1960; 44-63807 and three others were transferred to the Bolivian Air Force, and aircraft 265 preserved at the Museo Nacional de Aviación.

NORTH AMERICAN T-28A (SUD FENNEC)

Eighteen aircraft acquired 1979-1980 from Argentine Navy stocks, serialled 401 to 418.

PIPER AE-1 (L-4) CUB

Three were delivered in 1944 and later given the serials 700 to 702; 701 is displayed at the Museo Nacional de Aviación.

PIPER PA.18 SUPER CUB 150

Two aircraft only, originally 530 and 531 but later reserialled as 730 and 731.

PIPER PA.23 APACHE 235

One aircraft, serialled 503, apprehended from smugglers. 503 has also been reported as a Piper PA.12 Super Cruiser !

RYAN L-17B NAVION

Three aircraft serialled B2-521 to B2-523. The B2- prefix, indicating Base Aeronáutica N°2 was later omitted.

Uruguayan Navy

Although some of the first Uruguayan aviation pioneers were naval officers, the naval air arm, or Servicio Aeronáutico de la Armada (Naval Air Service) was not formed until 7 February 1925. An air station was planned at Isla Libertad, but bureaucratic complications delayed its activation for many years. Flying training began at the Escuela Militar de Aeronáutica in 1926, but the first naval aircraft were taken on charge four years later in September 1930, being three flying boats of Italian origin: two Cant 18 trainers serialled A-1 and A-2 and powered by a 250hp Isotta-Fraschini Asso 200, and a reconnaissance Cant 21 serialled A-3, with the 520hp Asso 500 engine. They initially operated from the Santa Lucia river, with a bare minimum of facilities - the ground crews had to carry the aircrews on their shoulders to the aircraft, there being no slipways or boats, and budgetary restrictions prevented their transfer to La Teja, where the Servicio's tiny headquarters were located.

The three flying boats were deployed to Isla Libertad, facing Montevideo, in June 1934; the island had been transferred to Navy jurisdiction in August 1932, but was not suited for operations until 1934 and did not in fact become operational until 1940 ! The Isla Libertad naval air station (Base Aeronaval) was officially inaugurated in June 1938 by which time a Cant 18 had been lost (A-2 which crashed on 5 January 1935) and the two surviving machines formed the whole of Uruguay's naval aviation. The other Cant 18 was grounded in 1940 but the Cant 21 remained in service until the arrival of six Vought OS2U-3 Kingfisher floatplanes which, together with three Fairchild PT-23 primary trainers and one interned Grumman J4F-2 amphibious transport, were part of a post-Pearl Harbor agreement between the United States and Uruguayan governments. The Kingfishers had a long operational life being finally retired in 1958. During 1942, consideration was given to the establishment of another

Base Aeronaval at Laguna del Sauce, with Laguna Negra and La Paloma scheduled for use as flying boat stations. Construction work began at Laguna del Sauce in 1945, and it was activated as Base Aeronaval N° 2 in September 1947.

No further aircraft were received during the war or in the immediate postwar years as there were simply no funds available. However, US aid was resumed in 1949 with the delivery of ten Grumman TBM-1C Avengers which arrived in December and were followed by another six TBM-1C and TBF-1 in May 1950; the latter were accompanied by a trio of North American SNJ-4 Texan advanced trainers. During the same year, the Isla Libertad base was reduced to depot status and seaplane facilities provided at Punta del Este. Lagune del Sauce then became the main base.

A reorganisation in 1951 changed the Servicio's name to Aviación Naval; the Uruguayan Air Force handed over a Fairchild PT-26, to which standard the three PT-23, initially radial-powered, had been converted; and plans were made for the formation of an operational element, which materialised on 22 April 1952 with the arrival of ten United States Navy surplus Grumman F6F-5 Hellcat fighters. The Hellcats equipped a fighter squadron until grounded in 1961, no replacements being procured.

The Aviación Naval's first helicopters, two Bell 47G, were delivered in 1955 at the same time as a pair of Piper Super Cubs were obtained; another two Bell 47G-2 and two Hiller UH12E-4 were later delivered as were three additional SNJ-4 Texans. The first of three Martin PBM-5 Mariner flying boats arrived in May 1956 from NAS Pensacola (the other two followed in 1957), mainly to replace the Avengers on coastal patrol duties and allow them to be allocated to the Escuela de Especialización Aeronaval (Naval Air Conversion School), which had been activated in June 1952 with a few Avengers and Texans. The Escuela, which is still very much operational, was named after Capitán de Corbata (Corvette Captain) Mayo Villagrán in December 1970.

Re-equipment on an extensive scale, although still limited through financial shortages, began in the early 1960s. The Avengers were withdrawn in 1960 and the Grumman S-2A (S2F-1) Tracker was selected as their replacement; crew-training began in 1965 and three aircraft were delivered in 1969-70. A transport flight was formed with three Beechcraft SNB-5 (C-45J), and a single Beechcraft T-34B Mentor arrived in 1966. There was a requirement for transport helicopters, and the Sikorsky SH-34J with ASW capability was selected as ideal for the job; two were obtained in 1971 but crashed after only a few weeks; two replacements were delivered later. The Argentine Navy also gave some assistance to the Aviación Naval. In 1970 two North American SNJ-5 Texans were presented, and more recently, in November 1979, three Beechcraft TC-45J.

The present-day Aviación Naval Uruguaya is made up of a training element with a single Beechcraft T-34B and three newly-delivered T-34C, three Beechcraft TC-45J (which double as light transports), four SNJ Texans and two Piper Super Cubs; a helicopter flight with a Bell 47G-2, two Sikorsky SH-34J and a new SAR Bell 222; three Grumman S-2A Trackers for ASW and rescue duties and a new maritime patrol Beechcraft Super King Air 200. The main base is Base Aeronaval Capitán de Corbeta Carlos A Curbelo, Laguna del Sauce, on the River Plate estuary, where the Escuela de Especialización Aeronaval Capitán de Corbata Mayo Villagrán is also based.

Aircraft Review

COLOURS AND MARKINGS

Uruguayan naval aircraft have similar markings to those of the air force, but have the national flag (Sun and Stripes) painted on their rudders, and sometimes an anchor marking on the wings, and/or the inscription *Armada*.

AIRCRAFT SERIALS

Three digit serials are used, the A- prefix having been dropped of late for newly-acquired aircraft. Equipment known to have been used during postwar years by the Aviación Naval Uruguaya is :

BEECHCRAFT SNB-5 (C-45J)

Three were delivered :
A-210   ex Bu.39759
A-211
A-212   Bu.51041
Three ex Argentine Navy TC-45J were taken on charge in November 1979 :
215
216
217

BEECHCRAFT T-34B/C MENTOR

One T-34B Mentor, delivered in 1966 :
A-260
Three T-34C-1 Turbo-Mentor delivered May 1981 :
270
271
272

BEECHCRAFT SUPER KING AIR 200T

One aircraft delivered in October 1980 and equipped for maritime patrol :
AU-871   c/n BT.4 (ex c/n BB.408)   ex N2067D

BELL 47G

The first two Bell 47G were delivered in August 1955 :
A-051   c/n 1411
A-052   1444
Two Bell 47G-2 later obtained :
A-053
A-054

BELL 222

One helicopter obtained late 1980 for SAR duties.

FAIRCHILD PT-23/PT-26

Deliveries comprised three PT-23A in 1942 (A-201 to A-203) later converted to PT-19 standards, and a former Uruguayan Air Force PT-26 (A-204) which crashed in 1957.

GRUMMAN F6F-5 HELLCAT

Ten aircraft in all, A401/406 and A-451/454 ferried from the USA by Aviación Naval crews and arriving on 22.4.52. Withdrawn from use in 1961.

GRUMMAN J4F-2 WIDGEON

One only, A-751, received in 1942.

GRUMMAN TBF/TBM AVENGER

A total of nineteen Avengers were taken on charge. A-501 to A-510 have been reported as TBF-1 and TBM-1; A-551 to A-559 were TBM-1C. The last surviving machines were grounded in 1960.

GRUMMAN S-2A TRACKER

Three aircraft only :

A-851	ex Bu 133215	d/d	11.69
A-852	133239		11.69
A-853	133262		25.3.70

HILLER UH12E-4

Two helicopters serialled A-001 and A-002. One crashed in 1964; the other was withdrawn from use.

MARTIN PBM-5 MARINER

Three aircraft, all scrapped in 1963 :

A-810	d/d	12.5.56
A-811		2.57
A-812		3.57

NORTH AMERICAN SNJ TEXAN

Deliveries comprised six SNJ-4 serialled A-251 to A-256, of which A-254 is known to have crashed, and two ex Argentine Navy SNJ-5, A-257 which was written off, and A-258. Four remain in service; A-252 is on static display outside the Escuela de Aviación Naval.

PIPER PA-18 SUPER CUB 150

Two aircraft, A-754 and A-755, delivered in 1955.

SIKORSKY SH-34J

Two delivered during 1971 :
A-061   ex Bu 143934
A-062   143941
Both were written off on 4.11.71 and replaced by A-063 and A-064 which remain in service. Another aircraft A-065 was acquired but was withdrawn from use by 1978 and an A-066 was acquired for spares use only and did not wear its serial.

VOUGHT OS2U-3 KINGFISHER

Six were delivered initially with codes OP-1 to OP-6 (OP- for observation and patrol); these were later serialled A-601 to A-606, and were ex US Navy Bu5926/5931. Another two arrived later, and were serialled A-752 and A-753.

Beechcraft T-34C-1 Turbo-Mentor 270 and 271, two of three delivered in May 1981.

VENEZUELA

Area	912,047 sq km
Population	15,200,000
Capital	Caracas
Civil registration	YV-

The Republic of Venezuela (Little Venice) was discovered in 1498 by Christopher Columbus and separated itself from the Greater Colombia Federation in 1830. It is a leading producer of oil (the world's fourth) but both agriculture and industry contribute towards maintaining a fairly stable economy, which reflects itself in a stable political situation, although there have been several military coups in the past and the problem posed by the Cuban-sponsored National Liberation guerillas has not yet been solved. Conscription is mandatory for males aged eighteen and over, although recruit intake depends on a government-controlled lottery system.

A Venezuelan military air service was created by presidential decree on 17 April 1920 and an Academia Aeronáutica (Air Academy) inaugurated in December at Maracay in the state of Aragua. A French air mission arrived in January 1921, at the same time as the service's first aircraft — twelve Caudron G.III and G.IV, two Farman F.40 and two F.70. When the French left in early 1923, the Servicio de Aeronáutica Militar was fully established although flying was suspended until another French adviser was signed on in August 1924, by which time there were airfields at Maracay, Caracas, Carabobo, San Juan de los Morros, Ocumare and Puerto Cabello. The second half of the 1920s saw a slow expansion of the service due to the meagre financial support provided by the government, and aircraft procurement was limited to four additional Caudron G.III to make up attrition and four Caudron C.60, followed in 1928 by the first combat aircraft, twelve Breguet 19 A2 (reconnaissance) and 19 B2 (Bomber) biplanes which saw limited use during the 1929 revolution. Additional airfields were inaugurated at Ciudad Bolívar, Barinas, Baraquisimeto and San Fernando to mention but a few. A Curtiss JN and an Italian SAML Aviatik were also obtained during the 1920s for evaluation.

In 1930 provision was made for the creation of a tactical force but the idea had to be put aside until 1936. During the early 1930s German emigrés were busy establishing airline services all over South

America and the Venezuelan government was far-sighted enough to follow this lead. A specialist engineer was obtained from Junkers Flugzeugbau to found what was to become the Aviación Nacional Venezolana (Venezuela National Airline) and eventually the LAV, Línea Aeropostal Venezolana (Venezuelan Air Mail Airline), initially as a military airline with military crews. The idea was to pioneer an airline network throughout the country at the same time giving the Servicio crews much-needed operational experience and familiarising the Venezuelan public — still rather dubious of the practical use of military aviation — with the enormous possibilities of aviation. Curiously enough, the airline's first aircraft came not from Germany, but from France, possibly because of financial limitations, being second-hand (ex Compagnie Générale Aéropostale) Latécoère transports — two Latécoère 28/1, three 28/6 and three 28/9. It is interesting to note that LAV did not become widely accepted by the general public until it introduced a rather unusual publicity campaign — for a limited period, seats were available at no cost!

Three Morane-Saulnier MS.147 and three MS.230 trainers were procured in 1935; from France also came nine Breguet 273 reconnaissance aircraft to supplement the three Breguet 27 acquired in 1933 for evaluation. Three Lioré et Olivier-built Dewoitine 500V monoplane fighters ordered in 1934 arrived late in 1935, just before a major reorganisation, brought about by a more air-minded government, took place in January 1936. Provision was now made for the establishment of a Regimiento de Aviación Militar (Military Aviation Regiment), comprising an Escuadrilla de Caza (Fighter Squadron), an Escuadrilla de Bombardeo Nocturno (Night Bomber Squadron), an Escuadrilla de Reconocimiento y Bombardeo (Reconnaissance and Bombing Squadron) and an Escuadrilla de Vigilancia y Defensa (Surveillance and Defence Squadron). The Regimiento was to operate alongside the training school, now known as the Escuela de Aviación Militar, still at Maracay but with Fleet 10 and 11 primary trainers. The Escuela's duties were reduced

in 1937, when a civil flying school was created — until then, the military were in charge of all flying training — but the much-needed replacement aircraft took some time to arrive, again because of the usual lack of funds.

Three North American NA.16-1GV (NA.45) basic trainers — the forerunners of Lend-Lease AT-6 Texans — were ordered in December 1937 (c/ns 45-693 to 695) followed by three improved NA.16-3 (NA.71) in January 1940 (c/n 71-3074 to 3076). During 1938, an Italian air mission arrived to reorganise the Regimiento de Aviación Militar, bringing along three Fiat CR.32 fighters and a BR.20 twin-engined monoplane bomber, but little was accomplished until September 1939 when war broke out in Europe and the Italians left. From then on, a logical change of policy took place — Venezuela was to obtain most of its military aircraft and technical know-how from the United States, by then actively engaged in expanding its influence in Latin America.

Initial purchases included a Lockheed 12A, a Fairchild 82B and a Bellanca 31-50 Skyrocket (c/n 809, ex NC15015, later sold as TI-69), but no real expansion took place before the United States government agreed to provide some assistance. Orders were placed in 1940 for three Waco UPF7 (c/n 5313 to 5315 delivered on 20 March), three North American NA.16-3 and three Stearman A75L3 (c/n 75619 to 75621) followed late in 1941 by another four A75L3 (c/n 752687 to 752690), five A75B4 (c/n 752682 to 752686) and five armed A76B4. C/n 752686 was eventually sold as TG-CEP-37). Venezuela had by then become eligible for Lend-Lease deliveries in exchange for defence facilities, and these included three Aeronca L-3B and three Piper L4B liaison aircraft, twenty Fairchild PT-19A, twenty-three Vultee BT-13B and twenty North American AT-6 trainers, plus a few Beechcraft AT-7 and AT-11 crew trainers, and a Cessna UC-78 Bobcat light transport. No combat aircraft were supplied, the USA theoretically assuming the country's air defence; but the La Carlota air base in Caracas was inaugurated in 1946.

It was not until Venezuela signed the 1947 Rio Pact that a combat element became reality, mainly due to the changed postwar strategic requirements which demanded that the country be responsible for its own defence. Some twenty Republic F-47D Thunderbolts equipped Escuadrón de Caza N° 10; fourteen North American B-25J Mitchells were received for Escuadrones de Bombardeo N°s 3 and 7, and an effective Escuadrón de Transporte was activated with the first few Douglas C-47. United States instructors and advisers also arrived, and at the same time Venezuelan air and ground crews began to receive training in the USA. When the service became independent from the Army as the Fuerza Aérea Venezolana in 1949 much had been achieved, although there were only a hundred aircraft in the inventory and personnel strength a mere three hundred. Modernisation, made necessary by the renewed importance of oil-producing areas in the postwar world, began in 1950 with an order for twenty four de Havilland Vampire FB.Mk.5 which equipped Escuadrillas A to C of Escuadrón de Caza N°35, activated at Boca del Río (Maracay) in December 1952. The F-47D Thunderbolts were at the time operated by Escuadrón de Caza N°36 and were destined to serve until 1956. The survivors of Escuadrones de Bombardeo N°s 3 and 7 formed Escuadrón de Bombardeo N° 40, which in 1952 received an additional ten B-25J Mitchells to bring it up to full three-Escuadrilla strength. Six English Electric Canberra B.Mk.2 were ordered in 1952 for the new Escuadrón de Bombardeo N°39.

More than two years later, a change of government made extra funds available, and two major orders were placed during 1955 — one for twenty-two USAF surplus North American F-86F Sabres which eventually re-equipped Escuadrón de Caza N°36, and the other for twenty-two de Havilland Venom FB.Mk.54 (the export version of the FB.Mk.4), which formed a third fighter squadron, Escuadrón de Caza N°34. In the mid-1950s, the FAV was already substantially more than a token force, with three fighter, two bomber and two transport squadrons, an efficient training organisation which, apart from the Escuela de Aviación Militar then flying various AT-6 models, included a technical training school and a specialist crews' school. There were five major air bases — Boca del Río (Maracay), Maiquetía (Caracas) and Anzoátegui (Barcelona) were suitable for operation by jet aircraft, whilst Coro (Falcón state) and Maturín (Monagas state) were not. The original transport squadron, now redesignated as Escuadrón de Transporte Nº 1 flew a mixture of Douglas C-47 and Beechcraft D18S/C-45 in addition to a pair of Douglas C-54; and an Escuadrón de Transporte Nº 2 had been formed with eighteen Fairchild C-123B Providers supplied by the USA. An Escuadrón de Reconocimiento was later activated with a mixed complement of Sikorsky S.51 and S.55 and Bell 47G helicopters, with detached Escuadrillas at each of the main air bases.

As the country's economy improved, so did the FAV's expansion plans. Late in 1957 the first of eight Canberra B(I)Mk.8 and two T.Mk.4 arrived for Escuadrilla B of Escuadrón de Bombardeo Nº 39, the earlier B.Mk.2 being allotted to Escuadrilla A. In mid-1959 five Vampire T.Mk.55 trainers were taken on the charge of Escuadrón de Caza Nº 35 and forty-one Beechcraft T-34 Mentors began to replace the Texans of the Escuela de Aviación Militar, although in the event seven were assigned to the Miguel Rodríguez Civil Aviation School under the control of the Ministry of Communications. Despite several military coups and counter-coups between 1958 and 1961, some of which saw limited FAV involvement, aircraft deliveries continued at regular intervals — and at least the 'quartelazos' provided a good excuse to test the operational efficiency of both aircraft and crews! A reorganisation took place in 1961: Escuadrones de Caza Nº 34 *Caciques* (dH Venom), Nº 35 *Panteras* (Vampire) and Nº 36 *Jaguares* (F-86 Sabre) formed Grupo Nº 12, Escuadrones de Bombardeo Nº 39 (Canberra) and Nº 40 (B-25J Mitchell) formed Grupo Nº 13, and Escuadrones de Transporte T1 and T2 formed Grupo Nº 6. Although fifteen Hunting Jet Provost T.52 trainers were ordered in 1962, making Venezuela the second South American

country to acquire basic jet trainers, the political unrest reflected itself in a temporary shortage of procurement funds. Royal Air Force surplus Canberras, already needed as early as 1961, were not ordered until 1965, twelve B.Mk.2 (including some B(I).Mk.2 with gun packs) and two PR.Mk.3 bringing Escuadrón de Bombardeo Nº 39 up to five Escuadrilla strength being received.

The main problem was to find replacement fighters; times had changed and the United States government of the day was not willing to make fighters available to a country showing so little internal stability. Britain could not help at the time, but West Germany agreed to sell fifty-one North American F-86K Sabre interceptors. These were delivered in 1967-68 and re-equipped Escuadrones de Caza Nºs 34 and 35, although a number were kept in storage (four unused examples were sold to Honduras in 1969). New helicopters were also needed and these came from France, twenty Sud SE.3160 Alouette III being ordered. A few light aircraft were purchased in the United States — including twelve Cessna 182N which were to be shared with the Army — and an HS.748 executive

Bell 412 3137, an IFR-equipped aircraft with pop-out floats.

transport came from Britain.

Another modernisation programme was launched in 1971, reflecting a change in US foreign policy as much as Venezuela's understanding of its own needs. A brief evaluation of France's Dassault Mirage and Sweden's SAAB 35X Draken ended with an order for nine Mirage IIIE, four Mirage 5V and two Mirage 5DV (operational trainers). Canada agreed, with United States approval, to supply eighteen Canadair CF-5A and two CF-5D from CAF stocks; and US aid was made to four Lockheed C-130H Hercules for Escuadrón de Transporte Nº 1, sixteen Rockwell OV-10E Bronco close support aircraft to replace the obsolete Mitchells of Escuadrón de Bombardeo Nº 40 and finally twelve Rockwell T-2D Buckeye jet basic trainers for the Escuela de Aviación Militar. Some reorganisation was again called for, and thus the next few years were spent with relatively few new aircraft being ordered — though single examples of the Boeing 737, Douglas DC-9 and Cessna Citation were obtained for executive use, another twelve T-2D arrived in 1977 and an order was placed in 1978 for twenty SAAB-MFI 15 trainers. Assistance was also given to the Army and Navy in the establishment of their own air arms.

The most recent acquisitions have included small numbers of the larger Bell helicopters, the 214 and 412, and a Gulfstream II executive jet. In 1981 a major re-equipment plan was under consideration, and was said to include seventy combat aircraft, perhaps made up of forty-eight F-16 and twenty-two A-7 or A-10 (subject to US approval), twenty or so extra T-37C, seven more Hercules, and forty-eight BAe Hawks, twenty-four of which would be for training and twenty-four for light attack. No order for the Hawk has been formally announced at the time of going to press, and Venezuela's open support for Argentina in the Falklands Islands dispute makes it perhaps unlikely that the contract will in fact come to fruition, but there are aircraft in production marked as being for Venezuela. Two aircraft which are more likely to be delivered in 1982 are two Aeritalia G.222 transports for which an order was announced in April 1982.

Current Organisation

The present-day Fuerza Aérea Venezolana, with some 250 aircraft and a personnel strength of about five thousand all ranks, is controlled by the Ministry of National Defence through a Comandancia General de Aviación (General Air Department) and comprises the following units :

COMANDO AÉREO DE COMBATE (Air Combat Command)

Grupo de Caza Nº 12 - Base Aérea Teniente Vicente Landaeta, Baraquisimeto

Escuadrón de Caza Nº 34	Canadair CF-5A/D
Escuadrón de Caza Nº 35	Canadair CF-5A/D
Escuadrón de Caza Nº 36	Dassault Mirage IIIEV, 5V, 5DV

Grupo de Bombardeo Nº 13 - Base Aérea Teniente Luis del Valle García, Barcelona

Escuadrón de Bombardeo Nº 38	English Electric Canberra
Escuadrón de Bombardeo Nº 39	English Electric Canberra
Escuadrón de Bombardeo Nº 40	Rockwell OV-10E Bronco

COMANDO AÉREO LOGISTICO (Air Logistics Command)

Grupo de Transporte Nº 6 - Base Aérea Francisco de Miranda, La Carlota-Caracas (recently detached to Base Aérea El Libertador, Palo Negro)

Escuadrón de Transporte Nº 1	Douglas C-47, Lockheed C-130H Hercules
Escuadrón de Transporte Nº 2	Fairchild C-123B Provider
Escuadrón de Helicópteros Nº 42	Bell UH-1N, Bell 412
Escuadrón Presidencial	Boeing 737, Douglas DC-9, Cessna Citation, Grumman Gulfstream II, Bell UH-1N

Grupo Mixto de Enlace y Reconocimiento (Mixed Liaison and Reconnaissance Group) at Base Aérea Teniente Vicente Landaeta, Barquisimeto, with a detachment at Base Aerea Francisco de Miranda, La Carlota-Caracas, with Beechcraft Queen Air, Bell 47G, UH-1D and 206B, Sud Alouette III.

COMANDO AÉREO DE INSTRUCCIÓN (Air Training Command)

Grupo de Entrenamiento Aéreo - Base Aérea Mariscal Sucre, Boca del Río-Maracay

Escuela de Aviación Militar	Beechcraft T-34 Mentors at BA Mariscal Sucre for primary training
	Rockwell T-2D Buckeyes at BA El Libertador for advanced training

The FAV headquarters is at Base Aérea Francisco de Miranda, La Carlota-Caracas. There are fighter units at BBAA El Libertador and Luis del Valle García, bomber units at BBAA Teniente Vicente Landaeta and Luis del Valle García, and transport units at BBAA Francisco de Miranda and Mariscal Sucre. BA Francisco de Miranda also houses the Escuela de Aviación Civil Miguel Rodríguez and the Aeroclub de Caracas, and is also the main Army and National Guard airfield.

Military Air Bases

1 Caracas (Francisco de Miranda)
2 Maracay
3 Palo Negro (El Libertador)
4 Maracaibo
5 Coro (Halcón)
6 Barquisimeto (Vicente Landaeta)
7 Barcelona (Anzoátegui)
8 San Fernando de Apure
9 San Cristóbal
10 Maturin
11 Santa Elena
12 Puerto Ayacucho

Aircraft Review

COLOURS AND MARKINGS

The Venezuelan flag, like those of Colombia and Ecuador, is similar to that of the Gran Colombia federation, and its national markings are, not unexpectedly, quite similar to those of Ecuador, although the proportions of the colours are different and the wing roundels now have US-style tricolour bars, and the blue rudder stripe displays seven white stars representing the seven provinces which formed Venezuela in 1811. Roundels currently appear in four positions only (fuselage sides, port upper wing, starboard under), with FAV, in USAF style, on the starboard wing upper surfaces and port wing undersurfaces. Camouflaged aircraft have fin flashes instead of rudder stripes.

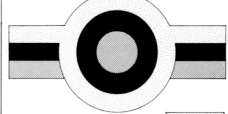

Camouflage schemes follow the current US practice of using two shades of green plus tan with light grey undersides, with one main exception: the Canadair CF-5s supplied retained CAF camou-

flage (green 34052 and grey 36118 with light grey 36270 undersides). Trainers have red areas or are white and red, much like US Navy trainers. Transports are marked *Fuerza Aérea Venezolana*.

AIRCRAFT SERIALS

Venezuelan Air Force aircraft are identified by a four digit serial; allocations appear to random, but there may be some rationale to the system which eludes researchers !

There was at one time a code system which provided an immediate identification of an aircraft's Escuadrón and Escuadrilla. The codes consisted of a plane-in-flight number, an Escuadrilla letter (sometimes followed by role letters) and the Escuadrón number. Thus, aircraft 5B40 was the fifth aircraft of Escuadrilla B of Escuadrón de Bombardeo Nº 40; 4BT1 was the fourth aircraft of Escuadrilla B of Escuadrón de Transporte (hence T) Nº 1; and 6AHR1 was the sixth helicopter (H) of Escuadrilla A of Escuadrón de Reconocimiento Nº 1.

Aircraft known to have been used by the FAV in recent years are :

AERITALIA G.222

Two ordered April 1982 for 1982 delivery, with options on a further six.

BEECHCRAFT C-45/D18S

About ten believed delivered. Known serials are 2187, 2228, 3099 and 5210, the latter preserved at the Museo del Transporte, Caracas.

BEECHCRAFT AT-7C NAVIGATOR

At least three delivered, ex USAAF 43-33603, 49998 and 50065.

BEECHCRAFT AT-11 KANSAN

Six were delivered, ex USAAF 42-37146, 37389, 37510, 37683, 37881 and 43-10413. One was serialled 3341.

BEECHCRAFT B45 MENTOR (T-34A)

Thirty four of the forty-one delivered were for EAM use and were initially coded E-001 to E-034. New-style serials known are 0007, 0022, 0054, 0072, 0302, 0860, 0890, 1696, 1728, 1758, 1944, 4470, 4673, 4703, 5355, 5385, 6192, 6222, 7246, 7276, 8083, 8113, 8486 and 9230.

BEECHCRAFT TRAVEL AIR 95

Two believed delivered; no details known.

BEECHCRAFT QUEEN AIR

Two Queen Air 65 were delivered in July 1960 :
2345	c/n	LC.23
4939		LC.25

Four Queen Air B80 delivered April-May 1966 :
1864	LD.290
7662	LD.293
8215	LD.289
8888	LD.294

Three Queen Air B80 at a later date :
3168	LD.444
5702	LD.445
7815	LD.446

BEECHCRAFT SUPER KING AIR 200

Two aircraft delivered in July 1979 :
2840	c/n	BB.520
3150		BB.522

A third aircraft noted at Opa Locka in April 1981 :
3280

BELL UH-1 IROQUOIS

About twenty UH-1B and UH-1D were delivered. The first four UH-1D initially flew with codes CHR1 to CHR4. One UH-1D was serialled 0947.

BELL 212 (UH-1N)

Two delivered, one of which for Escuadrilla Presidencial use.
0929	c/n 30538	ex N2912W	d/d 4.72
1972	30539	N7978J	5.72

BELL 47G/47J

A small number of 47G were delivered, as were four 47J :
5-HR-1	c/n 1771	d/d 8.59
6-HR-1	1782	8.59
7-HR-1	1783	9.59
8-HR-1	1784	9.59

A Bell 47J was later serialled 7387.

BELL 214ST

Two ordered for delivery April/May 1982.

BELL 412

Two helicopters ordered for 1981 delivery; one is serialled 3137, c/n 33013

BOEING 737-2N1

One only, serialled 0001, c/n 21167, delivered 30.1.76 for the Escuadrilla Presidencial. Another, c/n 21168, to have been 0002, was cancelled.

BRITISH AEROSPACE HAWK

The Hawk is reported to have been chosen as meeting the requirement for 24 advanced trainers (a further 24 may be required for light attack) though no order has officially been announced. However, build numbers 241 to 243 are allocated to Venezuela on the production line as we go to press.

CANADAIR CF-5A/D

Sixteen ex Canadian Armed Forces CF-5A were delivered initially, one of which, FAV 9456 was subsequently converted to RCF-5A :
2950	ex CAF 116781	d/d 12.4.72
3274	116780	12.4.72
3318	116779	12.4.72
5276	116778	12.4.72
6018	116777	12.4.72
6323	116776	12.4.72
6539	116774	11.2.72
6719	116767	11.2.72
7200	116773	11.2.72
8708	116789	7.6.72
8792	116787	7.6.72
9124	116775	11.2.72
9215	116788	7.6.72
9348	116786	7.6.72
9456	116783	12.4.72
9538	116782	12.4.72

Known losses took place on 1.10.74 and 2.3.76. There were also two CF-5D :
1269	116803	11.2.72
2327	116808	11.2.72

Two additional CF-5D arrived later, ex CAF 116827 and 116828; one became 5681.

CESSNA 180

Two only, delivered in 1954 :
0469	c/n 31321	ex N9222C
0845	31316	N9217C

CESSNA 182N

Twelve aircraft delivered around 1970 :
0345	c/n 60689
0777	60692
1836	60695
2265	60698
4283	60690
4441	60693
5554	60696
6702	60699
6827	60691
7106	60694
9368	60697
9555	60700

CESSNA CITATION

One Cessna 500 Citation for Comando Aéreo Logistico, delivered about 1972 :
0222	c/n 500-0092	ex N592CC

One Cessna 550 Citation II also for Comando Aéreo Logistico, delivered around 1979 :
0002	550-0011	N98875

Bell **UH-1D Iroquois** 0947 photographed at Palo Negro on 12 July 1976.

Beechcraft T-34A Mentor 8113 seen at Boca del Rio in July 1976.

English Electric Canberra B.82 1233 was shown at the Greenham Common Air Tattoo in June 1979.

English Electric Canberra B.82 1437 in a contrasting colour scheme at Barcelona in July 1976.

Canadair CF-5D 1269 seen at Baraquisimeto in July 1976, one of four two-seaters.

Douglas C-47 Skytrain 1923 at La Carlotta in July 1976.

Dassault Mirage IIIEV 7381 photographed at Palo Negro in July 1976.

Cessna 182N 4283. A batch of twelve aircraft were delivered around 1970.

Cessna 500 Citation 0222 at La Carlotta in July 1976 is the first of two Citations with the FAV.

DASSAULT MIRAGE

Nine Mirage IIIEV were delivered in 1972 and a tenth in 1977. Known serials are 2473, 2483, 7381 and 8940. Four Mirage 5V interceptors (including 1297, 7162, 9510 and possibly 1207) and two 5DV operational trainers serialled 5471 and 5472 were also delivered.

DE HAVILLAND DH.104 DOVE 2A

One only, coded 3-CR-1 and later serialled 2531, c/n 04382 ex YV-T-FTQ. It is preserved at the Museo de la FAV at Maracay.

DE HAVILLAND VAMPIRE

Twenty-four FB.Mk.5 were delivered in 1952 with codes 1A35 to 8A35, 1B35 to 8B35 and 1C35 to 8C35. A few were eventually serialled; one became 2534. The Escuadrón provided Vampires and crews for the FAV's aerobatic team 'Las Panteras' (The Panthers).

Five T.55 two-seat conversion trainers were delivered in 1959, all later receiving serials:

1E35	became 0023 (was temporarily 2A36); now preserved at the Museo de la FAV.	
2E35	0053	
3E35	0055	
4E35	7029	
5E35	7060	

They were used by the Escuadrilla de Entrenamiento of Escuadron de Caza N°35.

DE HAVILLAND VENOM FB.Mk.54

Twenty-two aircraft for Escuadrón de Caza N°34, coded 1A34 to 7A34, 1B34 to 7B34, 1C34 to 8C34. Most were later serialled, known serials being 0099, 0325, 5232, 7090, 7125, 8331 and 9418.

DOUGLAS C-47 SKYTRAIN

Some twenty were used, including 42-24183, 92090, 93165, 43-48003, and coded 1AT1 etc and 1BT1 etc of Escuadrón de Transporte N°1. Known new-style serials include 0030, 1023, 1127, 1162, 1250, 1311, 1330, 1544, 1547, 1570, 1593, 1633, 1660, 1923, 2111, 2122, 2315, 4984 of which 1544 was wfu in 1978 and 1250, 1311 and 1633 were

transferred to Línea Aeropostal Venezolana in 1972, presumably for spares, being temporarily stored at Maiquetia. 4984 was preserved at the Museo de la FAV, Maracay.

DOUGLAS C-54 SKYMASTER

Two aircraft only. One, a C-54A coded 7AT1, c/n 10287 ex 42-72182, NC51877, was delivered in June 1949 and was for a time the presidential aircraft.

DOUGLAS DC-9-15

LAV airliner YV-03C c/n 47000 has been loaned to the air force on occasions, operating with FAV titles and markings but retaining its civil registration amended to YV-03. In late 1981 however, it was noted carrying the serial 0003.

ENGLISH ELECTRIC CANBERRA

Six B Mk.2/B(I) Mk.2 were ordered in October 1952 and delivered during 1953 :

1A39	ex RAF WH708	w/o 5.56
2A39	WH709	to 6315
3A39	WH721	to 6409
1B39	WH722	w/o 8.11.54
2B39	WH736	to 3246
3B39	WH737	w/o 17.1.63

Three were converted to B.Mk.52 in 1971 :

3246	as G-27-157
6315	G-27-159
6409	G-27-158

....and later to B. Mk.82 :

3246	as G-27-309	re-delivered 15.4.80
6315	G-27-303	11.7.78
6409	G-27-304	22.8.79

Another twelve ex Royal Air Force B Mk.2 were delivered as B Mk.82.

0129	ex WH877	to B Mk.82 as G-27-301	d/d 18.6.80
1131	WH647	G-27-257	28.9.77
1183	WJ570	G-27-258	7.7.77
1233	WF914	G-27-302	27.6.79
1280	WH881	G-27-305	17.5.79
1339	WH649	G-27-259	16.3.78
1364	WD993	G-27-260	3.5.78
1425	WH712	G-27-306	7.11.79
1437	WH730	G-27-307	7.2.79
1511	WH862	G-27-261	8.9.77
1529	WH732/G-27-3	G-27-263	14.6.78
2001	WJ980	G-27-262	1.2.78

Two PR.Mk.3 were delivered at the same time :

2314	WE172 to PR Mk.83 as G-27-264		13.9.78
2444	WE171 w/o 9.3.76		

Two T Mk.4 were delivered in 1957-58 :

1E39	became 0619	to T Mk.84 G-27-310 d/d 5.3.80	
2E39	0621	G-27-265	12.4.78

They used the nose sections from WD944 and WJ863 respectively.

Eight B(I) Mk.58 were delivered in 1957-58 :

4A39	became 3216	w/o 28.1.69	
5A39		w/o 20.4.60	
4B39	0923	to B(I)Mk.88 as G-27-308 d/d 12.3.80	
5B39		w/o 19.11.64	
1C39	0240	G-27-254	23.11.77
2C39	0269	G-27-255	4.1.78
			w/o 14.11.78
3C39	0426	G-27-256 d/d 22.2.78	
4C39	0453	G-27-311	21.5.80

FAIRCHILD PT-19A

Known deliveries included ex USAAF 42-83413, 83657, 43-31394, 31396, 31424, 31434, 33667, 33672, 33720 and 33837.

FAIRCHILD C-123B PROVIDER

Eighteen were initially delivered with codes including 1AT2, 4BT2 and 8CT2; they were ex USAF C-123B-20-FA 57-6185/6193 and C-123B-21-FA 57-6194/6202 (c/n 20281 to 20298). Known new style serials are 0120, 1003, 1150, 1191 (ex 3AT2), 1245, 1290, 1323, 1342, 1352, 1430, 1449 (ex 5AT2), 1445, 1646, 1673 (ex 3CT2), 1675, 1718, 1777, 1780 and 1830, which suggests that additional aircraft were delivered later. Some aircraft were named, examples being 1290 'Uribante', 1675 'Araure', 1780 'Unare' and 1803 'Caroni'.

GRUMMAN GULFSTREAM II

One aircraft, 0004 c/n 124 ex N203GA, first reported in August 1981, presumably with Comando Aéreo Logistico.

HAWKER SIDDELEY HS.748 Srs.2

Two aircraft have been taken on charge :
0111 Srs. 223 c/n 1591 d/d 1.8.66

6201	215	1578	9.77 ex YV-C-AMI to YV-05C 5.80

HUNTING JET PROVOST T.52

Fifteen aircraft, believed delivered as E-040 to E-054; E-040 and E-041 were ex G-23-1 and G-23-2 respectively. They were subsequently re-serialled, one becoming 6780. The survivors were replaced by Rockwell T-2D Buckeyes during 1977-78.

LOCKHEED C-130H HERCULES

Seven aircraft were delivered to Escuadrón de Transporte N°1; all are model L.382C - the suffix is shown in the second column below :

3134	84D	c/n	4801	d/d	20.12.78
3556	20D		4406	c.1970	w/o 4.11.80
4224	42D		4556	2.75	
4951	20D		4407	c.1970	
5320	42D		4577	4.75	
7772	20D		4408	c.1970	w/o 27.8.76
9508	20D		4409	c.1970	

4951 is named '24 de Julio'.

NORTH AMERICAN AT-6 TEXAN

Apart from half a dozen early NA.16-1GV and NA.16-3, about thirty Texans of several models were delivered, including AT-6C ex 41-32339, 42-4180, 42-44018, 44242, 48841 and AT-6D 44-81085/81089. They initially flew with EAM codes such as E-71 (c/n 78-6445) which is now preserved at the Museo de la FAV, Maracay. A number were serialled, including 0034, 0993, 1072, 2175, 2501, 2506, 4008, 4568, 5389, 6444, 7401, 7525, 8703, 8922 and 9350, most, if not all, being T-6G.
Harvard II N20240, c/n 81-4128 was bought on 4.12.80 from Leeward Aeronautical Inc., presumably for display purposes.

NORTH AMERICAN B-25J MITCHELL

Twenty-four were delivered in 1948; known codes include 5A40, 6A40, 5B40, 8B40, 15B40 (ex 44-30812). Quite a few were later serialled, known serials being 0953, 1480, 3741, 3898, 4115, 4146, 4173, 5851, 5880 (ex 44-86725).
43-28096 is preserved at the Museo Aeronáutico at Maracay.

NORTH AMERICAN F-86F SABRE

Twenty-two were delivered with such codes as 1A36 and 5B36; previous USAF identities included 52-4614, 4660, 4682, 4689, 4690, 4736. Known examples of serialled aircraft are 0310, 0493, 0674, 0900, 1382, 1465 (ex 6C36) 3335, 4549, 4741, 6271, 9478 and 9518. Nine aircraft were later passed to the Bolivian Air Force.

NORTH AMERICAN F-86K SABRE

Fifty-one were supplied from West Germany in 1967 and 1968; not all were actually placed into service, and four crated examples were sold to Honduras in 1969. Known aircraft are :

0002	ex USAF 55-4895	
0005	55-4896	
0011	55-4907	
0014	55-4911	
0019	55-4912	
0026	55-	
0028	55-4925	
0042		
0050	56-4116	
0056	56-4117	
0059	56-4118	
0074	56-	
0132	56-4124	
0140	56-4125	
0178	56-4126	
0325	56-4127	
0375	56-4128	
0389	56-	
0597	56-4131	
0748	56-4135	
0807	56-4136	
0881	56-4137	
0926	56-4139	
0931	56-4140	preserved at BAM Mariscal Sucre
0943	56-	
0960	56-4141	
0967	56-4143	
0977	56-	
0984	56-4146	
0991	56-4147	
1011	56-4149	
1014	56-4150	
1107	56-4151	
1130	56-4152	
1135	56-4153	
2166	56-	
4341	56-4155	
5627	56-4158	
6422		

Other known previous USAF identities are 55-4845, 4866, 4878, 4881, 4882, 4888, 4889, 4898, 4899, 4901, 4904, 4908, 4909, 4910, 4913/4919, 4922/4924, 4926, 4927, 4929, 4931/4934, 56-4119, 4122, 4123, 4160.
An unidentified aircraft crashed on 21.2.72.

PIPER PA-31 NAVAJO

An aircraft serialled 8215 was noted at Miami in May 1981.

REPUBLIC F-47D THUNDERBOLT

Twenty were delivered in 1948 for use by Escuadrón de Caza N°10, later Escuadrón de Caza N°36, and coded 1A36 to 10A36 and 1B36 to 10B36. They were withdrawn from use in 1956-57, and P-47D-30-RA 10B36 ex USAAF 44-32809, preserved at the Maracay museum.

ROCKWELL T-2D BUCKEYE

Twenty-four aircraft delivered in two batches. The first twelve were :

0048	c/n 358-1	ex Bu. 159330
0219	358-2	159331
1316	358-3	159332
2155	358-4	159333
3499	358-5	159334
4821	358-6	159335
5612	358-7	159336
7532	358-8	159337
7744	358-9	159338
8763	358-10	159339
8991	358-11	159340
9187	358-12	159341

The second batch of twelve, delivered in 1977, had no previous US Navy serials, and included 3605 and 4290, which was written off on 14.7.78.

ROCKWELL OV-10E BRONCO

Sixteen aircraft :

0076	ex Bu. 159058
0194	159061

Fairchild C-123B Provider 1780 seen visiting New Tamiami, Florida in July 1978.

Lockheed C-130H Hercules 4951, one of seven which have been delivered to the Escuadrón de Transporte N°1.

Rockwell OV-10E Bronco 2312 seen at Palo Negro in July 1976.

Rockwell T-2D Buckeye 3499 at Boca del Río in July 1976, one of the first batch of twelve.

1367	159065	
2312	159069	
2641	159057	
3923	159062	
4035	159066	
4159	159070	
5709	159059	
5847	159063	
6280	159067	w/o 14.7.78
7435	159060	
7970	159071	
8578	159064	w/o 15.4.76
9744	159068	
9988	159072	

SIKORSKY S.51

Two believed used; no details known. One is preserved at the FAV Museum, Maracay.
Westland Dragonfly WG725 was acquired from the AAC Museum at Middle Wallop in October 1981, allegedly in connection with the Venezuelan Air Force anniversary celebrations, and may appear in spurious markings.

SIKORSKY S.55/UH-19

At least ten helicopters. The few from USAF stocks retained their USAF serials as call-signs, although they were given FAV codes. Known aircraft :

1AHR1	c/n 55.889	
2AHR1	55.903	
3AHR1	55.904	
4AHR1	55.911	
5AHR1		
6AHR1	55.891	ex 52-7522
4BHR1		52-7578 preserved at Museo de la FAV, Maracay.

SUD SA.316 ALOUETTE III

Twenty were delivered, c/ns as listed below :

1201	serialled 0085
1224	ex F-WKQC
1225	0104
1228	
1229	0790
1321	
1348	F-WIPC
1349	

1352
1373
1404
1405
1411
1412
1413
1424
1425
1426
1432
1433

One of these was serialled as 1852.

VULTEE BT-13B/BT-15

Twenty-three were delivered, including BT-15 ex USAAF 42-41642, 41644, 41694, 41738, 41740, 41742, 41744, 41921, 41940, 41955, 41972 — and flown with codes (one was ET-4, preserved at Maracay). A few survived long enough to receive serials; one such aircraft was 6006.

Venezuelan Army

The small, but expanding Servicio de Aviación del Ejército Venezolano, with headquarters at Caracas, is basically a helicopter force, although there are a few fixed wing aircraft, principally the IAI Aravas. The Army's main airfield is BA Francisco de Miranda, La Carlota-Caracas, and the aircraft and helicopters are used for artillery spotting, liaison and rescue/evacuation duties.

Army aircraft serials are prefixed EV-, for Ejército Venezolano, and then, unlike the air force, comprise a simple system where the first two digits indicate the fiscal year of acquisition, and the last two are sequential digits. Known allocations are:

EV-7701	Beechcraft Queen Air B.80 c/n LD.441			
EV-7702	Beechcraft Queen Air B.80			
EV-7703	Bell UH-1H			
EV-7704	Bell UH-1H			
EV-7705	Bell UH-1H			
EV-7706	Bell UH-1H			
EV-7707	Bell UH-1H			
EV-7708	Bell UH-1H			
EV-7709	Bell UH-1H			
EV-7910	Beech Super King Air 200		BB.489	
EV-7911	Britten-Norman BN.2A-6		851	ex G-BEVZ
EV-8012	IAI 201 Arava	d/d 2.80	0062	4X-ICI
EV-8013	Bell 205A-1			
EV-8014	IAI 201 Arava	2.80	0063	4X-ICJ
EV-8015	Bell 205A-1			
EV-8016	Bell 205A-1		30305	
EV-8017	Bell 205A-1		30300	
EV-8118	IAI 201 Arava	8.81		4X-CVC
EV-8119	IAI 201 Arava	8.81		4X-CVD

Other aircraft delivered to the Army have included an additional three Bell UH-1H, a Bell 47G (possibly two), six Bell 206B (one of which was reported as EV-3001, a non-standard serial), and an executive Bell 206L. An order was placed in 1979 for eight Agusta A.109A.

The Venezuelan Army (28,000 all ranks) is made up of eleven infantry and three Ranger battalions, in addition to a small armoured force. The Grupo de Paracaidistas 'Aragua', although part of the Army, is controlled by the Air Force. Based at Maracay, its maximum strength is two paratroop battalions.

National Guard

The Venezuelan Fuerzas Armadas de Cooperación (Paramilitary Forces), commonly known as the Guardia Nacional, have a total personnel strength of about 15,000 and are controlled by the Ministry of Defence. Eleven Coast Guard vessels, theoretically owned by the Navy, are operated, and there is a Destacamento Aéreo (Air Detachment) with a small number of light aircraft for internal security and customs duties; the duties have recently been expanded to include forestry patrols.

The aircraft serial system is similar to that of the Army, with GN- prefixes for Guardia Nacional and the first two of the four digit serial indicating the fiscal year of acquisition. The earliest known aircraft was Beechcraft C-45 GN-5210, an ex-FAV machine. More recent allocations include :

GN-7427	Beechcraft Queen Air B80		
GN-7428	Beechcraft Baron 95-B55		
GN-7429			
GN-7430			
GN-7431			
GN-7432	Britten-Norman BN.2A-9	c/n405 ex YV-C-AKL	
GN-7839	Beechcraft King Air E90	LW.260	
GN-7842	Bell 206		
GN-7952	IAI 201 Arava	0049	d/d 17.3.79
GN-7953	IAI 201 Arava	0051	d/d 17.3.79
			w/o 23.7.79
GN-7954	Cessna U.206G	05019	
GN-7955	Agusta A.109A		
GN-7956	Agusta A.109A	7119	
GN-7957			
GN-7958	Bell 206B		
GN-7959			
GN-7960	IAI 201 Arava	0064	d/d 26.1.80
GN-7961	Agusta A.109A		
GN-8168	IAI 201 Arava		d/d 3.81

National Police

The Police is known to operate a couple of aircraft with FAV serials prefixed PN- indicating Policía Nacional. One was Cessna TU.206B PN-0877 (c/n 206-0799) delivered in March 1967.

Britten-Norman BN.2A-6 Islander EV-7911 at Oxford in July 1979 in pre-delivery marks as G-BEVZ.

IAI 201 Arava GN-7952 delivered to the Guardia Nacional in March 1979.

Beechcraft King Air E90 TR-0201, the sole example of this type with the Venezuelan Navy.

CASA 212A Aviocar TR-0204, one of a pair delivered in 1981.

Grumman S-2E Tracker AS-104/149865 displays a strongly US Navy flavoured colour scheme.

Douglas C-47 Skytrain ARV-12 photographed at Maiquitia in February 1968.

Beechcraft T.34A Mentor MR-27, one of the fleet of the Escuela de Aviación Civil Miguel Rodríguez, at Fort Worth in February 1959.

Venezuelan Navy

The small Venezuelan naval air service, although only formed quite recently, can trace an ancestry as far back as November 1922 when a Centro de Aviación Naval (Naval Aviation Centre), controlled by the Army, was inaugurated at Palmita on the Laguna Valencia, not far from Maracay, with two float biplanes, a Caudron G.IV and a Farman F.40.

The Venezuelan Navy currently has a personnel strength of about eight thousand, including about four thousand marines in three battalions. No ships have provision to carry aircraft, but there is a growing Servicio de Aviación de la Marina Venezolana, its current duties being limited to transport, search and rescue and anti-submarine patrols. The United States is the main source of equipment.

Aircraft are marked *MARINA* (Navy) and have their serials prefixed ARV- for Armada de la República de Venezuela, or according to their rôle, such as AS for Anti-Submarinos, and TR for the transports.

Aircraft known to have been used are :

AGUSTA-BELL AB.212AS

Ten were ordered. The first two, MP-0301 and MP-0302 were delivered in July 1980; further examples serialled MP-0303 to MP-0306 were noted during mid-1981.

BEECHCRAFT KING AIR E90

One only, TR-0201, c/n LW.264, but reported as ARV-0201 late in 1981.

BELL 47G

Two reportedly in use; details unknown.

CASA 212A AVIOCAR

Two aircraft delivered in 1981 :
TR-0204   c/n A27-1-177
TR-0206   AV27-1-183

CESSNA 310

At least one earlier model, serialled ARV-15. Two new 310R delivered in 1980 :
TR-0207   c/n 310R-2120   ex (N6832M)
TR-0208   310R-2124   (N6833D)

CESSNA 402C

One aircraft, serialled TR-0202.

DE HAVILLAND CANADA DHC.7

One 'Dash Seven' ARV-0203 c/n 68 delivered late 1981; it was test-flown as C-GFBW.

DOUGLAS C-47 SKYTRAIN

Four aircraft, ARV-12, ARV-14, TR-0102 and TR-0202, due to have been retired in 1980, but two remained in service early in 1982.

GRUMMAN HU-16A ALBATROSS

Four believed to be in use; no details known.

GRUMMAN S-2E TRACKER

Six aircraft from US Navy stocks :
AS-101   ex Bu 150603
AS-102   149867
AS-103   149878
AS-104   149865
AS-105
AS-106   149080

HAWKER SIDDELEY HS.748 Srs.215

One only, TR-0203, c/n 1579 ex YV-06C, delivered 23.7.77.

PIPER PA-23 AZTEC 250

At least one, serialled ARV-11, believed wfu.

Escuela de Aviación Civil

Mention must be made of the Escuela de Aviación Civil Miguel Rodríguez, which operates from La Carlota in co-operation with the armed forces. Initially equipped with such types as the Vultee BT-13A (including YV-E-MR-17 c/n 9491) and the Champion 7EC (examples being YV-E-MR-4 c/n 320, YV-E-MR-20 c/n 346 and YV-E-MR-23 c/n 348), it currently flies modern trainers identified by their MR numbers, the YV-E- prefix now being omitted. Recent acquisitions include eight Cessna 182RG (MR-43 to MR-50). Other aircraft known are the following :

MR-25	Beech T-34A Mentor	c/n GC.286	
MR-26	Beech T-34A Mentor	GC.287	
MR-27	Beech T-34A Mentor	GC.296	
MR-28	Beech T-34A Mentor	GC.297	
MR-29	Beech T-34A Mentor	GC.298	
MR-30	Beech T-34A Mentor	GC.299	
MR-31	Beech Travel Air B95	TD.297	
MR-33	Cessna 150D	60101	ex N4101U
MR-34	Cessna 150D	60112	N4112U
MR-35	Cessna 150D	60131	N4131U
MR-36	Cessna 150D	60141	N4141U
MR-37	Cessna 150D	60739	N6039T
MR-38	Cessna 150D	60741	N6041T
MR-39	Cessna 150D	60743	N6043T
MR-40	Cessna 150D	60744	N6044T
MR-41	Cessna 150F	62581	N8481G
MR-42	Piper PA-30 Twin Comanche	30-1429	N8291Y

Champion 7EC YV-E-MR-20 is preserved at the Museo del Transporte, Caracas.

The Falklands Conflict

The most recent happenings during the preparation of this book have been the invasion of the Falkland Islands and their dependencies by Argentina in April 1982 and the subsequent British re-taking of the islands during May and June. These actions have had significant effects both in the overall relationships in the area and its effect on future dispositions of forces, and of course in the short-term losses of aircraft and equipment. Many aircraft were lost or damaged in the conflict, and though at the time of going to press it is too early for full details to be to hand, the following is a summary of what is known from various press reports. It should be noted that claims from the two opposing sides are at considerable variance, that it is usually unclear as to which service a particular aircraft was operated, e.g. Argentine Skyhawks could be from the Air Force or from the Navy, and that is equally impossible to draw distinctions between Mirages and Daggers.

In the occupation of South Georgia on 2/3 April a Puma and an Army Lama were lost to British resistance. The Air Force used Boeing 707s for long-range reconnaissance of the approaching British task-force in April, and the 1 May attack on Port Stanley airfield by a single Vulcan followed up by Sea Harriers destroyed several aircraft on the ground including Pucara A-528, probably a Hercules, and several helicopters including two A.109s and a Chinook. A similar attack at Goose Green airstrip claimed several Pucaras and helicopters. One Mirage/Dagger was shot down and another probably lost to Argentinian fire. Retaliatory attacks on the British fleet on 1 and 2 May by Canberras with Mirage/Dagger escorts resulted in the loss of one Canberra and three Mirage/Daggers to the Sea Harrier defenders.

On 4 May a second attack was made on Port Stanley airfield by another lone Vulcan and Sea Harriers, one of which was shot down, and on the same day HMS Sheffield was sunk by an Exocet missile launched from a Super Etendard. On 9 May an Argentine Puma was shot down by a missile near Port Stanley and a Hercules with a Mirage/Dagger escort was intercepted and forced to return to the mainland. On 12 May two Skyhawks were shot down by Sea Wolf missiles from HMS Brilliant and another flew into the sea whilst taking evasive action. An attack by British ground forces at Pebble Island on 15 May resulted in the destruction of six Pucaras and five other aircraft, one of which was a Prefectura Naval Skyvan.

UK forces landed in strength on 21 May, on which date about twenty attacking Argentinian aircraft were lost (nine Mirage/Daggers, five Skyhawks, two Pucaras and four helicopters). On 23 May further Argentinian attacks were made with the loss of one Puma, one UH-1 Iroquois, six Mirage/Dagger (plue one probable) and one Skyhawk (plus two probable). Two days later HMS Coventry was attacked by three Skyhawks; two were shot down but the third was successful in attacking and sinking the British ship. On 25 May the Super Etendards appeared again and an Exocet launched from one of these aircraft (some of which were rumoured to have been destroyed on the ground in Argentina by a clandestine attack by ground forces) sank the requisitioned container ship Atlantic Conveyor which had discharged its cargo of RAF Harriers but was still carrrying at least three Chinook and about a dozen Wessex helicopters. The 25 May saw two Skyhawks brought down by Sea Darts and a Puma destroyed on the ground by an RAF Harrier.

On 1 June a Hercules operating as a crude form of bomber (i.e. pushing bombs out through the open rear door), was shot down by British aircraft. A similar mission was flown by another Hercules on 7 June when a Liberian registered tanker ship was bombed about 500n.m. from the Falklands. British landings at Bluff Cove on 8/9 June were opposed by Argentine Skyhawks and Mirage/Dagger aircraft, and during the day eleven of their aircraft were lost, including at least four Mirage/Daggers shot down by Harriers.

It should be noted that because of the lack of detailed information we have largely not included details of the losses sustained during the conflict in the 'Aircraft Review' sections of the Argentine entry in the main body of the book.

Space for Notes:

Space for Notes:

Military Air Arms

UNITED STATES MILITARY AVIATION: THE AIR FORCE

This widely-acclaimed book by Robert J. Archer is the largest in our series; as well as the expected historical and current organisation sections there are 117 photos, seventeen of them in full colour, also a massive section giving individual aircraft details on upwards of 22,000 of the 54 types now in service or under evaluation. Tail-codes, bases, badge colours etc are featured in appendices. 302pp, A5B.

Softback £6.95; Hardback £9.95

LATIN AMERICAN MILITARY AVIATION

John Andrade's review covers twenty-nine countries, in many of which military aviation harks back to the 'Mustang era' but on which so little has previously been published. Histories of each air arm are included, with details of current units, insignia, bases and equipment. Illustrated with over 220 photos, including a colour section. 284pp, A5B.

Softback £7.95; Hardback £10.95

This series has been acknowledged by reviewers and enthusiasts the world over for the depth of original research, quality and quantity of relevant illustrations, accuracy of content and also for the high standard of presentation and production in a subject-suited A5 landscape format. Usually included are a history of the Air Arm concerned, its organisation, unit histories, considerable detail on the individual aircraft involved - including unit allocations and codes, construction numbers and fates etc; all backed-up with extensive photographic coverage, details of unit markings and a number of useful appendices. Titles are offered, subject to availability, in both paperback (glossy card cover) and hardback (cloth cover for longer life, and silver blocked) versions, as follows:

German Military Aviation 1956-1976 by Paul A Jackson (152pp, 101 bw ph)	Hardback £5.95	0 904597 04 0	Softback £3-45	0 904597 03 2
Belgian Military Aviation 1945-1977 by Paul A Jackson (120pp, 87 bw ph)	Hardback £5.95	0 904597 05 9	Softback £3-45	0 904597 06 7
Spanish & Portuguese Military Aviation by John M Andrade (128pp, 111 bw ph)	Hardback £5.95	0 904597 08 3	Softback £3-45	0 904597 09 1
Dutch Military Aviation 1945-1978 by Paul A Jackson (134pp, 98 bw ph)	Hardback £5.95	0 904597 10 5	Softback £3-45	0 904597 11 3
French Military Aviation (2nd rev.edn.) by Paul A Jackson (208pp, 113 bw ph)	Hardback £6.95	0 904597 17 2	Softback £4.95	0 904597 18 0
United States Military Aviation : Air Force by Robert J Archer (302pp, 100bw ph)	Hardback £9.95	0 904597 28 8	Softback £6.95	0 904597 29 6
Latin American Military Aviation by J.M.Andrade (284pp, 216bw ph)	Hardback £10.95	0 904597 30 X	Softback £7.95	0 904597 31 8